MISS YOU

Mollie Lee Pryor

MISS YOU

The World War II Letters of Barbara Wooddall Taylor and Charles E. Taylor

Judy Barrett Litoff · David C. Smith
Barbara Wooddall Taylor · Charles E. Taylor

The University of Georgia Press · Athens and London

Designed by Sandra Strother Hudson
Set in 10 on 14 Linotype Walbaum by Tseng Information Systems, Inc.
Printed and bound by Thomson-Shore

The paper in this book meets the guidelines for permanence
and durability of the Committee on Production Guidelines for
Book Longevity of the Council on Library Resources.

Printed in the United States of America
94 93 92 91 90   5 4 3 2 1

Library of Congress Cataloging in Publication Data
Taylor, Barbara Wooddall.
Miss you: the World War II letters of Barbara Wooddall Taylor and Charles E. Taylor /
Barbara Wooddall Taylor, Charles E. Taylor ; [edited by] Judy Barrett Litoff,
David C. Smith.
p. cm.
Bibliography: p.
Includes index.
ISBN 0-8203-1145-6 (alk. paper)
1. Taylor, Barbara Wooddall—Correspondence. 2. Taylor, Charles E. (Charles
Eugene), 1919– —Correspondence. 3. World War, 1939–1945—Personal narratives,
American. 4. World War, 1939–1945—United States. I. Taylor, Charles E. (Charles
Eugene), 1919– . II. Litoff, Judy Barrett. III. Smith, David C. (David Clayton),
1929– . IV. Title.
D811.5.T34 1990
940.54'8173'0922—dc20
89-4874
CIP
British Library Cataloging in Publication Data available

Contents

Preface

More than thirty-five years ago, the distinguished southern historian, Bell I. Wiley, published two path-breaking books on the lives of "ordinary" soldiers during the Civil War. His penetrating studies of "Johnny Reb" and "Billy Yank" were based largely on soldiers' letters, which had received little attention before his research. Since the publication of these volumes, a number of books of letters by "ordinary" soldiers have been printed. For the most part, these works have not examined the wider questions of life in the military and the experience of war so carefully detailed by Wiley.

Our book is based on an extraordinary private collection of World War II letters which recently emerged from a battered trunk long in storage. Two young people from the southern part of the United States met in the summer of 1941. They fell in love, were married, and had a family. He was in the United States Army and she became a "war bride." Together, they endured the war, even though they were often physically separated. While they were apart, the couple wrote each other almost every day. Nearly all of their correspondence survives, even her letters to him. In total, this treasure trove amounts to about four thousand typed, double-spaced pages.

When the letters emerged from storage, Barbara began the process of sorting, organizing, and transcribing them so she could eventually give them to her children as Christmas gifts. This complicated and time-consuming task took more than two years. During this period, Barbara showed the letters to her niece, Judy, who was overwhelmed by the extent and historical significance of the collection. Barbara told Judy that she and Charles had long thought that the letters might serve as the basis for a book on young people and World War II, and asked Judy if she would like to help. Further discussion led to Judy's suggestion that her close friend and colleague, Dave, be included in the project.

As the transcription of the letters progressed, it became increasingly clear that the letter writers were, very probably, representative of millions of other young people of the World War II period. The great wealth of detail in these letters, complemented by many written memoirs, lengthy discussions about the meaning and significance of the couple's wartime experiences, and research in primary source materials, reinforced the view that what happened to Charles and Barbara was, in fact, prototypical.

What makes these letters unique is that they tell both sides of this human story. While soldiers' letters have been published, the letters from their sweethearts, wives, and mothers have yet to appear in print. Letters from home were read and re-read, but space, time, transfer, and above all, combat, meant that they often had to be discarded or burned, no matter how precious the content.

Barbara's letters, however, were saved. Some were tied up in bundles and shipped home. Others served as emergency stationery when Charles used the blank sides to write to Barbara. The end result is that nearly every letter written by either Barbara or Charles is available. This valuable collection of detail, question, answer, comment, and controversy tells a story never told before.

These letters describe the difficulties of a wartime couple and the stresses created by the war on each partner. Like thousands of other young people in similar circumstances, Barbara and Charles Taylor were forced to conduct their courtship by mail and experienced a wartime marriage on the move. Through their correspondence they shared her life on the home front and his experiences on the western front. And, although separated by thousands of miles, they planned for his homecoming and worked to meet the challenges of the postwar world.

Barbara grew up in Fairburn, Georgia, a small town just south of Atlanta. She entered first grade at four years old and completed the eleven years of public school at the age of fifteen in June 1938. After graduating from high school, she worked for a year in her brother-in-law's dry-cleaning business in Fairburn. She attended North Georgia College in Dahlonega, Georgia, for a quarter, but returned home because of financial stringencies and homesickness. She next attended Chrighton's Business College in Atlanta.

After completing the secretarial course at Chrighton's, Barbara had hoped to find work at Metro-Goldwyn-Mayer in Atlanta, where her sister was employed. Company rules prevented this, however, and she found work at Twentieth Century-Fox instead. Another sister worked at Warner Brothers, so the three sisters were all on "film row" at the same time.

Charles grew up in Gainesville, Florida, and graduated from high school in 1938. He entered the University of Florida in the fall of 1939 and later, after registering for the draft in October 1940, he received a student deferment. For people like Charles, a depression child living in a university town, college was simply a continuation of high school— the same friends, the same ideas, even the same subjects. He hunted, fished, dated, and had a good time.

A series of incomplete grades, a minor automobile accident, and "girl problems" led Charles to withdraw from college and to volunteer for enlistment in the Army in July 1941. He also spent one summer in a Civilian Conservation Corps camp, where he became familiar with the rudiments of Army discipline.

After Charles's enlistment, he was processed into the Army at Camp Blanding, Florida. He did his basic infantry training at Camp Wheeler, near Macon, Georgia. His cousin, Virginia Edwards Kitchens, and his grandparents lived in Fairburn, approximately ninety miles north of Macon. Virginia promised to get Charles a date with Barbara Wooddall, "the prettiest girl in Fairburn," during one of his weekend passes from Camp Wheeler. On the third weekend pass, Barbara broke a Saturday night date so that she could meet Charles, and this book began.

While the letters themselves form the core of the book, the making of *Miss You* requires further explanation. The four of us live in three different places: Gainesville, Florida, Providence, Rhode Island, and Bangor, Maine. Others live in our houses, depend on us in varying ways, and share our time. We also are history professors, college students, and employees of the Florida Department of Agriculture. Yet this powerful and absorbing correspondence melded us, all strong-willed individuals, together.

Aspects of this cooperative endeavor made the effort humorous, were at times frustrating, and probably also delayed publication. As an example, we used three different computers and word-processing programs, and we learned to use them as the book progressed. The public libraries we visited to read popular women's magazines were also havens for bag ladies and the homeless seeking shelter. We now know how desperately understaffed these establishments are. But these magazines are seldom found in university libraries.

Judy and David, responsible for the major efforts of the interpretive sections, learned to work under great time pressure, in an intense manner, often in airports, in planes, in hotels at conferences while surviving room service meals, and in brief visits at each other's homes. As a beleaguered child once remarked to us, "When you two workaholics can stop for a moment, I have something to say." In fact, we have adopted the slogan of the Thirty-ninth Infantry Regiment, Charles's combat unit, as our own motto: "Anything, Anywhere, Anytime, Bar Nothing."

We made telephone calls by the hundred, wrote letters, and three times all four of us met for marathon sessions in Gainesville. At these meetings, we faced the difficult process of selecting those letters to be included in this work. This was an extremely challenging task. All of the letters contain insight or information about the wartime era, but space restrictions limited the published selections to less than 10 percent of the total correspondence.

It says much for those to whom the book is dedicated that the end result is what it is and that we all remain friends. Openness, honesty, frankness, and affection made that possible. Our joint authorship does not imply compromise. We dealt with each other's questions and doubts, but we all agree on the contents of this book. It is our statement of mutually perceived truth.

The experience has also made clear the need to locate and preserve other letters and correspondence of "ordinary" people. These stories are at the center of American history and life, and they need to be told.

Acknowledgments

When is a book completed? For us, the easy answer is the day you sign your page proofs. The real answer is never. For, in truth, there is always a new insight, another bit of information, or a better way to frame your ideas. Research and writing a book can be all-consuming, tiring, tedious, exhausting, and frustrating. It can also be exhilarating, exciting, and lots of fun. One of the more satisfying aspects of writing a book, however, is the time when you finally let it go. Then you can sit down and thank those individuals who shared in your work and helped make its publication possible.

We have been generously supported by our institutions, Bryant College and the University of Maine, with funds for travel, research, typing, and the reproduction of materials, as well as sabbatical leaves and reduced teaching loads. We could not have completed this project without help from understanding librarians at Brown University, the University of Maine, Bryant College, the Providence Public Library, the Bangor Public Library, and the Worcester Public Library. We also wish to offer special thanks to the interlibrary loan offices of the University of Maine and Bryant College for patiently fulfilling our hundreds of requests for materials which were often obscure and difficult to locate.

The many individuals who commented on our presentations at the Popular Culture Association meetings in Atlanta, Montreal, and New Orleans; the Missouri Valley History Conference meeting in Omaha; the Duquesne History Forum in Pittsburgh; and the talks and seminars at Bryant College and the University of Maine provided us with great insights and posed new questions for us to ponder.

Several colleagues read this manuscript in various stages. Their comments sharpened and focused the results. We would like to thank especially William J. Baker, James P. Ingraham, Lee Kennett, Glenda Riley, Ron Slawson, and Martha Swain. One very dear friend and colleague who gave "above and beyond" is Larry Malley.

Malcolm Call, director of the University of Georgia Press, catered to our idiosyncrasies while still demanding that we meet his high standards—no easy task. We could not have asked for a better copy editor than Mary McFeely. Her sensitive approach to our work is deeply appreciated. Special thanks are due to Sandra Hudson, the book designer.

Government documents are an arcane science. We were led through their mysteries by Frank Wihbey. Donna McKinnon located the military photographs which appear in this volume. Sarah Wendell shared her wonderful collection of World War II posters with us. We also wish to acknowledge the contributions of an anonymous seatmate on a flight from Boston to Montreal. In addition, we have been fortunate in knowing and working with two superb professionals: Jackie David and Kathy Moring. They always know the answers to our questions.

Jim Ingraham is a prince of a department chairman. He has been incredibly supportive of this project, making certain that Judy's teaching schedule allowed maximum time for working on this book—to say nothing of helping her obtain better office space, secretarial help, and a new computer.

This book is based on letters from World War II. We wish to thank the United States Post Office for its services during that conflict as well as in our time. We cannot forbear from writing that overseas mail is often slower now than then, but dependability of delivery continues—even without the use of V-Mail!

We salute the brave members of the Thirty-ninth Infantry Regiment of the Ninth Infantry Division with whom Charles served and whose valor in World War II has not yet been sufficiently recognized. The stress of the war years was lightened for Barbara by her close friendship with other war brides: Jenny Bradley, Maxine Dew, Ina Hartman, Emma Johnson, Eleanor Longino, Helen Plunkett, Lillian Pruchnicki, Martha Sanders, Emily Thompson, and Barbara C. Wooddall, as well as her childhood companions, Miriam Gordon and Evie Shannon. They, and others like them, also deserve commendation.

If there is a single person who is ultimately responsible for this book, it is Charles's cousin, Virginia Kitchens. She was instrumental in arranging Barbara and Charles's blind date. Barbara's older sister, Dot Barrett, also deserves thanks for easing those first few awkward moments on the side porch that warm August evening in Georgia nearly fifty years ago. Since then, her role has been one of providing love and companionship. Although he might not have wanted others to know it, the late Pip Barrett always cared.

While they have expressly asked not to be acknowledged, two other people have endured it all: Sylvia Smith and Hal Litoff. *Merci bien, Nostra Culpae,* and *Shalom.*

Chapter One

COURTSHIP BY MAIL

August 1941–August 1942

Overleaf: Barbara on her way to work in Atlanta,
August 1941

Camp Wheeler, Georgia, 27 August 1941

Dearest Barbara:

I had not forgotten you, just haven't had time to do a thing on my own hook. They have really put us through this week. Late to bed and early to rise—

I am in hopes that you are holding a few words and actions sacred; they should mean as much to you as they mean to me. I know you are wondering just what last weekend meant to me—(Well)—last weekend was one of my happiest since I have been in this man's army. . . .

In this letter I have to sort of feel you out to see whether or not you were only infatuated or whether you are in love with me. Frankly (real Frank?), I am not infatuated. I am definitely in love with you. In fact, you have been constantly on my mind ever since I left you on Sunday. I am hoping you and I can keep the flame burning from now on. You know it takes the two of us to make this affair beautiful—so if you will only meet me halfway, we will have something that no one can tear up or change.

Not such a pretty letter but I have only a little time. So please forgive my scratch and spelling, I can do better.

Darling, please don't be kidding me. I don't think I could take kidding like that.

All my love,   Charlie

P.S. Write soon what I want to hear.

When twenty-one-year-old Private Charles E. Taylor of Gainesville, Florida, wrote this letter to Barbara Wooddall, he could not possibly have known that it would mark the first of approximately eight hundred letters he would write to her over the course of the next four years. Nor could he have known that as a newly enlisted man, or later as a lieutenant, in the United States Army, he would travel thousands of miles within the United States while he trained for combat. It would also have been difficult for him to predict that he would eventually be called upon to fight in the war then raging in Europe, which the United States had not yet officially entered. What he did know in August 1941, however, was that he was "definitely in love" with an eighteen-year-old, brown-eyed, blond-haired beauty from Fairburn, Georgia, whom he had only recently met.[1]

Barbara Wooddall was equally in love with Charles Taylor. In a letter of July 16, 1942, to Private Taylor, in which she described her impressions of their first date, she recalled:

> About the night we met—I'll never forget how you looked when you walked in the living room. You were smiling and I knew from the start that I had loved you all my life. I wanted to go out with you, but I was almost afraid to. I knew that if you told me to jump I would do so and quick too! Then the next thing I liked about you was the fact that you liked good hot swing bands. Then out at Jennings, I'll never forget how your eyes looked right through me—I felt as if you could tell me what color underwear I had on. You felt as if you were insulting me because you were in your uniform and if I had just told you (but I wouldn't) I was proud to be with you. I didn't want to go home—I wanted to stay with you all my life because I knew that night, without you I would never be completely happy.

Although the Selective Training and Service Act was approved by Congress in September 1940, Charles was not drafted. He had volunteered for the Army in July 1941. He was the only man in uniform at Jennings, a popular "juke joint" near Atlanta (soldiers were then required to wear their uniforms both on and off duty). After Pearl Harbor, of course, the oddity was a man who was not in uniform.[2] In recounting the circumstances of his first date with Barbara some forty years later, Charles further elaborated on the significance of his being in uniform that evening. He wrote:

> We went into Jennings—which was nothing but a big barn-like room with tables, and a dance floor, and a band. I felt very conspicuous—for there were a lot of guys my age—a few with dates—but I was the only person

there in uniform. Since the draft had only started . . . the population of such big cities as Atlanta had hardly been touched. Nevertheless, everyone was in a draft category—1–A, 1–B, etc., or 4–F, with or without deferments. All eyes turned our way when we came in. I knew that part of the attention to us was because Barbara was so pretty, and I was immediately jealous and subconsciously on guard to protect her. I also knew that the uniform was another part of their interest. The girls—'cause they liked uniforms; but the boys—'cause a lot of them knew such a fate as to be in the service of their country was certain in their not-too-distant future.[5]

Like thousands of other young couples caught up in the exigencies of World War II, Charles Taylor and Barbara Wooddall experienced a whirlwind romance, followed by marriage. Although their courtship spanned eight months, from their first date in August 1941 until their secret marriage on April 5, 1942, they were rarely able to be together. As long as Private Taylor was stationed at Camp Wheeler, in Macon, Georgia, he could arrange for occasional weekend visits to Fairburn. When he was transferred to Fort Leonard Wood, Missouri, in October 1941, however, trips to Fairburn became much more problematic. In fact, the young couple saw each other only once between October and their marriage in April. In total, they probably spent no more than four weekends and a brief furlough in each other's company prior to their secret marriage. Because the opportunities to be together were so limited, Charles Taylor and Barbara Wooddall relied upon their letters to supply such fundamental information as their ages and the names of each other's parents, sisters, and brothers, and most important, to develop and nurture their love.

Surprisingly, historians know more about the personal meaning of courtship in earlier times than in this century. Letter-writing between courting couples had, until the twentieth century, been a "mainstay of courtship," providing the chief means of getting acquainted. Telephones and ease of travel after 1920 made letter-writing less necessary, and, consequently, historians have been forced to rely on published material on dating and sexual behavior when studying recent courtship practices. However, during World War II, sweethearts and lovers, separated by the wartime emergency, took to pen and paper once again.

Unfortunately, millions of wartime letters which were written remain hidden away in attics and closets, or, in many instances, have been destroyed. Charles and Barbara's wonderfully detailed letters now give us a needed intimate look into modern courtship.[4]

Both Charles and Barbara repeatedly acknowledged the importance of each other's letters in the growth of their love. For example, in a letter of January 6, 1942, Barbara recounted a humorous incident which clearly underscored the importance she placed on Charles's letters:

> Sunday Daddy got the mail for me and there was a letter from *you*. I was right in the midst of it in the Sunday School class when my teacher asked me to read something for her. I got so frustrated that I dropped my pocketbook one way, gloves the other, and almost started reading the letter out loud. Boy, did my face get red.

But, on a more serious note, she confessed:

> Your letters mean a great deal to me and my outlook on life. They make my day happy or sad. If I don't hear from you I'm *bad!* All inside I mean. I suppose you've just spoiled me in that respect.

Charles concurred. On January 9, 1942, he declared:

> Dear, there is doubt (*a very little doubt*) in my mind *only* when I do not get a letter from you. Please let us both be true and keep each other happy. The only way we can keep each other happy is by letters. I feel nearer to you every time I get a letter from you. I feel so warm inside and so very happy and contented when I read lines that *you* wrote.

While Charles Taylor and Barbara Wooddall knew that their deep attraction for each other represented much more than a frivolous wartime romance, their courtship did have its difficult moments. When they first began dating, Charles was involved in a rather serious relationship with another young woman. In a letter written on July 16, 1942, Barbara poignantly reminded Charles of the pain and heartache which she had suffered upon learning of this earlier liaison:

> Then that awful weekend that you brought, er, I don't know her name (not much!!) to Fairburn. I knew that there was too much competition for

me, sooo I made up my mind to forget you. I wouldn't answer your letters, and I burned yours up as fast as I could read them.

Charles's early letters to Barbara are interspersed with his disavowals of love for this "other woman." On one occasion he stated, "I am in your hands and you know it. I would not trade a hair off of your head for two [of her] complete." A week later, he reiterated, "[She] is completely out of my life as far as I am concerned. You have completely taken her place and built yourself up in my mind and my heart, and no other woman will have a chance at me."[5]

On the other hand, Charles had his own concerns about Barbara's social life, and Barbara found it necessary to reassure him that the many young men whom she was seeing meant little to her. In a letter written February 4, 1942, she stated, "Remember what you said about my having dates? You know it's funny—in a mild sort of way! When I'm out on a date, I feel as if something definite in my life is missing. It's you, Charlie." One week later, on February 11, she announced: "Our YWA [Young Women's Auxiliary] leader is planning a social for us. She wants to invite some *selected* men from Fort McPherson. Of course, I think it's *nice* to be *nice* to *nice* boys in the Army, but what do you think? In case she does this, honest I won't give a '*soldier a break!*'"[6]

Dating, the modern practice of young people of the opposite sex pairing, had emerged in the new social mores of the post-World War I era. Throughout much of the nineteenth century, the formal act of "calling" was one way that couples were able to meet. In addition, group activities, such as contra and square dances, box socials, and sleighing parties, had offered young people the opportunity to pair off, but not in a regular or formal way.

By the 1920s, however, changes were occurring rapidly. As informal get-togethers became "dates," another casualty was the chaperon. Now the extent of activities was determined by the peer group rather than by the fixed rules of an outdated system. The differences in mores can be seen in the successive editions of Emily Post's standard work on etiquette, as chaperons diminish in importance and then disappear entirely, along with such conventions as group dating.[7]

Changes in dating practices continued to take place in the 1930s. Movies, dance halls, restaurants, the radio, wider and better education, shorter working days, increased leisure time, and especially the automobile, had all appeared in the twenties, but they expanded throughout small towns and rural America and well beyond the social elite in the next decade. Charles and Barbara came from more conservative backgrounds than the persons discussed by such well-known observers of the day as Frederick Lewis Allen, Helen and Robert S. Lynd, and Willard Waller. Nevertheless, the circumstances of their courtship mirrored these changes.[8]

In the case of Barbara Wooddall, group activities continued to be more important than paired dating, but Charles was still bothered by the frequency with which she chose to go along on these outings. The exasperation he felt was reflected in a letter dated February 25, 1942:

> you tell me how much you love me, but everytime you write, you just came in from a date or you went someplace with someone. You don't have to make me jealous, 'cause I already am. But where I come from a girl that is *in love* with someone does not run around as much as you claim to be doing. Yes, I realize that you are there and I am away up here, but I don't go out like that, I sit.[9]

After their secret marriage on April 5, 1942, the question of whether or not Barbara should date took on new significance. In a letter written on April 12, Barbara related a special problem she encountered when she announced to a girlfriend that she was no longer dating:

> Evie called, and she couldn't believe that I didn't have a date tonite. I told her that I wasn't dating anymore and she just laughed and laughed. Finally, I made her believe me in a mild sort of way, and she said that if I really didn't date anymore she would know I was married. Dopey, huh?

A similar announcement to her parents brought forth the comment that for once, "We'll know what it is like to have a daughter." [10]

Even after Charles and Barbara became "officially" engaged in June 1942, the question of Barbara's going out with other men occasionally arose. The following passage from a July 13 letter demonstrates that Barbara even experienced brief pangs of regret at having to turn down dates.

> I'm going to tell you something 1 know that I shouldn't but it's so very seldom that I just give-away to my feelings that I feel that you should know. This afternoon about 5:00 I was dressing to go have something to eat before I went to BTU [Baptist Training Union]. A guy called me and wanted me to go to the show tonight. He said he knew that I shouldn't go out and furthermore he shouldn't call me, but if I'd go he'd be very glad and be good to me. Well, I didn't accept his invitation, of course, but it made me want to go somewhere terribly. Well, I . . . saw him riding with one of my girlfriends and they were laughing and seemingly having such a good time. I know you understand what an empty feeling I had. I went in . . . and cried for about twenty minutes. Mother was so sweet. She said she knew exactly how I felt, and she talked to me about how much I had to look forward to etc., and soon I got all right.

Although Barbara may have let her feelings "give-away" on this one occasion, her letters reveal that she usually was able to keep her emotions in check. One week later, on July 20, she offered:

> Charlie, now you listen to me, it is *not* hard for me to stay home when my girlfriends are all going out. Why I feel sorry for them, yes, they have my deepest sympathy, because they do not have a beautiful love like ours, and they do not have a darling Charlie like I have. So there!

One of the ways that Barbara managed to endure the long periods of separation from Charles was by continuing her busy routine. In addition to maintaining a full-time job as a secretary at Twentieth Century-Fox Film Corporation in nearby Atlanta, she took a leadership role in the local Cotillion Club and was an active member of the Fairburn Baptist Church where she sang in the church choir, taught Sunday school, and served as president of the Young Women's Auxiliary. In leisure time she went roller-skating, biking, bowling, and swimming, and played tennis. She was determined, in her own words, to keep her "chin up." On February 20, 1942, she wrote:

> Yes darling, I'm keeping my chin up. You wanta' know why? Why because I have the finest man in the world! He's backing me in what I do and I'm

backing him in what he does, rite or wrong, good or bad! He's true to the good 'ole USA and what it stands for, and I love him, yes, I love every part of him.

Both Charles and Barbara recognized that the times required that they make quick decisions about their future together. In her first letter to Charles after Pearl Harbor, Barbara exclaimed:

> Well, what about this WAR business! Oh, Charlie, will you still get your Christmas leave? You must get it because I'm counting big on being with you again. . . . What's going to happen to us? There is no doubt in my mind as to who shall win the war, but how long will it take us? It makes you feel like getting the best of everything before it's all gone. Now I know that isn't the right way to feel, is it Charlie?!?!?!? [11]

Charles, too, recognized that war had sped up the pace at which time was passing for them. In discussing his upcoming Christmas furlough of 1941, he remarked:

> Barbara, I want to impress you with the fact: I have but seven days off—four of them on the road to Florida from Missouri and back. Things will have to happen fast. Remember that.[12]

At the same time, however, both Charles and Barbara went to considerable lengths to insist that their love for each other was *not* a casual wartime romance. Early in 1942, when the topic of marriage began to be discussed seriously, Charles made it clear that they were not rushing into a wartime marriage. In a letter of March 5, he emphasized this point:

> I am not afraid of war and you (if you were afraid) are over your war fright. Therefore, this would not be considered as a *war* marriage. Too, we have had quite a test *of our love*. I believe if we were married that it would be a *lasting* one.

One week later, on the twelfth, he noted: "I am well aware of this war, but it has not made this love of mine any different. I would have loved you just as much had there been no war."

Barbara also worried that others might think that their love was nothing more than a wartime fling. On June 2, 1942, she expressed her concern: *[handwritten: also see p.147]*

> Some people criticize "war loves and marriages" but as for me, I would do the same thing again. As a matter of fact, I don't know but what this war is going to reform this whole world. It's teaching us the importance of real, true love.

As she was only nineteen at the time, Barbara also felt compelled to respond to the often-repeated charge that she was too young to get married. The following passage, from a letter dated May 21, 1942, shows that Barbara adamantly discounted such arguments:

> A lot of people have told me I was too young to settle down to one boy. Does that infuriate me! I mean it does. Gee, I don't call it "settling down," I call it starting life anew with new vim and vigor.

An almost continuous discussion of wartime marriage took place in the United States during this period. The speed of the changes brought on by the war, especially in the length of engagements or the formality of the wedding ceremony, worried some. Others felt that marriages might provide stability and add an ethical edge to wartime relationships and counseled that marriages were all right as long as true love was the force in speeding up events, not casual encounters or sexual hungers.[13] Special counseling was often available for prospective couples at the United Service Organizations (USO), and wartime fashions which would maintain traditional aspects of weddings were featured in the popular press. *Life* magazine gave its approval to war marriages in 1942, when it featured on its June 22 cover a war bride carrying a Victory-stamp bridal bouquet. The fiction of popular magazines added a further dimension to discussion as plots dealt with every possible controversy.[14]

An equally significant discussion of the pros and cons of war marriages took place in the scholarly press. Sociologists noted that the immediate effect of war was the acceleration of the marriage rate, followed by a decline, as more and more men went off to war. In actuality, there were one million more marriages from 1940 to 1943 than would have been expected at prewar rates. Scholars expressed concern that "hasty marriages" followed by long separations could mean that family life was "more fictitious than real." One sociologist went so far as to claim that "there was a greater dispersion of family members and families as groups between 1936 and 1942 than in any other six-year period in the history of the world." [15]

Family and marriage counselors as well as home economists focused on their role in helping young people to make up their minds about marriage. With proper counseling, they were optimistic that war marriages would last. As one home economist concluded: "Generals and armies may win the war, but they can never win the peace. A lasting peace will have to be won on the home front by the kind of family which we evolve during the present crisis." [16]

Charles and Barbara were undaunted by the vociferous public debate on wartime marriages. They undoubtedly discussed the possibility of matrimony during their brief 1941 Christmas holiday together. In a letter dated January 4, 1942, written just three days after they had parted, Charles left little room for anyone to question his intentions on this matter:

> I intend to marry you on my next trip or furlough, even if it is not the best thing. You said you did not want to marry me when I was there because you did not want to tie me down. Can't you see, just as you said you wanted me to boss you, I want to be tied down by you.

Barbara, however, displayed a bit more restraint when she discussed the prospective marriage. On January 29, she replied to his comments:

> You know that I want to be Mrs. C. E. Taylor worse than anything in the whole wide world, now, don't you? But it seems to me as I just couldn't marry you in Feb. Now don't get the idea that I am letting us down but you said to help plan and that's just what I'm doing. I have quite a few small bills that I would like to get paid up first. And also, if you get a short leave, your Mother will want you to come right home. You know, you've never told me how she feels about me. But, darling, we will continue planning. Maybe there will be some light on the subject soon.

During the first three months of 1942, both Charles and Barbara grappled with the financial and logistical problems of arranging their marriage. Hoping that he might be stationed in Fort Benning, Georgia, Charles applied to Officer Candidate School. When his application was turned down, his spirits reached a low point. For the next two weeks, his letters reverberated with bitterness toward the Army as he attempted to reconcile himself to the fact that he would not be going to Officer Candidate School. The prospects of receiving some time off at Easter, however, helped to raise his spirits. On March 12, 1942, he wrote that he had "high hopes of being on furlough."

Barbara was equally excited about the possibility of their being together again. Upon learning that Charles had been granted a two-week furlough, she exclaimed, "Darling, I am actually too excited even to write! I love you so very, very much and just the thought of being with you again seems entirely too good to be true. I can hardly wait!!!" When Barbara asked for time off from her job at Twentieth Century-Fox so she could be with Charles, her understanding and patriotic boss replied, "I'd do anything for the boys in the service!" [17]

After spending most of the Easter furlough together, Charles and Barbara were secretly married on April 5, 1942. In a letter written June 29, 1942, Charles recounted the events of that momentous occasion:

> You know, I remembered every part of the night we were married. When we started and everything. Remember how excited both of us were. When I read over our marriage certificate, I felt like I was again back in Bronson, Florida, on April 5 at 1:15 a.m. watching the Rev. Waldon write the certificate up. Remember how you felt after you stumbled through, "I do,"?? I will cherish that night until I die.

After their marriage, the couple immediately returned to Charles's home in Gainesville and retired to separate bedrooms. Because of the stress of the war, they felt the need to be officially married, but they were satisfied with just the ceremony for the time being.[18]

The decision to keep their marriage secret was mutual, but on more than one occasion Barbara expressed regret that she had not been able to be open and honest with her parents about the marriage. When she learned that Charles had given the Army her name as his wife so that she could receive an allotment check, she became extremely upset. In an uncharacteristically curt note, dated June 22, she stated:

> Received your letter this morning and I certainly think you were foolish to turn my name in as your wife. Mercenary, aren't you? If you have to give them my address, have them send it to the P.O. in Atlanta—General Delivery!! Please don't get that messed up!

What Barbara did not understand was that Charles had acted under orders when he submitted her name for an allotment. Failure to comply might have meant court martial.[19] In June 1942, Congress had enacted the Servicemen's Dependents Allowance Act to provide family allowances for dependents of enlisted men in all branches of the armed services. Each family allowance was determined by a contribution from the federal government plus a voluntary allotment authorized by the enlisted man. The government allowance was fixed at the monthly rate of $28.00 for a spouse, $12.00 for the first child, and $10.00 for each additional child, up to $60.00. The enlisted man could, if he so chose, also allot $22.00 from his monthly pay. This grant was applicable up through the grade of sergeant, with staff sergeants and above allocating funds at their discretion. By June 1945, 4,000,000 family allowances were being paid, and 3,800,000 family allotments had been authorized.

The Office of Dependency Benefits, which administered the Allowance Act, located at Newark, New Jersey, soon became one of the largest branches of the Army Service Forces. It attempted to go far beyond bureaucratic routine; it often sent checks to different addresses when people moved, mailed checks to the mothers of soldiers when wives were able to find temporary war jobs, and even responded to queries concerning possible uses of the funds. These green checks, modest as they were, often provided critical financial support to a population on the move, and also boosted morale. Information about the system appeared in the press. Barbara was not aware that "even at the risk of overpayment," the government mailed checks promptly to all who were named as recipients.[20]

Shortly after Charles and Barbara's secret marriage, they began to make plans for a public ceremony. In June 1942, Charles's parents purchased and mailed him an engagement ring, which he quickly sent to Barbara. In a flourish of excitement, she wrote that it was the "prettiest, loveliest, and everything goodiest ring that I've ever seen." The following month Charles wrote to Mr. Wooddall, formally asking him for his daughter's hand in marriage. Before he could send the letter, however, he had to find out the full name of his future father-in-law. On July 10, he told Barbara that he was "ashamed to say" that he did not know her father's initials and requested that she provide them.[21] Even in these rapidly changing times, however, some formalities could not be forgotten. The letter Charles wrote is a significant expression of the efforts of this young couple to retain a sense of propriety in their new world.

14 July 1942

Dear Mr. Wooddall:

Perhaps this letter from me will come as a surprise to you, but it seems to me that even in these extraordinary circumstances in which we find ourselves today, formalities should still be observed.

I realize that you are completely aware that Barbara and I have plans for marriage upon her arrival in St. Louis, but before we go any further in our plans, I would like to have your consent. I already have the consent of my family, they are very proud to add such a wonderful person as Barbara to their family.

Sir, I am sorry that we are in War, which does not afford Barbara and I time, under the circumstances, to have the luxury of a normal peacetime wedding. However, there could be nothing about a big formal wedding that could have any effect upon the life and beauty of Barbara's and my life as husband and wife. . . .

Needless to say, I am looking forward to the day when I shall become a member of your happy family.

Respectfully yours,
Charles E. Taylor

Barbara, who had arranged for vacation time from her job in Atlanta, now made preparations to travel by train to St. Louis, Missouri, where she and Charles would be married in early August. The July letters of Barbara and Charles teem with excitement as they look forward to their forthcoming public marriage. Barbara's last letter to Charles before leaving for St. Louis reveals just how much significance she placed upon this public ceremony:

> As I told you, I wrote to the Clerk of Superior Court and a Mr. McAtier in St. Louis answered my letter. I have to be 19—you have to be 21. No waiting, no physical exam, no witnesses, no *nothing* required. . . . We can find a Baptist preacher and get married in his study and then we can wire our folks and everything will be nice and clean and good in the sight of God and man.[22]

The wedding occurred as planned on Sunday, August 2, 1942. However, in a letter to her parents, Barbara gave the date as August 1, the date of her arrival. Later that week, Charles and Barbara had a candle-burning ceremony in which they burned the April 5 marriage certificate. They then changed the date on their second certificate from the second to the first of August. Barbara and Charles kept the knowledge of their first marriage a secret for more than forty years. Not until the early 1980s, when they began to think of publishing these letters, did they reveal the full details of their first and second marriages.[23]

After their weekend in St. Louis, the "newly married" couple headed to Waynesville, Missouri, and Fort Leonard Wood, where Charles was required to report for duty on Monday morning. After enjoying eighteen days together—the longest time they had ever spent with each other—Barbara returned to Georgia. It would be more than three years, however, before Barbara and Charles would have the opportunity to lead a normal life together as husband and wife.

Their experience was eloquently captured in a poem, written by another young person, describing her own life during this same era.

LOVERS, 1941

I'll tell you how it is with John and me;
We build ourselves a small security
Within the present—plant those garden flowers
Whose bloom is swift; we snatch more happy hours
To swim and hike, hear concerts, see our friends,
and money's something now that each one spends
on silly, tender gifts that warm the heart.
We make great effort not to be apart.

We never talk of fear or death or sorrow
Knowing how close and awesome looms tomorrow.[24]

Francis Hall

Letters, August 1941–August 1942

[10th Trn. Bn., Co. D., 4th Platoon]

Camp Wheeler, Georgia, 23 September 1941

Dearest Barbara,

Once again I sit down to write to the little girl. The one with the brown eyes, black eyebrows and black eyelashes, combined with that blond hair, and once again I am so sorry that I could not make it this past weekend.

This time I hope you think it is good news. The Captain called a selected group, in which I was placed, to his desk to break easily but surely to a little news. We are chosen to fill or replace the Cadre's* places that are leaving. Some of us stay here in Wheeler when the Company leaves for Missouri and some of us leave with the Company for Missouri to be made corporals when we arrive there in the new camp. Please wish me luck. . . .

I am in a kinda rush now; have to do a little studying before I get to bed at nine and it is now eight-thirty.

Please hurry and drop me a real sweet note, for I may not be leaving after all.

All my love,   Charlie

[Hdq. Det., 2nd Bn., 63rd Inf., 6th Div.]

Fort Leonard Wood, Missouri,
21 November 1941

Well My Dear:

You are sure slow with yours truly's letters, are you not? We will forget it for I know you are going to keep the flags flying. . . .

---

*Cadre: a selection of trained individuals for key slots in units in a division.

I am going to be with you Christmas if I have to break out to do it. I love you, I love you, I love you a thousand times I do, so return it in the same way I give it out. My heart, my soul, and my being all belong to just Barbara. Please remember that and see if you can pass it all back as it was given out; from the bottom of my heart. I am true and serious with you. Barbara, I will go nuts if you do not tell me what I have to know.

In a hurry, but if I feel this way Christmas (and I think I will) you had better look out, for you may be somebody's girl for life. Please be good for,

I love you,   Charlie

P.S. Barbara, I mean it, I love you truly and I can say it to the world now for I am out of the noose. My hands are not tied, so please do not hold your love or your emotions back. Remember when I see you Christmas our time will be limited and we will have to make every minute count. Please be true and love me with all your body and soul. Can you? You are the only one for this boy Charlie, *Your Charlie.*

Love forever,   Charlie

What a wonderful, precious, dear letter.

Fairburn, Georgia, December 11, 1941

Dearest Charlie,

I had started thinking that you were not going to write me again. I am certainly glad you did.

Well, what about this WAR business. Oh, Charlie, will you still get your Christmas leave? You must get it because I'm counting big on being with you again. I hope I feel just the way I did the first night I had a date with you, remember? We had such a good time and I've never been so knocked for a loop. I remember exactly what I thought about you and I wonder if I will think it again when you come. We must be sure and we will be sure. . . .

A man here in the office just said that Italy had declared WAR on the USA. What's going to happen to us? There is no doubt in my mind as to who shall win this WAR, but how long will it take us? It makes you feel like getting the best of everything before it's all gone. Now I know that isn't the right way to feel, is it Charlie????

Charlie, please don't threaten me. I just want to wait until I see you and I already know what I'll say and do. I can hardly wait.

Must close now,

Sincerely,   Barbara

Fairburn, Georgia, January 6, 1942

Darling,

. . . Darling, you'll never really know how much I miss you. And, by the way, you almost missed the train. The more I think about it, the "funnier" I feel. Do you realize that the train was *moving?!?!?!*

You know what? I have no desire what-so-ever to go anywhere, with anyone. Now that's not good for me so perhaps I had better make myself want to. But, Charlie, I want to be with you forever and ever. I love you so much. You're the best, aren't you, hon? Please write me as often as possible so that I may really know you're mine forever. Please darling.

And, another thing, if ever there's the slightest doubt in your mind, let me know. If we could *really* be together for a little longer time, I'm sure we'd never forget what we mean to each other. That day will come, so let's be patient and wait for it.

Remember, darling, I'm always with you and I love you,

Barbara

Fairburn, Georgia, January 10, 1942

My Darling Charlie,

I hope you don't mind if I call you "my Charlie," because I feel that you are mine. I never stop thinking about you and never stop wanting you to be with me forever. I'm really in love with you, in fact, I'm crazy as hell about you. (Pardon).

I received your wire this morning. It was telephoned down. I'm so glad you sent it because today is Sunday and it makes me feel good all over to hear from you on Sunday. By the way, how long does it take for an Air Mail letter to reach you?

You said in your letter of the 13th that you were only going to write me on the days that you received a letter from me. Now that's all well and good, if that's the way you want it, but, just remember, Charlie, when I write you it's because I want to and not because I feel it my duty.

Quoted from your letter—"I am inclined to think that you love me as much as I love me"—that's a good one, you conceited devil, and I'll never stop kidding you about it! Am I being mean? Well, really, I'm just acting real silly, believe me!

Please let me know what your Mother said about us. . . .

By the way, you didn't send the match cover you were speaking of. And I'm not 20, I'm 19. . . .

I love you entirely too much and I know it and you know it. Therefore, be good to me and for me, and I'll do the same for you.

Love always,   Barbara

What an incredible letter, so much love.

[Hdq. Det., 2nd Bn., 63rd Inf., 6th Div.]

Fort Leonard Wood, Missouri,
15 January 1942

My Darling,

They say that the Civil War is not still on, well I sure am finding out different. When I came to Missouri there were six boys to get into the detachment at the same time—we were all from the south. There were three of us due for ratings, but did these Yankee dogs play the game fair? No, they moved boys out of one section to another to give the ratings to. The boys were full-blood Yankees. Man, do I hate them. It is not for myself, but some of these boys on my side need the money. I hate to see a double cross. Maybe there will be a day of reckoning. I will feel better after a good night's sleep. That is quite enough of gloomy words.

My Dearest, just keep your fingers crossed, maybe word will come soon about my OTS.* I sure hope so. By the way, my papers on the OTS

*Officer Training School. This is Barbara and Charles's term for Officer Candidate School.

have to go to the Adjutant General's office, Washington, D.C., after they go to the board. Maybe I will hear about it soon.

You are such a dear for answering my letters so quick. May your letters never stop rolling. You know I just couldn't wait to get back from the show. I had to talk to you and tell you about everything. I actually feel better about it already. You are the girl for me. You are truly the one I have been dreaming about for so many years. Will our dreams come true? They will have to, Barbara, for I do honest to God love you. Please believe me, for I swear it by all that is good. My life is sure an empty one without you with me in person, but you are still here near me. You would laugh if I told you about how I talk to you when we (you and I) are alone. I tell you a thousand times a day that I love you. Please be mine forever, for I need you as I need nothing else. *Sweet.*

Remember me to your Mother and Dad. Give my love to them all. I hope they appreciate *us.*

I love you,   Charlie

P.S. Let's be careful about *our* love, Darling. CET

Fairburn, Georgia, January 20, 1942

My darling Charlie,

May I bother you a few minutes? Just felt like I had to talk with you for a little while. Darling, I surely do wish you were here. I love you so very much. I mean it, Charlie, I mean it more than anything I have ever done or said.

The letter I should have gotten Sunday was here at the office Monday and then I got one in the ten o'clock mail and another Air Mail last nite. I believe I felt better yesterday than anytime since you have been away. I'm living for you and your letters, darling, so keep the good work up! . . .

I wish you didn't feel the way you do about Yankees. I can really be no judge because I've never had so many words with them. However, darling, just remember that they are people just like yourself and want to get ahead just the same as you do. Try not to hate them, Charlie, because by hating them you are making yourself hard and hateful.

Maybe they are getting the breaks now, but your time will come, so just be patient and wait for it.

Yes, Charlie, I am being very good. Not only for you, but for us. You see, I believe, in fact, I know—that if I should write you everything I do in detail that you would agree with me. As long as I love you I could never be bad or even halfway bad.

Whatever you want to ask me is all right. I shall do my best to tell you the very truth to the "nth" degree. I have nothing to ask you because I love you just as you are and I want no doubts ever.

Please be mine forever and ever and darling, I do want to marry you. Definitely!!

Love always,   Barbara

[Hdq. Det., 2nd Bn., 63rd Inf., 6th Div.]
Fort Leonard Wood, Missouri,
31 January 1942

Darling,

Here another day has gone by. There is snow all over the ground and it is cold as can be. Wish I were back in good ole Georgia or Florida for a little while, at least.

We went to town last nite, it was sure raining when we left. When we got to town, it sleeted and the snow fell. Sure got cold then. Joe and I saw a show but missed our streetcar and did not get home until two o'clock a.m. Had only half hour sleep before we went out to the TNT Plants.* Sure am getting to be tired, but maybe we will get some rest in a week or so, I hope. We are now on an alert and can't go to bed 'til we get orders. . . .

Just finished an article on war marriages by a couple of Experts. I thought you would like to read it so I clipped it out. He has the right idea all right. He said if you two are sure it is real love and not infatuation and there is some means of visible support of the wife-to-

*Charles was sent to Jefferson Barracks in St. Louis to guard the TNT plants for several days.

be, then let nothing or nobody stop you from marrying and don't wait, for the soldier does not know where he may be the next day—he can see no further than the orders of the day. . . .

Please "keep the mail flying" as it is the one thing that keeps my chin up. I can never tell you how much I love you, but all I want is for you to be mine truly and because you want me to be yours. Don't worry, but pray as you have been doing and I know things will turn out o.k. soon.

Powerful words!

All my love forever,   Your Charlie

P.S. Shall I change the subject of my letters or what do you want??? ANS.

Fairburn, Georgia, February 18, 1942

My dearest,

Am *sorta* listening to Bob Hope. He's broadcasting from some Army Camp and really it's a scream. I get a big kick out of anything concerning the Army. Darling, I love you so very much!

Skated for awhile tonight but didn't enjoy it much. When it rained so hard this weekend, a lot of dirt washed up on the skating rink. You know—made it rough!

Darling, sure hope I hear from you tomorrow. You see, I received no letter today, but I'm not kicking because you've been swell to write to me so much.

A lot more boys here are in the service now. Really doesn't seem like the same place. No use to have a dance or party because there wouldn't be a stag line and probably not enough boys to go with all the girls.

I was reading what the paper had said about drafting girls. Suppose you have read up on it, yes? "Golly"—I don't know whether it's such a good idea or not. There are a lot of advantages and disadvantages.

Don't worry about me tempting the soldiers. I wouldn't for the world. No stuff! . . .

We have more work in the Contract Department at 20th Century-Fox than the law allows. Wish we could get caught up just *once*.

Darling, I'm with you always and loving you like I do, I'm sure things will work out all right.

Please keep writing and let's be good.

Love always,   Barbara

[Hdq. Det., 2nd Bn., 63rd Inf., 6th Div.]
Fort Leonard Wood, Missouri,
25 February 1942

My Darling:

. . . Well, I can't apply for the Air Corps for a whole month, for they aren't taking any more applications until they have the boys placed they have already accepted.

I guess I needed you today more than I ever have needed anyone. My intuition of last nite was correct. The Lt. Brunswold called me in this a.m. and informed me that I had been *dropped* by the board for *OTS*. You realize what I said—I don't go to OTS at Benning. So, what is there left. No OTS, no Air Corps, but I can try to transfer, that is all I have left. My brain is still a little numb from the information and the realization of what I have lost. I guess I am hurt more than I ever have been. I guess I feel more like crying than I have since I was twelve, for I have lost all hope. They whipped me but whether it was fair or not I don't know. However, I shall endeavor to take this like a man. . . .

This place will drive me crazy as a loon, in no time now. Honestly, I have worried so damn much, that I have got a case of "nerves." I have just got to get South, but I wonder if I ever shall see it again.

Pardon me, but I am in the lowest spirits I ever have been in. I am getting quite a contempt for myself. I always almost make the grade, but *not* quite.

I still have your love to guide me, but do not hurt me for I could not stand that, too. . . .

I have worked my brain overtime to figure a way back but no results. If I had an emergency I could probably get to get a furlough for awhile. I can think of no emergency, can you? I can't tell a lie for the American Red Cross checks up on all cases. Gee, I would like to see you. If I only had an emergency perhaps I could go—I would have enough money, I get paid Saturday. . . .

I love you and only you and have had but a few dates since I left you, but I don't want another, unless it is my Barbara.

Your Charlie

[Hdq. Det., 2nd Bn., 63rd Inf., 6th Div.]

Fort Leonard Wood, Missouri, 1 March 1942

My Darling,

Barbara, I guess I have sort of let everyone down for the last few days, for I have not written any letters. I have not had the heart to write. Trying to get over this battle with myself. When that damn board kicked my papers out I guess it took me down too many steps, for I sure did get a very low estimate of myself. I am about to get over it now and my letters will come every day as usual, from now on.

Still can't figure out what is so wrong with your Charlie that keeps him from being a somebody in this Army. Perhaps I counted on going to that damn school too much. Well, my chance of going is past and I guess I did not measure up to qualifications or something. The thing still remains that they threw my papers out and there are several reasons that could have caused them to oust them.

Some of my recommendations could have been a little *too* much on the political side; I am only 22; I am from the South. I just can't get the hate of disappointment out of my mind, but I have myself back in the old groove. I will be o.k. soon, a day or so.

I have all of my stuff for the Air Corps but I have not put my application in, nor do I think I will. Perhaps all of this was for a purpose and from now on I will let fate deal the blows and head me where I am supposed to go. At any rate, I am going to stick with the Infantry for a while and see what I can see.

Yes, I did fight a hard fight but I was not the winner, maybe it *was* my last fight. It could be that if I did stick with this old Infantry and show them that I like it and intend to stay that they will give me a rating and perhaps send me out on a Cadre. It could be that they would place me on a Cadre that was to be sent South. At least, I am going to try it that way. I could not be in a worse place than I am here. I think that if I had five more months in this Camp I would go completely insane. I sometimes wonder about my sanity now. I know you are as tired of all that mess as I am, I am so damn tired I don't know what to do. So let's, you and I, pretend that it all did not happen.

I know that my chances of getting back to Georgia or even near Georgia are pretty slim, if there is even a chance, but that should not have an effect on our love, should it? It will only make me want to be near you all the more. I would have given a million dollars just to have seen you for ten minutes—ten minutes of happiness with you. I'll swear I don't think I could stand this Army if it were not for my love for you and the knowledge of your love. . . .

I sent you a telegram last night to help you know that even though I am up here, I am also back in Fairburn with the girl I love. Darling, I love you so much and I know even though the future looks very dull that God is still looking out for both of us. Just keep your chin up and always know that your Charlie is your Charlie, and will remain yours until you don't feel as if you want him. Even though we have nothing to base our plans on, I still love you and know that I shall be there sometime to make you my wife.

All my love,   Your Charlie

P.S. Darling Barbara, I really do need a nice picture of you.

[Hdq. Det., 2nd Bn., 63rd Inf., 6th Div.]
Still, Fort Leonard Wood, 5 March 1942

No Man's Land to—God's Country

My Darling:
Your sweet letter came this afternoon and I was so glad to know that you were still, my Barbara. Darling, I do know what that telegram meant or rather I sure hope I knew. You sure are the most inspiring

person I could have ever hoped to have had as mine. You fulfill every dream I have ever dreamed of. "My Barbara," that is the girl I want and shall be true to until I do not exist. . . .

Dear, Barbara, will you please tell me that you really and truly love me over and over, because I so love to hear you say you love me. Barbara, I guess if I will ever be a man I am a man now. I have had life pretty easy up until I got here in this Army. Perhaps this Army is changing me a little. Perhaps I am getting to like the Army *but* I don't like it by myself. I want you to be with me. No, darling, not now, but when I get to the place where I can provide the necessary things of life and the things that will make you happy. How long that will be is something you and I do not know.

However, in the meanwhile, we can get married, and you can go on as you have been with your job and there with your folks. Things would go on as usual until I can manage to take care of you and the other things. Does that sound rash to you? To me, it is one of the sane things to do. I am not afraid of war and you are (if you were afraid) over your war fright. Therefore, this would not be considered as a *war* marriage. Too, we have had quite a test *of our love*. I believe if we were married that it would be a *lasting* one. That would be the only way I would want to get married. *If you do marry me* I will never give you a divorce; I hope you understand this, do you? Nor shall I ever ask you for a divorce. I sure love you. . . .

Darling, you know just how I feel. I have been sorta waiting to write this letter. For a while I had the idea that I might make OTS and could tell you how I felt but things do not always *go* as planned, so—I had to write it. What do you say?

Love forever,   Your Charlie

P.S. Write soon, yes?

Beautifully written

[Hdq. Det., 2nd Bn., 63rd Inf., 6th Div.]

Fort Leonard Wood, Missouri, 9 March 1942

My Dearest Darling Barbara:

Yesterday made the last day of eight months in the Army for me. Seems like I have been in longer than that. I guess, I am just feeling old. . . .

Boy, oh, boy, am I sorry I was up for OTS before now. You know my Detachment Commander was Lt. Brunswold. Well, about a week ago an order came out for all non-coms* (corporals, sergeants) to sign up to OTS and a special board was gotten up for the purpose of testing these boys. Thursday, an order came out for all men that had been through high school to sign up for OTS and meet the board too. Incidentally, Lt. Brunswold was on the board and all the men in this Detachment got through with the board perfectly. I cannot sign up again now, for I was tested by the board before. Yes, they take boys that have been through high school and yet I don't get a chance because of I don't know what. Me, I went to college and had two years of ROTC with my college work. My, but these boards are a poor way of testing. Perhaps it is the way God thinks things should be, but I can't grasp the reason. Dad wrote me that he had rather have a good buck private as a son than a bad general. Perhaps it is best that I remain as a buck private. . . .

By the way, don't get overexcited for this could be only talk, however, the clerk in the office tells us we are *probably* going to get Easter furloughs. I know that is just too good to be true, so I am going to wait until they do give me a furlough. If they do get big-hearted and give furloughs Easter, maybe that will be the time for us to be married? Will you have your things straightened out by then. You said it would be summer before you would be straight.

I hope you intend to marry me and are not just talking. Sometimes I think you are backing out on me and then other times I feel that you are right. When and if I get back do you *know* for sure that you will still love me and are not just living in a dream?? I know after I have been away so very long you wonder is there *really* a Charlie. You think

*Noncommissioned officers.

I am just a make-believe in your mind and then other times you know I am really here and yours. Maybe we should not think so much. . . .

Darling, I must stop and write to Mother for I have really neglected her in the past week. You know how much I love you. I don't think I can do without you much longer, so please don't give up hope. I will be back someday.

I love you, Your Charlie

P.S. *How about that picture of you??*

Fairburn, Georgia, March 17, 1942

My darling Charlie,

Oh, Charlie, I'm getting so excited about your leave. I know I cross bridges much too quick, but just the thought of your coming back to Georgia is entirely too much for me. Darling, I love you so very, very much! I do, honest, I do. There's just so much that I do love about you. You're so swell about writing me and you really don't know what your letters do mean to me.

I told Virginia* about your (maybe) leave and she's just as happy as I am.

I only hope and pray that everything works out so that we can be together as much as possible.

Well, our work is "doubling" up! We have to work a half-hour longer each day and on Saturday. Perhaps by the time you get here that will be changed. We also have some extra help in the office. . . .

Did I tell you that I was going to a First Aid Class every Monday and Thursday nite? Well, I am, for two hours each nite. . . .

Believe it or not, Charlie, I do not want date *one* until you come back.

I'm going to write again tonight. Be good!

Love always, Barbara

---

*Virginia Edwards Kitchens was Charles's cousin. She lived in Fairburn and arranged Charles's first date with Barbara.

[Hdq. Det., 2nd Bn., 63rd Inf., 6th Div.]
                    Fort Leonard Wood, Missouri,
                    21 March 1942

My Darling,

Well, you still keep surprising me with your phone calls. I was really surprised last night. You asked me if I was alone, well, I was to a small degree. See the Sergeant slept only a few feet away from the phone, for the damn orderly room is but a few feet wide and he can hear all that is said. . . .

Dearest, I just want to be able to tell you over and over that I love you above all else and really I mean this with all that is in me. Darling, did you know that you have changed me into a man?? I guess you broke me of being a child. You started me to thinking and working hard to get up in life. No, not to get up in life visually, but inside myself. You have stopped me from experimenting with my future and with my life. I love you so much that I believe in you always. . . .

I talked to the clerk today and he said he was certain that I could get my furlough as soon as someone comes back. There are three boys due back Tuesday, so I am in hopes of getting my furlough to start Thursday (26th). I am sure going to plan on it at that time. I will wire you as soon as I leave Newburg, if I get it. I am sorry that we never know anything for sure, but I guess that is the Army for you.

Darling, I am tired tonight for I worked hard last nite and all day yesterday as table waiter and room orderly and today all day as KP. I sure will make some sweet girl a good housewife. I must close and get to bed.

Give my love to your Mother,

Lovingly,   Your Charlie

P.S. We have WSB,* Atlanta, on the radio right now. 9:00–10:00 p.m. your time. Pall Mall Program. CET

---

*A popular Atlanta radio station. The initials stood for "Welcome South Brother."

Charles was granted an Easter furlough in late March and early April 1942. He and Barbara spent most of the furlough together and were secretly married on April 5, 1942.

[Hdq. Det., 2nd Bn., 63rd Inf., 6th Div.]

Fort Leonard Wood, Missouri, 9 April 1942

My Darling Barbara:

How long has it been since I left you at the station? To me it has been years and years and in reality it has been but two days. Yes, it was a long trip but I wish it were starting all over today instead of being over today. You know if I were leaving today on furlough, I would want everything to happen just as it did. I can't tell you how much I feel the change and how happy I am to be able to realize the change. Things could have been a little different but I could not have been any happier. . . .

Barbara, you told me not to write about certain things, but I must talk around them, if you think it is all right. You know the only newspaper that had come since I was gone was the one of Sunday, April 5th. I was glad they sent that one. Perhaps there are people, things and days that are sacred to me as I hope they are to you. . . .

Barbara, could you be happier; are you sorry or unhappy about anything? Do you want nice long letters often? Do you want (   )?????

I know who my life and all belongs to so please just love and trust,

Your Charlie

P.S. Don't forget that picture.

Fairburn, Georgia, April 9, 1942

My darling sweetheart,

You'll never understand what this past week has meant to me. We've been away from each other about twenty-four hours and it seems to me that it has been ever so much longer. I love you more than I ever dreamed it possible to love anyone or anything. Darling, my whole life has been changed, my whole world now *"revolves"* but definitely around you and you alone. As long as I can make you happy and content then will I be the same. I'm living just for you, Charlie, I am now in your hands forever and ever.

May I complain a moment? Well, I couldn't go to sleep last night for love nor money. This morning I got up with a terrible headache and about ten minutes after having a piece of toast and coffee, I lost it. But I went to work and after about an hour began to feel some better. I suppose I just need a lot of rest, don't you? . . .

Darling, I'm going to do my best to write you every day. It seems that I should be able to but if I shouldn't, please remember that I wanted to and just couldn't.

Oh, darling, I love you so darn much. Gee, I wish you and I could be together tonite, but we have so much to look forward to, to work for, and to count on. I shall never forget anything that was said or done these last few days, and, Charlie, when I get to feeling so low and so downhearted that I can't stand it, I'll get off by myself and shut my eyes real tight and *remember*. We have so much to remember—good and bad. I will not forget the bad, for it is bad things that make good things so outstanding and sweet and important. You are all the good and the bad things that I've ever wanted, all rolled into one. I'm so thankful that we have each other and I pray that *nothing* will ever come between us. Honest, darling, you're all I ever wanted. I hate to think what my world would be without you. It's *our* world now, forever, 'til death do us part.

I must go to bed now. I really am a tired chicken and "definitely off the beam!"

Darling, above all, be a good soldier. By being good, I don't mean just be true to me, but to the Army. It's all been worked out to a fine point and regardless of how black things may look to you, try to see a broader view of it. Show those dumb nuts that you are just as smart as the next one. Do your work well and don't argue with your buddies. Be smart, but by being smart—well—in my opinion, it is smart to appear very dumb sometimes. Inside you know what the score is but don't let the other fellow know. Anyway, if you do have to go up the hard way, take *it* and like *it* because there's a reason for *it!* Show everyone what you can do without a pull from anyone. *You've got what it takes, let's see you use it!*

Darling, I don't regret anything, I love you too much. Oh, yes, it was simply swell of you to wire me. Darling, I love you, I love you, I love you. Every part of you and every one of your mean little moods. . . .

Remember to be good and most of all remember that I'm yours and I'm very proud of you and I'm right there with you, pulling for you.

Love always,   Barbara

[Hdq. Det., 2nd Bn., 63rd Inf., 6th Div.]
Fort Leonard Wood, Missouri, 11 April 1942

My Darling Barbie:

I received your note of Thursday and your letter of Wednesday both this afternoon. I can't begin to tell you how much joy a letter from you gives me. My heart just runs away when they call my name at mail call. If it is a letter from my Barbara I just read it over and over. You write so much like you talk that I can almost hear your voice. . . .

Darling, did you know that you and your Charlie have so much in common? To begin, both of us want the same things; like making each other happy, wanting to be near each other, wanting to be changed as we were Easter, just waiting for that little house and the trimmings, living and loving each other as we do. The things you said about last week, what it meant to you, well, it means just that much to me. . . .

Just remember at all times that I am yours and you are mine. I have been living for just you, Barbie, just as I will do 'til I have to meet my Maker. I am good, I have been good, and I am going to be good. You do not have to worry about your Charlie, for he will be dateless until he is with his Barbie again. Too, I know you will use the best judgement on your behalf. I mean, if and when, your folks begin to wonder why you aren't giving the boys dates. I only hope you don't ever have to for I don't know how it will affect me. You use your best judgement and I know that everything will work itself out o.k. I will let you worry about that part.

By the way, there is no one that reads my mail but me, so you may write anything that you should, or should want to write. . . .

There is a lot to be explained about me and this detachment. The detachment is divided up into sections: Intelligence, Message Center, Headquarters (truck drivers, clerks, etc.), Ammunition and Pioneer sections. When a man gets into any section and remains in that section for over four or five months, he generally stays there. Then, to get a rating he has to wait for the other fellows to move out. Now, I have been in the Intelligence section for over five months. The Staff Sgt. is going on Cadre; the two corporals are going to OTS. One man has been moved to the HQ* section, the other three privates have been sent to OTS, too. I told you about this man, Smith, coming back (over 28 years of age) well, he has really been in the Intelligence section longer than I have, and so he is in front of me for a rating. If things go as I am hoping that I get a Corporal rating soon. As you see, there is not or will not be anyone left in the Intelligence section but Smith (the new man), and your Charlie. There are but two ratings in the section and they will both be open in a week or two. I don't hardly see how I can miss getting a rating. . . .

We get free mail now, I guess you know. No stamps are needed, you just put free. . . .

Neither of us regret our love or our actions. I am really too proud of everything that has happened to me in the last week or so. Actually, I can feel you near me, it gives me more belief in my own action and outlooks. I can go through anything as long as you are my Barbara.

As never before,   Your Charlie for life

P.S. They are playing "Miss You" on the radio. Do I? More than anything I can ever know.

*Headquarters.

WESTERN UNION

Miss Barbara Wooddall   Waynesville, Mo.
Fairburn, Georgia   5:10 p.m. 12th

Sure miss you but we have our Easter to remember. Love,

Charlie

Fairburn, Georgia, April 22, 1942

My darling sweetheart,

   . . . Darling, I can't take it! Oh, I can too, but you have no idea how hard it is. I'm so irritable at times and like today when I didn't get a letter! It's more than I can stand. I didn't hear from you Saturday or Sunday, *but* I received four letters Monday. I'm so glad that you wrote me. When I got home last night the letter waiting for me was the sweetest and best yet. . . .

I had the YWAs* tonite and I thought they would never, never leave. I wanted to talk to you so bad and when they finally left Mother wanted to fix a couple of dresses for me and then I had to have a bath. It's now eleven o'clock and I'm so clean and pure in every way but my thoughts. They're mean and black 'cause I'm in a very bad way!! and I can say that again! . . .

Our Sunday School class is having a "Mother/Daughter" Banquet May 15th. I'm Chairman of the Program Committee. I wasn't at the business meeting, so that's what they wished off on me. They also elected new officers and asked me to be president of the class. They said that they chose me because I was such a good BTU† president (HA!). If I accept it will mean having charge of the opening devotional program (15 minutes) every other Sunday. At least that would keep me busy, would it not?

Some things have happened that I'd rather not mention but I must (in a mild sort of way). Well, a boy from Griffin came over Saturday

*Young Women's Auxiliary.
†Baptist Training Union.

nite. He's o.k. and everything was all right. Well, Daddy told me the next morning that he bet my conscience hurt me. Scared? I was scared stiff! I just knew he heard that I was——(get it?). Well, a little later Mother told me that Daddy said he did hope I was going to tell you about that, because if I was truly in love I shouldn't keep anything from you. So, now I don't have to go out to blind them because they sorta know how things are between us and that's what matters.

Darling, I love you and only you and when this War is over we shall start all over again—but until then we shall be good and true and loyal. I shall and I know you'll do the same.

When I can adjust myself to the fact that you are 'way 'way off and that you are loving and missing and needing me just as I am you and when I can realize that all this pain and sadness and sorrow is temporary, I know my sweet (if you could call it that) disposition will conquer this ugly and mean way I now feel and I shall be happy and carefree just waiting, waiting for you.

Your letters mean a great deal to me and my outlook on life. They make my day happy or sad. If I don't hear from you I'm *bad!* All inside I mean. I suppose you've just spoiled me in that respect.

Darling, if I could only see you for five minutes. Oh, shorter than that—if I could only see you! I need you, baby, so just don't forget that if you're not true or if you lose your love for me or anything—just remember that all this time I'm building myself up and I couldn't stand for it to be an awful let-down. I couldn't, Charlie, without you I'd be dead!

I love you, darling, with all there is in me. My heart cries out to you. Please, darling, let's be real! real! good.

Love always,   Barbara

The strength of her love is wonderful admirable and awesome.

[Hdq. Det., 2nd Bn., 63rd Inf., 6th Div.]

Fort Leonard Wood, Missouri, 25 April 1942

My Dearest Barbara:

Well, at last I get a chance to sit down and talk to you again. You will never know what last night's telephone call meant to me. I was so happy that you called, I was just thinking what a wonderful thing it would be to just talk to you when the phone rang and there you were. See, Darling, you just make my small dreams come true; I love you so much. We never do get to finish our conversation, always after we hang up there is a thing or two that I had forgot to say or tell you. Well, anyway, I can say them in a letter. You act as if it were a sin to let people find out about us. Why don't you think about it and see just how wonderful it is to know that you have come so far in life hunting for the right person and had success to find that *one* and he loves you as much as you love him, besides being otherwise attached to you. I am not in the least bit ashamed about our secret, are you? I am proud to be yours and I think you are proud to be mine, are you? Hope you will answer all of my questions and truthfully. . . .

Darling, I too believe that our God has been extra good to you and I. We are living a pure, clean, waiting life that shall always be true. I'll tell you now, I will be true to you until I find that you have been untrue to me. I am going by the Golden Rule as much as I can: "Do unto others as you would have them do unto you."—Shall that be *our* standard? Darling, you will not ever break my heart, will you? *Answer.*

His awesome strength and love were wonderful

You know sometimes I get afraid a bit, maybe of you, perhaps of my love for you. See, I am just putting my all up for you. Everything I do is for you, I am living for you and I have no defense up against you. It used to be that I played my girls like a game—always having two—and always fooling both of them, but when I found you I said that you were the one for me and if so, all of the tactics I had used on other people should never be used on you. When April the 5th came along, I told myself a lot of things. I just set the law down on myself, so to speak. This love of ours now is no game and should not be played or treated as such. Our love is serious and for life. It will never be anything less sacred to me than my religion or my God. Do you look at it in that way?

Moving words

There are a lot of unwritten laws attached to a man and his wife. I shall always respect you and those laws as long as you act the part of a *true wife*. I realize that it may take some time for each of us to adjust ourselves to this new life. There are a lot of little habits of thought and action that we both shall have to break away from because they are selfish and not for two persons in love.

By the way, you did not explain a thing about that date. Anyway, I guess you had to date him to keep the secret but not again. Am I right? *Answer*. I can't help it if people do talk and ask why you don't date, you are mine and I really don't want you going out. You would not want me going out, would you?? *Answer*. Anyway, this is *our* life you and I are living so it will hurt no one to let the town talk a little, will it? At least we knew what the score was before we got this way, didn't we, darling?

These weekends sure get me down, everyone about leaves for home or to see their girls and mine is too far away for me to go see except on furlough and we get furloughs so seldom. Wish I was getting one now so I could be with you on our Sunday. Tomorrow makes three weeks, yes?

When did you say your birthday was? I want to put a few dates down so I won't forget them.

Looks very much like rain outside and it is pretty cool. I am glad I don't have to go anyplace tonight, I hate to get all wet in the rain up here. It's funny too, because I used to like to get out in the rain back in Florida. Perhaps I have grown up to be a man. . . .

My Barbie, would it not be wonderful to be back five years, but the same age as now. We would sure have had a beautiful time. Just you wait 'til this war is over, then we will show the world what a love a man and wife can have. Until then we will show the whole world how a real *true* love is kept true. I am so happy and content that I found you. I do thank God every day for being good to me. You can bet that I will be the best person you could have chosen, just wait and see.

I love you,   Your Charlie

P.S. Tell me if these long letters bore you. I just can't stop when I get started.

Fairburn, Georgia, April 27, 1942

My darling sweetheart,

Well, how is the sweetest boy in the whole wide world tonight? I hope you have rested by this time and also that your head doesn't hurt. Darling, don't you think you should find out the cause of your headaches? I know it's caused from something more than fatigue and I wish you would see the doctor—please, darling, just for me if nothing more.

Have I been refusing dates!! Well, I won't brag—because you'd know I was "fibbing," wouldn't you? Well?! Don't agree with me!! Anyhow, I had a chance to go out tonite and tomorrow nite (with different boys)!! But I said "Thanks, but I'm not dating"—aren't you proud of me?

It's funny tho', I used to *never* stay at home. If I didn't have a date I'd go somewhere, it really didn't matter where, so long as I was going. But now I work as hard as I can and on Saturday and Sunday I ride my bike or do something that uses up a whole lot of energy—then by night, why, I'm glad to write you and then hit the hay for a good nite's rest. Not bad, eh?

This being away from you is terrible. Gee, how I wish you were here tonite. Oh, baby, you just don't know!

21 days!! since————!!

Tonight three weeks ago we were riding in beautiful Florida with Betty and James.* Remember how pretty the moon was? And weren't we panicky and excited and poor Betty was just about as bad as any of us. She's a swell girl. Do you remember that dope's name in Ocala? The screwball! I'll never forgive him as long as I live. He sure could have saved us a lot of time and energy etc. Anyway, I actually get goose-pimples just thinking about the wonderful nite of the 4th and especially the morning of the 5th. . . .

The radio is on and they're singing "My Buddy" and that doesn't help me a darn bit! Charlie, I love you so damn much. Sometimes I wonder how I stand this, but every day I go right on with my working, eating, and sleeping, and then another day is gone and I love you twice as much as I did the day before. How can I do it? . . .

Sweetness, I want a *real* love letter. I want one that will make me feel so close to you that, well, that I'll cry or do something drastic. Did you know that I tho't you were very, very sweet to write me so much? It means a lot to me—more than you know!

---

*The couple that accompanied Barbara and Charles on the night they were secretly married.

I sho' does need yo', honey chile! Gosh, oh, gee, what I wouldn't do —if you were only here.

Wasn't it fun talking last nite? I'm real proud of myself for being able to carry on a conversation for a change. Hon, you sounded so good—it really helped me in more ways than one! . . .

Until next time, darling, remember that I love you and I'm being very good and true, so you do the same, will you?

Your loving wife,   Barbara

Fairburn, Georgia, April 29, 1942

My darling sweetheart,

I love you, darling. You're so sweet to write me such nice letters and so often too. The one I received today was the nicest yet. It seems to me that they get better and better, and Charlie, I adore the long ones. Do you like to get long ones from me? . . .

In reference to your letter:

(1) I'm not ashamed of you and I don't think it would be a sin for people to find out about us—*BUT*—it was our agreement not to tell for more reasons than one. In the first place, it would hinder us both—you in the Army and me at home and especially at the office. In the second place, our parents would lose all trust in us. I know how Mother and Dad would feel towards you and surely after such a wonderful week, your Mother and Dad would think me terrible! Now, if you'll apply a little common sense to the whole affair you'll understand perfectly. Charlie, we've got to keep it a secret for a while anyway! I mean it!

(2) Yes, I believe in the Golden Rule, and if everyone in the world were living by it right now, we would have a much prettier world to live in and a peaceful one too.

(3) If I ever even hurt you in the smallest way it won't be my fault. I'm living just for you and my greatest desire is for you to be happy.

(4) No, I don't have to date again and I hope I don't. I certainly am not planning to—I don't want a date—and I meant it! Double plus!! It's o.k. by me if the whole state talks—why should I care?

(5) My birthday is September 14—when is yours?

Darling, we shall keep our secret. We've got to! . . . And it would hurt [Mother and Dad] to know that I wouldn't confide in them, because I always have, especially Mother. At least they know it's the real thing, this love of ours, so please try to understand why I had rather not let anyone know.

Darling, I love you so much. I miss you too. By the way, what are we gonna do about meeting each other somewhere. Why I have day-dreamed more about coming out there or meeting you half way. Won't it be wonderful when we do?! I can hardly wait to see you again and I know it won't be so very long. Will it?

Let's be good,

Your loving wife, Barbara

Fairburn, Georgia, May 5, 1942

My darling, dearest sweetheart, *wow! I love all the endearments!*

Gosh, how I do miss you! What I wouldn't give to be with you tonight! Darling, your letters are getting few and far between—why? I know that you must be busy all the time and when you aren't working, you're probably dead on your feet. I just declare, I didn't know I was capable of loving anyone like I love you. Wish I could put on paper just how I do feel about you, darling. I can hardly wait until this ole war is over and we're together. My Intermediate BTU is doing swell now. There are 16 on roll and 14 were present last Sunday nite. We're planning a social. I think it's going to be a bicycle-picnic. Should be fun. I just wish you were here to help me with them.

I was talking to Martha,* my sister, Saturday, and asked her what she'd think if I was married. She said that she wouldn't be surprised, but Mother once told her that if any of her daughters married secretly she couldn't stand it. I laughed and said that Mother hadn't counted on a War when she said that.

Yesterday all of the gang went out to Stinchcomb's Lake and went swimming. I swam (after a fashion) out to the raft and back and got out.

*Martha Wooddall Gastley.

The water was so cold and I was afraid to sit up on the raft very long because I was already so blistered. After everyone got out, we played the "juke" and danced. After church we played tennis. I came home and fell in the bed and felt very bad about not writing you. Forgiven? . . .

The Cotillion Club meets tomorrow nite down at Eleanor's. We are planning a dance at the USO Headquarters. I was appointed to talk to Mr. Cobb, the manager, and that's why I asked you about it first. A lot of our girls are married, but they're planning to go. I will keep you posted on the progress of it.

Mother and I have had such fun tonite. We went out on the porch after supper and she helped me embroider some things. Then, we had Coca-Colas and talked about everything and everybody, including my darling Charlie.

There are lots of things I'd like to tell you, but it's too much to write and you wouldn't like it anyway, maybe. Don't forget to have me tell you when I see you.

Darling, I must close now and take a bath and go to bed. I'm in need of sleep—bad! It's only 9:30, so I should be able to make it by 10:30 at the most.

Be real good for us and I will too. Don't forget that I miss you and love you more and more each day.

All my love forever,
Your loving wife,　　　　　Barbara

[Hdq. Det., 2nd Bn., 63rd Inf., 6th Div.]

Fort Leonard Wood, Missouri, May 9, 1942

My Dearest Darling,

I received a very sweet letter from the one girl of my life, you. Your letters get a lot sweeter as the weeks go by, I love you for every nice thing you ever say. . . .

The roster came out for the Intelligence Section this a.m. Can you guess what was beside my name, no?? Well, it was written:

"Section leader—PFC Smith"
"Ass't Section leader—PFC Taylor"

Now get this straight, the section leader is supposed to be Staff Sgt. and the Ass't Section Leader is supposed to be a corporal, but at the present time we are overloaded with rated men and as soon as they leave then Smith and I will get rated. We are losing four men out of my section, but besides these four we have a Staff Sgt. that is going on Cadre as a 1st Sgt. who is still attached to our section. The corporal of my section is due in Benning May 18th, so his rating will be open week after next. Besides this PFC Smith is up for OTS and will more than likely go in a month or two—as soon as he has served 3 months at continuous service as an enlisted man.

Understand what that means? Well, it means this, as soon as this Staff Sgt. and these 4 men leave (probably this month) Smith will go to Staff Sgt. and I will go to corporal. Then, as soon after that as Smith is called, it will put him in OTS and then I will go to Staff Sgt., I hope. Does that sound good to you, darling?? Boy, O, boy, perhaps I am going somewhere at last. I had almost given up hope but things do look brighter, don't they? Do not misunderstand this above—I am not a corporal yet—but in all probability if my work continues to be good as ever I will make corporal as soon as these men leave on the 18th. Will keep you posted.

Darling, I feel like I am making good for us, please be patient with me. Anyway, if I am climbing up the ladder, I worked for it and got it the hard way—no one pulled me up because I acted a yes man or laughed at their jokes. I can be proud of that when the time comes to be proud of myself, can't I??

Dearest, I am glad that you do enjoy my letters for I have tried to make them as interesting as I could, but at times I wonder if you get tired of reading the same old thing over and over. I write how things are and what I think about this and that and how I miss you and love you . . .

Barbie, I would give all I have to be with you this weekend. I need you to love forever. I can wait and be good for you and us until our day gets here, so don't worry. I love you more than ever.

Love forever, Your Charlie

Incredibly sweet.

Fairburn, Georgia, May 21, 1942

My dearest, darling sweetheart,

I have so much to say to you tonight that I hardly know where I should begin—I guess I love you more tonight than I ever have, even when you were here. I know you must be thinking about me rite now! because never before have I felt quite so close to you. Gosh, how I wish you were here. Darling, I have a *good case of the blues* now, but I'm not going to show it. It isn't right for me to make others around me unhappy just because I am, but I feel that it will help you to know that I am missing you more than I can ever say. I honestly believe that you know exactly how I feel, don't you? . . .

A lot of people have told me I was too young to settle down to one boy. Does that infuriate me!! I mean it does!! Gee, I don't call it "settling-down," I call it starting life anew with new vim and vigor. I'm so proud of you and everything you stand for. I just wish I was with you tonight.

Your idea of my taking my vacation soon is fine, but just to have it so I won't forget who I love and to whom I am married is undoubtedly the silliest and most absurd thing I've heard of a grown man saying. I'm sure you didn't really mean it that way. . . .

Your Mother and I have quite a correspondence going on between us and I do believe she likes me a lot. I hope and pray that she thinks half as much of me as Mother does of you—that way all concerned will be happier.

I know I must have been sitting here for an hour. I will close now but not before I tell you that I love you more and more. I'm always with you, Charlie, just as you are always with me. I am good and true, don't worry, please. Everything that I say or do is done or said because I feel that it is right. I wouldn't intentionally hurt you for anything in this world. We're each other's, darling, forever, and I'm very, very glad.

With all my love,

Your Loving Wife,   Barbie

[Hdq. Det., 2nd Bn., 63rd Inf., 6th Div.]

Fort Leonard Wood, Missouri, 24 May 1942

My Darling Barbie,

It is about eight-thirty—"our day." I am always a little happier and a little prouder on Sunday, because it was Sunday that I promised to love you and be just yours the rest of my life. I hope it will always be that I shall keep all of those Vows. I think now that it will be easy for that is all I am living for—to be yours and help to live *our* life and make you happy. . . .

I am good at daydreaming and have often been called a dreamer, but it sounds good and too, it gives me a lot of hopeful ideas. Let us dream awhile, suppose you had come up here Friday and I had met you Saturday evening, we could still be sleeping, about ten we would get up and get all prettied up and eat breakfast and then off to church. After church we would probably go have dinner and then take a nap til around four. Then go out in the woods for a nice walk, might even have a camera and take a few pictures. . . .

Barbie, please check up and see if you can come up on or around the 5th of June. If you can't come up then, or you feel it would be better to come at an earlier date, well, you just decide and let me know so we can make a few plans. You know the dates that you aren't feeling well and you could say when it is better for you to come up. Anytime you can come will be o.k. with me. . . .

I have to go bathe and shave and get ready to go to church. Will think about you all day and all the time until you get here.

I love you truly,   Your Charlie

Fairburn, Georgia, May 29, 1942

My dearest sweetheart,

For quite some time I have been trying to write you that I can't come out there. I'm up at the office now and have plenty to do, but I'm going crazy! In all your letters you seem so "enthused" about my coming out there, but, darling, I just can't afford it. I'm so sorry—guess I want to come worse than anything I have ever wanted to do in my whole life. I'm very unhappy about the whole situation, but I just plain don't see how I can come. I'm sure that you will understand. Sweetheart, perhaps it won't be long before this WAR is over and we'll be together forever. If you are still at Fort Wood later on in the summer perhaps then I can come.

Gosh, darling, I want to see you so bad. I love you more than life itself.

I know Mr. Mac* is going to fire me if I don't get to work, but I did so want to get this off at lunch.

Don't forget that I'm yours as long as you want me.

Love always,   Your loving wife,   Barbara

P.S. Will write you a long letter tonight.

Fairburn, Georgia, June 2, 1942

My darling Charlie,

I'm definitely going to burn up before this summer is over! I'm so hot right now. You said in your last letter that it was hot in Missouri, well, brother, you have my sympathy!

What I wouldn't give to get a letter from you tonight. I feel sure that there will be one at the office tomorrow.

Darling, what are we going to do? This being away from you gets worse by the minute. Gosh, I love you. It can't be so very long before we see each other again. I do wish that I could come up there but it's very foolish and "impractical." But, for that matter, isn't everything foolish in time of WAR.

I know I shouldn't talk about things like this, but, you know, sweetheart, I'd never forgive either of us if you were shipped out before we were near each other again. It's something to think about, isn't it?

It makes me so happy to know that we're married. I know I couldn't stand it if we weren't. Don't ever lose faith or trust in me 'cause I'm yours, hon, and you'd have a harder time than you think if you ever

*Mr. Mac was Barbara's boss at Twentieth Century-Fox.

tried to get rid of me. Everything I do is done because I know that's what you'd want me to do.

We're strong enough to take anything this ole WAR tries to push off on us, aren't we?

Some people criticize "war loves and marriages" but as for me, I would do the same thing again. As a matter of fact, I don't know but what this WAR is going to reform the whole world. It's teaching us the importance of real, true love. We're both facing the greatest test in our lives. I know that as long as we both live good Christian lives that we're sure to come out on top!

I'm a little on the blue side tonight, darling, so I'm sure you'll understand if I don't talk anymore. Will write again tomorrow night and until then—

I love you and miss you more than anyone else ever has, or will.

Love always,   Your loving wife,   Barbara

Fairburn, Georgia, June 18, 1942

My dearest sweetheart,

Darling, I received the rings this p.m. and I'm so very, very happy. I've never seen an engagement ring exactly like this one and I'm thrilled to death with it. I tried my best to write your Mother and Dad a sweet, conservative letter, but I'm so thrilled—that I know they won't be able to get a sensible phrase out of it.

When I got the registered mail notice this afternoon, our porter had gone for the day, so I flew out of the office and up to the Post Office without a bag, hat, or even permission to leave. Well, first, I didn't have any sign of identification about me, soooo, after much deliberation they let me have the package, threatening me with the FBI, NRA, FDR, and what-not! I opened it the minute I got back to the office and I was so excited and thrilled that I didn't do a lick of work all afternoon. I tried to work but there was no point in it. I showed the ring to four of my closest girl-friends and tonight I fixed my nails to a "fare-thee-well" and boy, will I knock 'em all cold tomorrow!!

Darling, I just know that it is the prettiest, loveliest, and everything "goodiest" ring that I've ever seen.

Mother and Dad had to sit down when I showed it to them, and Martha and Dot* are green with envy because it's much prettier than theirs. Dot almost cried because she said it sure did make her feel old to think about her kid sis getting married. They both contended that I was already married and they said they were going to write you and tell you that I confided in them, etc.—soooooo, if they do, don't you believe them, 'cause I didn't and furthermore, I'm never going to. . . .

I hope that you can get a little sense out of this but I'm happier than I've ever been in all my life and I can't seem to keep my thoughts straight.

How I do love you!! I wish you were here, darling, I'd eat you up, I just know that I would.

I just can't write anymore because I can't sit still any longer.

I'm so proud of you, of my ring, and right now I'm sitting on top of the world. Let's always be just as happy as we are now, regardless of what may come and go.

I thought my eyes were strained from looking for the ring, but I didn't know what the word meant until now. I just can't keep my eyes off of it. Don't blame me, do you?

I love you, darling, and I always, always will.

Be good (no use to even mention that, huh?).

Your loving wife,   Barbie

[Hdq. Det., 2nd Bn., 63rd Inf., 6th Div.]

Fort Leonard Wood, Missouri, 18 June 1942

My Darling:

This letter will have to be short and I hope clear.

This *bill* came through (more pay bill) and all men who were married secretly or otherwise had to turn their names and their wife's name and this was an order. I turned your name in. You are allotted $22.00

---

*Dorothy Wooddall Barrett was Barbara's oldest sister.

out of my pay and the government adds $28.00 to this, which makes a total of $50.00 per month you will get. There is a catch to it however, this money will not be paid to us until November 1st, when at that time we will get a total of $250.00 in a lump sum. This is payment for June, July, August, September, October. See?? Darling, what do you think of this? I hope it is o.k. by you.

I will write you more tomorrow, but it is now ten-thirty and I must stop for I have a 12-mile hike with full field equipment, I am tired already.

Please don't worry about this for I know they (the government) will not make inquiries for some time. If I have to turn your address in, which do you want, home or office—you know if the government writes to you they will send it to Mrs. Charles E. Taylor, so let me know.

Gee, I love you more each day. I wished today that you had sent me a letter. . . .

All my love,   Your Charlie

[Hdq. Det., 2nd Bn., 63rd Inf., 6th Div.]

Fort Leonard Wood, Missouri, 19 June 1942

My Dearest Darling:

What is your middle name or do you have one? If you do have one, please let me know what it is, don't guess I ever heard it. They called me down this a.m. and I signed the Class "A" Allotment to you as my wife. Now you will have to send me the marriage license pretty soon or as soon as you can think to do so. I have to prove my certification with it. This allotment was made compulsory, so I had to do it, or if they had found out I was married and had not made this allotment I would be subject to court martial.

Perhaps it is not plain so I will tell you over. Each month starting the month of June, the government takes out $22.00 from my pay and adds $28.00 to my $22.00, which gives a total of $50.00 and this is given to you. However, you will not receive the fifty dollars for June to Nov. 1st inclusive until Nov. 1st. On Nov. 1st we will be paid $250.00 in a lump sum, which will be payment for June, July, Aug., Sept., Oct. All of this is clear to me, but I do not know how well I have explained it to you. All I know is that this money will come in handy. You know with this money you will be able to come up here, but I would hate to wait until November 1st to see you.

Could it be that we could make a loan from the bank and pay them back in November, around the 15th?? If we could borrow a hundred and fifty dollars, I know that would cover your coming up and all of our expenses for the two weeks you were here. Would that be wonderful or would that be wonderful? Just think I could be with you every nite from retreat to reveille and all Saturday afternoon until Monday a.m. Gee! that would be wonderful. Darling, with this new bill passed, a Staff makes $96.00 per month plus $35.00 for a wife, if he has one. I think we will be able to live on that, don't you? I just have to make the grade on this Cadre, don't I?

I sure hope we can arrange for you to come up for I think it would be a very good idea for us to plan when we are going to announce everything and what we are going to do after we do announce it. We have to decide if we are going to tell the folks (mine and yours) that we are *already married* or if we are going to do it over again. We have a lot to talk about and we can't get it thoroughly discussed and settled in a letter or on the phone. Do you see what I mean? I hope, for your sake, that we can be able to keep our marriage secret as you want it, but I don't know if we can or not with this new bill.

What if you get a letter addressed to Mrs. Charles E. Taylor at the office or at home. The cat would, then, be out of the bag. I think the sooner you get up here and we get married (as far as the rest of the world knows) the less grey hair either of us will have. Barbie, it will not worry me but I am afraid you will worry yourself half sick about anything getting out of the bag. Will it? . . .

I must stop and go to class now for it is almost about time. Please write me a nice long sweet love letter answering a lot of my questions.

Do you think you will ever be able to come see me?

Love forever,   Your Charlie

Fairburn, Georgia, June 22, 1942

My darling sweetheart,

I received four letters from you today—one of which I answered in a big hurry because I was scared to death. . . . Have you given them my addresses yet? Darling, what will I do. If we positively *have* to tell everyone we're married, I certainly don't want it to "leak out." Besides, if a letter came to this Post Office I would never get it because the postmistress wouldn't know who in the heck to give it to! And, if it came up to the office, I swear I'd never go back there again! I'm just about to go nuts even thinking about it! I can hardly believe the allotment was made compulsory, but, of course, I do, if you say so. How on earth would they ever have found out we were married? It puzzles me!!

Sure the money will come in handy, but is it worth it? I'd die if Mom and Pop knew we have been married all along. They'd lose trust in both of us. I know that they wouldn't object to my marrying you tonite if you were here—but they believe in people being fair and square. . . . I shouldn't even think of this—but somehow I wish we hadn't married. Not that I don't love you a million, million times more than I ever could love anyone else, but just for the simple reason that this is all so 'low-down'!!

By the way, I write you as often as is humanly possible and I do try to answer your questions as best I can.

My middle name is Louise!!

No, sweet, I don't care whether or not I stay two weeks—I just want two weeks' vacation so I'll be sure to have enough time with you, after my traveling time is subtracted!!

Yes, I can save $35.00 and also borrow some. My clothes will be beautiful!! HA!! and it's not funny, but I'll manage somehow, so don't you worry. Ole Barbie can do anything—you know, she makes such a handsome salary and has no expense or responsibility whatsoever. And, if nothing happens, I'll be in St. Louis, Saturday, August 8. Regardless of the cost, I refuse to go by bus—I'll come on the train. I'm not sure that I can get to St. Louis by 6 p.m., but as near that time as possible.

I don't believe there would be many sights to see around Waynesville, Missouri, so I'll be very conservative in my thoughts and not even wonder what it looks like on the other side of the tracks.

I can read your letters one way and you sound as if you're sitting on pins and needles for me to come out there and another you wish I wouldn't come but you know it's proper for you to act accordingly considering my plight!!

Do you remember one of the reasons we didn't want to tell when we were married? It was because it might hurt you in your work!! Well, I can't understand it! Darn it, why did it all have to happen this way! . . .

I know that I'm going nuts!! It's a bad situation any way that one looks at it.

Well, I won't worry too much—surely it will all come out in the wash!! I could just scream to think that it all had to happen this way— and I wish wash day would hurry up and come.

The more I write the less I say—

Until tomorrow night, I love you, darling, with all my heart.

Your loving wife,   Barbie

[Hdq. Det., 2nd Bn., 63rd Inf., 6th Div.]

Fort Leonard Wood, Missouri, 5 July 1942

Barbara, My Darling:

My sweet, I hope you can read this letter with the tenderness I am trying to put in it. . . .

We got back from St. Louis about noon, we are all really tired. Yesterday we paraded about *10* miles, 5 of which were marched at attention, that sure tires a man out. The temp. in the shade was close to a hundred, boy, the soldiers sure did pass out from heat exhaustion. They were all drunk about but the parade came out *good*. We had a good crowd for the parade. It sure made me feel good to march along and hear all of the applause and exclamations from the people.

Barbie, I went to town (St. Louis) last night with the purpose of sending you a dozen *red* roses, but it seems that all the florists were closed for the 4th, so no flowers. I had planned all week long to be sure and have you some roses on the 5th, our day, three months after "I do."

I guess I love you more than anything else in the whole world, so please don't ever try to get away from me ever for it would be a hard job. I guess you knew you had changed a few of my habits already—yes, now I smoke Chesterfield ciggs. and don't drink whiskey, other than Tom Collins, at a nice respectable hotel bar with my Barbara.

I wish you could see all of these men here in the Detachment—they are all drunk and have been drunk since yesterday after the parade. It was funny at first to see them stagger around but after a day or so I get sick of looking at them.

I am glad you talked to your Mother about our getting married upon your arrival in St. Louis on the 8th of August. I felt like she would understand just as I know my folks are going to understand. What did your Mother say, Barbara?? I hope she likes me and is glad that you are mine. Has she told your Dad yet? Do you think he will object to it? . . .

You had better learn something about birth control 'cause that is one thing I am not up-to-date on. I think your Mother can help you there more than any books or anyone else.

Barbara, you said something about my writing your Dad, perhaps you had better help me draw a letter up to send him. What should I say and how should I say it? I guess you mean for me to write and ask him if I may have the permission to take his daughter as my wife, "til death do us part??" I wish I were there so I could talk to him and to your Mother as I should. I am not so good at expressing myself very well in a letter.

Barbie, I got a cute letter from Dad yesterday and he said that he and Mother had fallen so very much in love with Barbara and he did not ever want any of us to ever let her down. Too he said, "We are pulling for you and I know that beautiful brown-eyed girl is going to be very proud of you and your work." I hope so, darling.

I will write both Mother and Dad a letter apiece and tell them that you and I have decided to get married when you come here in August. Will let you know what they write me but whatever it may be we will do as we have planned. I asked you before, are you going to put the announcement in the paper and set the date?

I know I haven't said all I want to say in this letter, so I may write you again tonight before I go to bed. I know that letter of July 1st was the sweetest letter I have ever gotten. I am so glad too that you were able to get two weeks instead of one. We are going to be so very happy for two weeks. I just know we will, for I do love you so much. Darling, I am yours forever and ever, so please, just trust me and love me 'til death do us part.

    Lovingly,   Your Charlie

"Our Day"
Fairburn, Georgia, July 5, 1942

My dearest sweetheart,

Well, here it is—our third anniversary—can you believe that we've been married three months!! And can you believe that it's only been a little longer than that since we were together although it seems like years. Oh, Charlie, I love you so much. I am so glad that you're my husband and I'm your wife. Isn't it heavenly to know that we are in love and we are each other's!!

Well, by now, practically everyone knows we're to be *married* in August. Mother and Dad are still all for it and Dot and Martha have been just lovely about it. They're being so swell about helping me plan about things and stuff. All of my girl friends are twice as excited as I am (they think) and Miriam is already planning a shower for me. I'm so glad that we planned to get married this way instead of telling everyone we were already married. It's so much fun this way, darling, I just know I'm the happiest person in the whole wide world.

By the way, you'd better find out if we can get married in St. Louis —me being 19—you see, Mother asked me if she and Dad would have to sign a paper, so for our sake, you'd better find out about it.

What have your Mother and Dad said about our getting married?? Darling, will they think any less of me for 'tying you down'??

I wonder if I'm strong enough to wait until August to see you. Of course, I will wait, but, gee, do I want to be with you! . . .

I'm sitting on my bed and let me know if you can't read this. Darling, if and when we have a house, let's have a good place to write letters, you know, good lighting etc.!! What's say!?!

I don't know how to say I love you except to write those three words, but, please, read them real slow and understand that no matter how cold and bleak they look on paper, that I mean them. I do love you. . . .

Wish you'd write me and tell me definitely to quit smoking. I'm smoking too much and I haven't will power enough to quit by myself. Wouldn't you like me to quit?? I'm not taking good care of myself either. What I mean is I've quit taking my exercises at night—I never drink any milk—and I haven't had a yeast tablet in months. You are the only person that can tell me to do something and I'll do it or vice-versa —sooooo—how about giving me a good talking to!! And, I don't know what the word sleep means. I'm not kidding. Charlie, if you will tell me a thing or two I'll appreciate it. Do you think I'm crazy??

Hon, I'm just living for August the 8th—I hope you're just as excited and thrilled about it as I am!!

Darling, I love you so much—almost too much—

Your loving wife,   Barbie

[Hdq. Det., 2nd Bn., 63rd Inf., 6th Div.]

Fort Leonard Wood, Missouri, 6 July 1942

My Darling Barbie,

How are you tonight, well and happy as ever? I have thought about you constantly all day and I feel so near and, oh, so very happy. Our love has been the sort one reads about in a *Saturday Evening Post*. Shall we talk about our love for awhile—I am on Charge of Quarters and have just to sit here in the Orderly Room until ten o'clock, wish I could talk to you the whole time, for I am lonely tonight. I get Charge of Quarters every 14th day.

Darling, do you remember that wonderful nite you and I met for the very first time. Perhaps you have a letter from me while I was in Wheeler, Georgia, that would disclose to us the date of our first few hours together. Why I am thinking of that night is, I was just trying to remember how I really felt about you the very first time I saw you. I do remember how I felt. Virginia got me the date, and I don't think I had ever seen you before that night, even though I distinctly remember Virginia telling me all about you. She told me that you were just the sweetest girl she knew and she felt sure we would have a good time dancing for you liked to dance as well as she knew I did. I remember just as well that whole night.

I remember how sweet and cool you did look when we came in Dot and Pip's* house. I liked both of them from the very start. Too, there was that boy from next door (can't seem to think of his name now) anyway, he was there. Believe it or not, but I was afraid he was your boyfriend when we got there, and it sorta made me angry, and I know it must have been jealousy right off. . . .

As I started, before you so graciously interrupted me on the phone, to tell you about our first nite. When you first walked into the room, I was a gone goose. I fell in love with you the minute I laid eyes on you. Guess I never did change. Remember those nice long walks you and I took on the Sunday afternoons I came up from Wheeler to see you. Barbara, I love you so very much sometimes it is awful hard for me to think. Really, I guess I am counting on your coming up more than I ever have counted on anything else. I will just go crazy before you get here. I am glad that it is not any more than 34 days before the 8th and I don't think I will be able to wait that long, do you? I am thanking God that it shan't be any longer. see p53+50

Darling, I have written before and asked you, are you going to announce our engagement in the paper after we hear from Mother and Dad?? *ans.* . . .

I think we will splurge on the 8th and spend the night at the Statler Hotel or the Jefferson Hotel. Both of them are the best hotels in St. Louis. Have nice grills and bars. The Statler is my choice, seems more like a Florida hotel than the rest. Anyway, I hope and pray that we both are able to make it o.k. I don't know as yet what would be best for you to do after you get there. Perhaps if you get to St. Louis around

---

*John "Pip" Barrett was married to Dorothy Wooddall Barrett.

12 noon, it would be best for you to catch a cab at the station and tell the driver to take you to the Statler Hotel and wait for me there. By the way, if you haven't eaten dinner by the time you reach St. Louis, they have delicious meals right there in the station. You will go to the Union Station, I think.

I do not know as yet what time I will be able to get there, for the first bus to St. Louis is at 6:45 in the afternoon, but there are a lot of boys that have cars who go to St. Louis on weekends, so probably I can get there sooner. Perhaps there are buses leaving Waynesville sooner. I will try to get there as soon as I can anyway. I will let you know in a later letter exactly or as near as I can find out when Saturday, August 8th, I can get there. Tell me if you are going on to the Statler Hotel when you get there, so I will know where I am to meet you. There must be a train that leaves Newberg about 1 or 1:30 for St. Louis but it doesn't put me there until about 5 o'clock that afternoon. Pittenger's girl came up on it last Saturday. I just talked to Fuller and he said I could get a train out o.k. that would put me in St. Louis about 5 p.m. Maybe I can get a 1-day furlough and meet you at the train. Anyway, I am sure we will get to meet there o.k.—I really can't wait to get there.

I saw some cute p.j.s in St. Louis, but the stores were closed. The p.j.s had short sleeves and bottoms, I'll bet I would look real sweet in a pair of baby blue ones, don't you??

Darling, please write me often for I need a letter from you every chance you can write one. I always want to read the sweet things you write, so never fail me. You know I am living just for you and nothing else. I know God will give us those two weeks of happiness together if we keep on praying and being true as we should. I love you 'til the skies fall and the mountains wear all away for I am yours in the eyes of our Lord.

Lovingly,   Charlie

WESTERN UNION

PFC Charles E. Taylor   Atlanta, Georgia
Ft. Leonard Wood, Missouri   July 13, 1942

Have had to change vacation. Arrive August first. Let me know immediately if this suits you. Remember that I love you and miss you.
Love, Barbara

[Hdq. Det., 2nd Bn., 63rd Inf., 6th Div.]
Fort Leonard Wood, Missouri, 24 July 1942
My Dearest Darling:

Here I am at the USO in the big city of Waynesville. I came down to reserve a room at the hotel from the 2nd of August on. I got the job done. I tried to get a room in a private home, but without success, I was very lucky to even get a room at the hotel. Facilities are so bad here in Waynesville for anything. I know you will hate the place before you leave, but it is the best I can do. We will stay at the Belle Hotel, one of the only two hotels here. The Belle has pretty nice rooms and the only persons that stay here are soldiers and their wives. There is not much to do during the day but sleep and maybe go to a show but that is much better than having no show at all.

They are having a dance here tonight and here I am listening to the pretty music while I write to the only girl I ever think about.

Barbie, I can't wait for you to get here so I can be near you. Darling, I love you so much I really hurt deep in my heart from loneliness for you. How I feel for these other soldiers that have no girl or wife like this perfect one that I love so very, very much, you. My dreams are but for you, just as everything else I do is for you and you alone. I know I am very lonely tonight; as the days grow longer as in reality the time grows shorter. Just think, 'tis only seven more days before I will be in St. Louis with the most perfect person I have ever seen.

Darling, I don't remember how much money I figured I would have by the time you get here, but—I will have only about $80.00. I think before I figured that I would have around $95.00 but I forgot my living expenses for this month, that will run about $15.00. By the way, our room will cost $15.00 per plus the deposit I paid. I checked on the places to eat. You can't eat at the hotel, for they do not serve meals, but there is a nice place right down from the hotel that has the best food in town. I am worried a little about this financial situation, but perhaps it will all be o.k. We sure will have to be conservative, won't we? Well, you see, we will have our expenses in St. Louis for Saturday —transportation from St. Louis to Waynesville and from Waynesville back to St. Louis. Then, I have to come from and back to Ft. Wood every day. Well, I guess we can make it o.k., I do wish they had given me about a 12-day furlough, but no such luck. . . .

Not as yet have I bought me any p.j.s. I was never any good at picking out any clothes so perhaps you had better start your job as a wife by buying the kind of p.j.s you would like for me to wear. Yes???

I wish I were able to talk to you tonight, I have so much to say. I don't know as yet if I will be able to meet you at the train or not—I have tried for 2 whole days to see our Cadre Officer and have been unsuccessful. If not, I will leave Ft. Wood at 12:30 noon and get there about 5:30 that afternoon. By that time you will be rested. If by chance I need to send you a wire it will be to *Mrs. Chas. E. Taylor*, c/o Statler Hotel. Too, if you get to the Statler before I do, you register as Mrs. Chas. E. Taylor and bring our marriage certificate. I would like for us to get *married* on Saturday *again*, but I don't see how we can get a license, for the City Hall or wherever you get the license will probably be closed and I can't get one until you get here for you have to sign it too. We can get one and get married in Waynesville, after we get here. . . .

I hope you have learned a lot from your Mother and at least your Doctor. Keep your thoughts for me and me alone for I love only you.

Your Charlie

P.S. Will you bring your picture when you come?

[Hdq. Det., 2nd Bn., 63rd Inf., 6th Div.]

Fort Leonard Wood, Missouri, 27 July 1942

My Dearest:

Guess what, I am going to be able to get a pass for Saturday a.m., so I will be able to meet you at the station. I talked to the Cadre Officer this afternoon and he said for me to get a pass from my Detachment and he would o.k. it for me. Boy, was I happy when he told me—sooo, I will be at the station when you do get there.

Well, Darling, I may have to do some studying while you are here, but I can study at the Hotel some nights. See, they are going to give us our Division tests next week, but don't you worry for I have been hitting the old books. . . .

Just think, by the time you get here, you will be officially known as Mrs. Chas. E. Taylor. Will you really like that? I know it makes me proud to have a person such as you to share my name as well as my life, I only hope I can make you proud of me, I am already proud of you.

It's now six-thirty, in five days at this time I will have been with you for about six hours. I am just like a kid waiting for Christmas to get here, I can hardly wait. Barbie, you know a lot depends on the outcome of the visit. What I mean, neither of us know what it really, really means to be married and we have a whole lot to learn. This life (married ways) will be a new life to both of us and we will have to learn what it is. I know I have and you have an idea of what you think it is, or more than likely just what we want it to be. I pray to God that you are just as happy the day you leave here as you are the day you get here. . . .

The radio is playing, "I'll Always Remember," they just finished playing, "Oh, Baby, How I Baby You"—Barbie, are you as happy and thrilled as I am; no, you could never be as happy as I am. God knows I have never been as happy and thrilled in my life. I'll bet I have planned what I would say, a million times—the first glimpse I get of you. Gee, I would not take a whole million dollars for you and my life in the future, just wait 'til this damned war is over, we will show this old world what real happiness is. No matter how tough the old go is after this war, we will be happy and just as in love as we are now. Let's always be in love with each other—don't ever let our love grow old or stale as the years go by. We can keep it young and we will. *How sweet, wise, and tender.*

Darling, this is probably the last letter you will have time to get before you leave for Missouri, so I must review you on your few instructions. I think for sure I will meet you at the station—in case your train is early—you come in the station and get a seat near the "Information Desk." If I am not there by 1:00 (one o'clock) you go on to the Statler Hotel and check in—don't forget to sign as Mrs. Chas. E. Taylor. When you get there (Hotel Statler) check and see if you have a wire for if something happens that I could not meet your train, then I will wire you what time to expect me in. Now, keep your chin up and don't get afraid, but be very careful how you blink or wink at people especially when I am around for I think I would have to break your neck. Now please be careful, and I will see you soon.

Lovingly,   forever,   Your Charlie

P.S. I can't wait to see you, I have missed you so badly.

Fairburn, Georgia, July 29, 1942

My dearest sweetheart,

. . . I'm sure I'll be nuts about the city of Waynesville. Why any place with you will be seventh heaven and you know it!! . . .

You worry about money entirely too much. Gosh, if we aren't going to have enough perhaps I shouldn't come. But, I am coming if nothing happens to prevent it. I was proud to hear that you didn't want a furlough because you didn't want to miss out on your school.

Darling, I love you a million times more than I did when you were here. I'm actually starved for you!! and I'm not kidding!!

About your p.j.s—I'll wait and see what kind of taste you have and if I don't like them, well, I'll see that you have some "pretty" ones.

I'm going to register in the name of Miss Barbara Wooddall because something might happen and the folks at home might call me and then —oh, you understand. I wanted to explain all this last night but Mother and Dad walked in just before I got to talk to you and then I couldn't say anything. . . . I don't want to get married in Waynesville. I want to get married in St. Louis, Saturday, August 1.

Of course I will want to see you the minute I get to St. Louis, but I'll also be very tired and worn out and dirty. So, if you don't meet me, it will be fine, because I can go on to the hotel and rest, bathe, and be all refreshed when you get there.

I won't get my pix until Monday and of course I won't be here to get it. Mother will get it for me however.

Why?? I haven't learned anything from Mother is because she has yet to tell me *anything*, she always took it for granted that I knew everything. And as for seeing my doctor, well, no. But I can say that I know what's what etc. Everything's really up to you, or didn't you know??

One of my girlfriends, who has been married since March, came by Saturday afternoon. She told me everything from the time she began dressing to be married until the present date. Well, she practically scared the stew out of me!! I'll tell you all about it when I come out there. I only hope and pray that our honeymoon will not be anything like theirs was. I'm going to do my best to do just the right thing, 'cause I want our marriage to have a good foundation. After that we can build our love "sky-high!!" And even if a little of it tears down now and then we can cheerfully and successfully rebuild it. Oh, darling, I love you— I can hardly believe that we'll be together on Saturday.

This is a rather long letter but I just feel as if I could talk all night!!

Darling, I'll have two pieces of luggage, a make-up kit, and a hat box. I could take everything in one bag, but Virginia said that I would look crazy going on such a long trip with only one bag. . . .

Guess I'd better close, I've got so much to do.

I love you—very much. Just can't wait until Saturday.

Your loving wife,   Barbie

Chapter Two

MARRIAGE ON THE MOVE

August 1942–June 1944

Overleaf: Barbara, Charles, Sandra Lee, and "Junior" in Gainesville, Florida, May 1944

THE ARMY WIFE

We've something in common,
The Arab and I—
We make up our beds
Wherever we lie,

I've lived in a tent
And an old slave house,
Divided my roof
With a Chinese mouse,

I've rolled out my rugs
On historic floors,
and polished the brass
Of a hundred doors,

I've picked up the chips
Of Grandfather's chest
And toted them east
and toted them west.

My curtains, like Alice,
change stature at will,
My garden has grown
On a window sill,

We've something in common,
The Arab and I—
We fold up our tents,
And depart with a Sigh.

Alexa Byrne Ford,
Saturday Evening Post,
May 31, 1941

By the time the Taylors celebrated their public marriage in St. Louis, Private Taylor had served in the United States Army for thirteen months. After Congress passed the draft law in September 1940, Charles had reported to his draft board for classification. He had also taken an Air Corps Cadet examination at Maxwell Field in Montgomery, Alabama, that fall, but failed it because of poor preparation in mathematics. His experiences as a freshman at the University of Florida, where he received a series of incomplete grades, and a summer in the Civilian Conservation Corps, which taught him the rudiments of military discipline, prompted him to enlist in July 1941 rather than wait to be drafted.

After enlistment, Charles was sent to Camp Wheeler, near Macon, Georgia, for basic training. He learned that, in the Army, having a name near the end of the alphabet reduced one's choices in many areas. As a recruit, he drew pay of $21.00 per month, which did not go as far as he hoped. His commanding officer was from Gainesville as well, but this coincidence proved to be only amusing; although they knew each other casually, they passed without speaking at the camp. On October 14, Charles was sent to Fort Leonard Wood, Missouri, as a member of the Sixty-third Infantry Regiment, part of the Sixth Infantry Division. He underwent more training while helping to build a bridge out of green wood, with poor equipment. His fellow soldiers, mostly "Yankees" from Ohio, were different types to this young man. He began to meet new ideas, new attitudes, and different moral standards. He also confronted veterans of the peacetime Army, who had their own ideas and ethics. Charles, like thousands of others, matured rapidly.[1]

The press was filled with stories, photographs, cartoons, and serious pieces about the dramatic change in the lives of these young men. Books on the experiences of men in World War I, slang dictionaries, advice on survival, and Marion Hargrove's best-seller, *See Here, Private Hargrove,* all helped both soldiers and civilians to adjust. The recently founded company, Pocketbooks, Inc., provided inexpensive, easy-to-carry, paperbound books for soldiers and civilians.[2]

As early as November 1941, Charles began to discuss applying to

Officer Candidate School. After being turned down in February 1942, he was accepted for Officer Candidate School as part of Class 121 at Fort Benning, Georgia, the following August. He began his training in early September, graduated on December 9, and was commissioned as a second lieutenant in the Infantry.[3]

When the Army began mobilization in 1940, there were only 14,000 professional officers on active duty. As mobilization continued, the officer shortage became more pressing, reaching near-critical proportions during the summer of 1942. In response to this shortage, enrollments in Officer Candidate Schools, which had been established in July 1941, leaped upward. By the end of 1943, approximately 300,000 officers had graduated from OCS, outnumbering regular Army officers by a ratio of 40 to 1.[4]

Among the many Officer Candidate Schools which were established, the most well-known and highly respected was the Infantry Training Center at Fort Benning, to which Charles was assigned. A report in *Life* magazine described the thirteen-week training program at Fort Benning as "the largest, most efficient, and most ruthless educational institution in the world." The rigorous program included instruction in the use of weapons, field and tactical training, map work, and, most importantly, the development of leadership skills. Approximately two-thirds of those accepted into the program made the grade and received their gold bars. Charles Taylor's training prepared him well for his later combat experiences in Europe and throughout his military career.[5]

When Barbara headed back to Fairburn in mid-August, the shape of her future with Charles remained uncertain. Charles, anxiously waiting to learn the outcome of his OCS application, reported to Barbara that he was praying "to make this 'cause I want this more than a lot of other things I have tried for." If he went to Fort Benning, they would "be in the same state," only 120 miles apart, with the opportunity to meet "for a few hours" each week.[6]

During the three months Charles underwent training at Fort Benning, the couple saw each other nearly every weekend and telephoned each other at least once a week. They also continued their correspondence, writing almost every day they did not actually meet.

These letters and the reported telephone conversations are filled with their happiness at being so near. Some weeks had passed before they began to realize that the travel, Charles's classes, Barbara's work through the week, and the tension surrounding finding a room and obtaining meals each weekend were weighing down their lives. But as frustrating as their "rushed" weekends seemed then, they had no idea of the extent of the pressures still to come. After the commissioning ceremonies, Lt. Taylor was stationed at Camp Gordon in Augusta, Georgia, and assigned to the Twenty-second Infantry Regiment of the Fourth Infantry Division. Charles hoped that Barbara would quit her job and join him in Augusta, even though she had recently written that she was "nuts about the work" and especially proud of her promotion to head of her department. Charles, however, came first, and she yielded to the need to be with him before he shipped out. After they spent Christmas together in Augusta, she decided to resign from her job and follow him.[7]

In making this decision, Barbara did not differ from other war brides of her generation. Millions of people were on the move in the United States as one of the major demographic shifts in recent years took place. The Census Bureau estimated that 15,300,000 civilians moved during the war, over half of them across state lines. People hurried to new jobs opening up in shipyards and war plants. Families sought out the precious times they could steal together "for the duration" or as long as would be granted them at the military bases where their husbands and fathers were in training.[8]

"War guests" were a commonplace near military installations and defense towns and cities. The press frequently offered suggestions to nonmilitary families on how to make space in their homes for service wives. Articles recommended taking in boarders and renters, both to supplement income and to ease the pain of travel for others. Magazines encouraged women to practice "old-fashioned neighborliness" by inviting war brides to clubs, teas, and into their homes. Nevertheless, wartime housing shortages meant that service wives sometimes had to double and even triple in tight quarters.[9]

Not everyone agreed that service wives should follow their husbands to military bases. Citing the pressures on already overcrowded travel facilities, the Office of War Information urged wives to remain at home. At least some observers described those women who went anyway as "selfish," pointing out that prices were high and conditions near military camps far too crowded. Wives often arrived at bases just as their husbands were about to be shipped overseas. Nevertheless, most wives, including Barbara Taylor, felt it was important to be with their husbands as long as possible.[10]

The popular press repeatedly discussed the subject in every detail. The *Atlantic* published articles condensed from Barbara Klaw's best-selling book, *Camp Follower: The Story of A Soldier's Wife.* Klaw reported on train travel, the difficulty of finding hotel rooms, the shortage of rental rooms, the "camaraderie" with others in the same circumstances, and "the shock of seeing your husband in uniform for the first time." (Of course, this latter did not apply to Barbara.) Klaw, like most other wives, found wartime housing grossly inadequate. She also discovered that some landlords charged outrageous prices and expected her to be a maid-of-all-work.

The wives Klaw wrote about banded together, giving each other baby showers, sharing information, doing anything to fill what she termed "the daytime void." Food was a particular problem: prices were high, quantity was often low as rationing took its toll, and quality and choice diminished as well. Some people found that they had to cook in shifts, as they shared kitchens with other service families. Such "delicacies" as Victory Sherbet and the ubiquitous macaroni casserole stood out as monuments to perseverance. However, life could be wonderful, particularly on special days like anniversaries, promotion celebrations, and moments together, swimming, talking, riding in a borrowed automobile, drinking "Cokes," and learning to cope with circumstances. Of course, there was the inevitable move to another posting, and, eventually, saying good-bye to your husband as he left for overseas.[11]

As Barbara contemplated following Charles across country, he tried to warn her of the conditions she might find. He cautioned: "Just wait 'til you get about 1500 miles away from home and have an Army uniform on; everything costs more to soldiers and the people in the towns near Army camps are there for a gold rush. Soldier's Money. They all get together and sorta set the prices to suit themselves." Other letters described long searches for high-priced rooms, and his fear that Barbara might have to remain all night in the bus station. Letter after letter used such phrases as "I am in hopes that things work themselves out but I have doubt of that statement." They yearned for the funds to buy a car and wondered whether or not they could get tires and gasoline, all now rationed. Charles groused about the lack of facilities and said, "I think it is a shame the way they treat the soldiers here—no place to put their wives—or no place or time to be with them 'cause they (the wives) are so far away." [12]

Women like Barbara could find a great deal of advice in the press and even in books on how to ease the difficulties of traveling. Wives were told what to pack and "how to live in a trunk." The many items to take included corduroy bed covers, valances, chintz curtains which could be cut to any length, slipcovers for battered furniture, cocktail shakers, game boards, tablecloths, napkins, electric grills, clocks, radios, ashtrays, toasters, percolators, and folding ironing boards. This may seem like a lot, but paper products such as handkerchiefs, towels, and tablecloths only began to be widely used during this period. Authors were also concerned about maintaining the morale of both parties as they moved about, and they worried that service couples might fall into "slothful habits." One writer remarked, "Now is the time to prove to your husband (and to yourself) that you have the stuff in you that our pioneer ancestors had. You'll be on your mettle to prove that you are every bit as good a manager and decorator as you are a sweetheart." [13]

Decorating and making a place homelike kept wives busy for a time, but filling in the "the daytime void" soon became paramount for most of these service wives. They joined the Red Cross, drove in motor pools, worked as volunteers in hospitals and at military service centers, gave blood and helped at blood centers, and took nurses' aide courses. They attended lectures run by the extension services of the state universities, where they learned about first aid, treatment for common diseases such as colds, and how to provide proper nutrition in wartime. Many war wives found temporary employment; approximately one-half of service wives worked for wages at some time during the war. However, it was often difficult to find jobs because employers were hesitant to hire transients.[14]

Wives and husbands benefited from a chain of service clubs, United Service Organizations, and the ever-available Traveler's Aid booths located in train and bus stations across the country. The USOs are remembered today chiefly from the film *Stagedoor Canteen* or from accounts of the huge facilities in Chicago, New York, San Francisco, or at "Rainbow Corner" in London. In fact, every town near a military base or on a major travel route had some sort of facility for travelers, and often the wives of servicemen operated and ran these clubs. Holidays, especially Christmas, were times of great excitement as well as homesickness, but group activities allowed the young people to overcome shyness, obtain helpful advice, and relax.[15]

The wives of servicemen were on everyone's mind. Dorothy Thompson seized the opportunity to preach an effective sermon directed to those in the limelight:

> The young war wife is invested with a social dignity and a public mission, if she cares to assume it, namely to be a supporter and preserver of American civilization. She must live for what her man is fighting for, and not betray him, his cause, her country and herself. He endures terrible hardships and undergoes unaccustomed disciplines for his country. She can share his endurance and his discipline. The young woman who sees herself as part of a community, with a duty toward it and a standard to uphold in its behalf, will find it easier, much easier, to meet her problems for she can to some extent depersonalize and sublimate them.[16]

If Barbara Taylor had read Thompson's injunction, she would have agreed, and certainly would have thought that she was meeting this standard.

In March 1943, Charles was transferred from Camp Gordon, Georgia to Fort Dix, New Jersey, and Barbara went with him. She was four months pregnant. As the date for the birth drew closer, they decided that it would be best for her to return to her parents' home in Fairburn.[17]

Barbara deeply regretted not having Charles nearby as she made the final preparations for the baby. While she and her mother were setting up the baby's crib, she "almost wanted to cry, just seemed like you should be here fixing it." Yet there were also a number of advantages to being in the familiar surroundings of her parents' home. Her mother was a constant source of comfort and help to her. As Barbara remarked on July 17, "Mother just won't let me turn my hand at any 'strenuous' work." A surprise baby shower given by her high school friends also helped raise her spirits.

Just as important, Barbara was extremely pleased with the medical care she received at nearby Fort McPherson. After her first trip to the doctor, she wrote:

> Oh, you know how I always feel when I go to the doctor—just sort of 'let down' or 'tired.' It was certainly nice out there at Fort McPherson. And there's no comparison to the Pre-Natal Clinic at Fort Dix. The nurses and the doctor (Dr. Gardner, First Lieutenant) just seemed to have all the time in the world to take care of each individual. In fact, I went in at 8:15 and didn't get out until 11:30 . . . [Lt. Gardner] was so nice—and after the examination he talked for a long time, telling me what to do and what not to do, what to eat, how to rub my breasts at night, etc. He thought it grand that I had been drinking a quart of milk each day, getting up early, resting during the day, and walking so much. He said it was very good that I had only gained 17 pounds (I weigh 134¾) because it was much easier to make a little baby gain than it was to have a big baby. All in all, it was really nice going there and I believe the main reason was because there wasn't any rush about it.[18]

A ten-day "delay-en-route" enabled Charles to go to Georgia in early August. He drove from New Jersey to Georgia, getting only a few hours' sleep during a roadside stop. When he arrived in Fairburn on August 7, Barbara was in labor. She was rushed by ambulance to Fort McPherson, where the baby, a girl whom they named Sandra Lee, was born just two hours later.

It was a welcome coincidence that Charles was with Barbara at the birth of their child. At precisely this time, he was accepted into the Army Air Corps and received orders to report, on August 18, 1943, to the classification center in Nashville, Tennessee. His delay-en-route came between the two assignments.

The new duty in Nashville was an answer to his long-expressed hope to be part of the Air Corps. At the classification center, the prospective students were given a battery of tests to determine whether they qualified as pilot, navigator, or bombardier trainees. Charles described the tests as "the toughest tests I have ever had since I left college." Among the tests was a psychomotor examination, the purpose of which baffled him.[19]

Charles was assigned to preflight school at Maxwell Field near Montgomery, Alabama. He remained at Maxwell from August 31 to October 2. This was a difficult program with much work in mathematics, aircraft identification, Morse code, maps and charts, as well as vigorous physical conditioning.

Barbara remained in Fairburn to nurse and care for Sandra Lee. Charles reported his progress and the difficulties he was having, remarking that "Perhaps I bit off more than I can chew. . . . I must be a little too damn dumb for this sort of thing. A lot of the boys are in the same boat. . . . There is a lot of cheating going on."[20]

Barbara filled her letters with queries about the Air Corps. She asked about the tests, the other candidates, and his sleeping arrangements; she wanted explanations of Air Corps slang. Above all, she urged him to get plenty of rest in order to do well on his tests. Her letters also included detailed descriptions of the baby's life: from nursing to her bowel movement in the bath, her first visitors, and her first carriage ride.[21]

Despite the grueling schedule Charles was maintaining, he took every available opportunity to make weekend trips to Fairburn. The train ride, normally four hours, often took much longer because of delays. Since Charles's classes lasted until 5:45 p.m. each Saturday, the earliest that he could expect to arrive in Atlanta was 10:00 p.m. The trip was "pretty rough," and "they only had fifteen hours together." On one occasion, Charles left Atlanta on Sunday evening at 8:30 p.m. and did not arrive back at Maxwell until 1:30 a.m. On Monday, after his usual early rising, the time was spent on gunnery and the "darn math which is swamping your husband," and he was "pretty tired."[22]

With all this travail, Charles still managed to complete his preflight training. The next stage was primary flight training at the Lafayette, Louisiana, School of Aeronautics. The question of whether or not Barbara and Sandra Lee should go to Louisiana immediately arose.

Even before Sandra Lee was six weeks old, Charles had begun to discuss the possibility of his wife and daughter "following the ole Army." Barbara was initially reluctant to join him. Articles in the popular press discussed the special hazards of traveling on crowded trains and busses with young children, exhorting mothers to take extra precautions and carefully prepare for the trip. Mothers must avoid the logistical problems associated with carrying too much luggage and, at the same time, provide sufficient diapers, bottles, baby food, and other necessities. They should also get enough rest and sleep. The title of a wartime publication on this topic, issued by the federal government, *If Your Baby MUST Travel in Wartime*, emphasized the difficulties. Nevertheless, women continued to travel all over the country with their babies.[23]

In mid-October, Barbara decided to join the growing ranks of traveling mothers and babies. Sandra Lee was now two months old, and Barbara felt that both she and the baby were strong enough to make the long train journey to Louisiana. Realizing that it would be "too much to come alone," however, she hired a young black woman to accompany her and help care for Sandra Lee. Barbara's letters to Charles about the preparations for the trip indicate that she was well aware of the complexities of the situation she faced. She wrote Charles that she planned to make "a complete list of my clothes and everything, so that when I begin to pack I won't leave something out. I shall bring as little as possible – now, I *will* need the cover for her cradle, won't I?" Four days later, she noted, "I need more than my two bags for both our things. I may send the coffee maker and bathinette on ahead of me. You have an alarm clock, don't you? Let me know."[24]

From mid-October until the completion of primary flight training in early December, Barbara and Charles were in Lafayette together. After that, Charles was transferred to Walnut Ridge, Arkansas, for basic flight training. The couple bought a used 1938 Buick, packed up their belongings, and drove the four hundred miles to Walnut Ridge. After much searching, they found a room in a private home. They shared a bath with five other couples. Sandra Lee slept in a foot locker. At first, Barbara ate the noon meal at a nearby boarding house. Soon, however, she was invited to eat all her meals with the family where they lived.

Unfortunately, basic flight training did not go all that smoothly for Charles. A bout with pneumonia in early January, which caused him to fall behind in his training, coupled with difficulties with his instructors, resulted in his "washing out" on February 12, 1944. Historians of the Air Corps have focused attention on the instructor problem, but just as important was the fact that Charles was in flight training when the number of pilots had reached saturation. In fact, in December 1943, seventy-four thousand students, the highest number of any time in the war, were involved in various aspects of training. In the entire wartime period, 40 percent failed to receive their wings, and "whenever substantial backlogs of trainees accumulated . . . higher headquarters stressed rigid maintenance of proficiency standards." [25]

Barbara was no longer with Charles when the washout occurred. After he was hospitalized with pneumonia, the couple decided that she and Sandra Lee should return to Fairburn. Barbara's mother, "Miss Mae," came to Arkansas to accompany her daughter and granddaughter on the return train trip. Upon learning of the washout, Barbara was supportive as usual. Her Valentine's Day letter to Charles began:

My Dearest Sweetheart:

It's been so hard for me to sleep, eat, or anything since Friday. (Not because you didn't make the grade, but because we don't seem to be as close as we should be.) Why, everyone says they more or less expected it because of your sinus and pneumonia—why, there are too many pilots now, therefore they just have to get rid of some of them, and it so happened your sinus etc. showed up and made it easy for you to be one of them. At any rate, you've surely learned a lot and they can't take it away from you. Both of us know it's for the best, now don't we? [26]

Over the course of the next four months, Charles spent very little time in any one place. He was stationed at Camp Joseph T. Robinson, near Little Rock, Arkansas, with the Sixty-sixth Infantry Division for about a month. In early April, he was transferred with his division to Fort Rucker in Alabama.

After Charles was transferred to Fort Rucker, Barbara and Sandra Lee moved to Newton, Alabama, near the post, where they found a one-room apartment with kitchen privileges. Both Barbara and Charles knew that the Sixty-sixth would receive orders for overseas duty very soon. Charles preferred to avoid serving in combat with the Sixty-sixth, so he volunteered for an individual overseas quota levy. Within a week, he received his overseas orders, and Barbara and Sandra Lee returned to Fairburn.[27]

In late April 1944, Charles was able to spend several days in Fairburn with his family. After he left, Barbara was required to address her mail to him to an Army Post Office number, although he had not yet been shipped overseas. Charles was at Fort Meade, Maryland, for a short time and was then transferred to Camp Patrick Henry, Virginia. While at Camp Patrick Henry, he telephoned Barbara nearly every night and continued to write her almost daily.

In May, Charles was transferred, preparatory to going overseas, to Camp Kilmer, New Jersey, near New Brunswick. Censorship restrictions prohibited him from informing Barbara of his whereabouts. However, he devised a code to evade the censor. He simply referred several times in a letter to "the 6th or 7th of last month, as a year ago," telling Barbara "that would be a very restful place to go and sorta get to feeling better. Your mother would keep the baby and thus you would have nothing to worry about at all." Barbara understood that he was referring to New Jersey, where they had lived when he was stationed at Fort Dix. A few days later, Charles sent a telegram to his sister-in-law, Martha, in which he instructed Barbara to come to New Brunswick, New Jersey, and register at the Roger Smith Hotel. He addressed the wire to his sister-in-law so that military authorities would not realize that he was actually telling his wife where he was.[28]

Barbara made the necessary arrangements and traveled by train to New Brunswick. She and Charles spent two weeks together there in late May and early June, enjoying a "second honeymoon" on the eve of Charles's departure for combat.

Just as Barbara and Charles had to say good-bye when their "second honeymoon" came to an end, they also had to think thoughts usually suppressed. What would be necessary to put his affairs in order in case of death or severe wounding in combat? The Army provided forms for wills, but it was also necessary to discuss insurance, debts, available funds, possible education, and a thousand other details which crowded in on their precious last hours together.[29]

As Barbara went back to Fairburn and Charles boarded his troopship, the *USS Argentina*, for Europe, they could look back on nearly three years of romance and love. In a time of great stress and anxiety their marriage was strong, sure, safe. And, as a wise observer of the day pointed out:

> Marriage at best is a tussle of wills. Given time, long, solid leisurely time, understanding and good faith emerge from the bout. War deprives marriage of time. It strips it of all opportunity to forgive and forget. It reduces it to quick, uncomplex unity. Marriage today has to do with simple sincerities. With love, understanding, patience.[30]

Those were, in fact, the hallmarks of their "marriage on the move."

Letters, August 1942–June 1944

Evansville, Indiana, August 16, 1942

My dearest sweetheart,

I am now in Evansville and it is 3:10 p.m. Guess you are well on your way to Fort Wood and I would give all I have to be with you. Darling, how will I ever do without you—even for a day!!

I went over to a cafe right across the street and got a breakfast. Sure did feel strange to be ordering for myself and not to have a pair of beautiful blue eyes looking right through me, and, oh, darling, I'm already so lonesome.

You are the most wonderful husband that I could ever have hoped or prayed for. You are so smart—you do everything just the way it should be done. Why, I could sit here and flatter you for a couple of hours or longer.

I was so proud of you when the train started moving in St. Louis. There you were smiling at me and waving, and, darling, it just made me feel good to know that you were my husband and I was your wife. When I couldn't see you any longer, well, I cried *just a little bit* and the lady sitting with me started crying. Jimminy cricket!! say I, everything happens to me!! Soon I found out that she had been to see her husband at Jefferson Barracks for the weekend. There were two girls across the aisle from me whose husbands are at Jefferson Barracks and Fort Wood.

By the way, the lady sitting with me asked me if you were an officer. She said that surely you must be because you certainly did look like one. Naturally I agreed with her!!

I'm here with a girl from Kansas who is going to see her boyfriend at Macon, Georgia. She's rather cute and I'm glad she's here. At least it's nice having someone to talk with.

You know, we have the most beautiful love in the whole wide world. These last two weeks mean a lot more to me than happiness at the moment—they mean that I have a husband who loves me just as much as I do him—they mean that I don't have to live from day to day any longer, but that *we* can live for the future when the WAR is over and we are together forevermore.

You certainly did more than your part to make our honeymoon a success and I love you for everything.

I still have your pen, but I will mail it to you "pronto." You forgot to give me your camera—suppose you have already discovered that by now, yes??

I have a whole tablet of paper, so I won't bother writing on the backs —now you won't have to hunt forever and a day to find the consecutive pages. . . .

Well, darling, I have been writing you now for an hour and 30 minutes. I'm tired of sitting so I think that I will sign off until tomorrow.

Although I know that I will miss you and sometimes be so lonesome that I can't stand it—I know also that I am very lucky to be married to such a perfect person as you are. We have so much to look back on and look forward to, and I just want you to know that you've made me very, very happy.

I love you,

Your loving wife,   Barbara

P.S. A conductor just called a St. Louis train and it took all the self-control and willpower I have not to jump up and run to the train that would take me back to you.

P.S. If you don't get any sense out of this letter, please don't blame me—I'm sorta tired. Perhaps by Tuesday nite I will be able to write a sensible letter.

I love you, B.

[Hdq. Det., 2nd Bn., 63rd Inf., 6th Div.]

Fort Leonard Wood, Missouri,

19 August 1942

My Dearest Darling:

It seems that I miss you more as the days go by but I guess you and I will be able to stand to be lonesome for a little while. After all, we did have the most wonderful time two people ever had in two weeks. I have thought so much of things that happened while you were here. You know, things like my watching you put rouge on your cheeks or like looking at you across a table. You are really so much with me even though you are far away (in miles).

I went up to the hospital for my final physical for the Officer's Candidate School this afternoon. Only got half through, so I have to go back in the a.m. Only have a Wassermann to take. I think the Division Board is to meet some time this week. At any rate, I hope they do. Would sure like to go on and meet them so I can know I will not have to go on maneuvers. The boys that meet the Divisional Board and pass to get on this month's quota will not be taken on maneuvers, but will be left here to go to Benning on or around the 15th of September. May God just let me be one of those men to make the grade. I have a good chance, for I have such a good grade from the Battalion Board, but still a prayer would help. You know, if I get to Benning I think I would be able to get the first two or maybe three weekends off, rather Sat. afternoon and Sunday, and after that I know I could have Sundays off. We could see each other some at least. How would that suit you?

That 25-mile hike is up for tomorrow, but I may get out of it because of this physical examination tomorrow. I still have not made up my mind about submitting my air corps papers—I think they need some thought. . . .

Barbie, to me our love is: beautiful, calm, clean, pure, warm, hot, cold, cool, sweet, lonely, happy, contented, and all of the other things we feel and learn to respect in this life of ours. I do know that our love is everything to me and it must go on and live and grow as the years go along. We have just started our life together. We did not have an ideal place to have our so-called honeymoon, nor was our honeymoon taken under ideal circumstances, *but* I can't see how we could have had a more perfect honeymoon anywhere else or at any other time. To me our honeymoon was perfect. Thinking back I can think of nothing that could be more beautiful than a life with you as beautiful as our honeymoon was. What made our honeymoon so perfect??? I'll tell you —we both more or less respected the will and the feelings of the other. We both tried to go more than halfway. Let us always have the same judgement and action, neither of us can lose that way. . . .

Just keep your chin up and say a silent prayer for our being together real soon.

All my love,

Your loving husband,   Charlie

Fairburn, Georgia, August 24, 1942

My darling,

We've just had a "black-out" and it was a grand success. I've just heard a report over the radio and it said that all over the county everything was dark except defense plants—they were allowed to keep on working. It started at 9:50 and lasted 50 minutes. I had to work tonight and also brought some work home with me.

I can't get my picture in either Atlanta paper because of the paper shortage. They aren't allowed to put any pix in the paper unless it is sent in within two weeks after the marriage. . . .

You certainly did write me a sweet letter Friday nite. Sure did make me want to see you, but surely if we pray hard and sincerely enough and it is the Will of God, it won't be very long until we are close to each other again.

No, I haven't seen my doctor but I will if I ever have time. IF!!!!!!!!!!

I love you more than ever. Gee, how I hate to cut off the light and go to bed alone, but I'm sure that all these lonely days and nights we're spending are proving to us more and more what we really mean to each other.

I love you, Barbie

[Hdq. Det., 2nd Bn., 63rd Inf., 6th Div.]
Fort Leonard Wood, Missouri,
24 August 1942

My Dearest Darling:

. . . Guess what?? Well, I don't know for sure and I will not ever count on anything in this Army again until I have *the orders* in my hand; but, I talked to a boy who works up in Division today at noon. Division is where all of the eligible lists for OCS come out. I told the kid that I met the final division board Friday nite and about the board calling me up here on the phone Saturday. He said—"more than likely you passed for if you had not they would not have been interested in your history the day after." (The radio is now playing "Miss You"—and I miss you "since you went away, dear—miss you, more than I can say dear—do you ever miss me as I miss you?" etc. etc.). . . .

Think of me often and talk to me lots when you go to bed for I will be listening to the winds for your voice. (Do you think I am crazy?)

Tell your folks hello, wish I could see them all.

Lovingly,
Your husband, Charlie

[Hdq. Det., 2nd Bn., 63rd Inf., 6th Div.]
Fort Leonard Wood, Missouri,
29 August 1942

My Dearest Darling:

Well, I have the good, good, news—I am due at Fort Benning, Georgia, on or before the 10th of September. That is but 12 more days. I am going to try and get an en route furlough, but I know before I try that I

*= I bet that the 1944 movie classic title SINCE YOU WENT AWAY was taken from the song MISS YOU. I never had really ed this fact.

will not be able to get one. I guess I should be satisfied by getting to go
to OCS. Isn't it just too wonderful. I am just tickled to death about it, I
am really happy about getting to go. I feel sure I can make the grades
at Benning. I was sorta worried that my orders might not have gotten through before this Division went on maneuvers. They leave about
three days before I am due in Georgia, so it was really close, for my
orders just came in today. God did answer our prayer, didn't He?? . . .

I love you dearly,   Your Charlie

P.S. So you think 2nd Lts. are the lowest things on earth. What will
you think of me??? Perhaps I better not go, yes????

Fairburn, Georgia, September 1, 1942

My dearest sweetheart,

. . . Tomorrow week you will be in Georgia! I do believe that God
answered our prayers and He certainly has been good to us. You know,
we're very lucky and I'm so happy about the whole situation. Every
time I think about it (which is all the time) I get weak all over. Imagine it—just being with you for ten minutes or five minutes will mean
everything. Mother and Dad and the girls send their congratulations.
Martha and Reese* are already planning to go down to see you. I'll be
so glad when you get better acquainted with my family.

You should have been in Atlanta today to see the parade. The Moving
Picture Industry has to sell *one billion* War Bonds by October 1st, and
today we had a parade and everyone on film row and at all the theatres
had to parade. We all met at the Capitol City Club and just as we
got there at 12:00, it started raining. Of course, we had floats and
banners, Red Cross cars, Marines, high school bands, Coast Guards,
plus, soldiers, *jeeps,* and *scout cars.* When it started raining the man in
charge hollered, "Hop a jeep, girls!"—so we all made a dash for them.
I got lost from the crowd I was with and the next thing I knew someone
was pushing me in a Marine station wagon. I didn't know a soul in

*Martha and Reese Gastley were Barbara's sister and brother-in-law.

there, so I got out and ran up and down the line looking for the Fox crew. Finally I found nine of them in a scout car, so I piled in and had to sit on the lap of one of the men from the Ad Sales Department. When the driver got in—it made eleven of us. Boy, was it fun!! and did I get kidded about sitting in Nick's lap!! Everyone said they were going to write you!!

Honey, I've got to close. I'm listening to the "St. Louis Serenade" and just wishing we were in St. Louis and it was August 1 instead of September 1!! Or do I?? At any rate, it won't be too long until we're together.

I love you so darn much. Boy, I've got my chin high—how could I be any other way with such a wonderful husband as you.

I love you,   Barbie

[Hdq. Det., 2nd Bn., 63rd Inf., 6th Div.]
                    "Our Day"
                    Fort Leonard Wood, Missouri,
                    6 September 1942

My Dearest:

. . . I can hardly wait to get to Benning. At least you will know where I am for a couple of months. Had I gone out with this outfit Lord only knows where we would have ended up. I guess I was just born lucky and never did realize it until I met you. Why, just this year I have married the swellest person in the whole wide world. Now I am going to OCS, something I have wanted to do ever since I got in the Army. Too, if I had gone to OCS when I really tried hard to go—I wonder where I would be now?? I think most everything happens for the best. . . .

I know it will be pretty hard on me to be so near you and then perhaps not be able to see you, but even if I see you twice while I am there, it will be better than if I had gone on maneuvers and not seen you at all. You and I are so very lucky for we always have each other near even though we are miles apart.

Lovingly,   Your Charlie

Fairburn, Georgia, September 5, 1942

My dearest sweetheart,

Oh, darling, I know I'm the happiest mortal this side of anywhere. I have soooo much to talk with you about tonight that I know I will never be able to stop!! I'll just start talking and I sure hope it all makes sense to you.

First, I want to tell you how sweet I think you were to send me the perfume. Just thrilled me to death, and, honestly, I've got all the girls at the office green with envy because they haven't got as attentive a husband as I have. You think of everything, darling, oh, how could I help but love you. If it's anything I like better than perfume or any kind of cosmetics, it's more cosmetics.

I got the schedule from Atlanta to Fort Benning and vice versa and it's just alike:

6:00 a.m.	1:30 p.m.
8:00 a.m.	3:00 p.m.
10:00 a.m.	4:30 p.m.
11:59 a.m.	6:00 p.m.
	7:30 p.m.
	9:30 p.m.
	11:59 p.m.

The ticket is $1.89 one way and $3.41 round trip. Takes about four hours to make the trip. And, darling, did you know that it only costs 85 cents to call Fort Benning during the day, not to speak of the 65 cents at night. It's just too wonderful, isn't it?? . . .

Emily* had the shower for me tonight and it was perfectly lovely!! The contests were precious—I'll send you a copy of them, also a copy of the way I got some of the gifts, also a copy of, oh, well, everything. On the back of one of the contests everybody had to write you a letter of advice, on the condition that I would mail them to you. I promised to, but don't fail to mail them back to me—because I want to keep them forever. Some of them are real cute, I think. I just wish you were here

*Emily Wooddall Thompson was Barbara's cousin.

to see all the pretty things. May I wait until tomorrow night to send you a list of them—I may?? Oh, thank you, darling, I'm so, so tired right now. . . .

It is one o'clock. Where has this nite gone!!! Why it's just flown by— the first time that minutes haven't seemed like hours since I left you!!

I'm so in love with you. Gosh, how I wish you were here tonight!! Your letter today was perfectly grand.

Well, I'll see you in my dreams—so until tomorrow,

Goodnight darling,   Barbie

Fairburn, Georgia, September 18, 1942

My dearest sweetheart,

How close you are to me this evening! Sometimes it seems that I would only have to turn around and you would be right back of me. I dare not turn around because I don't want to be disappointed. I should be at choir practice now, instead I took a bath and now I am talking to my husband. I'm so very glad that you're at Fort Benning—I am also glad that you are my husband and that our love is great! If you were here I'm sure that you'd tire of me in three minutes flat! (and I'm not kidding!) because I'm in *some mood.* . . .

I really enjoy my work now—have just about the same kind of work to do—just a heck of a lot more and much more responsibility. Mr. Mac made me feel real good today—said that I did more work by myself than Jerry and I did together. I just laughed and told him no one was pushing him! All kidding aside, I certainly am trying hard and I just hope that I can continue to do the work! By the way, Mr. Mac hired a girl to help me and slow? oh, my gosh, she drives me nuts! She's a beautiful girl but looks are only skin deep as far as the Contract Department is concerned. Mr. Mac told me not to explain any of the work to her, just let her file and type (copy-work). Therefore, he evidently isn't planning to keep her permanently. . . .

I want to hear all about your school. Just what is it like? Had you forgotten how to study?

There isn't any news, so I'll close. I love you so much, darling. By the way, this morning, on the radio, they were dedicating all the songs to the boys at Fort Leonard Wood. I would have had ten fits if you had still been there.

I'm so proud of you, my dear. Really I never knew I could love anyone like I do you.

I'll be home Sat. at 5:00 until I hear from you. (That is if you don't come up). . . . Either way I'll be prepared for anything.

Can't wait to see you!

I love you,   Your loving wife,   Barbie

Fairburn, Georgia, September 22, 1942

My dearest sweetheart,

I sure do want to be with you tonight, but since it is definitely impossible I will talk with you for awhile. . . .

Last weekend was just perfect. I'm so proud of you! Quite a few people have called me and said some very nice things about you. Uncle Bob wanted to meet you and he said that next time he certainly was going to! It's just too wonderful to know that you're in Fort Benning —darling, you're in the same state I am (something tells me that you could take that two ways). . . .

You seem to be a little bit on the worried side about my not being just as blue, white, and perfect as a wife should be when her husband's away. Darling, I want you to know that *now* and *forever* I'll never do anything that would lower me in your opinion. Why I walk down the street and never even see anyone. Sometimes I catch myself looking for you. I even pretend that I'm meeting you for lunch and dopey things like that. Gee, I love you. Guess I love you a million times more than either of us will ever know!

Your loving wife,   Barbie

[7th Co., 1st STR, OCS 121]

Fort Benning, Georgia, 20 October 1942

My Dearest Darling:

I wonder how you are tonight, can't ever keep my mind from thinking about my Barbie. I really know how much you mean to me as the days go by. It is really so wonderful to love as *we* love, is it not??

Darling, I tried to make reservations so we could eat Saturday nite, but they will not reserve a place on Saturday night. However, the man said he would keep me in mind and he was sure he would have something about 8:30 p.m. for us. We will not worry too much about that for there are a lot of places we can go and eat. I just hope we both feel good and are both in a good mood this weekend. I do realize how hard it is on both of us to have to work hard all week and rush and travel and stew around and still be in a good humor when Sunday comes. But, we both must stop and think this way—this thirteen weeks of which 6 weeks will have passed by this weekend, will not last forever, so let us be strong and as good to each other as is humanly possible. I know that these little misunderstandings we have had were my fault. I promise to be a more thoughtful and loving husband for the remainder of our life. I said a few things Sunday nite that I am very sorry I even thought; I hope you have forgotten them and have forgiven me for each one. I love you, my darling, even more than life itself. . . .

Remember I told you how worried I was about that M–1 test and heavy machine gun test?? Well, I got my grade on the M–1 and I passed it. Now, the only test I am worried about that I have taken is the heavy machine gun. Isn't that wonderful—makes 4 grades I have and passed them all. . . .

I am going to have to get a fort driver's card and will have to register my car as a matter of form. Will wait 'til you get here so you can help me buy the shoes. Have a ¼ tank of gas but think it best if I try to get some more on Friday nite. Perhaps I can take you for a Sunday afternoon drive Sunday.

Do the busses have a new schedule as yet?? What time do you want to go home Sunday??

Guess Turner* will double date with us Sat. nite. I thought it would do us good to sorta have a party and get in a crowd for a change.

Here is the plan for Saturday. Of course, things will not run as planned to a "T" but we can have an idea as to what fun we will have.

In all probability I will get to town by 4:00, we will shop a bit, then go out to our room and clean up. Perhaps, rest for an hour. Pick Turner and his date up around seven-thirty. Go to the Hotel for a few cocktails and then go out to eat supper. Go by Tiffin's* around 9 or 9:30 and have a tip on his party—meet a few people—and then go home around 12:30 or one, or later, or what have you?? What do you think of that, my sweet??

Well, I must stop and get on the books, 'cause I sure want to see the bed early tonight.

Wish I was in a certain bed in a certain home in a little town with the sweetest little person in the world, (my wife, Barbie). Gee, Darling, how I do love you.

Lovingly,   Your husband,   Charlie

P.S. Bring a little dough—may run short.

Fairburn, Georgia, October 20, 1942

My darling sweetheart,

 . . . I can hardly wait until this weekend when again I will be with the only person in the world that *really* means anything to me. I love you so very much, darling, don't ever forget that.

I'm not sure about the bus schedule, but I believe a bus leaves around three o'clock and that's the one I'll be on. Boy, oh, boy, do I want to see you—oh, Charlie, what would ever become of me if I thought you would be gone forever? I love you more each second and I'm very glad. You're such a dear.

I really must close now, wish you were here. You know, when I'm

*Turner and Tiffin were members of Charles's OCS class.

with you I don't worry about a thing, I don't even think for myself—
I feel so secure and I know that you are capable to taking care of any
situations that arise.

I'm glad Turner and his girl are going with us Saturday nite. If
something happens and he can't go—please arrange for us to see him
Sunday. I would like to go out to the Fort again Sunday, too . . .'cause
I want to bring my new blue dress to wear to church. O.K.?

Well, darling Charles, I will see you Saturday p.m., and until then
remember that I love you more than life itself. My world is so complete
now that you have made it our world!!

Be good—if I had been in Columbus* tonight we would have been
together, yes?

I love you with all my heart,

Your loving wife,   Barbie

Fairburn, Georgia, November 2, 1942

My dearest sweetheart,

Your little baby doll is really a worn-out chick tonight. I'm ready for
bed so just as soon as I finish this I will go to sleep and dream about the
dearest person in the world—you. You are so sweet and good to me and
I love you more than life itself! I wish I were with you tonight—I wish
it so hard that I could almost cry—but I won't because good soldiers
can take it and certainly I'm a good soldier.

This being an Army wife is really tough, but when the War is over
we'll at least appreciate the peace and contentment of our love and
marriage. I hope that you are happy, Charlie. I'm very, very happy, even
now when you're almost 100 miles away. I don't wonder or worry about
your going out and doing anything that I wouldn't want you to. Just
don't forget to tell me about it. I will always tell you everything.

I have a good idea for next weekend. Let's just have a quiet Saturday
night—maybe go to a show or something like that—then early to bed

*Fort Benning is located near Columbus, Georgia.

and early to rise—have breakfast and go to church. After lunch we can have our Sunday afternoon together. Does a nice quiet weekend interest you, my dear?

Please study hard—you've got to make the grade—you know you have.

Remember me in your prayers and don't ever forget how much I love you. My gosh! I wish you were here. I love you so damn much—so very, very much.

Your loving wife,   Barbie

[7th Co., 1st STR, OCS 121]

Fort Benning, Georgia, 2 November 1942

My Dearest Darling:

Here it is still blue Monday but the only reason it is blue Monday is due to the fact that I am not where I can see you. It doesn't look much like I will be able to talk to you for I have been trying to get you since six. Would sure give a lot to be able to talk to my darling tonight.

Barbie, I have sure done a lot of thinking since last nite and I have convinced myself that we can be together without arguing if we would just stop and be a little conservative. I am the one that should do the most of this conservative thinking for I am the most stubborn person in this whole wide world. You may rest assured that the next time you come down that if you don't ever want to go home then that is the best thing. You see, every time you don't want to go home I have prematurely made up my mind when I think is the best time for you to go home. Most of the time (I am ashamed to say) it is not for the best. Just like last night, it was not best for you to go home at one, but I was so damn hard-headed and I guess self-centered that I could not see any side of the discussion but my own. Please forgive my nearsightedness. I swear and I promise that I will always be more reasonable and more thoughtful in the future. You may believe in those words.

Barbie, I do wish we could be near each other always every night. I know that I miss you more every time I see you and then I have to be away from you. Honestly, I will not treat you as an Army wife again, so don't expect it. I am realizing more and more that you don't like to be treated as an Army wife but you do like to be treated as Charlie's wife, don't you?? I love you a million, million times. To prove this may take me many years, but some of these days I shall be a somebody and then I can give you what you rightly deserve. . . .

I must stop for the lights are being cut out now.

Remember I worship you as ever. So don't forget to kiss yourself a good goodnight for your Charlie.

Lovingly, Your Charlie

[7th Co., 1st STR, OCS 121]

Fort Benning, Georgia, 10 November 1942

My Dearest Darling:

I was not feeling so good last night so here 'tis this a.m. I am talking to you. I don't think I feel any better this morning either. I have a much worse cough and my head aches this a.m. Oh, I hope I don't get sick.

Darling, we did have a wonderful weekend, didn't we? Anywhere we are we can always have a good time, can't we?? We just click as no other persons do. I know I love you more this week than I ever have. You are so perfect and we always belong together. Some of these days we will be near each other and for good. Why only last night I dreamed that the War was over and you and I had started our life anew with each other forever. At least you and I have more to fight for than anyone else in the world. You are honestly my perfect, wonderful, darling. There is no other love in this world as your love for me and my love for you. . . .

Well, darling, only 28 more days and I hope to graduate with this class. Just pray for me and I know everything will be alright. In all probability I can beat this old cold and be o.k. by the weekend. As yet I don't know if I will be able to come to Atlanta so we will have to wait a day or so to find that out.

Don't guess I have ever felt your nearness as I have this week. It seems as though you are here right beside me. You are here really and, too, you are up on my shelf smiling at me this very minute. If there was only some way I could measure out my love to prove to you how much

I do love you. You are the most wonderful person I have ever seen so don't ever leave me for I shall always need you and want you. . . .

Don't ever forget to kiss yourself goodnight each night for me.

Lovingly,   Your Charlie

Fairburn, Georgia, November 19, 1942

My dearest sweetheart,

Well, I worked a little while tonight—came home on the 6:45 bus—and was so tired, went directly to bed. Mother has just come home and brought me this paper and pen so that I could make myself better by writing you. If you can't read it, well, don't blame me.

We've gotten all of the contracts out of the department and Mr. Mac is so proud of us, he hardly knows what to do. Of course, there will be more and more everyday but at least we won't be weeks behind like we have been. . . .

Remember Jerry? The girl I used to work with? Well, she's in California now—got a card from her yesterday and she said: "Following the fleet has been fun, but I think this is my last port."

I'm getting so excited—just thinking about your graduating. Won't be long now, will it? . . .

Do we want to send cards? Christmas cards!? I would kinda like to, perhaps there are some you'd like to send from you, and me from me, and then some we could send from us both. Let's put five dollars on cards and mailing. Don't forget to let me know if this suits you.

Now about Christmas presents. . . . If we were smart and thrifty, and started looking around and putting things aside now, we could easily have a perfect Christmas, and a cheap one too. . . . Then we can figure out just about what we want to give . . . and approximately what we will pay. Then, we'll try to save a little on each one, because by starting early enough we should get in on some bargain sales. Let's be frank, etc. Sure is hard for me to plan etc. with someone, because I never have had to before. Guess you feel the same way. . . .

Well, sweetheart, I'll sign off now. I love you so much and always will.

Your loving wife,   Barbara

Charles received his commission as a second lieutenant in the Infantry on December 9, 1942. Shortly thereafter, he was assigned to Camp Gordon in Augusta, Georgia.

[4th Div., 22nd Inf., Regt. Hdq. Co.]

Camp Gordon, Georgia, 21 December 1942

My Dearest Darling:

Perhaps I should not have called you today but after thinking about the situation Saturday night and all day Sunday and today I finally decided that it best that you know just how the situation stood. I knew that you were going to be a little upset and I was sorta sorry I had to tell you things that would upset you. To tell you the truth I was very surprised to find the situation as I did. The real reason that made me decide to call you was the fact that if I did not tell you and things turn out that I do leave, as things look now, I knew that I would never forgive myself and you would not ever forgive me either had I not told you. . . .

I would hate to have gotten you all worried and have you quit your job and come up here and then me just go on a little maneuver or stay in the states. I say I would hate it, I would, for you might regret coming up here. Nevertheless, there is another angle to look at it, if you do not take into consideration Mr. Mac and Twentieth Century-Fox (Darling, I am not trying to be sarcastic or melodramatic, only trying to talk the thing over in a letter)—I think you and I had talked about your quitting work after you had gotten out of obligation to Mr. Mac and Fox, well, you must have planned on living on what I made, so why can't we do that now?? Really, if that is what you want, we can do it. Then, my darling, we can be sure to be together as much as is possible if we do get sent out the first of the coming month.

Don't let me persuade you for I am only suggesting. I don't know or not if you have any money in the bank. I have about $40.00 now and we are to get that extra for the clothing some time soon. Oh, we can make out o.k. Too, they are issuing C-ration cards for officers with their wives living in Augusta—that would clear transportation up. I went to Traveler's Aid and I think we will not have any trouble getting at least a room. The prices are very high but we can't help that. Strickland, the

Lt. I told you about who bought a house here, said he would rent me a room in his house until he and his wife packed their furniture up. I don't think he will pack it until about the 1st—by then we could have found us another place. Whatever you think best will suit me so use your best judgement. Just this, all of what I said, could be only rumor but when the *Col.* talks about it, it isn't usually rumor. Don't write my Mother or Dad about this and don't do any talking if you can help. Every time you speak, you may endanger me.

Darling, if you decide to come, let me know so I can get a place for us to stay. Living conditions here in Augusta are about as bad as they were in Columbus. . . .

Your loving husband,   Charlie

Barbara did join Charles in Augusta. They were together from late December 1942 until July 1943, while Charles was stationed at Camp Gordon, Georgia, and Fort Dix, New Jersey. As a result, they wrote very few letters to each other during this period. We include parts of one letter, written in March 1943, while Charles was on maneuvers.

[4th Div., 22nd Inf., Regt. Hdq. Co., Camp Gordon, Georgia]
                    "Mud Hole," South Carolina, 12 March 1943
My Dearest Darling:
                    "A Day of Rain"
How long it has been since I have seen my little sweetheart and her great big family. I am going in to Augusta in the a.m.—wish you were going to be there to meet me, but I don't see how it could be arranged on such short notice. The tires on my car should be checked and I have a chance to get in for about three hours so that is how I am getting in. I will go by the house and see how things are if I get a chance. I would like to get the tires checked and papers in for some more tire rations for then we could go in to the big city of Atlanta once in a while if I could get a Saturday afternoon off once in a while. . . .

I went into town today—shaved—had breakfast—came back before dinner. After dinner I went out and got a load of wood—fixed my tent —then played a game or two of horseshoes and had supper. Yesterday I went to town with Lt. Jones and we decided to have a hot dog and marshmallow roast. We bought a lot of stuff and the hot dogs tasted like a lot of paper. You could cook them and they would not even give any juice, like they are supposed to. . . .

There is really not much to write tonight, but I thought that I just had to write something so you would get a letter once in a while. I know what I do wish and that is, that you and I were in the good town of Augusta at our house and no one else was around to bother us for about a year. I'll bet that we could have a lot of fun, don't you?? I might add that the officers are free to go for the weekend as per usual, but don't let that bother you, for I think that it is a good idea for you to get a rest there at home as you are doing.

Do right and take care of yourself just for your Charlie. You belong to him and he belongs to just you and the time we have here on this earth and then some. Give yourself a hug and kiss just from me.

All my love, as ever,   Charlie

In early July, Barbara returned to Georgia to have their baby.

Fairburn, Georgia, July 9, 1943

My darling sweetheart,

It's three o'clock and I've just written to Mrs. Dessell* and your folks. You've been gone eight hours. I wonder where you are now. Probably near or in North Carolina, am I right? Gosh, I felt as if the whole world had crumbled right on top of me when you left this morning, but, gradually, piece by piece, it seems to be moving away, so it shouldn't be long until I'll be entirely recuperated. I know that I won't be convinced that you have actually gone until I get a letter postmarked New Jersey. Still seems as if you'll be home tomorrow and we'll go into Trenton and

*Charles and Barbara rented a room from the Dessells while living in New Jersey.

shop and see a show. Honey, I know that I'll miss you more now than I ever have and I hope and pray you'll be back soon. . . .

The cedar chest came this morning and it's ten times as pretty as it was in the store. It was delivered by truck. I'm ever so proud of it and can't wait to really put my wedding gifts away.

Just can't wait to get a letter from you. Don't fail to write me any and every chance you can because that's what I'll be living for, your letters. Now, don't worry about writing me, because I know it'll be hard to find the time. Tell me all about everything. Lord, I wish we were together. Really don't believe I can take it. However, it's so much easier on me than it is on you that I know if you can, well, I can too.

But you gotta be here when the baby comes!!!!! I just want to see you right now sooo bad. Wish we *were* together—even if we did have to live in "Yankee town." Did I do the wrong thing by coming home?

I've gotten through today all right, but when I think of how many days and nights I'll have like this I wonder if I can go on. Just being with you does me more good than a million other things. Who's going to keep me going now? Oh Charlie, love me forever. You will, won't you darling? . . .

It's most time I had some supper, but I wanta bathe first, so I'll close. Would rather keep writing you but I just can't.

Be real, real good for us and so will I.

I love you,   Your loving wife,   Barbie

Fairburn, Georgia, July 10, 1943

My dearest sweetheart,

Well, I'd just be willing to bet that you are in New Jersey right now. I do hope that you haven't had any kind of car trouble. Wouldn't it be swell if this was last Saturday this time! We'd have a week ahead of us. Oh, Charles, didn't we have the most perfect week possible. We can truthfully say that it was "our week," can't we? I don't see how I can go on without you. Surely you know by now just how much I do love you, in fact, I idolize the very ground you walk on. I know almost that it'll be impossible for me to ever follow you again, until this War is over, and when I think of being away from you for such a long time, it's all that I can do to keep from going crazy.

I wish I were at the Dessells and we had tonight and tomorrow. You could "fool" with the car, and Skeeter* could worry the kids—then, in the afternoon we could go out to the Fort to a show, or sumpin'. Why even think about it! I should be very glad that I'm at home because it is best, or is it? . . .

I do hope that you have time to write me tomorrow. I want a letter from you terribly. Charlie, I can't stay away from you long. If you could just walk in right now—oh, I love you entirely too much! I'm not at all sorry about the baby, in fact, I'm rather glad, but it is keeping me away from you. It won't always be that way, will it, darling?

Speaking of the baby, he's really been giving me some swift kicks today. Really had me "jumping" before I took a nap today. By the way, Mother got some calcium for me, and I'm taking it regularly. Haven't walked any yet, but will certainly start tomorrow.

Everyone sends you their love. Charles, you just don't know how much all the folks think of you. Makes me so very happy and conceited! You know, Pip was so mad when he found out that you had gone Friday —he tho't you were leaving at six p.m. . . .

Don't forget to write me about things and remember that I love you and will forever and ever.

Your loving wife,   Barbie

Dinkler Hotels, Greensboro, North Carolina,
10 July 1943

My Dearest Darling:

How I would like to be there by your side tonight. It has been such a lonely day today without you. Today was such a bad bad day for me— first I had to leave you and second I took the wrong road in Gainesville and went through Asheville—never have I been so tired of driving through mountains. The next thing bad was the fact that it rained on

*Their dog.

me all day long; not little showers, but a storm. I made it on here to Greensboro and then decided that I had better stop. I only hope I make it on up by tomorrow nite on time.

Well, I have already picked us a song out. It is: "You'll Never Know Just How Much I Miss You"—don't forget it.

Now, darling, you must stop all of that crying and think about how lucky you and I have been for the past two years. Really, all of this, our being apart, will only last for a little while. Only long enough for the baby to learn to travel. You know it can't last long.

Just keep your chin up and always remember that I love you truly and that I am always by your side.

Let me hear from you. This is but a note so don't give up. I love you as I always did.

Your Charlie

[Co. F., 22nd Inf., APO #4]

Fort Dix, New Jersey, 18 July 1943

My Dearest Barbie:

Darling, please don't ever get blue for really everything is going to turn out all right. In fact, everything is o.k., now, so please don't worry, will you?? You are home under the best of care and near Fort McPherson* in case anything happens and that relieves my mind of quite a bit. Still in all, I know it meant a lot to you and I both to be together all along, but it will not be but a short while before we shall be together again. By that time, we will have a baby and really something to build on. Barbie, did you ever stop to think how wonderful it is to bring someone into this wonderful life of reality and being. Besides being responsible for their being here, to have the job of being their teacher of all of the many things of life. Darling, can you see how that seals a marriage to a concrete stage of endurance?? How could anything break up our world after the baby gets here to really make us realize what this thing called marriage is. . . .

Your loving husband,　　Charlie

*Barbara received maternity care at nearby Fort McPherson.

Fairburn, Georgia, July 22, 1943

My dearest sweetheart,

Well, this time next month, you will be a "papa", we hope, eh? Won't that be simply grand! Honestly, I can't even imagine what it's going to be like to have a little ole baby, of our very own! I see Annie Sara (you know, Robert's wife), over there with Robertine now—she has the best time with her.* I just can't wait—really if something should happen—but we won't allow ourselves to even think about that, will we?

Charlie, I went to the doctor today and the funniest thing happened! But, first let me tell you that he said I was in perfect condition! Anyway, I got there at eight o'clock and when I walked in, there were about forty girls already there. Well, finally after standing up about fifteen minutes, I found a place to sit down. I waited and waited and the nurse kept calling in this one and that one. At 9:15 I was pretty hot and tired from waiting so I got up and went to see the nurse. I asked her if I could come back in the afternoon and she said they weren't open then. Well, I told her she'd just have to give me another appointment because I couldn't stand around and wait. She asked me if I felt bad, and I said, "Well, I don't feel so good this morning," and maybe that was a little white lie, Charlie, but even if I felt marvelous when I got up, I *did* feel terrible after waiting up there and, honestly, I was getting dizzy. Naturally, that irritated the nurse "no end," but she glared at me and asked my name. She found my record, and whether she looked at your being an officer, or the fact that I was eight months pregnant, I don't know, probably the two things together, anyway, she got terribly sweet all of a sudden and told me to wait a moment while she talked to the doctor. He sent word that he would see me next! How 'bout that! The funny part is that Lt. Gardner couldn't find one form thing the matter with me. He even went so far as to take my temperature!!!! I've gained ½ lb. since Monday a week ago. Anyhow, he finally gave up and said it was probably the heat. He said—I had nothing whatsoever to worry about—by all means for me to take it easy and not get overtired the least bit—to come back next Tuesday, for sure, but before then if I continued

---

*Annie Sara and Robert Johnston and their young daughter, Robertine, lived across the street from the Wooddalls.

to get dizzy—that I would be in the hospital from five to seven days, depending upon the number of cases they had—that he would most likely deliver my baby, but *certainly* if any complications arose—that very soon he wanted me to be x-rayed just to be sure—and by all means not to worry about the baby coming too soon or my husband (that's you) or anything. I was out of there by ten o'clock and I know if any of the women knew I got in front of them, they would have murdered me, but, fortunately, they didn't know. I just positively couldn't have waited, and I am surely glad I'm an 'officer's wife'—there's something about it that can't be beat!

We went on into town and I got practically everything I'll need for the baby. Didn't spend so much money, either. Will make a list (complete) and send you just as soon as I can. Right now, however, I'm "worn out" and my legs hurt and I certainly intend to have them rubbed down good tonight. . . .

Please continue writing the same sweet letters. Remember me to the fellers and darling, above all, do something for that cold.

I love you,   Always,   Just Your Barbie

[Co. F., 22nd Inf., APO #4]

Fort Dix, New Jersey, 22 July 1943

My Dearest Barbie:

I guess by now you will think that I have forgotten you. Really I haven't but you know how sleepy your Charlie is once in a while. Well, yesterday I got off from court at 5:30, I went to the barracks and ate supper. Then I went on up to my room and stripped off to my shorts. Really it was so hot and I was wet all over. I got my table all cleared off so I could write you a letter and I was so wet from sweating that I lay across the bed. Generally one does a lot more sweating right after eating. Before I knew it, it was this a.m. Gee, did I sleep. That was the same thing that happened the night before.

12:45—Well, guess what happened today? No, you don't know, for it is just what we have been waiting on. Yes, my warning order came in for the Air Corps. It says that my travel order will get here sometime before the 18th of August and that I am due in Nashville, Tennessee, on the 18th of August. How do you like that?? Well, I wish that the orders to the Air Corps had just gotten here a little sooner or later. See, now it may be that I will not be able to be there at the time you are supposed to have the baby. However, we will not worry about that for the baby will probably get here a lot sooner than we either expect it, don't you think??

Darling, I will have to stop for now and go to work. But don't worry, I will write you again tonight. . . .

Just keep your chin up and always remember I love you as ever and even more.

All my love,   Charlie

[Co. F., 22nd Inf., APO #4]

Fort Dix, New Jersey, 24 July 1943

My Dearest Darling:

Well, here it is old Saturday once again. Gee, but the weeks just drag along now. It's not like it was when you were up here.

Before I forget to tell you I had better write about the Air Corps stuff. I received my *orders* to report to the Classification Board on August 18, 1943, in Nashville, Tenn. I am going to try Monday to get Division to give me a ten-day leave about the 8th of August. I don't know if it is possible to get this or not, but it is worth a try. If I get the delay-en-route or leave it will mean that I can be there with you until time for me to catch a train and report to Nashville to take my exam. Now, darling, don't you even think about this or count on it too much, for it may happen that they will only give me time to go from here to Nashville, and that will mean that I will not get to see you, so don't get your hopes up too much, understand?? Now, there are some more things about the Air Corps—I am to report to Nashville to take an exam to see if I would make a bomber, pilot, or just what. It means, too, that I have to take another physical exam. There are chances for me to fail to make the grade so do not pass the news around about me being in the Air Corps too fast. You know how I feel—I have been wanting to get into the Air

Corps for so very long, and I am afraid that I may mess up even before I get there, so just hold your breath and keep your fingers crossed. See, if I fail the physical or do not want to take the school to which I am assigned, then I will be reassigned to the very same outfit I am in now —the 4th Division.

Now, there are a few things I am worried about for this coming month. We are sure going to have an expensive month and I wonder if our money will go that far or not. I will have the trip to pay for, the baby is coming, then the fixing up of the room, my bills here and I am going to have to get a tire recapped before I make the trip. I guess that will not be all before the month is up. I am sure that we will have to go in debt, but no matter, please don't you worry about a thing for we can work it out. I guess I have been doing too much thinking on the subject. . . .

Just you keep your chin up and save all of your beautiful love for just your Charlie for he needs it all for himself.

Love forever,   Your Charlie

Fairburn, Georgia, July 26, 1943

My dearest sweetheart,

I didn't write you Saturday or Sunday nights—therefore, I had Daddy call me when he left this a.m., so I could get a letter off to you in the first mail. I'm sitting on the back porch and Skeeter is out here with me. Mother is fixing breakfast and, gee, how I wish my Charlie were here. Oh, honey, I just miss you sooo much. You'll never know. . . .

Now, about the most wonderful and important thing! The Air Corps —gosh, aren't we glad your orders came at last. Why, I was tickled pink when I read your letter and then when I talked to you, and you said they were really here, etc., why, I was happier than ever! Oh, I surely hope that you get your leave. I'm already looking forward to seeing you. When will you know for sure? Let me know as soon as you do. I'm so glad the orders came, mainly because you really want to be in the Air Corps, eh?

Charlie, I had the nicest surprise yesterday! Miriam, Emma, and Louise* were planning to come down. Well, I had dinner with Martha and Reese and since they *said* that they were going to Brookhaven, of course, I had to come home shortly after dinner. They did say they'd like for me to go with them etc., but since Louise and them were coming, of course I couldn't. I saw Ninya' and Eleanor Saturday night and Ninya' casually mentioned that she might come down, if it wasn't too hot. Eleanor was standing there and she kept saying, "Well, can't you ask me!"—Then, yesterday afternoon I called Evie and asked her to come to see me. I told her that Louise might come but I didn't know when, and I surely did wish she'd come up here, 'cause I was so lonesome. She gave me some excuse about having to pack (she's leaving tonight for Delray Beach, Florida). Anyway, just about the time I finished talking to you, Mother came in. Boy, I was so glad to see her. Well, we sat on the porch and talked for awhile and before I even knew it—all the girls were coming up the walk with packages in their arms. Honestly, I was speechless! Just couldn't say a word. It was Emma and Miriam that gave the shower for me. They all stayed a long time and served refreshments and everything. What I liked the most was that it was a *complete* surprise. You see, I had positively refused to have a shower given for me, and yet, I didn't feel a bit self-conscious or anything yesterday. Just seemed like an 'ole-time' get-together, when we were in high school.

Here's what they brought the baby: Ninya'—towel. Dot—baby's first rattle. Emily—pillow for carriage she made herself. Martha—3 blue coat hangers. Eleanor—room thermometer. Evie—pink bed set (spread & pillow top). Louise—blue and white blanket. Miriam—white dress and undershirt. Emma—white and blue pillow top. Everything was wrapped so pretty and the little cards were precious. Am enclosing some of the paper. Dot's gift was the first I opened, which means she'll have the next baby and Emily's the last, meaning she won't ever have any?!?!

*High school friends of Barbara's.

Honey, I still haven't made you a list of *all* the things we have for the baby. It's so much now that I hardly know where to start. Anyway, I'll attend to that very soon. . . .

Well, I've more or less told you all the news and stuff, so guess I'll close for now. Hope I get a big fat letter from you this morning. Boy, when I didn't hear from you Friday or Saturday, I was sho' getting down, down, down. Honestly, I just live for your letters!

Be *real good* and always love me, for I'll never, ever stop loving you. Darling, you do still have a cold, don't you? Oh, *do* take care of yourself!

Write soon. I love you.

Your loving wife,   Barbie

A ten-day "delay-en-route" between assignments enabled Charles to go to Georgia for the birth of their daughter, Sandra Lee, in early August. He then headed to the Army Air Corps Classification Center in Nashville, Tennessee, where, after a battery of tests, he was assigned to pre-flight school at Maxwell Field, near Montgomery, Alabama.

Fairburn, Georgia, August 22, 1943

My dearest sweetheart,

I really was a happy woman today when I received your letter. No, I didn't think you had forgotten me—just didn't let myself look too hard for a letter until it actually came.

Charlie, what do you mean by being processed?? I'd love to be able to talk with you about the tests that you are taking. Just know you'll pass them—I'm praying for you every minute, so don't forget that. Maxwell Field is in Montgomery, is it not?? How long will you be there (in case you get through o.k.) and what happens if you don't make 'pilot'? Are all the men with you there—officers?? What does S/O on your address mean?? Where do you eat and sleep?? Do you need any money as yet and will you tell me the truth about it?? You know me, I'm always full of questions—just a nosey ole thing, eh??

Now for Sandra Lee—oh, Charlie, she is a zillion times cuter than she was a week ago. She's gained 3-½ oz. (now weighs 6 lbs 9-½ oz) and almost seems to know people now. I wonder how I ever got along without her. I'm proud of her because she's "us" all wrapped up in one. If something should happen to me or you, the one left would always have Sandra Lee. I'm so glad we had her while we're young—it'll be nice for her as well as for us. And everytime I look at her I see you and love you more and more. She has "oodles" of hair now. Today she sat in water for the first time and does she like it?!?!?! Won't it be fun when the three of us can be together forever and ever!!

I'm feeling perfectly wonderful!! Sat up Wednesday, walked around Thursday and Friday. Yesterday p.m. I tried on some last summer dresses and couldn't fasten any of them. Dot got me a girdle (ten bucks!) and now I have on a red and white dress I wore summer *before* last. Really I don't look bad at all—in fact, I probably look better because my breasts are naturally larger. I'll have to wear a girdle eight or nine months!! but it's worth it to get a figure back. Have been up and down all day—mostly down—but does feel so good to dress again and not have a great big stomach!! I'm still sore down 'round *possible*,* therefore I have to carry a cushion around with me all the time!!

Mother loves Sandra Lee more than she ever loved me, so you see, she isn't worrying her a bit. And Daddy got up three times the other night to see about her because she *wasn't* crying. She really has been a good baby at night. Just almost impossible to wake her for two o'clock feeding. Am going to cut that out pretty soon.

I just enjoyed your being here so very much. Really couldn't have had the baby without you. You do so much for me, darling, and I love you for everything. Please be good—take good care of Charlie—and love me always!!

Sandra Lee has lots more gifts and cards and *visitors!!* . . .

Surely do wish you'd call me today. Started once to put in a call to

---

*"Possible" and "impossible" were the pet names Barbara and Charles gave to their genitalia.

you, but don't know if I should or not. If I were there could I be with you today?? You know how much I miss you and I'm living for the day "we three" can be together!!

Write me when you have time and remember that I love you.

Lovingly,   Your Barbie

[Student Officers Detachment, AAFPFS]

Maxwell Field, Alabama, 31 August 1943

My Dearest Darling,

Well, here I am at Maxwell Field and I know it is a lot hotter here than it was in Nashville. We left Nashville about ten last nite and got here about ten this a.m. Rode a troop train up and had to bring about five thousand cadets along. No, I was in charge of a car and they were not a bit of trouble.

I went over to finance this afternoon to get my pay voucher straight so I could get paid. Remember me looking for the assignment to quarters for Fort Dix before I left Fairburn?? Well, now I need a termination of quarters from Fort Dix before I can get paid. I also have to have my leave papers put up in abstract form. I'll bet it takes me a full two weeks to get those termination of quarters from Dix. I guess I am a little worried about the money situation, but I suppose that is all I can do is worry, for I only have eleven dollars now. Too, my BOQ* fees, Club dues, etc., and chow is going to cost somewhere in the neighborhood of $65.00 per month. Now that is just the basic, too. Now, don't you worry for I know your $75.00 will come through o.k.

The situation up here has not all come through for we have not started classes and do not know what to expect as yet. The housing situation here is not bad at all, most all of the fellows have been able to get places to stay o.k. Now don't you worry because you can't come up here, because you and I both know that you can't travel with Sandra Lee for at least three or four months. And anyway, no civilians are able to ride the trains or bus lines for two weeks and I will only be here for

*Bachelor Officer Quarters.

21 days to a month, so that would be even too short a time for us to even get set up, I guess. At least, we will do our best to keep our chins up and take things as they come along. That is just about as good as we can do, right??

Darling, I hope we can get Sat. nites and Sundays off. Perhaps if I can get some money and the transportation facilities, maybe I can get to Atlanta to be with you and Sandra Lee for a few hours at least. Now don't you count on that too, because the money situation is sure bad, if I can see things as they are. Well, we will see what we can see. . . .

We have our first formation in the morning at 8:30. By the way, before I forget it I want to tell you about the food. I have been in the Army for about 2 years and honestly, this is the best food and the most of it I have ever seen. I really think I will get fat here, I hope. We even get milk 3 times a day—my, oh, my, I like that.

Well, I guess I better stop and get a little rest after riding on that train for 12 hours.

I hope you and Sandra are not suffering due to the lack of money or attention in the last two weeks. Now, you be good and keep the mail flying for I love you and all that keeps my morale up is you and Sandra's letters of that beautiful love.

Tell all hello and don't wait to write for I am waiting.

Lovingly,   Your Charlie

Fairburn, Georgia, September 4, 1943

My dearest sweetheart,

Received your package today, and, honest, darling, I'm just thrilled to death with all the insignias. I can identify all of them except four. You know I have a book on the US Army, etc. I really think it's the best hobby yet, and I'm awfully interested in getting more and more. I had two already—the 6th Division and the 2nd Division. I would particularly like one of the 77th Division—you know, with the Statue of Liberty on it. I'm trying to decide on a good idea of how to save them—any suggestions?? . . .

The baby didn't give me much time to do anything but 'tend to her today. No, she wasn't sick or anything, just didn't want to sleep and since she is a little spoiled she has to have attention when she's awake. She's just precious, Charlie. It's rather a big responsibility to always make decisions for her, but you know I shall do what I think is best. Then by the time the real work of raising her comes, we will be together, won't we??

I won't hardly let myself think about your coming home this weekend for fear you won't—but, Charlie, do come, by all means, if possible. Of course, you know the score better than I do, but I'm looking for you, anyhow. Gee, it'll be swell to talk to you, see you, and just have you close, real close to me. And, too, I want you to see your little gal baby. I kinda hope that in case you come, she'll have a sweet spell on her Sunday and will sleep a good bit. But it's just one of those things you can't plan on, you know.

It's after nine, but I sho' do hate to wake Sandra Lee because she's sleeping so good. However, I must, so I'm going to close and get this ready for mailing. Then if I have time, will add a few lines later.

Remember that I'm praying that you will come this weekend.

I love and miss you so much,

Your loving wife,   Barbie

and with loads of love from Sandra Lee

[Student Officers Detachment, AAFPFS]

Maxwell Field, Alabama, 7 September 1943

My Dearest Darling:

Gee, I hope it hasn't been as hot there today as it has been here. It rained all nite last nite and this morning it started off just as hot as the devil and has been muggy and the altitude is very low. I just guess it is too hot to feel too good, and besides I am a little lonesome for you.

This morning we took a three-mile run and that is not quite what one would call starting the world out right. Then we went to gunnery school, ate, and went to class. My, oh, my, but you have the dumbest husband ever. *I* made the lowest grade on the math test that was made in the room—45—. That stuff just doesn't sink into my little head. I will have to go to school at nite for an hour and get some extra help, but that is o.k., if that is what it takes to make me learn math. Too, the code did not go so well this afternoon. It seemed, the longer I stayed in there taking code the blanker my mind got. Maybe this ole school is just for real smart boys, of which I am not a part of. The longer I live, the more things I run into that I find I do not know. God, I wish now that I had gone to school and really studied. I think I would be all right if I get through this preflight, but it looks rough here for me now. I guess while I have been out in the field while in the Army, the rest of these boys have been reading and studying for they sure know a lot more than I do, and it seems, too, that they learn much faster. Don't you worry, for you know that your Charlie never quits and he won't quit this time. I hope he works hard and does not let his little gal or his sweet wife down, now that he has gotten this far. He will get through preflight, so keep your fingers crossed and say a prayer or two to that effect. We have a test tomorrow in ship identification and also in code. Before this week is out I may be going to classes all day and to make-up classes all nite. Well, anyway, I sure am dumb, 'cause I am trying hard to learn. . . .

I hope that me getting you so passionate did not have any ill effect on you or Sandra. Will your getting passionate affect Sandra through your milk?? I hope not, but let me know. . . .

Now, darling, the boys are ready to hit the books so I had better stop and get to work for it is already 8:30 and we will have to study for a couple of hours.

Please, please take care of yourself and write and love me with all there is in you, for honest to God, I am all yours. . . .

Give my little girl a kiss and tell her that I will more than likely see her Saturday nite late or Sunday morning early.

I love you a million, million times.

I am always   Your Charlie.

[Student Officers Detachment, AAFPFS]

Maxwell Field, Alabama, 17 September 1943

My Dearest:

Gee, I am sorta tired and a little bit lonesome for you tonight. I just got back from my *extra* code and identification of aircraft classes, and it is but a few minutes from ten o'clock. We had the third algebra test today. I studied from seven last nite 'til about midnight, and did not sleep so well last nite. However, I took the test and I think I made from about 85 to 95 on the test. I don't know yet, for the grades aren't out as yet. I seem to be doing a little better in all of my work, but I am getting pretty tired. Besides that the work just seems to keep piling up.

We have really had a full week; every morning we have three one-hour classes. It takes an hour of walking, going and coming, from these three classes, then we eat, and go to class at one 'til six, and then me and the rest of the dumb ones have had one to two hours after supper each night to go to classes. Look around and see how much time one has to write his wife and study on your lessons. That is why I am getting behind I guess, it's not because I haven't been trying. . . .

In all probability I will be here for another month 'cause I am really not as smart as most folks, but if I am we won't feel sorry, will we?? It will give us a little more time closer together. Too, Sandra will be bigger and you will be more able to travel—too, we will be more or less on our feet again financially. Maybe it will work out for the best all the way around. I hope so.

Well, I must stop and go back to the books. Please write the folks for me for I can't find time enough to shave.

I love you—adore you. Honestly, you are the prettiest, sweetest person in the world.

Lovingly,   Your Charlie

[70th AAFFTD, Lafayette School of Aeronautics]

Lafayette, Louisiana, 2 October 1943

My Dearest Darling:

We arrived here this morning about 8:30. Came on over and got a room in this hotel. Since we took a bath, we have scouted the town over, found a room and it is costing us but $7.50 each per month; however, the food cost is pretty high in this town. There are no used cars for sale at all, so I just don't know about a car. I really do need one here to get back and forth from the field 'cause there is but one bus that runs once each hour.

I have located an apartment, which is not the best in the world, one bedroom the size of the living room in your Mother's house and a kitchen with cooking utensils and dishes furnished. Too, the lady has a cradle she will loan to us. There are very few places to be had, in fact, after about four hours of looking we just happened upon this apartment and room. They want $25.00 per month for the apartment but the gas for the range is not furnished. There is an electric icebox, sink, 3-burner gas stove, pantry, kitchen table and chairs in the kitchen. The bedroom has a bed, 2 chairs, bureau, and a large closet and a little linoleum. Well, I don't think you would like it, but thought I would mention it. By the way, the bathroom down the hall is used by the apartment and the three other rooms there. Probably a better place will turn up. There are a couple of grocery stores down the street. This town does not look as advanced as Gainesville, even though there are a few more thousand persons.

Most of the people here speak English and French, too, sure does sound funny to me.

Well, we have a ride with a fellow to go out to the field to check in and get the lowdown on the place.

Keep the old chin up and stay on the ball and decide what you are thinking about doing.

We have to go now. Give my love to all.

Lovingly,   Charlie

[70th AAFFTD, Lafayette School of Aeronautics]
                              Lafayette, Louisiana, 2 October 1943
My Dearest Darling:

. . . Well, how would you like to come out here and be with me. I can't say that you would like the place I could get for you to stay but at least you would have a roof over your head and you would have a way and a place to keep little Sandra Lee all right and a place to cook or close enough to eat at a restaurant uptown. A very few nights would I have to be at camp and some days I could be home some of the day. Now do not act hasty, be sure that Sandra Lee can make the trip, and be sure to ask the doctor if the change in water, climate, etc., would hurt her or could she readily adjust herself to it all. Too, I want you to be o.k. before you come. Now if you plan to come be sure and let me know, so I can be sure and have a place to take you when you get here. . . .

Well, I am going to leave your coming or not coming entirely up to you, for you know better your condition and Sandra Lee's condition. May I say that I would be glad if you did come for I would sure like to have you near me from now on but you decide. If you do come bring every penny we have, including the bonds you have, for we will surely need more money in this Air Corp than we did in the Infantry. Also, there is one more of us, too.

I must go to bed, so please write me and let me in on your plans.

Lovingly,   Charlie

Fairburn, Georgia, October 5, 1943

My darling sweetheart,

I feel like the very devil this morning, for more reasons than one. It was so late when I got to bed last night, and Miss Taylor had me up at 4:30 a.m., but her Grandmother played the part of the good fairy, by taking care of her and letting me sleep until 6:30. Mother had to go to the store early because it's Monday, so that left me to amuse Sandra Lee and do a million other things, too. I haven't even had time to clean my room or even dress, but I did press some of the baby's clothes, fold diapers, and gave her a bath. It's after 10 and she eats at 10:30. She got *so* mad at me, because I wouldn't pick her up, that I had to hold her for about an hour after her bath. She is now waking up so I'll finish this letter later!! (Guess she slept fifteen minutes.)

It's twelve now. Had to fix the baby's orange juice and prune juice and then she wanted to be rocked. Have just put her down—she isn't asleep, but seems to be enjoying just kicking and talking to herself. . . .

Later. . . . Had to amuse your darling daughter again. Finally we both went to sleep and she waked me at one p.m. She has had her dinner and so have I. It's fifteen 'til two, and she's asleep again—and if she does as usual she'll sleep until four, but I'm keeping my fingers crossed. I'm gonna finish this if it's the last thing I do!! . . .

By the way, I went to the Southeastern Fair last night with a couple of girls. We had fun—but, of course, didn't ride anything. Saw some sideshows, etc. . . . Sandra Lee was asleep when I left and asleep when I got back—how 'bout that!! The most fun was just getting out again!! I have looked at these four walls until I'm practically nuts!!

Sure is a bad rainy day!! That just helps to make me feel lower than the lowest!!

Received your letter written Saturday today. I've been racking my brain ever since you called Sunday trying to figure out a way for us to come to Louisiana. I wanta come—HELLS BELLS!!—why not?? There isn't any future in what I'm doing now. However, I must say that I was completely shocked to think that you, of all people, would even suggest that we come, 'specially after the way you talked here last Thursday. Oh, I just don't know what to do—the baby's so young and wants so much attention—then her clothes have to be washed every day and that's a big job. I'm still off the roof* and no matter how much I eat and rest, nursing her just drags me down—'cause all I eat practically goes to milk—and that doesn't give me a lot of excess energy. Wish we could find a place where I could eat my noonday meal—that way I believe I could manage with breakfast and supper. And, too, we don't have a lot of money and we couldn't ever save a penny. But, on the other hand, we could be together and that's what is important, I guess. Well, anything you say, I'll do. Do you want me to go to Fort McPherson again?? I asked Mother about my going to Louisiana—and, of course, she said she'd rather not commit herself. Every time I think about it, I get a headache, I hate to figure out things by myself when there are so many angles to it. Why didn't we decide definitely when you were here??

*A colloquial expression for a woman's menstrual period.

You kept talking about "we" in your letter—who's we?? And do you live in town or at the field?? Where do you get your meals?? And what did you mean over the phone about cashing in our bonds, or did I misunderstand you?? . . .

Guess that's all the news for now. Will write you again soon. Let me hear from you, so I'll know what to do.

I love you,　　　　　　　　Barbie

Fairburn, Georgia, October 7, 1943

My darling sweetheart,

Ain't it wonderful!! Your two gals will soon be on the way!! How 'bout that!! Gosh, I just can't wait, honestly, I'm so thrilled and excited I hardly know what to do!! Am really looking forward to seeing you, being with you, and have you near again. Oh, aren't we lucky—just think, we're going to be together again—not just the two of us—but, now we have a lovely little daughter, who will make us twice as happy as we've ever been before.

Didn't we have fun talking tonight—guess we understand each other after all!! Now here's some things I'd like to know so write right back and let me know. How is the house or apartment heated?? Is it the same apartment that you told me about?? Is it upstairs and who else is upstairs and who is downstairs?? What about a bathroom and is there a rocking chair?? How much is it?? What are the people's names, etc.?? You see, I'm still "inquisitive!!" . . .

Tomorrow I will make a list of everything I will have to bring with me—a complete list of my clothes and everything, so that when I begin to pack I won't leave something out. I shall bring as little as possible— now, I *will* need her cover for the cradle, won't I?? Be sure to answer all my questions. After I get out there I can always send for additional things in case I need them. . . .

I'm just going to tell people that I'm coming to see you, so that if something happens and I have to come back home, well, it'll keep my pride, understand?? Oh, honey, it'll all work out swell, won't it?? Pray to God to watch over us and see us through these trying times. Mother and Daddy are so happy for us. I'm going to write Pop and Mama Taylor tomorrow, for I know they'll want to know.

Will go to town and get the tickets either tomorrow or Saturday. I'm going to see Mr. Knowles* for I feel that he will help me. You see, the Streamliner is always booked up so far ahead, but he can probably fix that up for me.

Well, I'll close now and get ready for Sandra Lee's 10:00 feeding. Let me hear from you real soon—I am very happy about the whole thing —and, oh, just to be with my darling Charlie again!! I won't believe it until I get there!!

Lovingly,

just,   Your Barbie and loads o' luv' from Sandra Lee

In early December, Charles was transferred to Walnut Ridge, Arkansas, for basic flight training. Barbara and Charles wrote the following letter to their parents shortly after arriving in Walnut Ridge.

                    Walnut Ridge, Arkansas, December 6, 1943
Dearest Mother & Daddy & Folks,

We're here because we're here because we're here because we're here—we're here because we're here because we're here because we're here!

                    Here's a word from the ole man: Quote

Well, the three vagabond Taylors arrived in one of the larger popula-tion (2,000) cities of the midwest or should we say Northern Arkansas. You've never seen a more comical sight—the old Buick puffing and blowing and coughing and spitting as we rode into the gallant city in immaculate form. All the farmers rushed out of the buggies and off their barrel seats and ran into the muddy streets to greet the haughty blond Lt., his blonde wife and blond baby, as they screeched to a quick stop in front of the huge Lawrence Hotel. 'Twas a sight they had never

*A friend of Charles's parents who worked for Southern Railways in Atlanta.

seen before—the Taylors and their loaded (*L O A D E D*) limousine. Mrs. Taylor hustling and bustling to get the blond brat out of the balmy breeze into the barny hotel; with little Lt. Taylor trailing back and forth many times to the huge black Buick (that has 3 cigarette lighters) and then to the hotel and with the millions of things that his wife and baby needed. Every third trip to the car being a pick-up trip for the things he dropped before. The Taylors had a pleasant surprise, after hauling things from the car in front of Room 45 (which was locked). The Manager—Lt. Taylor at the time—finally opened the door and to the Taylors' surprise found a gorgeous room, disastrously furnished with 5 pieces of furniture and a spittoon, not to mention the basin. The surprise was how they got so many pieces of furniture in such a little room. The baby still crying at a high *C* for two hours. The Taylors removed their presence back to the black Buick. They climb up on their high perches and screaming through the glass panel at James, the driver (Lt. Taylor, at the time), "To the USO and hurry please!!!" Again there's a mad rush by the farmers, from their buggies and barrel seats, into the muddy streets, to see the poor Taylors in their big black limousine, with James driving (Lt. Taylor at the time). With the clamor of the crowded midwestern city streets, on Monday afternoon, the Taylors dashed up into a stop in front of the old USO. This is one of the oldest USOs in the United States—founded for the veterans of the Civil War. It has four rooms, including the little house in the rear. Waddling around the front porch and side steps, they have a queer duck (not to mention the three that work inside). "Yes," said the lady inside (one of the queer ducks) "We have many rooms in town for rent." After driving for two hours and 47 minutes greeting most of the town's people on their own doorsteps (like the County Agent up for re-election or the city dog catcher trying to get a raise by kissing all the dogs in town), the Taylors cheerfully get a cheerful NO ROOMS FOR BABIES! Soooo, they clamber up into their great big black Buick and spur their powerful 8-cylinder home back to the ge-orgeous hotel!—to be greeted by the joyful farmers who have rushed from their barrel seats and out of their wagons into the muddy streets. The pretty "miss" of the family being fed, then gooing for a bed in which to lay her blond head, her command being fulfilled by an antique 1865 model that creaks because of the wooden screws—brought to her by the Manager, his faithful bell-hop, the housemaid (87 years old) and her helper, *all* being Lt. Taylor (at the time), drops off to deep slumber and dreams of the happy south and her Grandmother and Granddaddy. Lt. Taylor (after being knocked unconscious by his blond wife) stumbles down the 44-step staircase, helped by his wife, stalls himself over a chair and falls into a deep concentrative mood over a 15-page menu—which is five days old. The Taylors gluttening themselves over a 7-course dinner are now left holding the check.

Charles was hospitalized with pneumonia in January, and Barbara and Sandra Lee returned to Fairburn. The following letter was written shortly after Barbara and Sandra Lee's departure.

[Class #44, WRAAF]

Walnut Ridge, Arkansas, 15 January 1944

My Dearest Darling:

We sure did come close to missing that train this morning, didn't we?? We would have missed it had you not had everything in such good order to leave. Did not take us but a few minutes to finish packing everything and get to the train. You are about the smartest gal I have ever seen. I think your Mother is a wonderful woman too, so be extra good and sweet to her for your Charlie, won't you?? We are really a fast bunch when we do wake up, though.

I went back to the house and picked up what we had left and then I came back to Camp. Went to the Student Officers Quarters and got my pen and changed shoes, then came to the hospital. Got the ward boy to get me some coffee, then I went to sleep and woke up for breakfast. Now I am writing to my little darling. I sure hope you three take the trip o.k. I think you will for if and when you have to change trains, you will not have much trouble for you only have your little bag and those shopping bags, plus the baby, and there are two of you. I am sure glad that your Mother came out, so she could be on the train with you on the trip back.

I think my sleeping with you just those few minutes did my ole heart good, for I feel pretty good today. In fact, if the doctor knew just how good I really do feel he would run me clear out of this place. He will catch up with me one of these days, will he not??

You know, it has been wonderful how well you and Sandra Lee have been in all of this cold weather. I am certainly proud of my girls, for they are the best two gals a guy could have, and what is best of all, they are the only two like them in this whole wide world—the Doc just stopped in and asked me if I got you all off o.k. *and what time I got in.* I guess he was worried about *us!* Ha! This Captain here in this ward looks like one of the Marx Brothers. He sure is a sight to see and he acts like one of them too. He is o.k. I only wish there was some way I could thank Captain Polk for getting me that overnight pass last night. I guess if he only knew just what it meant to us, that would be thanks enough, right??

Now, Darling, don't you go and get sick there in old Georgia, just because you are where you have a lot of attention, do you understand?? Go up and get your hair waved and your fingernails fixed. Start back drinking your 1½ qts. of milk each day and if the weather is such, try to get a sunbath or two. Go on up to Ft. McPherson and get a physical, I'll bet those nurses that helped you with Sandra Lee at the hospital in August would be tickled pink to think that you brought her back to see them. In all probability, they would want to keep her while the Doctor gave you a physical—just back to my old planning once again. Too, perhaps you will be able to get that lady in town there that makes dresses to make you a few pretty nice dresses. You could run up to Atlanta and get yourself some material and the patterns of just the exact type of dress you should like. Then, perhaps you could go and buy yourself a ready-made dress or two, you know something nice and get the accessories to match, too. I guess you can get through the rest of the winter with your coat and what winter things you have, don't you think?? The things you will want to buy will be more spring stuff. You write me and tell me all of your plans so I can follow your line of intentions and thoughts pretty close. . . .

Now, my darling, I must stop and get the sleep that I lost last nite.

You follow my wishes to a "T" and I am sure I will always be able to call you my "T"-bone. Ha!—how is that for an original husband. Kiss Sandra Lee and keep me posted on how she is.

Give yourself a big hug and kiss,

from,   Your Charlie

Fairburn, Georgia, January 16, 1944

Dearest sweetheart,

Oh, Charlie, we had such a wonderful trip over here. Sandra Lee was precious—didn't cry hardly any until just before we got in Atlanta. Everyone on the train remarked about what a good baby she was. A major played with her quite a bit and he said she was nothing but a flirt!! We stayed in the Club Car until after breakfast and then had two spaces in the Pullman which made it just perfect for us. A lady in the Drawing Room invited us back there with her and she was so interesting to talk with. We weren't very tired last night and this morning we were all three just fresh as daisies.

Daddy and all her aunts and Uncle Reese just can't get over what a sweet baby Sandra Lee is. She has already been on her good behavior —she'll laugh, etc., for anyone. . . .

Charles, are you feeling o.k.?? I can't help but feel kind of mean about leaving you in the hospital, but everyone here agrees that you'll rest better knowing I'm o.k. Do write me in detail just exactly how you are and if any complications come up, remember I'll be there immediately. I'm mailing some cards tomorrow—haven't decided whether you'd rather have the new ones or old ones—anyhow, I'm mailing some. So you can be on the lookout for them.

While I was gone today, Mother washed and boiled all the baby diapers and dirty clothes and ironed the dresses. Honestly, she shouldn't have done it, but wasn't it good of her? Boy, she's too good to me!!

I just wish you could see Skeeter—if he isn't the biggest, prettiest dog—(right now he's muddy, but you can tell how pretty he is when he's clean). You can't imagine how big he is. We'll have to send you a pix soon. Can't wait to play with him awhile. . . .

Sandra Lee looks too sweet for words in her little bed, with the covers clamped down over her. I was surprised that she would sleep alone after sleeping with me. Daddy put her bed in here in our room, for it is unusually cold here now.

Oh, we saw snow!! deep snow all along the trip. The woods and farms were beautiful!! Bet it snowed in Walnut Ridge, yes??

I still don't know how we got to the station in Hoxie on time. We just couldn't have done it if you hadn't been so level-headed and all. But I had planned to wake up at three and enjoy a few minutes just knowing we were together and all—know what I mean?!? Charlie, I'm enjoying being here—so far—and I intend to rest and all just like you said. I won't take offenses to people, or cross bridges, I'll have a big time, etc. —*but,* I *do* miss you more than anything. I'll *try* to stay but it's hard to be this far away from you. Do get well and be real good, for I love you so much.

Sandra Lee also misses you and sends a great big hug and kiss—X.

I love you,   Barbie

Basic flight training at Walnut Ridge, Arkansas, proved to be very difficult. Eventually Charles "washed out." The story of the washout and Barbara's support for Charles was discussed in detail throughout their letters. The highlights of this difficult period follow.

[Class #44 WRAAF]

Walnut Ridge, Arkansas, 21 January 1944

Dearest Barbie:

My darling, here it is nine o'clock in an Army Air Basic School of Walnut Ridge, Arkansas, and there is sure one lonely little boy. I guess I had a bad day on the old flight line. This Lt. who is my instructor is a yelling expert too—just as Rex—oh well, perhaps I will be able to take it for after he hits the ground he is a gentleman and Rex wasn't. I went to ground school this afternoon and passed an eight-word check, so I felt pretty good about that. I don't know but all the code I learned in Maxwell suddenly came back to me and I passed it o.k.

Well, tomorrow a.m. we don't have classes—only PT*—then we fly in the afternoon and I sure do hope I do better than I did earlier today. Boy it sure hits me hard—all of these guys I started out with in Nashville are up to around 70 hours here and me I am reverted and don't get out 'til a whole month after them, if I get out at all. I only pray to God that I am able to fly this plane the way this instructor flies it or the way he likes it flown. Oh I can fly it o.k. for myself, but everyone flys differently and to get by you have to suit your instructor and I hope I can suit him. One more boy washed out today. I can't tell but they are sure washing a lot of the revertees out. Gee, I hope they don't catch me until I am confident. If they would only solo me I would be o.k. after that, I know I would. Well, time will tell. I only hope I do not lose that old Taylor willpower for that would sure do the trick.

Barbie, I guess if I do wash out you must promise not to hold it against me and not let it get you down 'cause if I do it will not be because I quit. Well, I only thought that in case they are washing all of the reverts out I would get you set for the occasion, understand?? No, not as far as I know, I am not washed nor do I intend to, I am pretty convinced that I want to fly and it is pretty hard to buck me when I get this one-celled mind made up, understand?? . . .

24 January 1944

Your sorry husband got a check ride by the Squadron Commander this afternoon. I'll tell you all about it. I guess I may wash out—perhaps after all, this is just a formality, this keeping a man back a class and giving him a check on his 4th hour. They don't seem to start us all over, do they?? Well, perhaps I have not put in enough for it is said that one gets out just as much as one puts in. Whichever way my ride happens to turn out in the morning, we will not shed a tear or think that God is

*Physical Training.

being unfair to us, will we?? Let's take it on the chin and give a laugh.

I went to the flight line at noon and waited until about 4:30 to get my check ride:* the Captain was a real nice fellow, he tried to make me feel easy, but you know me, I get one idea and nothing in this whole wide world can ever change me. We started off and I made a very bad take-off, anyway, I got it off of the ground and climbed up to 4,000 ft. (Before we went up he told me to take off, climb up to 4,000 ft., level off, do a power-off stall, a characteristic stall, gliding turns, go into the traffic patterns at Phopshunters,† land, take off and come back home to the field). I leveled off, cleared myself, after I trimmed the ship up and did a stall just as I popped the stick, I hung my arm in the wire to my headsets and did a damn sorry recovery, but the stall was fair. I immediately cleared myself and did another, then I did the characteristic stall pretty fair, too, then I glided down to 1500 ft. and came over the field, checked the "T", and went out and let down— there was another plane there and he did not see me, but I saw him, and before I could move the Captain was all in a bluster and trying to get up out of the way—the other plane was nowhere near us, but the Captain is a sort of cautious guy, well, I came in on the 45 and landed and taxied up to the ramp and parked. The Captain got out and so did I and he and I talked. He said: "The ride was not bad; your air work is not bad, you know your stalls and your procedures, your pattern was good. Fundamentally, your flying is all right but you are timid and not aggressive enough. Your coordination is good and your planning was fair. Now I will ride with you a nice long ride in the morning and if you can prove to me that you can be more aggressive, then o.k.!"

Well, that was it and so tomorrow I go up and I guess I wash, for if I am aggressive, he can then turn around and say that I am reckless, and so on throughout the night. Well, I am trying hard and the rest will have to be left up to God. Sure makes me shudder every time I think of washing out, but if it is in the book for me, then I know it is best. I only pray to God that I do not start crossing my bridges in the

---

*On a check ride, an instructor flew with a student to observe his progress.

†Phopshunters was a practice and landing field near Walnut Ridge, Arkansas.

morning before I get up on that deck—Well, now what do you think of me?? Honestly, I have done my best and I guess that is all I can do so maybe you will get your old outfitted husband back. I hope that I can contact Fulton, if I wash, and he can get me back in the old sightseeing 4th, 'cause maybe then I would get to go over and cause some of these damn Japs a little of the trouble that they have caused me.

Darling, don't you worry, my dear, for I am in pretty good shape tonight—I am going up in the a.m. and show that damn Captain that I can fly as good as the best, they can't get this kid down. . . .

7 February 1944

Well, another day, another ten dollars. The days sure do go by slow now that you are gone and all I have to look forward to is check rides. I got another one today with the Major. I must have done much better for he is to ride with me tomorrow. I shot two landings at Biggers Field and one on the home field and they all were really good three-point on the first third of the field landings. I was sorta proud of myself for that. I did a better job of controlling torque and when we got back to the ready room we had our usual chat. He said all I did wrong was let my plane slip and skid here and there but that was all he said about my flying. I asked him if he thought I had air sense and if my judgement on my pattern and landings was o.k. and he said it was good—so there too. Well, at the end of our chat he said that he would ride with me and that we would go over and shoot a few landings, so perhaps he will get the heart to solo me—if he doesn't I don't know whether or not I will make it on through or not. I am doing my best so I guess that is all I can do. Don't you get disgusted or anything for it will all come out o.k. If the good Lord thinks it best then I will get through here and also Advance. It will all come out for the best, so don't worry. . . .

12 February 1944

I sure would like to be in Georgia tonight for I would like to see everyone pretty bad. Would sorta have to bow down a little if I did get there for I am sorta ashamed of myself for getting a wash job. I guess I knew from the very first day in Walnut Ridge that I would never make it through. I tried but I did not have the stuff, so I know it is all for the best—all I hate is letting you down in front of everyone, but I guess you will get over it.

I better stop and go to bed for I don't feel so good tonight—guess I don't like winter weather too much anyway.

Keep your chin up and write me when you have a lot of time.

Lovingly,   Charlie

Fairburn, Georgia, January 28, 1944

My dearest Charlie,

Wasn't it just too wonderful talking together last night??!!?!?! I'd been kinda blue and after our chat I really felt much better. . . .

Guess by now you've shown those guys that you *are* air-minded. Why, I'm not worried one bit—I know you'll make it o.k. However, in case Fate has another road for you to travel, then we'll realize it was meant that way and just be thankful for the training you have already gotten. Golly, we certainly won't let anything mar our happiness, will we, honey?? Oh, I love you so much and I'm so proud of you. Why, Dot said to tell you that in her opinion (and she was very sincere) you had already shown this ole world what you could do and she is proud to say you are her brother (in-law) and a whole lot of other nice things that I can't think of right now. Pip said if you washed out that he'd be sure that it wouldn't be 'cause you couldn't fly, but that they needed you somewhere else more. Martha and Reese are pulling for you and Mother and Daddy are always saying nice things about you. Even Sandra Lee said just today that she really wasn't interested in much else except her Daddy and most of all she wants to see him right this minute. So, you see, in case everything doesn't work out just like *we* think best (with what *we* know about it, *which isn't much*), there isn't a soul who'll think you're not still tops!! and 'specially me—for you're my all—and I do love you so very, very much. . . .

February 9, 1944

Sandra Lee and I were so very, very happy to hear from you today. We received your Sunday and Monday letters—and it was so wonderful hearing you almost speak. You're just swell about writing. Charlie, even when you're down in the dumps, you still write a sweet letter. Oh, I'm so glad that you miss me—I was scared that you wouldn't. . . .

Hope you are getting along all right. I know how "nerve-wracking" it must be for you to be under such a strain all the time, but, honey, I know also that you can take anything they dish out—you told me so yourself. Why, it never crosses my mind that you'll actually ever wash out. Why, all this will just make you appreciate your 'wings' more—ain't I right??

I wanta see you sumpin' terrible!! Oh, just seems like I've been here years and years. Boy, I wish all this mess was over—DAMMIT!! Why did we have to get in all of this anyhow—oh, well, doesn't do any good to stew about it. . . .

February 14, 1944

. . . Please don't worry about the fact that you washed out, for, honey, you're still the sweetest, most thoughtful, smartest, best, and everything good and wonderful person in the whole wide world. I'd give anything to be in Walnut Ridge, honest, I do mean it!! I love you, Charlie, and a pair of wings isn't going to come between us. Please, honey, don't let it!! You do love me, don't you?? My dear, you've just gotta!! If me and the baby were just out there, then I know you'd be o.k. Sooo, just write me *right back* what to do. I'm waiting for your letter before I do one thing. You've always been the boss and I certainly don't intend to start making decisions now, for you've always planned things just right.

Remember—when I wanted to go to New Jersey and no one exactly agreed?? Well, you said I could go—I did—and everything worked out swell. Remember—you told me when to come home and that was right. You told me when to go to Louisiana—I didn't think I could and nobody else tho't so, but you did, and I went and *could*. Also, the trip to

Arkansas, etc. etc. So, now when there's another situation exactly like the other—it's only natural that you should decide again. Honey, you're my man—and my boss—and Sandra Lee's boss. So, tell me what to do and I'll love anything you say. Honestly, Charlie, I won't be happy until you tell me. Reminds me of what Mother said—I was trying to get something out of her and she said that—well, she'd like to tell us just the very right thing, but she and Daddy had always made their own decisions and she felt like after all it was our life (mine and yours) and no matter what, that we should do exactly what we wanted to. Now, Charlie, remember I'm waiting for your answers to these questions, so, honey, oh, I love you and wanta see you and love you, so please write me right back.

Sandra Lee had a big Valentine's Day. Lots of cards and War Stamps, etc. She's surely a big girl now and is getting some sense. You will just eat her up, I know!!

Write me, darling—oh, I love you.

Lovingly,   Barbie

[Co. I., 262nd Inf. Regt., 66th Inf. Div.]

Camp Joseph T. Robinson, Arkansas,
19 March 1944

My Darling Barbara:

. . . My Barbie, I know things could be a lot worse but what condition couldn't anyway—all we can do is sort of exist and hope that as the days go by they will bring us a little closer.

What I meant the other day by this outfit being Cadred by the 6th Division is that a lot of the supply sgts., 1st sgts., etc., are boys who were in the 6th at Fort Leonard Wood. They sure like your husband, but my nickname by the men in the Company is "Hard-man-Taylor." I guess I am pretty rough at that, but I really don't mean to be. I just want things like they should be. I am just trying to incorporate in these men the things I know about the army that they should know—at least they can show me respect and they don't other Lts. that I know. Well, I will have been commissioned for 16 months on the 10th of April.

Aren't you proud of me, I am so very smart that I stay a 2nd Lt. so long. Lt. Thompson in our Company is a 1st Lt., and I was commissioned ahead of him—1200 commissions. But he ranks me, ha! ha! At least he comes to me for advice as to what he should do about this and that. I guess there is but one 2nd Lt. who ranks me in this Camp and it is Lt. Pheiffer who was in my class 44D of the Air Corps. I say, DAMN THE DAMN AIR CORPS. I think I hate them more now than I ever did before. I hate to get cheated out of things that belong to me. Barbie, if this war is not soon over I will surely have a twisted mind. Sometimes I think I will just go crazy or something—I sure hate a lot of things.

Barbara, I have never wanted to see you more than I do now. I have never missed you more than I do now. Why don't we have enough money to be near each other or enough time or whatever it takes. I hurt inside for you and I just can't help it. My whole soul is crying for Barbara and Sandra Lee, please darling, don't forget me for what would I ever have without you to share it with me. Barbara, isn't there some way we could figure out so we could be together. . . .

Lovingly as ever,　　　　Your one and only,　　　　Charlie

The following are excerpts from a serial letter which Barbara wrote while Charles was en route to his port of embarkation.

Fairburn, Georgia, April 30, 1944

My dearest sweetheart,

Friday . . . Did the usual thing in the a.m. (trying to ignore Sandra Lee saying "Daddy"—"Daddy"—all day)—and in the afternoon I put on your coveralls and fooled around in the yard—washed *at* the car, really you couldn't tell any difference—had the brakes tightened ($ .75)—they need relining ($10.95)—and Friday nite went to the Senior Play with Martha. Came back by the store and Daddy didn't have any help so Martha and I pitched in until the 'play-crowd' left.

Saturday . . . Mother and I took Miss Taylor to the doctor—she's gained, weighs nineteen pounds now. She started screaming the minute she

saw Dr. Davenport. He gave her her last shot and now she is free from
the worry of whooping cough (I HOPE!) She has an appointment for
May 31st and he's going to test her for diphtheria. We came back by
Rich's and Mother got some shoes. Came on home and Emily and I
went over to Martha's and watched she and Reese work in their yard.
Sure does look nice. Emily had supper with me, and then Martha and
Reese took me to see "As Thousands Cheer." It was about a fella in the
Infantry and bye, bye, etc. Surely did wish that I hadn't gone to see it.

Sunday . . . Had lunch with Emily and Martha and Reese took Sandra
Lee and me to Piedmont Park. Reese's niece and family met us there
and we had ice-cream and coke because it was Patricia's birthday.
Sandra Lee was a perfect little doll all afternoon. She really knows
"how to win friends, etc." Bless her heart—just let her see an Army
fella and of all the squealing and pattacaking and anything to attract
their attention—she does it! Now Sandra Lee is fast asleep and I soon
will be.

Oh, Charlie baby, do take care of yourself and trust in God. I firmly
believe that He's watching over you, for I couldn't go on without you.
Someday we'll have that little home we want—just me and you and
Sandra Lee. Wouldn't do us any good to have it now for we couldn't
enjoy it; so we aren't out anything—are we? I love you, my dear, and
always will. . . .

Wednesday—My dearest Charlie—For some reason or other I feel so
close to you tonight. Perhaps you are thinking about me more than
usual. What makes me this way, I don't know, but I feel as if I could
close my eyes a second and when I opened them, you would be here.
I would definitely keel over in a dead faint! Wouldn't mind knowing
what's cookin' now—gee, won't I *ever* get a letter! No, I'm not down—
still got my chin up, but I do wonder, ya' know how 'tis! . . .

Darling, I'll have to mention this once more—I miss you dreadfully,
Charlie. Guess maybe I'm not such a good soldier after all.

I love you more than you know,   Just your Barbie
me too!!!!   Sandra Lee

[Co. T., APO 15302, NY, NY]

10 May 1944

My Dearest:

It is now eleven o'clock—and I just got back from calling you and darling, it was so wonderful. I know there is really no one who could ever ever take your place. I have really never thought before how it was going to be without you for a while. At least I wish at the present that there was no WAR and that there never had been.

While I was waiting on our call tonight I remembered the time I was in Fairburn, before I left Wheeler, back in my first days in the Army. Really I can think of nothing that could have made you fall in love with me. I was just a green cocky private among a lot of civilians. I thought at the time that I was pretty cute and I knew you were. What did make you fall for me? I can well remember our first date as if it were only yesterday. . . .

Can you remember how on Sunday afternoons you and I would go walking down by the creek and sit on the creosote rails on the bridge? I have a pair of pants on now that has some of that bridge tar on them. It sure does remind me of brighter days. Don't think that I am in the least bit gloomy, for I am not. But, really, we had a good time—all of it so clean and beautiful.

Barbie, even if you think you know where I am it would do you no good to come near, for you would not be able to see me. You can see that it is for my own safety not to even tell your own guesses as to where I am, so always think of that while I am gone. It is all right for you to guess, and I think you are pretty good at the G-twoing*—but please be cautious with your talk for it means a lot. . . .

Since Aunt Cora can't go out,† I guess you are right about not seeing her. Best just to forget it.

I will sign off with a kiss. Give Sandra Lee a kiss from her Dad and say a prayer of thanks for us.

    Lovingly,   Your Charlie

---

*G-2: the intelligence section of Army units.

†Barbara's Aunt Cora lived in Richmond, Virginia. This was a way of Charles telling Barbara that he was in Virginia.

[Co. T., APO 15302, NY, NY]

12 May 1944

My Darling:

So much happened to me today—I talked to my wife around three-thirty and then I got two letters from you about five. They were mailed on the eighth, so it did not take too long, only four days. My, but there is no way to tell you how wonderful it is to talk to you. Really, Barbie, I know there is no other person in this wide world like you. You are a good soldier, so do not start telling me so soon in the game that you are a poor soldier. Just you take care of yourself and Sandra Lee and, by all means, get a good tan. . . .

I was quite surprised at your letters—they were so much like you talk. Really it was almost as if I were listening to you talk. Please make your letters frequent and long—tell me everything that you do and everything that Sandra Lee does—don't spare the pictures for I can look at pictures most anytime. You can sure bet that we will have a wonderful life when we do get back near each other again, so don't worry just plan. Why don't you keep a diary and let me read it when I get back—by all means don't fail to tell me that you love me every day in it. . . .

By all means, be sure not to ask me any military questions for it is for my own safety to adhere to censorship regulations—by the way, after a few weeks do not write on both sides of the paper and do not number your letters as you have done. You can number your pages when you desire but not the letter itself. There should be but three things on your letters—address—stamp (6 cents) for air mail for letters with an APO (not 8 cents)—and your return address in the upper left hand corner of the letter—no xxx's or ooo's for hugs and kisses, and no letter such as sealed with a kiss—if they are there they will be cut out, also no blank sheet of paper. Sorta forget the army when you write me and the censor will not cut much out of your letters.

Really, Barbie, you know as much as I do and I know nothing much. Too, if I knew anything I could not tell you, just you don't worry about a thing. This is some hot weather but I guess it [censored]. I really hope I do not have to stay here long but guess only God knows the answer to my guesses. . . .

There is really not much to do here—only two clubs—one for permanent officers and one at the hospital. This is a nice camp and the P.X.s really stay open long hours which gives a guy a chance to buy something. . . .

Oh, Barbie, I love you too damn much but God knew best when he let me fall for I guess he sorta knew what we had in store. Do not ever fall down on me. You haven't since we said "I do" and I know you will break faith with me never. I swear to God that I am only yours in every respect.

Lovingly,   Your Charlie

Fairburn, Georgia, May 14, 1944

My dearest sweetheart,

I have so much to talk about tonight that I just know I won't be able to get it all in. First of all—I received your letters of the 8th and 10th today —and although I read between the lines of your letter of the 8th and found out that you were sick physically and mentally, and more or less disgusted because you hadn't gotten any mail—it just made me want to be with you all the more and hug and kiss you and hear all about everything that was worrying you and help you see the bright side of the situation. But, on the 10th, I read that you were in a better mood and feeling some better physically. Gosh, honey, I'm awfully sorry that you had a sick headache—I really know how to sympathize with you. I have read your 10th letter so much that it's almost worn out. It's another letter that I shall put in my box of beautiful letters. You have to read my "trash" while I get your wonderful letters—poor you!?! . . .

Gee, I always think about how you looked the morning you left for Nashville and I was here with Sandra Lee. When you came to the door I don't believe I've ever seen a more handsome fella in all my life. Guess I'll always remember those few minutes when we were saying "good-bye." It will surely be grand when this war's over, won't it, my dear? . . .

I was so glad you called—I could *understand* you perfectly. I just wanta be with you so terribly bad. Seems like everything goes wrong when you're away—I even feel and think differently—damn everything anyhow!! . . .

Emily and Emma and I decided to go into town on the bus and see some show, but after I got home I had changed my mind, as usual. Mother tried to get me to go on for she felt that getting away would do me good, but I told her I needed to chatter awhile to you tonight worse than seeing any ole picture show. 'Sides it's no fun without you, Charlie, nuthin' is, honey. I really should try to get out of that but somehow I just can't. They say that time cures all—but it'll take a long, long time to get accustomed to being away from you. . . .

I love you truly and of course I'm all yours. Don't ever worry about your Barbie not being true to you for she loves you too much to ever displease you.

Be as careful as possible and write often,

Lovingly,   Your Barbie

Prior to Charles's departure for combat, he and Barbara spent two weeks together in New Brunswick, New Jersey. The day after they parted, Charles wrote Barbara the following letter.

Camp Kilmer, New Jersey
DAY AFTER—D-Day 1944

My Dearest Darling:

I know that you married the sleepiest-headed man in the whole wide world. Why yesterday I came to camp, ate breakfast, went to work, and worked until five, stood retreat, ate supper, and then went to the BOQ, pulled off my clothes, and lay down, the next time I knew anything it was six a.m.—boy, did the time fly. Remember you said (and bet me) that there would be no D-Day, well, there was, and so I guess you now owe me a bet. I heard about it on the way back to camp after leaving you. Really, I was a little surprised myself. Well, one never knows, does one?

Barbie, you will never know just how big a task it was for me to walk out of that room. Gee, I hated to go, in fact I started to just stay and put you on the train and then go back to camp. . . .

All said and done we really did have a good time, even though we did not go anyplace or do anything. I am glad we were able to go juking once or twice, weren't you? Just about now you are giving little Sandra Lee a bath and I can imagine what a wonderful time you are having. I know how much you love her, for I love her just the same way. Oh! it would be so good just to see her. Barbie, please take good care of her and don't ever stop loving her for a minute.

You know what I wish you had done now that your stay up here is over—I wish you had kept a log on what we did each day—would sure have made nice reading for Sandra Lee when she is up and grown, don't you think?

Barbie, I know that this letter looks as if I jumped around in my thoughts, and perhaps I do, but I will have to get back in the old swing of writing letters once more. Now here are a few things about the car on a little slip of paper. It is best, too, to keep the gas tank full as possible at all times because of condensation which will allow the gas tank to rust and cause you gas line trouble later on. Well, you just go by this paper and you will be o.k. Now when you go on a trip and plan to leave the car, be sure that you have the tires checked and the car in the garage, o.k.?

Oh, Barbie how much I already miss you—well perhaps it will not be too long now before we are through with all of the damn war and can come back home. . . .

I love you, Darling, so write often. Give my little gal a big birthday kiss for me.

Lovingly,   Charlie

Fairburn, Georgia, June 8, 1944

My dearest sweetheart,

Well, here I am back in ole Fairburn. Sandra Lee is a dream girl, honestly, she's much sweeter and cuter than I even remembered. She has three teeth that really show up! and a fourth on the way. She does a lot more things and is just a darling.

Am sending you a money order for $40.00. Guess you can use it.

This is just a short note. I love you and miss you. Oh, how I wish this ole war was over and that we could be together—me and you and Sandra Lee.

Had a nice trip—"nuff said."

Let me hear from you often and tell me anything you can.

I love you,   Barbie

Chapter Three

THE HOME FRONT

June 1944 – August 1945

When the classic work on the history of women comes to be written, the biggest force for change in their lives will turn out to have been war. Curiously, war produces more dislocations in the lives of women who stay at home than of men who go off to fight.

Max Lerner,
Public Journal: Marginal Notes on Wartime America

After Barbara and Charles's "second honeymoon" came to an end, she returned to Fairburn, knowing that she might never see her husband again. From now on, like wives and sweethearts since wars have been fought, she could only wait and hope. One difference was that she and others like her in World War II maintained close contact with the fighting men through the speed of mail delivery and through widespread reports from war correspondents, often themselves in action with the soldiers. Reporters dispatched copy for newspapers and magazines and provided commentary for home-front radio broadcasts, photographers sent pictures to newspapers and magazines and newsreels to movie theatres with breathtaking speed. People at home, whether wives, sweethearts, family members, friends, or "armchair generals," could and did follow the war in detail. Nearly every house had its bulletin board with maps to follow the navies and the armies. Stories on home-town boys were carried in the local press. In this war, relatives and friends on the home front knew what happened with an almost hypnotic immediacy.[1]

Servicemen and their loved ones anxiously awaited the arrival of "mail call" or the mailman. As the war expanded, the volume of mail rose enormously. Following British precedent, the American government began to experiment in 1942 with reducing mail to microfilm size for shipping and then enlarging the photographs for distribution to the addressees. Victory Mail, or V-Mail as the procedure was more commonly called, saved much-needed space in scarce wartime transport. Letters with a bulk weight of 2,575 pounds could be reduced to a mere 45 pounds when processed in this manner.

V-Mail letters were written on specially designed 8½-by-11-inch stationery, available at all post offices. Each piece contained space for about seven hundred typewritten words. After shipment, the letter was delivered to the recipient in the form of a 4-by-5½-inch photograph. The original letters were kept on file so that they could be rephotographed in case the film was lost or damaged in transport. Early in 1943, a Canadian RAF plane carrying thirty-two rolls of V-Mail, or more than fifty thousand letters, from United States soldiers stationed in England and Ireland crashed in Newfoundland. The original letters were rephotographed and the new film was dispatched on a later plane.

The Army Signal Corps microfilmed the V-Mail, and mail for all service people was distributed through Army and Fleet Post Office centers. The mail from servicemen went through the regular United States postal system once it arrived from overseas. Censorship was applied at the source for this mail, and most officers spent part of every day reading and censoring soldiers' letters.[2]

At first, people were reluctant to use V-Mail. Some thought it slower and more cumbersome, some were concerned that others might read their mail. The letters seemed short and, as Charles Taylor expressed it, left the reader feeling incomplete, "like a postcard would." Many letter-writers, including Charles and Barbara Taylor, used V-Mail for ordinary correspondence and air mail for more significant mail. Despite its drawbacks, the Postmaster General estimated that more than one billion V-Mail letters were dispatched during the war years.[3]

Civilians paid 3 cents for V-Mail postage and 6 cents a half ounce for airmail letters sent outside the continental United States. This uniform postage rate was established to insure the secrecy of troop locations around the world as well as to be fair to those who had loved ones stationed in remote areas. Beginning in March 1942, all ordinary mail, that is V-Mail and surface letters, sent by members of the armed forces was accorded free transmission.[4]

The quantity was immense. In comparing the volume of mail processed during World War I and World War II, the Postmaster General reported that "during 1918 . . . there were sent to the American Expeditionary Forces in France 35 million letters and 15 million parcels and papers. During the month of October 1944 alone there were mailed overseas to our forces more than 65 million letters, exclusive of air mail or V-Mail." The total volume of mail sent overseas rose from 571 million pieces in 1943 to 3.5 billion pieces in 1945. The quantity of mail sent by soldiers and sailors to loved ones and friends at home was equally staggering. In 1944, the United States Post Office Department estimated that the 11,500,000 men and women serving in the military at the time dispatched 3,611,920,000 pieces of first-class mail. During the entire period of American involvement in World War II, the number of pieces of mail handled by the Post Office increased from approximately 28 billion in 1940 to almost 38 billion in 1945.[5]

The speed of delivery, whether air or V-Mail, is still astounding. Occasionally, Barbara received Charles's letters from Europe in about ten days. Although her letters took longer to reach him, especially during his period of frequent transfers, the mail was usually delivered regularly and efficiently. This couple wrote nearly every day, so they were especially conscious of delivery speeds.

Military officials knew that "mail call" was one of the most important morale-builders in the soldier's life, so extra care was given to the mail, even to drying and photographing letters retrieved from the sea after a plane crashed. Well-known military cartoonists, such as Bill Mauldin and George Baker, poignantly emphasized the importance of the mail in their drawings. As one combat Marine remarked, mail was truly "the best reward that can be given to a fighting man . . . manna from heaven." A Red Cross doughnut "girl" stationed in North Africa reported that "mail [was] even more important than food. On entering a hospital the first thing a soldier says is 'How can I get my mail?'" Ernie Pyle, whose wartime dispatches probably most accurately captured what life was like for the "ordinary" frontline soldier, placed "good mail service" at the head of his list of soldiers' needs.[6] In June 1944, the *Saturday Evening Post* featured on its cover a soldier finding in his mail from home the bootees of his newborn son. *Woman's Home Companion* noted that "the right kind of letter from you means everything to that man in uniform," while *House Beautiful* emphatically informed its readers: "You *Can't* be too Busy to Write."[7]

Popular magazines and government publications published numerous articles on how to write a good letter. They encouraged those at home to report everyday events of home life, along with much family detail. A widely syndicated newspaper cartoon, "The Neighbors," by George Clark, depicted a war bride cleaning up after her baby and saying to her friend, "I write his dad everything he does. Only in the letters I make it sound cute." Writers were urged to be judicious in conveying bad news. *Ladies' Home Journal* cautioned service wives who were feeling blue or depressed against writing their husbands, and instead urged them "to take your tears to a stirring movie where you can really let yourself go. Then when you have got it all out of your system, go home and write your husband the swellest letter you can compose, with not a hint of a sob in it." The "lost art of letter writing" and the "dos" and "don'ts" of writing a good letter were frequently discussed.[8]

On occasion, domestic mail was censored in an effort to locate saboteurs or to prevent sensitive information about troop training and transport, the location of war plants, and even the weather from reaching the enemy. Publications instructed letter writers on how to avoid running afoul of the censor and urged them to write on only one side of the paper so that censorship cuts would not obliterate other parts of the message. During holiday periods such as Christmas, an immense amount of information on how to package goods for overseas travel, when to mail in order that the goods would arrive on time, and even what to put in the packages appeared.[9]

Magazine covers featured war brides, mothers, and children receiving mail from their loved ones. After visiting family members of his friends still in combat, a returning soldier astutely remarked, "A letter from the front . . . means just as much to the recipient as a letter to the front." *Woman's Home Companion* began publishing a regular monthly column, "Share Your Mail," in May 1942. The editors remarked: "This is directed to you proud and lucky receivers of mail from American boys fighting on all our far-flung fronts." Each month, first-prize winners received $75.00 in war bonds and $25.00 war bonds were awarded to the recipients of other letters which were printed.[10]

During the height of the war, almost every issue of *Life* magazine contained an item on mail. These ranged from photographs of the lips of young women who sent kisses in their letters to the fighting men overseas to letters written by officers and enlisted men to their loved ones. In October 1943, *Life* published a full-page photograph of Christmas presents which had fallen apart because of poor preparation by the senders. The caption read: "The sorry sight . . . represents lots of Christmas affection to U.S. troops overseas, but little or no practical attention to proper packaging." Even more heart-rending was a large photograph, published in *Life*'s January 1, 1945 issue, of hundreds of Christmas packages strewn across the floor of a New York City post office, which had not been delivered because the addressees either had been killed in battle or were missing in action.[11]

Advertisers were quick to use "mail call" to promote their products. As one might expect, pen and paper companies developed a variety of ads which focused on the importance of the mail. The makers of Sheaffer's pens advertised "our letters keep us together," "write him a letter often," "let your pen bring you nearer this Christmas," "home sweet home on a bugle . . . that's mail call," and "like a short furlough home . . . your letter." These advertisements also featured special Skrip V-Mail Ink. An ad for Parker "51" pens stated persuasively, "OUR letters are mental food and ammunition for your man in service!" and urged the public to buy a "gift with a 'lift' for fighting spirits!" A Zenith pens' ad simply proclaimed: "Writing Is Fighting, Too!" Sample letters, with pictures of soldiers and loved ones writing to each other, advertised Crane's paper, while Montag's Coronet ads reminded those on the home front, "Only you can write the letters he wants . . . cheerful, understanding, reassuring letters, bringing home and you into faraway places."[12]

Even when there appeared to be no direct relationship between the product and the mail, advertisers ingeniously invented one. A popular Chesterfield ad picturing a sailor carrying a sea bag filled with letters from his sweetheart also featured a package of cigarettes. Not to be outdone, Camel cigarette ads depicted a mother reading a letter from her son and saying to the postman: "He doesn't say *where* . . . but he got the Camels!" A picture of a soldier carrying a box overflowing with company mail carried the comment: "Word comes back again and again from those who have been at far-flung fronts that next to wives, sweethearts, and letters from home among the things our fighting men mention most is Coca-Cola . . . Coke." Using the maxim, "Morale Is a Lot of *Little* Things," the Brewing Industry Foundation published a medley of full-page ads on the importance of letter writing. Martin Aircraft emphatically declared: "The Next Best Thing to a Leave * * * is a LETTER," and a Dole Hawaiian Pineapple ad asked, "Can You Pass a Mail Box with a Clear Conscience?" Remarkably enough, companies manufacturing products as diverse as Hamilton watches, Borden's milk products, Kotex sanitary napkins, Scotch tape, Pacific sheets, Kodak film, Nescafé, General Electric dishwashers, AC spark plugs, Sergeant's dog medicines, Maytag washers, International sterling, Listerine antiseptic, and many others all devised advertisements which linked their merchandise to the mail.[13]

While the government did play a significant role in propaganda, endorsing more than twenty-five specific campaigns ranging from the employment of women to salvage and rationing, none of these efforts focused on mail and morale. The government limited its publications on mail to information on what to send, advice on how to deal with prisoner-of-war mail, and releases that urged letter writers to use V-Mail because it was "fast, safe," and saved "cargo space."[14]

It is almost impossible to overemphasize the role of mail both at home and away. The arrival of the mailman, the bugle call to mail distribution, or the opening of the mail deposit box in the local post office were precious times in everyone's life.[15]

Charles Taylor's letters, the focus of the next chapter, tell us much about his reactions to his wife's world, their young child, and small-town life in the South as well as his military and combat experiences.

In this chapter, however, we examine Barbara Wooddall Taylor's wartime correspondence and what it tells us about young wives of servicemen. Between four and five million women, eight percent of all wives, and forty percent of wives under twenty, were married to servicemen during the war years. Barbara Wooddall Taylor exemplifies the young war bride. Her letters comment about rationing, shortages, war bonds, blood drives, Red Cross work, and the news of the day, both domestic and military. Their real significance, however, lies not in her comments on public matters, but in how she reveals her private and personal feelings. They provide a rare and intimate first-hand glimpse at the ways in which service wives endured the lonesome days of separation.[16]

Professionals who dealt with such matters spent a good deal of time on the problems of separated, lonely, and emotionally deprived war wives, as well as the anxieties of their soldier husbands. The Army sponsored several investigations of the issue. The anxiety of soldiers over furlough, transfer, impending combat, or "the seeming waste of time," and the fears of wives about accidents or death, the possibility of future wars, the difficulties of raising young children alone, and eventually, "readjustment," all came under scrutiny.[17] The many letters which Barbara and Charles exchanged, with their openness, detail, and frank discussion, helped them to deal with these problems.

After Charles was sent to Europe in June, 1944, Barbara set aside a special time each evening to be alone with him and have her nightly chat, "the best time of each twenty-four hours," as she phrased it. Sandra Lee had been put to bed, and she could now recall past events, tell him about her activities and those of their growing child, discuss the whereabouts of relatives and friends, even symbolically smoke "the last cigg before cutting the light off" as they had done when he was home.[18]

Barbara's letters to Charles about the progress of the child gave information, brought him back into the family circle, and took the place of the lengthy talks which parents have while watching their children grow. Once Charles was in combat, Barbara made a special effort to include all sorts of information about the child's world: her walking and early words; the news that she called his photograph "Daddy"; her two-year-old birthday celebration; and Barbara's worry that she would "grow up" before he returned.[19] Sandra Lee also soon learned that writing to Daddy and hearing from him was significant. Even before she was a year old, she began to participate in the daily ritual, and her father occasionally addressed letters to "Miss T."[20]

Barbara Wooddall Taylor often complained that she was not a good letter-writer. But she seemed instinctively to know what to write. In reading the letters, one is struck with their intrinsic strength and how they reinforced the marriage. She rationed out bad or sad news, usually providing only upbeat comments. The emotional endings, emphasizing her love for him, her dependence upon him, and her looking forward to the time when they could be together, all provided Charles with ballast.

As one would expect, Barbara's letters are filled with her longing for Charles and her anxiety over his welfare. She did not reveal the extent of this anxiety until the news came in late November 1944 that his combat days were over. Fear, longing and yearning remained an integral part of Barbara's letters long after Charles left the battle front. She dreamed that he was hurt and in a hospital, and she worried about his headaches and continued concussion, souvenirs of his war experiences. She underwent swings of morale and told him that his anxieties were transmitted to her. The combat dangers continued to disturb her even after the Japanese surrender. Over a month after the attacks on Hiroshima and Nagasaki, she read Ernie Pyle's book, *Brave Men*, and said to Charles:

> I'll bet there's a million questions I want to ask you—will you mind? So many people say that returned veterans don't want to talk about things they've been thru! I just can't see it that way—how is it.[21]

She often wrote to Charles about their early meetings and shared experiences. These themes not only cemented the marriage ties, but also helped her develop emotionally while he was away. At first, when they had weekends together and were able to set up housekeeping for brief times, these detailed memories were not as necessary. But as their separations grew longer, she increasingly relied on her memories for

Wartime poster using the idea of the importance of the mail in sustaining morale to sell war bonds

Courtesy of Liggett Group, Inc. Reprinted from
author's collection

Courtesy of Eastman Kodak Company. Reprinted
from *Collier's*, October 24, 1942

Courtesy of Sheaffer Eaton, Inc. Reprinted from
Collier's, August 28, 1943

Courtesy of Dole Packaged Food Company. Reprinted from *Ladies' Home Journal*,
December 1944

Courtesy of The Coca-Cola Company. Reprinted
from *Life*, August 2, 1943

Examples of World War II advertisements
that used the mail/morale motif

Examples of U.S. Army photographs taken during combat at the Western Front, 1944. *Top left:* Mail call at the Western Front. *Bottom left:* Road marker in Normandy near where Charles was in combat, August 8, 1944. *Top right:* A bazooka team in the hedgerow fighting, photograph taken the day Charles went into combat, July 18, 1944. *Bottom right:* A mobile post office converted from a German vehicle, France, June 1944

Printed by permission of the Estate of Norman Rockwell. © 1942 Estate of Norman Rockwell. Reprinted from the *Saturday Evening Post*, October 4, 1941

The Saturday Evening Post © 1943 The Curtis Publishing Co. Reprinted from the *Saturday Evening Post*, May 8, 1943

The Saturday Evening Post © 1944 The Curtis Publishing Co. Reprinted from the *Saturday Evening Post*, June 17, 1944

Magazine cover art frequently depicted the importance of the mail.

V MAIL

The Sad Sack® © 1989 Sad Sack, Inc.

"I'm sure it will be all right, I want it sent by V-mail"

V-Mail was the subject of many cartoons.

ADVANCE MAN Reconnaissance on New Georgia, page 3   MARCH 1, 1945 Issued 1st and 15th 10₵

The March 1945 cover of *Pacific Leatherneck*, a publication that was circulated in the southwest Pacific by the Marines, portraying the importance of the mail to the morale of men in combat solace and comfort. Shortly after returning to Fairburn to have the baby, she reminisced about their "last, most perfect week" together. She played tennis in May 1944 for the first time in nearly two years, which set off recollections. She dreamed about him frequently, especially after her last visit with him in New Jersey just prior to his embarking for Europe. During the Christmas season of 1944, as she and her mother decorated the tree, she kept thinking about their own Christmas in Arkansas together the year before and she exclaimed: "Don't we have a bushel of happy memories!" Three weeks later, when recalling their first meeting, she wrote: "I love you so—oh, honey, what would my life have been like had there never been a Charles E. Taylor to sweep me off my feet and carry me away up in the clouds. Ever since the first night we met . . . I've been walking on air." Her letters often described "enjoying turning over in my mind the many memories of you," including their frequent travels to new military posts prior to his departure overseas.[22]

Useful as these memories were in keeping up Barbara's morale, the support she received from her sympathetic relatives and friends and from other war brides helped her most of all. Her parents, sisters, brothers-in-law, aunts, and cousins all were ready to help. Her mother was "wonderful" to her during her pregnancy and Barbara told Charles, "Honey, let's make our baby feel the same way about us, o.k.?" She repeatedly acknowledged the special role which her mother played in her life. Once, when Barbara was away at church, her mother washed and boiled the diapers and ironed the clothes. ". . . she's too good to me," was Barbara's comment.[23]

The help the war wives gave to each other is of special significance. While Barbara at first thought it was difficult to be an Army bride, she was also able to say that "when the war is over we'll at least appreciate the peace and contentment of our love and marriage." She corresponded with war brides she had known at Army bases and told Charles their news. When combat took its toll from these earlier companions, she sympathized and provided her own support in their sorrow.[24]

The war brides enjoyed informal gatherings where they made ice cream and "swapped stories" of their situations. The women went to the movies together and saw *Thirty Seconds Over Tokyo, God is My Co-Pilot,* and many others. They played cards, went bowling and swimming, met at the local drug store, took leadership roles in the Cotillion Club, and participated in a variety of church activities. After V-J Day, Barbara and another young woman spent a much-needed vacation at Jacksonville Beach, Florida. She and two other war wives even celebrated their wedding anniversaries together. Once, during a visit to Charles's parents in Gainesville, she wrote that she very much missed that "crazy bunch of Fairburnites—I know we have the best crowd of girls anywhere."[25]

A 1944 feature story on war brides described them as "wandering members of a huge unorganized club." They recognized each other on sight, exchanged views on living quarters, babies, allotments, and travel, and demonstrated pride in their husbands. They reinforced each other and made life, if not pleasant, tolerable.[26]

Women's companionship helped Barbara through the dark days of separation. But the circumstances of the separation, as Max Lerner suggested in the epigraph with which we opened this chapter, changed her life as much as that of her Army husband. To put it simply, she "grew up," became an adult, and took on tasks she would never have thought of earlier. She traveled alone to distant places to be with her husband, cared for their young child, became a proficient cook and housekeeper, ably managed their finances, learned to repair their automobile, "Junior," and in many other ways demonstrated her maturity.[27] Late in 1944, she wrote to Charles, "This War has certainly made me realize just how foolish I was about a great many things. Guess I just hadn't really grown up before."[28] After the war was over in Europe, her mother took a two-month trip during the summer of 1945 to visit relatives in North Carolina and Virginia. It does not seem too much to suggest that her mother made this trip, at least in part, to help Barbara get ready to establish her own home.[29]

"Growing up" meant taking on many new responsibilities and becoming a more self-assured individual. Even though Barbara repeatedly told Charles that she wanted him to be "the boss," she also offered her own opinion of leadership, as when, in March 1945, she remarked, "we're grown now and certainly can't live on our folks always." She told Charles to buy war bonds for their savings, worried about his drinking and his general health, and encouraged him to return to college when the war was over because "someday you'd be proud you finished."[30]

As the war came to a close, planning for the future took on a new meaning in the young couple's lives. There was some chance that Charles would be shipped to the Pacific, but everyone in Europe hoped to have a stateside furlough before being sent away again. Barbara and Charles began to consider the use of a vaginal diaphragm as a means of limiting their family. She inquired of her friends about the instrument, and asked Charles "where you had learned so much about the article!" They discussed whether she should be fitted for one before he returned to the states and other potential problems. Barbara said the diaphragm would put things "on a business basis," but "better to have business than babies, eh?" After this, she went on to discuss how many children they would have in their postwar family.[31]

By the end of the war, Barbara knew her Charles well enough to deliver a blast when he didn't meet her standards, even though he was thousands of miles away. Although Barbara trusted her husband, she did expect him to describe his life while not on duty, and when these descriptions were not detailed enough, she let him know that she expected more elaborate comment than he had offered. After Charles had been to Paris, the city once described as the "silver foxhole," her new-found maturity and independence expressed themselves very strongly.[32] After remarking that she had not heard from him for several days as "you probably didn't have time to write me while you were in Paris— and for that I don't blame you one bit," she then went on to say:

> Although there was one short paragraph about the trip, I gather you had a *nice* time. What if I should go to the mountains or beach and when I returned say just a few words like you did. You'd probably think the same things I am thinking right now and I would doubt it if you would like it even as much as I. Do I make myself clear ole top? Since we are miles apart with an ocean between us there isn't a helluva lot I can do about it —as you well know. I am glad that you are 'rested mentally'—must be a great feeling—wouldn't know for ten months is a long time—and as you

have told me, 'It's all in your mind, Barbie'—and who knows?? You could
be right about it! Now that my speech is over I will write about happier
things.[33]

This outburst was uncharacteristic. In general, she worked hard to
make her letters cheerful, to provide news, and to nourish the marriage
that had begun under such turmoil and was now heading into the
unknown, but probably less dangerous, future. Yet the outburst is also
characteristic of the change the war had brought to her and to many
other service wives as they "grew up" during those tumultuous years.
The personal trials and social circumstances of World War II provided an opportunity for many young women across America to develop a clearer view of their capabilities while becoming confident,
self-reliant individuals. As Louise Paine Benjamin succinctly expressed
it in the January 1943 issue of *Ladies' Home Journal,* "Being a serviceman's wife is the hardest job of all." Or, to take another contemporary
comment from a nineteen-year-old war bride: "This is our life—but
we accept it. We are young, and strong, and can see it through. We acknowledge this life our own, in the faith that the work we do will help
—that the battles fought, the danger endured will help—to make the
future peace—to secure the life we have now for our old age, perhaps,
for our children and for theirs."[34]

Sherna B. Gluck, the author of a recent work based on the oral his-
tories of female defense workers in California, has sharpened our per-
ception of the long-term impact of World War II on the lives of women.
As Gluck has suggested, social change is not always easy to measure;
the stasis implied by Betty Friedan's concept of the "feminine mys-
tique" does not take into consideration the "slow, incremental process
of change, and, as a result, we underestimate the role that women's
wartime experience played in that process." Many women underwent
a subtle change in character and outlook as they drew upon wartime
experience to deal with the complexities of the postwar world.[35]

At present, it is only possible to speculate about the long-term and
ultimate meaning of World War II on the lives of service wives in
general. D'Ann Campbell has proposed that the stresses of wartime

separation hastened the evolution of more egalitarian, companionate marriages. Historians must scrutinize letters, diaries, journals, advice manuals, the popular literature, and a wide range of other materials from the 1950s and later before a significant assessment of this tantalizing hypothesis can be reached.[36]

What we have determined, however, is that the lives of war brides were profoundly altered by their World War II experiences. Indeed, Barbara Wooddall Taylor's letters serve as prototypical evidence of the turbulence experienced by many women in this period of great change and they give poignant illustration to Max Lerner's prescient observation.

Letters, June 1944–August 1945

Fairburn, Georgia, June 8, 1944

My dearest sweetheart,

I love you so very much—darn it! I just can't bear it—being away from you. Why, oh, why did we have to get here in this ole world just in time for this war.

Am enclosing a letter that was returned to me—dumb Barbara—she put APO #1303226!

This is still just a note. By the way, Mother kept a diary while I was gone so I'll get a copy of it and send it to you for I know you'll enjoy it.

Poo-foo! I wanta be with you. Honestly, I miss you more now than ever—Charlie, why do I love you so much. Guess it's because you're so wonderful and good-looking and so tho'tful and so good to me, and because you don't have a brain in your head (at least you make me think that just to evade answering questions). I know good and well you coulda told me sumpin'!!

Gee, I miss you, honey!

Really must close—*long* letter follows,

Love ya! Barbara

Fairburn, Georgia, July 8, 1944

My dearest sweetheart,

At last I have some Air Mail stationery—and I am certainly glad! Gee, I surely would like a letter—if I only knew that my darling Charlie was safe and well. Oh, do be as careful as possible—for I love you and need you so very much. Honestly, honey, I don't see how Ina* has been so brave for the past 27 months, do you? Merton† really can be proud of her. I wish I were more like she is, but perhaps I rely on you too much. But you're always so ready and capable to do little ole things for me. Surely "this war" or should I say "these wars" won't go on much longer. I just pray to God to keep you, watch over you, until you're safe at home again.

This time last year I was getting myself adjusted to being at home again and buying things for the baby etc. Now she's a little girl—and oh, so very much has happened in this past year, hasn't it, darling?

Tonight a crowd of girls went up to Martha Bledsoe's for awhile and made ice cream. (It's after eleven now, but I felt as if I must talk to you a little—gee, I love you.) Louise, Emily, Jean, and I went, and we enjoyed it. Just sat there "swapping" stories as to what we've done in the past year. Kinda makes me lonesome for you, you know.

Sandra Lee is darling. Everyday she gets smarter. And everyone in town just raves over her all the time. It's funny how many people know her name—(lots of people notice children, but they don't often call their names.) Emily calls her "Little Charlie" all the time.

You remember the little figures on her high chair pad? Well, one is a little girl and a rabbit. Miss T. thinks the rabbit is a dog. And whenever she sits in her high chair, she continually turns around and says, "Bow-wow-wow." She can do a lot of little things and she seldom cries, which is wonderful.

Well perhaps I'll say "goodnight" now. This won't go off until Monday anyway. I just felt as if I'd never go to sleep until we chatted for awhile. I love you so damn much, Charlie, and there's no point in my

*Ina Taylor Hartman was Charles's sister.
†Merton Hartman was Barbara and Charles's brother-in-law.

not saying that I miss you, for I do, *dreadfully*. Goodnight, my dear, don't ever, ever stop loving me, not even for a minute.

It's been swell talking to you tonight. I have your picture right here and it makes me feel good and bad at the same time to look at it. I do love you so much. Don't ever worry about my being untrue to you, for I'm not and you know it.

Sandra Lee says to tell you that she loves her Pop, too!

Always,   Your Barbie

P.S. Keep the letters coming and how 'bout having a picture or two made for me, o.k. Please, please do.

"Our Day"—Sunday
Fairburn, Georgia, July 9, 1944

Dearest,

I received two letters from you this morning and oh! my darling, it was so wonderful hearing from you. Felt as if you were here talking to me. Of course I've read them dozens of times. One was written June 17th on the transport and the other on July 2nd—*last* Sunday—isn't that grand! It was so interesting—descriptions, etc., and I do appreciate you taking so much time to write such a long letter. For I know that it does take a lot of time to write a letter, much less a long one—and I appreciate it so much and love you more than ever.

Clay* is 50 miles north of Manchester. Would be swell if you were close enough so that you could see him. And Jenny's husband, Freck, is somewhere around Plymouth. Well, who knows—you may run into lots of people you know over there, huh?

I think that I shall type excerpts from your letters when you describe the country or tell incidents like the English woman giving you a lift. Will not only be nice reading material for us when you return, but also will help you to remember other things that happened at the same time that you weren't able to speak of at the time.

*Clay Kitchens was married to Charles's cousin, Virginia Edwards Kitchens.

Does your sinus bother you? Don't fail to let me know when you're sick. When I know that you're telling me, it'll keep me from wondering, you know.

Am certainly glad the food is good. Gee, I'll never understand the difference in money. Seems awfully complicated. I have "one penny" —"half penny"—"2 shillings"—"sixpence." About your having more money than you need—perhaps it would be a good idea to start a separate savings account, and whenever you send any money, I'll put it in there. That'll be our "Post-War Account" and then the next time I go to meet you, wherever it may be ?? we'll have that money. You see, I can easily live on $150.00 per month, and as soon as I come back from Florida, I am going to start paying Mother and Daddy so much each month. We should be on easy street for a while when you come back— don't you think so?

About Gillette blades—I'm trying 'most everywhere to find them, and a girl who works at Fort McPherson is going to try there at the P.X. If it's possible for anyone to get them, you shall! And matches! Why, how on earth do you manage on a 1-cent box per week. Since hearing that it's really made me match conscious.

I know the country must be beautiful. Would surely like to see it with you. Somehow I feel so close to you tonight. Please pray with me that we shall meet again soon. Someone was kidding me today about sitting at home and waiting while you're over there having the time of your life with all the lovesick girls who go for Yanks in a big way. But I just laughed (for someday I may have more to worry me than that) but I know that you will never be untrue to me. You weren't here and you won't be there, for you know that I miss you, and I'm just as lonesome as you are. And I am so very lonesome—oh, my darling, if you were here tonite I'd just sit and look at you and wouldn't let you out of my sight—not even for a minute. You know, we've wasted a lot of time in the past; however, I've now learned that "time waits for no-one"— haven't you? . . .

Always,   Your Barbara

(Letter No. 1)

Fairburn, Georgia, August 14, 1944

My dearest sweetheart,

As you can see, I have had to start back on Letter No. 1—somewhere or other I got mixed up, so I thought best to start over. Also, excuse this pencil—for . . . I misplaced my fountain pen, and . . . this will have to do. I hardly feel up to laboring with that terrible pen I used last night. Anyway, a chat is what I want, pen, pencil or what have you, what about you? Gee, honey, Barbie sho' is missing you more and more. However, I'm taking it on the chin and even though I haven't had a letter I'm trying not to worry. Now, I don't want you to worry about not writing me, for if things are like Ernie Pyle says, it must be awfully hard to write. And, darling, when you do get a rest period—I want you to rest, for you will really need it. Now, don't worry one minute about anything at home, for everything is going fine here and I'll give it to you straight when and if anything comes up! Honest to goodness.

Today just went along fine. I had to wake your little daughter up this morning and she looked as if she would sleep all day if I'd leave her alone. We had breakfast and she had her bottle and then we got ready to go uptown. . . . I deposited the $44.00 in our Savings Account—think we had a balance of $2.00. Ha! Put $50.00 in the checking account— giving us around $75.00 there. I have about $15.00 in my pocket book. That is our fortune. Seems like I haven't done so good with our money —but I can account for all I've spent—THANK GOODNESS! That's one good advantage of a checking account! Anyhow, you know as well as I do that I'm doing and will do the best I can, o.k.?

Miss T. and I came home and Aunt Dot was here. She just adores Sandra Lee and we had such fun watching the cute little things she does. She wears a bow in her hair most of the time and she takes it out and tries to pin it back in. It's a show to see. She'll finally get it to stay on top of her head and then not dare move for fear it'll fall out. When Dot left I put Sandra Lee to bed and she was soon asleep. . . .

Dot, Martha, Mother, and Daddy are all as anxious to hear from you (via me, of course) as I am. They speak of you so often, and Charles, you just don't realize how much they love you. Be careful and stay mine, all mine, forever. I do love you and am praying for peace soon. . . .

Always,   Your Barbie

Fairburn, Georgia, September 17, 1944

My dearest sweetheart,

This has been a nice day. Passed so quickly—usually "Our Day" is the hardest one for me to get through—for I feel your nearness so strongly—until I hurt inside for you. Oh, my dear Charlie, I love you truly and am praying every day for your safe return home. Oh, everything is swell here—good food, shelter, nice clean clothes—all the comforts of home that you fellas are not getting—but somehow I feel that I could do without the comfortable living if only you were here with me. You'll have a terrible time getting me out of being such an old maid. Everything goes right on schedule and I'll be so glad when you're home to mess up that schedule. Gee, I just don't know how it will be to have you home. Will have to work awfully hard to make ends meet—and I'm not a good manager, but I know you'll be able to get us over the rough places until we're on our feet again. How I do love you and want you, Charlie.

I received your letter of August 30 yesterday and it was grand hearing from you. Letters mean so much, don't they? I was awfully glad to hear that you got some mail. Also enjoyed the usual clippings. Jenny Bradley says hello—her husband (Freck) is on a mine sweeper. If this means anything to you, just pat Freck on the back and let me know. What were you trying to say about a little scratch? Oh, baby, you haven't been hurt, have you? Please let me know.

I suppose by now you have received letters telling of Sandra's walking. In case you haven't and because you asked: she is walking—everywhere! She doesn't crawl at all. She wasn't one bit of trouble to put on a glass—doesn't even miss her bottle. Honestly, she is undoubtedly the sweetest baby in the world. And so very smart. She continually says "Daddy" and looks at your pix and claps her hands. This morning when she waked up I put her on our bed to dress her—and she pointed to your pix and said "Daddy"—then she pointed to me and said "Mama." I think she's awfully smart to know that Mama and Daddy go together. . . .

Well, after listening to the Army Hour . . . Martha B., Jenny, Ninya', Eloise Tucker (who is pregnant and husband on the way over practically), and Katherine Moon (a teacher here) and me all piled in Jr.* and he was such a good boy. Didn't give me one speck of trouble all the way to Atlanta and back. We had a coke and then went to the Rialto— saw *The Impatient Years*—with Jean Arthur. It was rather silly, but pretty good. Had supper and got home about 10:00. I was almost blind from watching the lights all the way home—but now I'm o.k. . . .

I enjoy getting out with a crowd but I always have an empty feeling when I return home. Somehow I feel so lost—gee, I miss you, Charlie. Be real good and wait for me for *everything*, for I'm waiting for you, honest! I know you're good, but there are so many stories about how cute the French gals are etc. etc., that I can't help but wonder. Anyhow, I trust you, just as I know you trust me. If we couldn't trust each other, there wouldn't be any point in our marriage etc., eh?

Keep praying and remember always that I love you more than life itself. We've started your Christmas packages and there'll be more.

I love you, Your Barbie

Kisses from Sgt. Taylor

(Letter No. 32)

"Our Day"

Fairburn, Georgia, October 1, 1944

My dearest darling Charlie,

There isn't any way for me to express my feelings when I received your Sept. 18 letter today. The letter itself was simply delicious—it wasn't just words on paper—they were straight from your heart. I could hear you talking, and see your beautiful, flashing blue eyes looking straight at me. Your sweet eye saying, "Barbie, I love you"—and your

*Junior was Barbara and Charles's automobile.

bad eye telling me all the things I like to hear and think when I'm bad. Do you comprehend? But to think, you—my own Charlie baby—being in Germany—well, that was almost more than I could take. Our news must be terribly slow, for the map in today's paper showed the Allies barely across the border. I know you're all right and that you'll be home before we realize it, but, of course I want you to know that I am most anxious about you every minute of the day and night.

Am glad to hear that you received some mail from me. My letters are terribly "samey," but so are my days, and not having too much originality, there isn't much I can do—eh? . . .

After I got the baby to bed last night I went over to Jenny's. All the gals were there cooking steak—but I got there for the gabbing. After so long a time we went to Stonewall for a drink and home. It was about 11:30 and Miss T. was wide awake—had been for about 15 minutes. I tho't first that I would rock her, but when she failed to go to sleep—I just put her in bed with me. I turned my back to her and she snuggled up to me, and really sawed the logs! When I waked up this morning she was in the kitchen with Mother and had finished her breakfast. We ate and then we straightened here and there and I got Miss T. and me ready for Sunday School. The funny part about it was that all morning I had been telling her that the church bell said, "Ding, Dong, Ding, Dong, Sandra Lee, come to Sunday School." And she would clap her hands and get so excited. Well, honey, when the bell really did ring I tho't she would have a fit. She ran to the door and jabbered and then back to me and Mother—back and forth. I tried to get her to understand bla-bla —but no sir, she wasn't happy until we went out the door. She was the cutest at Sunday School as I have ever seen her today. Went right in and started playing with the blocks and coloring. Didn't cry to go out or anything. She was precious! She played "Ring Around the Roses" for the little chillun' and told them who her sweetheart was ("Daddy").

Then when we all went in the church she sat in my lap and sang. Finally, she got down and walked around a little and started toward the door. Naturally I had to follow her for fear she'd fall down the steps. When I caught up with her, she took my hand and just as we got to the door—she turned around and said, "Bye"—so loud that everyone could hear her. . . .

My darling, I love you so—every minute I'm praying for your safety. Oh, my dear, you must be careful and come back to me. I'm waiting for you for everything—so don't ever forget.

You are my all,

Lovingly,   Your Barbie

P.S. Kisses from Sandra Lee

(Letter No. 42)
Fairburn, Georgia, October 10, 1944

My dearest sweetheart,

Sandra Lee and Grandmother went to the Post Office this afternoon and came home with two wonderful letters from you—written Sept. 25 & 26—14 days ago. Good mail service, don't you think? You sounded as if you might be a little blue or maybe fed up. At any rate, I do hope you're feeling better about all situations now, for it is bad enough for you to be there, much less to have double trouble. I'm just praying that the Germans will surrender in Aachen—I heard just now that the deadliest fighting of the war was going on in that section. Now, I don't know if you're even around there, but someone's loved ones are there and it's terrible I know. . . .

While I was reading your letters Sandra Lee came up and kissed them. No one told her to, understand, she just did it. She's finally catching on to what a letter means and she gets so excited over it. Now when asked where her Daddy is—she'll say, "Gone, gone." She never fails to kiss you "good-morning" and "good-night," so you may as well expect that from now on.

Do you not carry any extra clothes along with you? Gee, you must be about to freeze—for you get cold here the first day of fall. I would adore keeping your feet warm. You know what I'm going to do tonight?— sleep with socks on my feet. Yes-siree! They 'most froze off last night. I hope by the time you receive this that you are in a safe, warm place. . . .

Oh, darling, how I would love to go to bed with you tonight. I haven't forgotten how it feels to have your arms tight around me and my head on your shoulder. Do you know that I haven't been really comfortable since you left here! Gee, it'd be swell to be with you. . . .

This love of mine grows everyday. Why, when you come home you'll be wishing for the peace and quiet of active service after a few hours with me. JOKE!

Remember that I'm praying for you and I love you.

Always,   Your Barbie

(Letter No. 52)
Fairburn, Georgia, October 24, 1944

My dearest sweetheart,

. . . Emily came by and the three of us went to the P.O. Mother and Daddy received a letter from you written October 13 and so did I. I was more than relieved. But, somehow, I felt kinda bad, for there I had ten pages from you and sometimes I only write two. I certainly have more time and news to write, and I'm certainly in a better condition both mentally and physically to write. I've told you all along, my dear, that I didn't deserve you—I'm not half as good as the girl you should have married; but I'm awfully glad that you did marry me and I'm so proud of our little girl. Oh, Charlie, I pray that I might learn to be the wife I should be to you. I love you so very much, Charlie baby. . . .

You know, I was just thinking how grand it is that we are Americans. Sandra Lee looks at airplanes in the sky and claps her hands and says "Purty" (pretty). She'll never have to realize the terror of an enemy plane that might drop a bomb on her. She gets a thrill out of soldiers and she'll never see the ragged, bloody, dirty soldier who is tired and hungry but has to keep on the go, and that soldier might be her own Daddy. Oh, she'll hear all the terrible stories and read books on them and see movies of them; but it won't hit her as if she were a French or English or some other girl in the War Zones. It'll all be just a little exciting and romantic with enough sadness to make it good. I thank God for the fact that she is here in the United States. . . .

Darling, if I could only see you right now. If I could just look at you and you at me, if only for five minutes. I figure that it takes a month for you to receive my letters. So, on November 30th at 11:00 a.m. I shall think of you and talk to you. Will you do the same? Oh, just lots of times I can feel your nearness so strong that I know you must be thinking of me, but this once let's see how it works. Now, that is 11:00 a.m. my time, so can you figure it back to your time, wherever you are. O.K.? . . .

My dear Charlie, help me pray for God to see us through this War and for Him to let you come home again. I love you, truly I do.

Always,   Your Barbie

P.S. Sandra Lee sends her love too.

Fairburn, Georgia, November 5, 1944

My dearest sweetheart,

It seems to be getting colder here now, so perhaps we are at last in for some real winter weather. We have certainly been blessed with beautiful days these past few weeks. It's really been nice for Sandra Lee for she's happy—when she's outside. She's so like you in many, many ways. Today someone at Sunday School said I should have named her Charlie. I wouldn't take anything for her being so much like you. Sometimes when she looks up at me right quick, I can see you so plain.

The Army Hour was just grand this afternoon. I wish that it was compulsory for all Americans to hear it. It would certainly stop a lot of griping and optimistic talking. I'm almost fed up with these bla-bla-bla-bla-people. The Army Hour was mostly about the Infantry and I almost felt as if I were there with you. Oh, it's such a horrible War. I pray that God will direct us to Victory before long. How will it be when there is peace on earth again!? I don't ask anymore out of life except that me and you and Sandra Lee can be together forever. I love you so very, very much, my dear—and no matter where you are or what you're doing—always know that I am there beside you. . . .

Emily came down and sat at the table with us while we had lunch. . . . Mother suggested that we go to town and do some shopping, have supper, and see an early show. I wasn't much in the mood, but after talking about it, it sounded like fun, and it was. It did me a world of good to get away for a few hours. There's such a difference in the soldiers compared to several months ago. Back then they were cocky little boys in a uniform—"Hi, babe, whatcha' doing, etc. etc." Now most of them have campaign ribbons and are wounded men and they seem to know that all that before was kid stuff and that everyone has their one and only somewhere. See what I mean?

We shopped around—I got Sandra Lee three dress materials and patterns that I plan to make myself. Also got a box of peanuts for you. Bought this stationery. Got a patch for our collection. Oh, yes, and picked out some Christmas cards for us to be printed—50 with Lt. and Mrs. Chas. E. Taylor and Sandra Lee; and 25 with The Taylors—Charlie, Barbara, Sandra Lee. The cards are real pretty—but everything is so high and I hated to pay ($8.00 for 25) for cards that aren't worth that much. These are $9.00 (or around that) in all. So perhaps that isn't too much. I can remember when it would have been possible to get a much prettier card for that amount. Went by Holzman's and had a pair of figurines put on layaway. They're $10.00 each, but really look much prettier than that. They are about seven inches high—white and gold—and perfectly formed. So, by paying two or three dollars a month, we won't miss the money and we'll really have something pretty. Do you feel that way, too? By the way, if ever you think I'm doing the wrong thing, don't fail to let me know!

We had supper at Wisteria Gardens. Went early so that it wouldn't look awful for two gals to go in alone. Gee, they've gone ultra, ultra, swank up there. What with their hostess, photographer, and cigg girl—believe it or not! Went to see Wallace Beery in *Barbary Coast Gent* and it was good. He's really a character, isn't he?

Got home about 10 o'clock and Mother was waiting up for me. She said that Sandra Lee had been precious. Isn't Mother wonderful to be so good to us? Sometimes I get aggravated with her because she makes her plans to fit ours, when by rights it should be just the other way. Maybe someday we'll be able to do something really big for her and Daddy, but perhaps bringing them a granddaughter has been enough. They just worship her, Charlie. . . .

Gee, Charlie, my letter sounds so trite—but really I don't feel that way. Perhaps when you get a chance to read this it is better than a doleful, sad letter. I'm praying for your safety every minute. Do be as careful as possible. Don't ever forget for one minute how much I love and adore you. I'm all yours, Charlie, forever and ever.

I love you,   Your Barbie

P.S. A great big kiss from Sandra Lee

"Our Day"
Fairburn, Georgia, November 12, 1944

Dearest beloved,

This is the best part of each twenty-four hours—this time I spend chatting with you about all that happened, telling you my troubles, and letting my hair down, more or less. I'm so very thankful that I'm your wife and you're my husband. We have so much, Charlie, so very much. I love you truly.

Received three letters from you today—October 11 and 12. Naturally, I was glad, real glad to get them—but somehow your saying my letters sound restless and as if I'm not interested, sorta put a dampered feeling over me. You've mentioned this several times, and each time I try to think that maybe it's the way you read them due to the fact of working too hard, C-rations, rain, mud, etc. etc. However, there must be something to it for you to take up time and space and energy to mention it. Now, Charlie, all of us can't have the gift of letter writing that you have. I suppose when you receive your weekly letter from Ina and one from me at the same time, there is quite a difference. But, I do my best to write a good letter every time I write—I tell you what I've done and what Sandra Lee has done—and then there's nothing more to say, except the personal things I want to tell you. Somehow that makes me feel worse than anything—for I look forward to this time of day when I am talking to you and, honestly, I feel as if you're right here. . . .

Four months of combat is a long, long time. I don't see how you've taken it. Four months!! Oh, can't they ever send you back for a rest and let someone else take your place. . . .

That's all for now—I am all yours, my dear, and I love you, honest I do. I'll be so happy when all this is over and you're home again. Won't we be the nicest, happiest family in the world. Gee, how I'd like to see you, if only for five minutes!

I love you,   Your Barbie
Kisses from Miss T.

(Letter No. 83)
Fairburn, Georgia, December 4, 1944

My dearest sweetheart,

It has surely seemed strange for the past three nights not writing to you. Last night when I got home I was so sleepy that I just went straight to bed. I should be ashamed, I know, but that's the way it is. Please forgive me this time. I was fortunate though, for yesterday I received a letter from you and I always like a letter on Sunday—"our day"—don't you? It was written before the last one I received—on the 23rd—but I was still glad to get it.

Listen, don't think that I'm sorry that you aren't being sent back to combat. Of course I hate to think there is anything wrong with you, but the fact that you aren't going to combat is the best news I've heard in six months. I truly believe that you served enough time up there. But, the thing that sorta gripes me is that they didn't catch that in the overseas exam—it's supposed to be so good. Maybe that is just something that they couldn't tell about you until you got in that particular situation—but I do hope that by this time you aren't having any headaches, for I know how you feel. When I have a headache like that I just want to be where it is quiet and have you beside me to just be there. . . .

After thinking all of this over, I guess it happened the best way it could—for you would have never gotten over it had they turned you down and not let you go overseas—so now that you are there and have been in combat, and now you're out and safe—well, I know that God knows just what He is doing. . . .

What a glorious day it will be when you're home again. I don't care where we live or what we have to put up with—you won't ever hear me say a word—just as long as we are together and we are in love— the way we were when you left—and the way we always will be. "Our world" is such a beautiful, lovely place to live in and I don't want to ever have to leave it. I'm really all yours, Charlie, so regardless of the wild tales you hear about what fella's wives are doing—don't ever for one minute link your Barbie with them, for I'm just yours—because I want to be just yours, now and forever. And I know that you are mine for somehow I feel that I would know if something was going on. . . .

Write as often as possible for I live for your letters.

I love you,   Your Barbie

(Letter No. 91)
Fairburn, Georgia, December 15, 1944

My dearest Charlie baby,

Oh, I'm so excited tonight. You can probably imagine what it's all about. Yes, we got our Christmas tree today and now it's all dressed up, with piles of packages underneath. And, oh, Charlie, it's so very exciting and so wonderful. Every once in a while though, I get a great big lump in my throat and I wonder what's the matter—then all of a sudden I realize it's because you're so far away. If only you could be here Christmas Day. I have certainly prayed for it, should it be God's will. I shall think real hard about you and perhaps that way I can bring you closer to home.

Today as Mother and I dressed the tree, I kept thinking about us in Arkansas last Christmas. Don't we have a bushel of happy memories! Dot drove us to College Park this morning. The tree is just as high as the window in here in the living room—and it cost $2.00—we put it in a big can or bucket and propped it with rocks and bricks. Dot let us have her lights since she isn't having a tree this year—and with the strand of 'outdoor' lights I bought at Firestone—makes six strands we have on the tree. It was so funny, we put the lights on first, and we had them all on the tree except the outdoor lights. Mother was making an extension cord, for we were using the only one we had for the bottom string of lights. So, I put the outdoor lights 'way in the middle of the tree, for they're larger than the others—well, I noticed there was a socket in each end, so I connected it and when Mother and I looked, *all the lights were burning.* Do you understand what I mean? I hope you do. Anyway, I've been bragging ever since about what a genius I am. We put the icicles on like you and I did last year. One by one and made it hang straight down. Sandra Lee was so excited she could hardly stand it. She sat in her rocking chair and said, "Watch—watch." When we finished decorating, we put red paper over the can and on the floor. Mother made a big white bow and I pasted that on the paper and it breaks the distance between the floor and the top of the can. We pinned 'our' red/white/and blue stars on the bow. Remember them? Sandra Lee helped me bring the packages in and she looked darling. Dot came down and just raved over the tree. She put her packages on too. I wish I could describe them to you as they look under the tree. One especially that is so pretty—is one for me from Mama and Daddy —it's wrapped in metal (silver) paper with blue ribbon and stars on it and a glistening "Merry Christmas." I just wonder what's in it?! Gee, I guess you think you really married into a Christmas-loving family— and you did too. Oh, honey, how I wish you were here. I love you so much. Really I do. . . .

Well, I'm praying that you are safe and well. Would sure like to know *everything.* Do write when you can and remember that I am all yours and I love you truly.

Always,   Your Barbie
Kisses from Sandra Lee—
Will make up for this note over the weekend.

Fairburn, Georgia, December 18, 1944

My dearest sweetheart,

Well, I certainly looked hard for a letter from you tonight, but no go. No one went by the P.O. this afternoon, so perhaps there is one there now. I do hope so, more than ever. I've been wondering where you will be on Christmas day. Wouldn't it be swell if I could know that you were someplace where you could enjoy that wonderful day. Somehow I believe you will be, for if you try you can have a good time anywhere you are. . . .

Maxine has been down tonight. Poor thing, she misses Ray so much and is so unhappy. He is in England—and she is praying that he might be lucky enough to stay there.

The news is just on and ah, it's terrible! I am so thankful that you aren't at the front. Honestly, this is one time I'd just give up. Jerry has pushed back 20 miles in Belgium—oh, Charles, how and when will all of this end. It's such a big thing, and life is so short, and we're just two little people caught in the swirl of all this—when I think about it— well, it's unbearable. I miss you so, and need you, oh, we're missing so much time together. 'Course I know we have a lot to look forward to, but for how long. I love you so, Charlie, and really I'm not feeling sorry for myself—it's just that everyone's life is in such a mess and no one is living a normal life, whether they're actually in the service or not. Oh, Charlie baby, how I pray for your continued safety, only God knows. I want you so and Sandra Lee really needs her Daddy. Guess this won't make you feel any too good, but sometimes I have to talk to someone, and it seems you're always the one.

I love you truly, and I am all yours—even in my thoughts.

May God keep you safe and well.

Always,   Your Barbie

A great big hug from Sandra Lee.

Fairburn, Georgia, December 25, 1944

My dearest sweetheart,

It's impossible for me to say that this has truly been a "Merry Christmas," however, it has been fun. Sandra Lee has been a doll and has been just as a child should be on Christmas Day. Last night Mother and I fixed her Santa Claus—I just broke down and had a real good cry because everything was like it is. I hadn't cried in a long time, so it really did me good! I know that we have much to be thankful for—but I was hurt because you weren't here and all. Anyhow, all her toys were set out in front of the tree and I filled her stocking full of nuts, candy, and fruit.

This morning she slept late and when she finally waked up I began telling her that Santa Claus had come to see her, and she was so excited she could hardly eat breakfast. Martha, Reese, and Pip were to be here at 10:00 for the tree—so I dressed her up real cute—and by the time Mother and I dressed they were here. Emily and Jim came in about the same time—and after everyone had said "hello," we asked Sandra Lee if she would like to see what Santa brought her. She ran real fast to the living room door, just as if she knew that we had been waiting for the family to get here. Well, I just can't describe the way she did when she walked in. She was thrilled to death—and just couldn't see for looking. She would pick up something—then drop that—and start out with something else. Then she began jabbering about everything and showing everyone. She laughed and was truly a happy child. We then had our tree and she began helping everyone open the packages. Oh, everyone received such beautiful gifts. . . .

Everyone but me and Sandra Lee was planning to go to the hospital to see Dot and Judy. Well, that's something new to you, so perhaps right here I should go back to Friday. Well, Friday a.m., Aunt Jimmie called and asked if I would drive her and Robert* to the airport. . . . It suited me fine, for I was planning to go to Atlanta anyway to get something for Dot from Pip. So, we left about 1:00, and Mother kept Sandra Lee. Robert was here overnight—he was going back to Miami after having attended a conference in Los Angeles. The plane was two hours late and we didn't go into town until Robert left. Got to town about 4:30 and I selected a beautiful blue-and-white luncheon set and a white blouse for Dot. Aunt Jimmie did a few things. The stores were really

*Robert Wooddall was Barbara's first cousin. Aunt Jimmie was his mother.

jammed and packed. We ate and then went to a show, *Our Hearts Were Young and Gay*. Got home about 8:30 and then I found out the shocking news. Dot was in the hospital—Mother and Pip were with her—and Martha and Reese were here with Sandra Lee. So, Martha and Reese left immediately for the hospital—and Daddy and I anxiously waited for news. About 11:30 Mother called to say that Dr. B. had put Dot to sleep, and he expected the baby about daylight—so finally I got up the nerve to go to bed. Sandra Lee waked up when I went in the room and to tell the truth, I was rather glad. It must have been two hours before I could go to sleep.

About 4:30 or 5:00 Pip called to tell me he had a little girl—Judy Lynn—7 lbs.-1⅓ oz.—born 3:57 a.m.—December 23, 1944. He was simply shouting over the 'phone. Was just thrilled to death. They both wanted a girl. Well, Judy is beautiful—she has the sweetest little features—and, Charlie, she has a head full of black hair. Oh, I'm so happy for them. Dot really had a hard time of it—but she's feeling better every day. . . .

Well, since it's eleven o'clock and I've had a busy day, I shall say "good-night." Oh, Charlie, how much longer will it be this way—this suspense and wonder and waiting, waiting for a letter, or perhaps a wire—or anything, anything at all. My dear, I love you truly. I am all yours—just as I have always been—and always will be. . . .

I love you,   Your Barbie

Sandra Lee says she loves you.

Fairburn, Georgia, January 11, 1945

My dearest sweetheart,

Still no mail—looks like it's held up again. But I'm still reading the 17 letters I received last week. I get something new out of them each time. Oh, you're so sweet and always know just what to do and say and honey, I love you so. Gee, it's sure a big thing—this love of mine. Our love and our world has to be big and sure and strong to reach so far, doesn't it? Somehow it seems that you are right here in the room with me—maybe you're thinking about me right now. Wouldn't it be grand if we could know for sure that we're both thinking of each other at the same time. I'm sure we do.

Oh, I forgot to mention this, you were saying something in one of your letters about what I tho't about you going to Paris. Oh, honey, don't you know I've gotten out of that stupid way of thinking. It didn't worry me one bit—I was really glad you had the chance to go so much. As for Paris women etc.,—well, that is out of my control entirely and if you felt the urge to do something you will regret later on, then, that too, is up to you. You see, at last I've learned that all I have to account for is what I do and what I influence others to do—whatever you or anyone else does is nothing to me—so, that's what I think. I know that as long as I keep up my half of this marriage and do just what I think is right—then, I know that in the long run if something should happen to tear it up in a zillion pieces, that it definitely won't be any fault of mine. Should you say that you did go out with women while I sat home and waited, I really don't know what effect it would have on me—I haven't thought that far ahead. Anyway, all I expect is the truth, for that's exactly what I'll tell you. Can you? Honey, don't ever worry about my being untrue to you in any respect—for really I haven't the energy to go out and look for anything. It doesn't appeal to me that much. . . .

As for the postwar children—well, I'd like to have about a half-dozen someday—but that's out of the question. We'd never be able to send them all to school, have the right clothes and stuff for them. If we were rich already, that would be my one aim. But, since we aren't, and since everything is going to be in a big mess after this War anyway—I hope we don't have a child for several years after you come back. What's your opinion? It just makes me sick when I think about it, for if things were normal, we would already be established in some kind of business and more or less be on our feet. Then, I'd want to be well on my way to having another child for it would be swell not to have such a big gap between Sandra Lee and her little brother. Oh, well—you're 'way over there, and I'm 'way over here, and here I am talking about—nuts! . . .

I love you,   Your Barbie

Gainesville, Florida, January 23, 1945

My dearest sweetheart,

Oh, Charlie baby, it's so wonderful here in Gainesville. Yes, I'm really here with Sandra Lee. I swore I'd never try to bring her alone again—but I did, and honestly, the trip wasn't half bad. Emily and Jim took us to the station last night with Mother, and the train was only about thirty minutes late.

Sandra Lee was all excited over going on the "Choo-choo"—"see Bill."* She looked all over the berth and had lots of fun. It wasn't any trouble getting to bed, like I tho't it would be. She cried for water and the conductor brought it to her—then she wanted GaMama and kitchen. It only took her about thirty minutes to go to sleep. Then the train didn't rouse her until 6:00. I gave her her bottle and we dressed, and our berth was made up. The Porter told me we had about 1:30 from the next stop to Wilcox—but in two seconds he was back asking me if we were ready to get off. He was mixed up—when we stopped for water, that was only a few yards from Wilcox. I saw Merton and he came in and helped us off—and there was Ina and Bill. Well, we came on home. It's wonderful to be here. Sandra Lee has slept a great deal —she really isn't herself yet, but it won't take her long. Mama Taylor came in this afternoon and they had a letter from you written the sixth. Sure made me feel better and I was glad to know you had finally gotten some mail. Maybe by this time it's coming in regularly.

Charlie, when I looked out of the train window and saw Florida, I just wanted to cry. It's such a pretty place to be—and if only you were here. I always miss you so much more when I'm here.

You're going to shoot me for this short note but you must know how worn out I am. Sandra Lee is asleep now, but I don't know for how long.

But, let me tell you this—Sandra Lee had a fit over Pop. Everytime she gets a different toy in her hand, she has to go in his office and show it to him. She acts as if she really remembers him.

Darling, we both love you very much and we're thankful for your safety.

Lovingly,   Barbie and Sandra Lee

*Bill Hartman was Barbara's nephew.

Gainesville, Florida, February 20, 1945

My dearest sweetheart,

No mail today—but I really didn't expect any since I had so much yesterday. Boyoboy! it's really swell to get a lot of mail. I've just read some of the letters over again. They're just delicious—so like my own Charlie. . . . Sometimes I get to thinking—and I wonder if you will be bored with me and my foolish ways when you come back. I know we'll be changed in some ways—and I wonder if you'll be disappointed in me. We'll have to realize that time has made changes in both of us— and really, Charlie, we're living entirely different lives now. I can't get a clear pix of what you're doing—and you can see very little of what I'm doing. It's just through our letters to each other and what we get out of them. Now I have no idea that you realize even half the things I write. It's all so simple on paper—such as: getting up, dressing Sandra Lee, giving her breakfast etc. etc. Now, even that much includes—Sandra Lee hollering "Barba-Barba-get up!"—so, I try not to hear her, but in a minute, she starts all over. So, I get up and of course she's wet as a drowned rat—so, I take her to the bathroom and wash her real good. All this time she's squirming to get down on the floor. Well, back to the bedroom we go, and I find her some clothes. That's a full-time job —just dressing her. She wiggles and squirms and chatters and giggles. Finally, it's over and I get my clothes on. Then to fix her hair. Her hair is beautiful—fine as silk and shines like gold. And it turns up all the way around her neck—real pretty. Well, we go in to have breakfast and she isn't still a minute and doesn't like to eat anyway. So, she wants water, wants to color, wants to write to Daddy, etc. etc. That's just a mild pix of it. Oh, it's lots of fun and sure keeps me busy—I wouldn't take anything for Sandra Lee. It's just that I'm trying to say we are living entirely different lives. Therefore, when you come home we will have quite an adjustment to make. I'll have to realize that a home, wife, and baby is new to you—and you'll have to understand that a husband and boss is new for me—and I do want you to be the boss (as always)— no matter. Oh, I'm sure we'll work all this out and I'm not worried at all—just thinking. . . .

Well, honey, better sign off now—I sure do miss you and how I'd love

to be with you. Oh, I love you so and it's getting sorta hard to take—
this being away from you.

I love you, Your Barbie

P.S. Kisses from Sandra Lee

Fairburn, Georgia, February 25, 1945

My dearest sweetheart,

Well, here I am—'home' again—and it's sure hard to get adjusted
again etc. You know—guess I'll be living out of a suitcase for a couple
of weeks. Such a job to unpack and all. Anyhow, it's swell seeing all
the folks and I sure had a grand time in Florida. That's a swell place to
go and I hope it won't be long before I go back. . . .

Better sign off now. This is just to get up-to-date. I love you truly.
Will tell you so tomorrow night.

Always, Your Barbie

Fairburn, Georgia, March 25, 1945

My dearest sweetheart,

Charlie baby, I'm so lonely for you. Not a very pretty way to begin a
letter, is it??—but, that's just the way I feel. Maybe it's "spring fever"
—but more than likely it's just because I'm a bad soldier and just can't
take it anymore. I'm sure that you could cure me right away if you were
here. I should be so thankful that you are safe and well, that the fact
of our being apart would be overshadowed—but somehow even that
doesn't make up for the loneliness inside of me. It's strange—but all
day Saturday and today I've felt so close to you and yet so far away—
and I can get along o.k. until we sit down to the table for a meal—and
then all at once I feel as if I must scream—or to put it stronger, just get
outside and start running—and run—and run—where?? I don't know.
It's just inside of me. Guess I'm nuts for sure now, but I sorta feel like
you understand what I mean. I know you do. I wouldn't dare tell this
to anyone—but, Charlie baby, does it bother you when I talk like this?

I hope not—for it's just the mood I'm in—and really it'll pass off in a day or two and I'll be o.k. again. You know how 'tis!!

Oh, honey, when I opened your letter this morning with the small snapshots—I—well, I was thrilled to death and yet, oh, I just wanted you so. They're just grand of you—why, you look exactly like you did when you left, and Charlie baby, you look so good I'm sure I could take a spoon and eat you. I love you so very, very much—you'll never know how much. And let me tell you how it was: well, Daddy went to the P.O. and bro't the mail, and I opened the letter. We were at breakfast and after I spent hours (it seemed) drinking in every pix—it dawned on me that Sandra Lee might like to see them. So I said, "Who is this"— and she said, "Pop"—and sorta grinned—and I said, "Aw, Sandra Lee, who is it?"—and she laughed and said, "Pop" again. I said, "Sandra Lee, look at that pix and tell me who it is." Out of a clear sky, she said, "Charlie Taylor." Your name hadn't been mentioned—she knew—she recognized the pix. Isn't it wonderful? So I asked her where Charlie Taylor was and who he was—and she said "France" and "My Daddy." Now I know for sure that it's all straight in her mind. Here I have the pix all set up in the order I like best. I want to have some of them enlarged. In each one of them you have a different expression and I can remember so well what you have said to me when looking like that. I really like the one with your helmet—your eyes (the good one and bad one) are doing some tall talking—and you look as if you've just told me something and are now trying to find out if I believe you. You look so happy and I'm glad. I wouldn't take a cool million for the pix—oh, honey, thank you ever so much. I love you so, and I do thank you for the pix—so very much!! Oh, and your hair—Charlie, it's pretty—real pretty—and so nice and long too. Has a wave—oh, I'm so darn jealous of everyone that even so much as looks at you—really I am!!

I've just had a shower of mail from you written from the 15th to the 19th. Last Monday—it's simply wonderful to get new news—and hear what you did *last week* rather than *last month*. . . .

About the American girls running out—well, I really don't know, for I'm here with Sandra Lee all the time. None of my friends do, that I know of, but I doubt if they'd tell me, for everyone knows my view point too well. I'm a prude—but, gosh, Charlie, when I'm in doubt about something, I just don't do it—and then I know I'm o.k. I love you so that I wouldn't dare do one thing to make me look cheap or small to you, for I always want to be your Barbie and I want you to want me. See?? . . .

Well, my time is getting short. But I want to tell you about yesterday and today. After cleaning the house, and Miss T.'s nap, Mother, the baby, and I went to Fort Mac* for the laundry. Came back by the Airport and watched planes land—and then Sandra Lee stayed with Martha and Reese until dark. Pip asked Louise, Maxine, and I to go to the Auditorium and see Henry Busse and we did. Had fun and he has quite an orchestra. We all wished for our husbands so that we were more or less depressed coming home. . . .

Well, my dear, I'm already better—just talking to you helps!! And a good night's sleep is also a good tonic—

so until tomorrow—

I love you,　　　　　　　Your Barbie

Fairburn, Georgia, April 12, 1945

My dearest sweetheart,

We are all so stunned by the sudden news of our own President Roosevelt's death. It was such a terrible shock, almost unbelievable. I wonder just how it has affected you all "over there." We've had our ears peeled to the radio since hearing it first at 5:00—and right now a chaplain from Paris is telling us a bit of what is being done there. It's such a sad thing—it's a pity he couldn't have lived to see the results of all he has been working for. Charlie, I wish you were here with me, for I need you so. Of course, Truman has already been sworn in as President of the United States, but it will take some time for us to get it through our brains. We don't know much about him, for he has always worked quietly—however, we must stick by him—closer than we did

*Fort McPherson.

even Roosevelt, for he will need us. There'll never be another Roosevelt —we will miss him.

My letter will be short tonight, for it's hard to get my thoughts together.

Robertine and Sandra Lee played on the porch all morning, while I tore up a dress to make a skirt and midriff top. After Sandra Lee's nap, little Nancy came up and we went to the drug store with Dot, Judy, Miriam, and Lynn. Then Nancy and Sandra Lee played until five.

Sandra Lee has been awfully good all day. She got in a rose bush— and really scratched her face up!! She's a sight.

Darling, you will have to bear with me now, for we are all so hurt. I will write more tomorrow. Remember that above all, I love you truly,

Always,　　　　　　　　Your Barbie

Fairburn, Georgia, May 2, 1945

My dearest sweetheart,

Mother is all excited and thrilled tonight because her brother in Wilson, North Carolina, called her today. Her birthday is Saturday and that's the best gift she will get. It really did her a world of good. She's planning a trip up there either the last of this month or the first of June. What I don't already know about cooking, I will certainly learn while she is gone. I just hope she doesn't back out at the last minute—for if I were in her shoes, I'd just about die to go back 'home.' She's so good and sweet, and I hope nothing happens to break up her trip.

Sandra Lee has been a mess all day. It's been rainy and we only got outside once. She was all right, but she's ever so much better when we can play outside. Dot and Judy spent the day with us—and Judy is good as gold. She'll stay on the bed and play by the hour. . . .

I must not have my thinking cap on—but I can't seem to write at all. We are so thrilled over the surrender in Italy and Austria. I wonder if Hitler and Goebbels are really dead. It's confirmed, but still I wonder. Will save a lot of trouble and time if they really are. I will be overjoyed when it's all over and you are home once more. I want you here— here with me and Sandra Lee forever. We'll have such a wonderful time—working and planning and living—day after day. Oh, there'll be many rough spots, but as long as we are together we can surely get through anything. Gee, eleven months is a long time to be without the very one you live for—and when I think how brave Ina was to stand it thirty-three months, well, it makes me really ashamed. I get so low sometimes that I just don't know what to do. Anyway, it can't be much longer now—and we've been fortunate in many ways. Don't think I'm not grateful . . .

Be real good for me, for I'm just yours.

I love you,   Your Barbie

On May 7, 1945, the German army's representatives signed an armistice at General Eisenhower's headquarters in Reims, effective the next day. The war in Europe was over.

Fairburn, Georgia, May 8, 1945

My dearest sweetheart,

So, it's over in Europe. Even now it's hard to believe. Evie, Maxine, and I went to the church tonight for an hour of praise and thanksgiving. I wonder how the boys on the front lines feel now that the guns are silent. Guess it would be hard for even them to express. God has certainly been on our side—and I'm grateful to Him.

Now, as for us—wouldn't it be swell if we knew just when you'd be coming home. If only you don't have to go to the Pacific, we'll be o.k. I just couldn't stand that! In your letter of May 1st today you said, "even if Germany should quit tomorrow, it'd be a year before I would get home." Is that my dear Charlie's humble opinion, or is it an established fact?? 'Course I'm trying hard not to build myself up for an awful letdown, but I do hope and pray you'll be home soon. I surely did enjoy your letter of May 1st. It was grand! . . .

Mother is spending the night with Mrs. Reese* again—so I'm writing

*Mrs. Reese, a good friend and neighbor, suffered from diabetes and needed someone with her when she had a reaction from the insulin. "Miss Mae" often stayed with her when this occurred.

this in bed. Daddy is home and I'm glad. 'Course it's after my bedtime, but I just got a late start tonight—and I knew that you wouldn't mind if I stayed awake longer to write you. This is my way of celebrating, I guess.

One thing sure—I love you more than anything. I miss you every day a little more and when you do come home—I won't ever let you out of my sight again. They needn't send you home for thirty days— for they'll never get you back—if they do. I really slipped up when I let you leave the first time!!

I love you, I love you,

Always,   Your Barbie

Fairburn, Georgia, May 22, 1945

My dearest Charlie baby,

Oh, Charlie Taylor, I love you so good! You are really tops and I wouldn't take anything ever for having you for a husband, lover, pal, and everything else. You are my life, my all—and I cannot go on without you much longer. I miss you every minute just a little more—and *How Tender* I want you so! How will it be when we are together again?? Will it be simple for the three of us to fall into the future together?? I'm positive it will be as natural as it was from the beginning, for we always did manage to cope with any situation, and I know we can forever. We were really meant for each other—I'm sure of it. For who else but you could make me do the very things you want me to except you, Charlie —and you so far away, too. Why, I can almost hear you saying sometimes, "Think now, Barbie, is that the way to act!?!" I believe you'll be surprised at the way I have learned to control my temper or my feelings. I'm not half as sensitive as I once was. I can almost always laugh instead of pout or cry now. Really it's wonderful what one can really accomplish, if one tries hard enough. Maybe it's just growing up, but somehow, I feel as if you had a great deal to do with it . . .

We are all looking forward to General Hodges's* return Thursday. Have a parade planned and a big to-do at the City Auditorium. I take

*General Courtney H. Hodges, commander of the First U.S. Army, was from Perry, Georgia.

it you aren't in the First Army now—are you in any Army??—I mean, everyone is in some Army, are they not? Can you tell me? My guess is the 15th—right?? Just say "right of the 22nd"—if I am right, o.k.? . . .

Well, sugar, this is all I can think of now—so I'll stop chatting. I really do love you, so don't forget it—for one minute??!! Please be good!!

Always,   Your Barbie

Fairburn, Georgia, May 23, 1945

My dearest sweetheart,

Received your letter of May 13th today—and you gave me your *correct* address, only—you didn't have an APO on it—so I'm taking it for granted that it's 545. Hope I'm right.

I liked your letter very much. It was nice and long—just what I needed. Sure I want you to get out of the Army as soon as possible—and I don't think it's the wrong way to feel at all. You've done more than your share already—so it's time someone else stepped in your place—in my opinion.

I agree with you about the diaphragm—but, may I be so bold as to ask where you learned so much about the article! After all, Charlie. Anyway, it's a great idea—and although I do want *several* children—not just two, if you please—I would like to plan for the next ones. So, with a diaphragm it would be better, of course. Do you mean that you want me to get a diaphragm *now?* You once said to wait until you were sure of coming home—so let me know, I mean ans. this pronto! I do think they're well worth the money. No, I wouldn't feel funny getting pregnant on my second honeymoon—but, frankly, I'd rather not. Just re-read the above sentence "you were sure of coming home"—I don't mean it that way—for I'm sure you're coming home *someday*—I meant until you were really on the way home, see?

The only disadvantage of a diaphragm—if I am capable of explaining what I mean—anyhow, well, most sensible people (from what I hear) only have one sexual intercourse in one evening—but some others (me, for instance, when I really get excited—and I'm sure I will when I see you again—for it gives me goose-pimples to even think about your coming home!!). Anyway, as I started to say—well, in the case of more than one SI in an evening—it isn't satisfactory, on account of—well, guess you know what I mean. Therefore, *one* has to be good—therefore, you, my friend, will have to control your feelings, in order to make it good. See? So, it's all up to you, as usual. . . .

Sugar, I actually feel as if you are almost home—and I really will be glad when you are here!—for I truly love you. Can you still whistle "When Irish Eyes Are Smiling"!?!—bet you don't remember just unconsciously whistling it as you would drive along the road—but I do—and I'd surely like to hear you right now.

Write as often as possible and remember I love you.

Always,   Your Barbie

Fairburn, Georgia, May 25, 1945

My dearest sweetheart,

Have just been checking up on our War Bonds. We have a total of $625.00—Sandra Lee, $275.00. From the War Department you have not received a bond for Sept. or Oct. 1944. We have received $25.00 bonds for Nov. and Dec. 1944 and Jan., Feb., March, April—1945— plus a $25.00 bond for April 1945. Wonder what happened to Sept. and October, 1944? Guess it would be a good idea for you to check on it— however, it may still come in eventually. I've had the bonds in the bank —and just today got them out so that I could add the rest. I also keep a list of the serial numbers at home, in case something should happen. Boy, I really want to hang on to them, for we'll certainly be glad one of these days. Five bonds mature in 1952—and that isn't so long off now, eh?

It's about 1:30 and I am here in the side yard—getting a real sun bath. Sandra Lee is asleep—and I can hear her if she wakes up. Have on a blue bathing suit that I had five years ago so I must not be any smaller or larger than ever. However, I must admit, I fill it out more now—HA! I'm concentrating on my back today—for I do wanta get tan —real tan this summer. I'll really have to have a bath when I go in— for it's so hot and am I *sweating!*

This morning I cleaned (mopped, etc.) the front porch, Sandra's, mine, and the back bedroom. Would have cleaned the whole house—but I wanted to get some sun. Just didn't want to have to do the whole thing tomorrow. Sandra Lee played—just had the best time. We had lunch when Daddy came home—good ole string beans, cucumbers, onions, potatoes, corn bread, and buttermilk. Just the kind of a dinner I need! I got Sandra Lee some chopped junior foods, instead of strained baby foods, and she tho't the string beans were from the table—and she ate like a pig! These junior foods really do look like food—so perhaps she'll eat more now. She had a bath and then I gave her her bottle on the porch. We were talking about you and I said, "What do you think your Daddy will do when he comes home and sees you, Prissy?" She said, "He eat me up." I said, "Well, what will you do." She said, "My hug him good." And, she wasn't joking one bit—and you will surely want to eat her!!!!!

Charlie, I had the best time yesterday—it was just grand—seeing the parade and *General Hodges* and everyone. Maxine and I yelled our throats out, and it was all the Boy Scouts could do to keep the crowd from just going in the street. After the parade I had about three hours to kill—so I saw *Dark Waters* and then met Evie at 5:00. We had supper at the "Ship Ahoy"—and actually I was able to get some fried shrimp —haven't had any since I was in Gainesville, Florida. Then we went to the auditorium to hear General Hodges speak.

Sandra Lee is waking up—so I'll write more later. I surely do love you.

Always yours forever,   Your Barbie

Fairburn, Georgia, June 5, 1945

My dearest sweetheart,

. . . I'm having the best time keeping house. Daddy seems pleased with anything I do. I got up at 6:30 this a.m. to fix his breakfast—and he liked that. Had a good dinner and Sandra Lee was an angel. When I put her to bed this afternoon I did the dishes and washed clothes. Really had a lot of them. . . .

Miriam and Lynn came down this afternoon—Lynn is walking real good now—so it isn't so much work on Miriam. Lynn and Priss were real good together.

I had a hot supper for Daddy tonight. Hoecakes, potatoes, and onions, and bacon. He likes that. Sandra Lee ate most of her supper all by herself and I wish she'd learn to do it all the time. She was unusually hungry tonight. . . .

Tomorrow is the 6th. One whole year since we were together. I never shall forget how you looked that morning—rushing around—dressing —and finally telling me good-bye. I remember just what you said— and finally I heard you walking down the hall, and heard the elevator come up for you. To think that I let you leave like that. Just give me one more chance and I won't let you leave—no siree—I'll hang on to you and go where you go!! . . .

I do love you,   Your Barbie

Fairburn, Georgia, July 15, 1945

My dearest sweetheart,

. . . I've been ironing a lot today. Just decided for once and for all that I would get everything ironed up instead of sticking it back—so I did. Therefore, Prissy really has a nice lot of clothes. . . .

Jenny, Jean, and Martha B. came down tonight to discuss the Cotillion Club. We're all officers and it's lacking in sumpin', so we tried to figure out something to put some life in it. Quite a job tho' without you and the rest of the husbands. Sandra Lee went to bed after being real cute for them.

Since Mother has been gone, I have learned a lot. I mean little things that don't amount to much—but mean a lot to me. I feel sure that when you come home, I can take over my duties as a wife and handle the job considerably better than I did before. You must have tho't me terribly dumb—and I love you for putting up with me. I can make starch— and haven't failed yet getting the correct amount in Prissy's clothes. And I'm not a good cook (by a long shot), but I feel like I can cook a digestible meal now. I made biscuits Sunday a.m. and they weren't bad at all. Really, I'm looking forward to your return—and our settling down—and *really* keeping house right. . . .

Guess that brings you up to date on the news. Oh, I made an apple pie, Charlie, and it turned out real good. And tomorrow I'm going to try banana pudding. I love to try new dishes. Just can't wait until we have a place so that we can really experiment.

Oh, I had Jr. washed and greased and he runs like a top. I want to have a new top put on—and wanted to surprise you with it, but it's so expensive I guess I should wait until you get here to attend to it. Sure looks bad tho' and really dirty on the inside—spotty, you know. . . .

Please be good and come home in a hurry. Am real anxious to hear from you.

I love you truly,

Always,   Your Barbie

P.S. I wouldn't attempt to read this over, so just consider the source on the mistakes, o.k.?

Fairburn, Georgia, July 29, 1945

My dearest sweetheart,

. . . Well, at long last Mother is coming home—yes, Tuesday a.m.!! I can't believe it. I was just thinking—if I'm as excited as I am over Mother coming home—what will I be when I know that you are! Her train gets in at 7:00, and Daddy, Martha, Sandra Lee and yours truly are going for her. I have a zillion and one things to do tomorrow to get everything ready for her.

Charlie, I made the best lemon pie yesterday. Honestly, it turned out fine. And, this morning I made a banana pudding and it looks like a picture. So perhaps I've learned something these past two months. At least we won't go hungry when you come home. . . .

Ninya', Jenny, and I all have an Anniversary pretty soon—remember????—so, we're going to celebrate one night this week. Have dinner in town, and see a show, 'er sumpin'. Think it will be fun, especially after two months of confinement. . . .

Maxine has had a letter from Ray written the 21st—so I'm looking forward to one tomorrow. Hope it has good news, too. Honey, I love you so very much. Oh, how I do want to be near you.

All my love,   Your Barbie

3 years?!?
Fairburn, Georgia, August 1, 1945

My dearest sweetheart,

This is it!—the official day, eh? Everyone has been just swell, pretty cards and everything. Mother and Daddy are setting me up to dinner and a show in town, whenever I wish to go. Mama Taylor sent a sweet card and note telling me to buy four pieces of china and charge them to Pop and her. Hasn't been too bad a day. Martha B. and Emily came down this afternoon and we played poker. Then tonight Mother and I went to the show, *The Affairs of Susan*—and Martha kept Sandra Lee. Really I haven't been blue, just enjoying turning over in my mind the many memories of you. I love you very much, my dear, and I hope and pray for many, many more years with you in the future.

When I heard of your definite orders at Reims, I was, well, you know. Anyway, I immediately called Mama Taylor, for I knew that she was just as anxious as I to hear. As you say, we are still lucky and should be very thankful. However, that doesn't help much now, does it? I was hoping that you would get a 30-day leave, at least, just to see Prissy. But this world is mighty big, and we are mighty small—and surely, all things happen for the best. Man, I sure want you home. In five more days it will be fourteen months, and it might just be that long again.

So, now that Mother is home, and we are settling down once more —I suppose I'll start planning a trip to Florida real soon. Sure wish I could go to the beach first—and then to Gainesville. I do believe a week at the beach would really fix me up—but there doesn't seem to be any chance. Oh, I'll be o.k., soon as I understand that you are assigned to stay there awhile longer! I've heard: "that's better than the Pacific"—too many times, tho'!

Don't suppose I'll save much this month. Have to buy all of Sandra Lee's birthday—and if we go to Florida, we'll need new things here and there. What th' heck! . . .

I love you so good—and I'll never get tired of waiting for you, not in a zillion years. I'm all yours and always will be.

I love you,   Your Barbie

Fairburn, Georgia, August 8, 1945

My dearest beloved,

. . . Say, this new atomic bomb has set the USA on fire. Have you ever realized anything could be so powerful? I hope the Japs realize just what it means to quit now. And Russia has declared War on Japan. Of course the Japs don't have a chance—but if all this could stop now —we could start over in a peaceful world again. I'm just tired I guess, but it all seems so pointless in the first place. . . .

After supper Mother and I decided to take Priss to the show just to see what would happen. We had no idea that we would get to see the first reel. But, there's always a happy surprise where Sandra Lee is concerned—the li'l angel sat there and looked at the picture for a long time, saying, "What's that, Mama?"—and clapping her hands to the music—and finally she put her head in my lap and her feet in Mother's and went to sleep. Now isn't she about the smartest thing you've ever seen? I was surely proud of her.

And last but not least I want to tell you about her birthday. Well, early in the morning I gave her some of her toys and she had fun opening them and discovering new things. Pinky (our new maid) and I cleaned the house and yard extra good—and at three the family was here to help her open her family gifts. I had the living room shut up —so when we went in—there right in the middle of the room was the table and chairs from Daddy (you). Priss walks in—sits down—says, "Isn't this cute? Well, where are my presents?" We all just hollered!!

Then the fun began—and she was so excited she could hardly look at one gift before opening another. At four the children came—eleven in all—and fifteen grown-ups. They all brought a gift and you can't imagine how adorable Sandra Lee was thanking them. We took lots of pix and then Martha played games with them. Then we came inside and the smaller children sat at the table with Sandra Lee—Mother lighted the candles on her cake and everyone sang "Happy Birthday" —Priss blew the candles out, and we served the cream and cake. I had intended taking a picture with the cake—but it slipped my mind. The day couldn't have been better, except for the fact that you weren't here. . . . And our li'l girl is now 2!! Does it seem possible? She's such a dear, Charlie, and does she love her Daddy. She never fails to let you in on everything.

Charlie baby, you asked how long I'd be willing to wait for you. Don't you know, can't you feel it inside you, that I'm here and I'll be here forever and ever, just waiting for you. . . .

Be good and do be careful,

Always,   Your Barbie

Fairburn, Georgia, August 9, 1945

My dearest sweetheart,

Well, the news is going so fast now, it's hard for a dumb bunny like me to keep up with it. Everyone is calling everyone else everytime something new comes over the radio. As for me, well, I'm very calm, for I've passed getting so excited that it shows outwardly—'course, my insides are like a "jumping jack". . . .

You mentioned something about discontinuing our War Bonds when we reach a certain amount. Well, I don't know—'course we'll want the cash the minute you get home—but if we really need it, we can always cash the bonds over the certain amount in them. So, maybe it would be better to go on and keep them as they are. I wonder how long after VJ day it will be possible to buy War Bonds? In case they should stop them, then I think it would be better for you to make out a check thru' the government direct to the bank here, see? O.K.?

How will the Jap surrender affect (effect) us?—that's what I keep wondering. I suppose your job will go on anyway, eh? Oh, Charlie baby, I had the most delightful dream about you last night. Everytime I saw you, we got in a wonderful clinch—and my dear, it was heavenly to be in your arms again. I love you so good—you are mine, all mine. Don't ever change and please don't let me down.

Always,   Your Barbie

Chapter Four

WESTERN FRONT

June 1944 – August 1945

Overleaf: Charles in France, late 1944

In a long drive an infantry company may go for a couple of days without letting up. Ammunition is carried up to it by hand, and occasionally by jeep. The soldiers sometimes eat only one K-ration a day. They may run clear out of water. Their strength is gradually whittled down by wounds, exhaustion cases and straggling. Finally they will get an order to sit where they are and dig in. . . . Regardless of how tired you may be, you always dig in the first thing. . . . They had had less than four hours' rest in three solid days of fighting. That's the way life is in the infantry.

Ernie Pyle, "On the Western Front,"
August 12, 1944

J ust as Barbara's letters tell much about how service wives made it through the long days of separation, so the correspondence of Charles exemplifies the millions of letters from overseas to families in the United States. He wrote nearly every day, skipping only days in which his combat duties prevented him, and even then he tried to get in a line or two in a serial letter. Charles's letters were often written on the back of Barbara's because of paper shortages. This gave him the feeling of actual physical communication with her as he wrote.[1]

The letters were filled with daily minutiae, especially after Charles found himself invalided out of combat and assigned to training replacement troops. He retained his strong interest in soldiers and officers with whom he had served and young men he had known in his civilian days in Florida. He worried about Barbara's health. As he observed Barbara's "growing up" in her letters, he grew up himself. And as her letters sustained him, his sustained her. Their strong marriage now was being tested in a combat crucible. He knew it, and she did as well. To some degree, he welcomed the test, but he felt certain that their marriage would survive and he would be "coming back."

Charles's mail home was now censored. He was especially careful throughout his military career not to give away sensitive information, and when he had to act as censor for his own troops, he bent over backward to meet government standards.

Charles landed at Southampton, England on June 29 and was transferred in the back of an Army truck to Crewkerne, in Dorset. Here the officers were debriefed and given a few days' intensive training, mostly to restore their physical tone, before being assigned temporary command of replacement soldiers on their way to France. The fighting in Normandy was still fierce; the German army had bogged the Allied troops down in the hedgerow fighting, as well as near Cherbourg, a key area in the proposed supply line to the invasion forces. Although many troops were ashore and more were coming every day, the control of Normandy, three weeks after D-Day, was still in doubt.

While in England, Charles and other officers lived in pup tents. Occasionally they were issued two-hour passes to nearby towns. They were told about the training disasters in the area prior to D-Day to emphasize that they should remain alert at all times; danger was everywhere, even in training.

Charles's pay rose by 10 percent now that he was overseas. In addition, he became eligible for a longevity increase of 5 percent of his base pay. All in all, he drew $99.15 each month. He praised the Red Cross, which had provided the newly arrived soldiers with food and information when they landed in England, for "really doing a wonderful job . . . not at all like I had pictured." But it was still just a waiting time for what would soon come, and did, on July 18, when he arrived, with his replacement troops, in France.[2]

Replacement troops, led by officers such as Charles, came ashore in groups of 250 and were assigned to one of five recently established replacement depots. Charles spent several days at one of these depots (universally called repple-depples or repple-depots) before receiving his assignment as a platoon leader in H Company, Thirty-ninth Infantry Regiment, Ninth Infantry Division, one of the most heavily used units in the entire Army.

Only a minority of the sixteen million men who served in the armed forces during the war years saw combat. More than one-fourth of all military personnel remained stateside, known in the Army as the "Zone of Interior." When the number of American troops in Europe peaked at three million, only 750,000 were engaged in actual fighting. Charles was part of that small minority.[3]

No one has yet written the history of the Thirty-ninth Infantry Regiment, but its slogan, taken from the ranch brand of its commanding officer, was well-known. The men carried the legend "AAA-O" on their helmets, meaning "Anything, Anywhere, Anytime, Bar Nothing." Charles was entering into the elite of the Army forces in Europe. The Thirty-ninth had landed at Algiers in the invasion of North Africa in December 1942 and had taken part in the famous battle of the Kasserine Pass, when American troops were first introduced to the impact of modern warfare. It had fought well elsewhere in North Africa and was part of the invasion force which eventually conquered Sicily. The regiment had also been part of the attack force in Italy before being withdrawn to England to prepare for the assault on the German forces in France. General Dwight D. Eisenhower later described the Ninth Division, of which the Thirty-ninth Regiment was a part, as one of the two best under his command in World War II.[4]

A war correspondent who traveled with these combat troops for a long time in Italy and Normandy expressed his admiration for them with the following encomium:

> They held the line because others held. But no one could force them into the attitude they have assumed. Now they know that some of them will die. But it doesn't matter as much as it used to. Even their homes seem far away—dreamy places receding into the distance. They love their leaders. They love their outfits. They love each other, if I may say it that way. They don't know any other way to go about this business, so that's the way they're going into the dark mouth of war.[5]

The Thirty-ninth Infantry Regiment participated in the difficult reduction of Cherbourg in early July and arrived in the heat of the Normandy fighting on July 9, with orders to move along the highway running from Périers to St. Lô, on the way to Le Desert. In this hedgerow fighting, they were thrust into the thick of the battle. The regiment suffered heavy losses: the casualty rate among riflemen (both noncommissioned officers and privates) reached almost forty percent during these early days of fighting in France. The troops encountered a severe German counterattack on the twelfth of July and, as it rained very heavily on the thirteenth, they were stalled in place. Enemy resistance continued to be very heavy, and this unit, with the other regiments of the Ninth Division, was only able to consolidate its gains by the eighteenth, the day Charles arrived as a replacement officer. The regiment spent the next week in light combat, taking the time to recuperate from its battle losses and bring up replacements, while attempting to repair its weapons and make ready for the next assault.[6]

By the time of Charles's arrival in France, the manpower shortage was reaching critical proportions. The war in Europe had taken a direction which military strategists had not foreseen. Initially, planners had expected that air power and armored vehicles would make the infantry obsolete. Large numbers of qualified men had been taken into the Air Corps and armored units. The infantry, formerly known as "the Queen of Battle," now faced a potential shortage of combat-trained troops. In the first month of combat in France, the heavy casualties suffered by the invasion forces worsened the problem. The difficult fighting encountered on the Italian front (Rome did not fall until June 6, 1944) and in the jungle fighting of the South Pacific meant that many more combat infantry troops were needed there as well. Charles and many other candidates were washed out of the Air Corps and channelled into the infantry to help resolve this problem. The situation would not be entirely cleared up until after the failure of Operation Schmidt later in the year. By then, the necessity for properly trained and physically fit combat troops to take on the Germans was well-known, and both Selective Service intake and basic training programs were stepped up substantially to fulfill this need.[7]

The Thirty-ninth relied on veteran non-coms and well-known officers to deal with the shortage of experienced men. The regiment was

close to the heart of General George S. Patton. Its commanding officer, when Charles joined the regiment, was the famous Colonel Harry
S. "Paddy" Flint. Flint, who was sixty-three years old at the time of
D-Day, had trained many of the leading officers of World War II at
West Point during the interwar period. In combat, he showed little
respect for rank, especially for those men who had been his students.
Charles, soon after joining the Thirty-ninth, recounted an incident
which clearly demonstrated Flint's lack of reverence for ranking officers. Flint, Patton, another officer, and Charles were touring the front
lines in a jeep. Flint ordered Patton about as though he were a green
lieutenant, instructed the others to take cover, strode about with German shells coming dangerously near, and all the while, of course, set
an example of courage for the men in the area.

A few days later, on July 24, Flint was killed in combat not far from
where Charles was in action. Flint did not die immediately; the courage
he displayed after getting hit served as an example to those around him,
including Charles Taylor. Patton served as a pallbearer at his funeral.
He described Flint in his dispatches as exhibiting "personal leadership
of a very high order." Max Hastings, in one of the best recent accounts
of the fighting in France, remarked that Flint was one of the "great
characters" of the First Army.[8]

The Thirty-ninth Regiment's elite conception of itself worked in its
favor in meeting the manpower shortage. The high morale of this regiment meant that replacement troops, such as those Charles led, were
quickly accepted into the unit and did not suffer any greater percentage
of the casualties than the veteran soldiers.[9]

Logistical difficulties plagued the troops in France. One of these was
providing sufficient gasoline and motor oil for soldiers who traveled at
least part of the time in gasoline-powered vehicles. Eventually, a series
of temporary pipelines was constructed to help meet this problem. Ma-
teriel was also moved by truck convoy, including the famous "Red Ball
Express." To provide food for this Army on the move, new rations were
introduced. The famous C- and K-rations provided nutritious food in
the form of powdered, dried, and tinned products. The Army included
cigarettes, toilet paper, candy, and coffee along with beef stew, ham and

eggs, hash, and other items in the rations. Later, a ten-in-one ration was designed to feed a small unit while in the field. These rations were designed to be mixed with water and heated over a sterno stove or other small fire, but they could be eaten cold. Often troops with limited supplies of water simply combined the entire ration in a sort of stew, which went down well for tired and hungry combatants. The Army attempted to provide at a least one hot meal a day and did remarkably well under the circumstances.

Three weeks after D-Day, however, there still were not enough troops and supplies ashore. The problem remained until late in July, when it was reported to General Eisenhower that approximately 86 percent of the proposed troop strength was in France. The percentage of supplies was slightly better, as the capture of Cherbourg had freed an avenue to bring provisions ashore.[10]

Charles reported to the Thirty-ninth during the third week in July, just as preparations were being made for a major assault on the German lines in the area which became known as the Falaise Gap. The attack was given the code name "Operation Cobra." Very severe weather limited the air bombardment which preceded the attack, and when it did occur, an error in navigation caused many of the bombs to fall on United States troops poised for the assault. This failure meant that the resistance would continue to be extremely stiff, as the Germans were now alerted to the probability of a major Allied ground attack.

On July 24, the day of the mistaken bombardment, two battalions of the Thirty-ninth took eight hours to reduce a German stronghold, located at the junction road. They took seventy-seven casualties in that time, including Colonel Flint, and did not get across the Périers road for another day, finally advancing two miles. Fortunately, the regiment did not have to face the brunt of the opposition for the next few days; it continued to move slowly forward through the fourth of August. On the fifth it was able to consolidate its position, still meeting heavy resistance, while passing through the Fourth Division, which had been in the lead.

On August 7, the Germans counterattacked in force, compressing the United States forces near the River See. The Thirty-ninth, now under command of Colonel Van H. Bond, took the major force of the counterattack. The unit was separated from its main force, and while trying to break out and connect with the Division again, it was isolated for a time. The regimental command force was cut off as well. The Cannon Company, under very heavy attack and bombardment, was forced to dismantle its weapons and perform as infantry. Its company commander remained behind German lines and acted as an observer for the isolated troops, giving them information on the enemy. Armored units of the Second Armored Division, moving in the area, eventually provided "temporary stability" for the Thirty-ninth at the See.

The Thirty-ninth had been temporarily attached to the Fourth Division during this difficult period, but returned to normal status on August 9. The German counterattack, now remembered as the Battle of the Falaise Gap, is still the subject of strategic analyses that debate whether the general commanding the American forces proceeded with enough dispatch to deal with the German threat. On the twelfth of August, the Thirty-ninth went into reserve for a few days to recuperate from this arduous fighting. It saw limited action later in the month, but spent most of the period from August 19 to 24 south of Paris, regrouping and reassembling while taking on more new replacement troops, and then moved out on the twenty-fifth to encounter the enemy again.[11]

Charles became involved in action even before Operation Cobra began. Shortly after he arrived in France, his company commander picked him up in a jeep at a replacement depot; as they were moving to join the Thirty-ninth, they came upon a German tank in the road. The tank hit the jeep with a round that threw the two officers into a ditch. A bazooka with ammunition was in the ditch next to Charles, and he used it to put the tank out of action. He has said since that the immediacy of the problem, coupled with the strength of his training, led to his instinctive reaction.

Charles's unit was involved in the closing of the Falaise Gap, where, on August 8, he received shrapnel fragments in his hand, wrist, and leg. He went briefly to the rear for medical treatment. This qualified him for the Purple Heart.

As the Cobra assault advanced, Charles faced even heavier fighting.

He found that the German counterattacks, especially with his own unit suffering from ammunition shortages, tested him greatly. However, his first sergeant, another Taylor from West "By God" Virginia, a veteran of much combat, helped him become the sort of leader his troops expected and received. Early patrols and the experience of meeting Flint and Patton in the very first days of combat also helped him become a "veteran."

In late August 1944, Charles was hurt again. He and his troops were strafed by a Messerschmidt 109, and a fence post nearby, uprooted by a bomb from the plane, hit him, dislocating his shoulder and knocking him unconscious. From this time, Charles suffered headaches, which continued to increase in severity and eventually sent him to the rear. The shoulder, never properly attended, still bothers him more than forty years later.[12]

Charles reported his activities to Barbara nearly every night and whenever else he could find time. On July 25, the day after Colonel Flint was killed, he wrote: "The men I am with are good men and have done a lot of wonderful work. Don't you dare worry about me for they sure look out for me here." He was unable to write again until the twenty-ninth, but he reported then that although he was tired, he had had a hot meal and was feeling good. It was clear from his comments that he had been accepted into his unit. On July 31, he reported on the award of medals to some of his men and commented on his first sergeant (the other Taylor) and others under his command. He was careful to reassure Barbara that he was in no danger. In fact, he spent more time telling her about attending a USO show which he had already seen in New Jersey, the well-worn chestnut, "Up in Mabel's Room," than about his combat activities.[13]

The press, however, kept civilians well-informed about the war in Europe. Newsreels took some time to reach movie theatres, but newspapers and weekly magazines such as *Collier's*, *Life*, *The Saturday Evening Post*, and others regularly reported on the fighting. Ernie Pyle's dispatches on Normandy were published in the Atlanta *Journal* in the summer of 1944, and Barbara read them, knowing that they could be about Charles.[14]

Despite the attempts of Charles to reassure Barbara that he was not in any immediate danger, they both were all too well aware of the perils he faced. The official history of the United States Army in World War II states that the casualty rate among the five hardest-hit European divisions, which included the Ninth Division, was close to two hundred percent. During heavy combat, casualties reached one hundred percent every three months. The Army historian, Robert R. Palmer, laconically observed: "A severe mental strain was imposed on the individual soldier, especially the infantryman, who felt that no matter how long he fought, or how long he survived the dangers of combat, he must remain in action until removed as a casualty. Cases of battle neuroses multiplied as men simply became tired, and when tired were more easily killed, wounded or captured.[15]

While Charles was enduring these days of danger, he sustained himself by remembering his life with Barbara in Georgia and the other places they had resided. They had agreed to spend the hour from ten until eleven o'clock each night thinking about each other—though they knew the time differential would mean that these were different times in fact. She would smoke "that last cigg" in a ritualistic way, and he, when he could, would do the same, write her a few lines, and above all, think about her and Sandra Lee.[16]

Even under the adverse conditions of war, Charles could find much of interest about which to write, particularly the countryside and people of France. Just before he went into combat, he described the animals near his bivouac—cows and horses, "undisturbed by our boys." In the same letter, he observed:

> This is pretty country. It's all cut up into two or three hundred yard plots, these fields or plots are all fenced in by a mound of dirt, about three yards high, with hedges on top. Really, it makes a very good fence. There are small trees growing about like elderberry bushes, around two feet apart, along the hedgerow. It makes quite a pretty picture. Most of the houses are made of a stone like sandstone.[17]

By the next time Charles described the French countryside, he had seen all the hedgerows he wanted. In addition to their beauty, they made wonderful tank traps, places for small units to resist stubbornly the American advance—in the parlance, they were a "killing ground." He continued, however, to demonstrate his great interest in the French people and their way of life, writing in mid-August:

> There is a family of French people that live in the big house to my rear. You would laugh to see them for they sure look funny with their patched clothes and wooden shoes. Yes, they wear shoes just like you used to read about the Dutch wearing. I want to send a pair home to you, but there seems to be no extra pair around here. Here comes one of the little French boys with his wooden shoes, patched, short pants, long hair, dirty face, questioning eyes that see you, but don't, and last, but not least—two big quart bottles of cider, one in each hand.

A few days later Charles was able to take a bath and wash his clothes in a farmyard under a pump. Although his monthly whiskey allowance (to which officers were entitled, with funds deducted from their pay for the luxury), a bottle of Johnnie Walker and a quart of dry gin, was delivered the same day, he wrote: "Do believe I shall save them 'til— well, 'til it's time to do a little celebrating." As good as the bath was, it was not a big enough occasion to celebrate.[18]

During this period of heavy fighting, Charles's letters occasionally showed symptoms of what we now know to be combat fatigue. In late August, upon returning to action after spending a few days of rest with his unit in the rear, he wrote a long and unpleasant letter to Barbara, reflecting the fact that his morale had deteriorated with his return to the front. Letters such as these were few in number, but they do indicate the impact of combat on even such stable persons as Charles Taylor.[19]

One of the most important things for Charles in these difficult and dangerous circumstances was his mail. Mail equalled morale, and he reported the enlisted men saying, "Each letter is a ten minute furlough." When the mail didn't come, he was disconsolate and worried unnecessarily about Barbara being true to him. In a letter of October 1, he confided:

> Don't you ever think that I don't trust you—I do. See all I (we) ever hear about over here is all about how untrue the wives and girls back in the

states are. Too, there are so many fellows here that have been over for over two years and a lot of them were not married too long before they came over and their wives are crying for divorces, etc. Oh, I guess with so much on a guy's mind and not knowing how a lot of the girls are acting, it puts one to wondering. You know how the men like to tease each other to pass the time away. I do not worry, but I do like to have you tell me in your letters that all is well. You know that I'd not take anything for you and our love.

Only two days later Charles was disappointed to receive only a mimeographed letter from the Fairburn Methodist Church, a birthday card with a checked message, and "a note, a damn note, letter No. twenty-three." He wrote:

Now you are going to write me a long, newsy or love or any kind of letter, or don't write. It is better not to get a letter than to get a page and a half. Why can't you spare one hour to write. I know good and well if I can sit or lie down and write you long letters over here that you can surely sit down and write me some long ones. . . . Well, I want this little matter taken care of, understand? . . . Honey, please don't feel bad about the way I write at times, for I get a bit nervous, etc., and I just fly off the string or handle or something. . . . I need a lot of mail. That is all a fellow has to look forward to—is mail call. That's all there is to keep a guy's morale up or give him any morale at all. So, please, do write me a lot for you are all I have, and I do like to hear from you, really I do. I worship and love you so damn much that it is pitiful for a guy like me to be away from you.

Two hours or so later, after a hot meal, Charles wrote again, in an even more contrite mood, saying, "I am sorry I ever mailed that mean letter. I know perfectly well that you are really doing a good job getting me a letter off most every day and even when it is a note I honestly do enjoy it and I am ashamed of myself for ever saying that I don't. Forgive my blinding ignorance."[20]

From August 25 until early October, Charles was involved in stiff fighting, mostly in rapid pursuit of the German enemy. Finally, on October 5, when there was a lull in the fighting, he sent a V-Mail home. In it he tersely remarked: "My time is really put to use lately." It is remarkable that Charles wrote as much as he did, for the Thirty-ninth was involved in some of the fiercest fighting in the European theatre of war during the late summer and early fall of 1944. On August 27, the Thirty-ninth had moved out and crossed the Marne River, capturing the town of Mieux. By September 1, it had reached the border near Etraupont and Aubentan. The unit swung northeast near Charleroix and crossed the Belgian border on the second. After consolidating its position, it crossed the Meuse River on the fifth, and captured Dinant, an important stronghold, on the seventh, moving rapidly to the east before going in reserve briefly on the eleventh. Here the troops found themselves with an opportunity to take showers, clean up, repair their gear, and relax at Camp D'Elsenborn.

This was dangerous work. When the Thirty-ninth came to Charleroix, it found German Tiger tanks situated in a "killing ground" which had to be subdued. Charles and his troops experienced heavy shelling before they were able to eliminate this stubborn resistance. Crossing the Meuse was not easy, either, as the bridge at Dinant was damaged and German artillery was zeroed in on this site. Charles, with two sergeants, took out a German stronghold at this crossing, using grenades to subdue the well-emplaced machine guns. Here he received his first commendation for bravery. However, even as he and his companions viewed those last few days, it was obvious that it was not over; the famed West Wall—the Seigfried Line—was waiting.[21]

The next several weeks provided the Thirty-ninth with even more difficult fighting. On September 14, the unit was back in combat, driving along the Vicht River, moving east and southeast toward Roetgen and Lammersdorf. Charles, crossing into German territory for the first time, stopped and ritually spat on the ground before moving on. After turning north again, these troops were pinned down before the Seigfried (or as it was sometimes known, the Scharnhorst) Line. Lammersdorf was finally subdued after three days of very difficult combat. From the eighteenth to the end of September, the Thirty-ninth continued to meet extremely heavy resistance as it sought to capture the German strong point, Hill 554, just south of Lammersdorf. The main difficulty of this fighting was that a plateau saddle of land ran between the hill and another German stronghold, so the United States troops were always in view and under constant heavy fire. This was also a period of extremely poor weather, and it was almost impossible to provide bombing and air cover. Muddy, wet ground made the fighting more difficult. The first battalion of the Thirty-ninth was eventually detached and, working with the Sixtieth Division, attacked the enemy in the Huertgen Forest, near the village of Huertgen, on the twenty-fifth. Part of the second battalion was seconded there a day later, and the two battalions covered and held the road from Lammersdorf to Huertgen until they were able to overrun Hill 554. Over the next week, as the Thirty-ninth again recuperated with only limited patrol activity, plans were made for the next push, code-named Operation Schmidt. Schmidt was to be a major thrust of the forces in this area, designed to drive east and north, with its main objective to capture the dams on the Roer River at Schwammersaul.

Bad weather continued to plague the Allied forces. Even so, they moved out, leaving the Huertgen Forest on the eighth of October, heading toward their Schmidt objectives. Two platoons of the Thirty-ninth, with units of the Sixtieth Division, broke through the last German resistance in the Forest on the ninth, but they came under severe counterattack on the tenth. Eventually, the German advance was stopped, and the Americans (Second Battalion, Thirty-ninth Infantry Regiment) moved out again, capturing the town of Germeter late on the tenth. Much open farm land lay beyond Germeter, however, and the German forces were located in very strong positions.

An Allied attack across the open ground between Germeter and Vossenach failed on the eleventh, as the troops came under very heavy German fire, but some elements of the Thirty-ninth did succeed in crossing this difficult stretch of ground on the twelfth. German counterattacks were again successful, however, in driving the Americans back, and this time the main line of the United States troops was severed. Another period of consolidation followed, accompanied by continuous heavy fighting and artillery shelling. On the thirteenth and fourteenth the German attacks were finally repelled, and the Thirty-ninth reoccupied its lost ground. The toll on the American troops was too much, however, and the Battle of Schmidt was declared over, without reaching its main objectives at the Roer River. The battle design had failed primarily because of very stiff German resistance, but also because of what has since been termed a failure of command on the part of some of the higher American officers. In addition, the troops in the van of the fighting, including the Thirty-ninth, had simply taken too many casualties to continue on without major reinforcement and replacements for those who had fallen.[22]

Charles was recommended for a medal for valor after he, another officer, and two corporals captured an important German pillbox at Lammersdorf, which allowed the Thirty-ninth to make its advances. His regimental commander, however, chose to award Charles a battle-field citation promotion to first lieutenant because, "Medals don't buy beans, but promotions do."[23]

By the end of Operation Schmidt, both sides had suffered severely, but the Thirty-ninth did hold Germeter and the neighboring town of Wittscheidt, the forward position of the Allied forces, for the time being. The regiment stayed in place there until late in October, when it was relieved by the Twenty-eighth Division and sent back to Camp D'Elsenborn again to take on its replacement troops, recover from the strain of the battle, and recoup its losses. It had received savage beatings in the fighting, but it had also handed out some in return.

Throughout this period of severe fighting, Charles continued to avoid writing about the serious nature of the combat. He discussed the war bonds and allotments he was sending home, and lamented that he had missed a promotion during his Air Corps training. On October 12, he mentioned a "close call" and told her that was why his hand was unsteady in the letter written immediately after the incident. This revealing comment came after the very difficult days of October 8, 9, and 10 and the capture of Germeter. He urged her to look for the August 14 issue of *Life* magazine, in which a photograph of a very tired and dirty GI appeared. Charles told her that was exactly how he looked. He also threw in several attacks on the rear-echelon troops they all envied—"blue star commandos," as they were often called.[24]

By the middle of October, although the intensity of combat continued, Charles was in a dugout much of the time with a roof over his head. He was able to sleep a bit and even shave occasionally. He described, in detail, two wonderful meals that he had shared with civilians as well as a "feast" he and his fellow officers had enjoyed after butchering a "liberated pig" and cooking it over a GI stove which they also procured. On October 22 he had a hot breakfast, the first in two weeks, as the cooks were able to bring up oatmeal, hot cakes, syrup, and real coffee. There was hot food for lunch as well, and he was even able to describe his dugout foxhole to Barbara. In his next letter, he mentioned the award of the Purple Heart, and more importantly, told her of the battlefield promotion he had received.[25]

During this period Charles began to experience frequent and painful headaches. In early November, his commanding officer ordered him to go to the rear and get treatment. Although he was sure that he would be returning to his men, the medical staff at the hospital he was sent to in Belgium, after an extensive series of tests and observations, diagnosed the headaches as migraine attacks and ruled that he was no longer fit for combat. Charles had been in almost continuous contact with the enemy since July 18, about 115 days of actual combat, and it was time to rest and recuperate.[26]

The next two months were difficult for Charles Taylor. As he recuperated from the devastation of combat, he found himself undergoing great mood swings. He knew he would not be returning to the front lines; he yearned for his comrades and felt he was deserting them by becoming a "blue star commando" himself. Even more exasperating, as he was transferred from hospital to hospital and barracks to barracks, his mail always lagged behind him. He went the entire period without receiving any mail from home. Not until January 1945, after he was stationed at Fontainebleau, outside Paris, to train replacement troops, did he once again begin receiving regular letters from Barbara. Yet he continued his daily stint at writing, sometimes composing two, three, and even four letters to Barbara in a day. It is not too much to suggest that their regular habits of writing, even without knowing what was said in return, maintained the stability in Charles's life and provided sustenance that allowed his complete recovery from the combat experience.

Many of the letters Charles wrote during the latter months of 1944 included long discussions of his desire to obtain a ranch in north central Florida after the war. He thought about the possible house, the cattle, the need for an education, and a dozen other matters connected with the ranch. As it turned out, he and Barbara did not have enough money to go into ranching.[27]

While recovering at the First U.S. Army General Hospital in Paris, Charles received several passes and explored the French capital city. He was astonished at what he saw, especially the sexual opportunities which seemed available everywhere. He expressed disgust at some of the officers and enlisted men who seemed only to think of sexual gratification. As a white southerner, he was concerned about the mingling of races in bars and dating, but the sight eventually became commonplace enough that he stopped making comment.[28]

Charles read the *Stars and Stripes* avidly for news of his unit and friends. He sent Barbara many clippings, including cartoons by Bill Mauldin, whose "Willie and Joe" characters appealed to this combat veteran. He also sent clippings from a variety of other newspapers and magazines, even articles from the London *Daily Sketch*, especially its account of the Normandy fighting. He shipped home examples of German, Belgian, and French money, subway tickets from Paris, and every other sort of memorabilia he thought would be of interest.[29]

Charles reconstructed his combat experiences for Barbara in a series of "bedtime stories" in this period. His account of the bombing and artillery during the hedgerow fighting began, "Well, once upon a time, long ago, there was a little man and he was definitely in a war." On another occasion, he told the story of an attack on a pill box through a little dialogue play entitled "Whitey." It began: " 'My God,' said the sgt., platoon sgt. of the weapons company of Co. E, 'that was rough.' "[30]

In January 1945, Charles was transferred to Company F, 118th Infantry and assigned to train new troops and officers for replacement purposes at the installation known as "Little Benning" in Fontainebleau. He was charged with setting up standard infantry and heavy weapons problems on the firing range for newly arrived troops. The noise of the firing range did not help his headaches, but it did seem like real work, so he did not mind it too much. He continued in this duty until the early summer of 1945, when it was clear that there would not be much need for more combat training.[31]

At "Little Benning," Charles's mail caught up with him! On January 3, he received three boxes, three cards, and a letter, but nothing from Barbara. On the sixth he received a letter from her dated November 29, and on January 23, a bonanza appeared in the form of eighteen letters (one from as early as June 23, but also one from January 5). A day later, twelve more letters from Barbara arrived, as well as nine others from other relatives. This caused him to offer a long apology for the times he had criticized Barbara for not writing to him. The apology ran to eight pages, and he wrote another six-page letter that evening. On January 26, five more letters arrived, including the one about the birth of his new niece, Judy, in December. More letters came on the thirtieth, some of them written as early as July 17. He responded in serial form, attempting to answer briefly all the queries that he received.[32]

Life slowed down considerably during the spring of 1945 as the war dragged to an end in Europe. Charles wrote about the need to get along with the Russians after the war, mourned the death of Franklin Roosevelt, and expressed shock and horror at the news of German atrocities reported in the press. Mostly, however, he simply discussed his boredom. In an effort to break up the monotony of his routine, he returned to Paris in March. The visit was made memorable by the fact that General Charles De Gaulle saluted the young lieutenant before Charles had the opportunity to recognize him. By this time his battle stars, his combat decorations, and his combat infantryman's badge all indicated that he was no "blue star commando."[33]

Visits to Paris, even with this sort of thrill attached to it, did not eliminate the homesickness which Charles attributed to too much "garrison army" duty. His yearning for Barbara reached a new intensity; the longer they were apart, the more erotic his letters became. The pet names the young couple had given to their genitalia, "possible" and "impossible," reemerged in their letters. Charles informed Barbara that he would never get tired of sex once he arrived home, and she had "better get yourself prepared for a lot of Charlie Taylor." He blamed this last comment on the three "wolves" who shared his barracks room and talked incessantly about "women and shacking." Two days later he delivered his views on male and female sexual cycles and described his recent dreams of her as "very . . . warm I'd say."[34]

Yet Charles was also quick to reassure Barbara that his emphasis on his need for sexual gratification was intrinsically related to their strong love for each other. Early in May, he wrote: "Maybe I am wrong, I don't think so, but our life together is not built on sex itself, but it does make our lives together more, shall I say, blissful. We are closer together or nearer each other's inner being. . . . When I am there beside you I can feel everything you feel, know what I mean, Barbie? . . . We are really one, aren't we?" On another occasion, he told Barbara: "We have a love that is so pure and so true that no one can touch it—no, not war, or people, or distance, or time, or anything, even death could not touch it, for we would still live by the love we know—'our love.' "[35] *special words*

Charles also spent an immense amount of time discussing the point system for rotation back home to the states. Over and over again, he told Barbara how the system worked, as well as of rumored changes which might occur in the determination of points.

Most of his letters, however, were like that of April 23, which opened with this paragraph:

> My Dearest Darling:
>
> Another week in the ETO has started and it's really funny 'cause the weeks all sorta look alike. I can't get interested in anything at all. Same old problems, same reactions, same night, the only things that change is the bill of affairs on the show preview. Even the menu is the same at the mess hall. Same old "no mail" at mail call. That covers the same things in a week in the ETO, yes?[36]

Even when V-E Day came, early in May, Charles was quite blasé about it, telling Barbara, "all I can say is don't celebrate too hard for there is still another big war going that is far from over."[37]

In July, Charles, as a "high point man," was transferred to Reims, a city notorious for its black market activity, as it was a site of the redeployment camps for transfer to the United States. Once there, however, his shipping orders were changed, and he was charged with supervising the work of German prisoners of war who were beginning to clear up the debris of the fighting. As far as Charles was concerned, this was all bad duty, for he was not going home. In fact, he thought he might be sent to Germany as part of the occupation forces. He complained that he was tired of writing the same old letter over and over, or, as he phrased it on July 24, "The more I write the bluer I seem to get."[38]

Only with the final surrender of Japan in August did Charles's downcast spirits begin to rally, and even then, he was not sure there was much to celebrate. The atomic bombs at Hiroshima and Nagasaki had ended the war much sooner than he and many others had expected, but he worried about the ultimate meaning of this new and powerful weapon. As he said to Barbara on the day the Nagasaki bomb was dropped, "I do hope that it is kept in the right hands, for even a little Nation could surely harness the world with a destructive weapon like that."[39]

The war was over, and it would soon be time to go home, fulfill all those dreams, see Sandra Lee again, and find out if he and Barbara had "grown up" enough to face the future. However, the method of ending the war brought on its own anxiety. The future was here, but it was suddenly different and daunting in its own way.

Letters, June 1944–August 1945

[Co. T., APO 51323, NY, NY]

At sea, 21 June 1944

My Dearest Darling:

I haven't written you a letter for two days but it is the same for there is nothing much for me to write except the same old things. I was just lying there on my bunk last night trying to visualize you and Sandra Lee. Gee, it would be a wonderful thing just to see you two. My Barbie, you are so brave and good and oh, so nice to have as a wife. Darling, you must send me some kodak pictures and also some pictures of everything. Gee, I'd give a lot to see you all. . . . By the way, send my mail Air Mail or "V-Mail" so it will come in record time. Also

check the addresses on your letters and see that you have the correct
address on them. . . .

I am in fine shape now and I think I have gained a few pounds. At
least, I have eaten enough to have gained it. Are you drinking any milk
like I told you? Now, please do like I instructed you to do for I love you
so much and you must take care of yourself for me.

Barbie, I've told you at times just how much I was missing you and
Sandra Lee—add all the missing I have done together and you will
have an idea how much I am missing you at present. Darling, you
have got to know how much I love you for I do worship you, a million
times I do.

. . . Barbie, I don't want you to do any worrying at all. I am o.k. and
I know that I will be o.k.—I am quite able to take care of myself. You
must have faith in me and in God—when you are worrying you are not
keeping faith—remember that. . . . I really think that He is watching
out for us. I am grown and still I am sure that I am o.k. to live a long,
long time. You know me and my feelings, well, they are still with me
and now instead of just feeling I am coming back, I know I will be back.
I'll keep up the war front—you keep up the home front, o.k.?

Barbie, listen to the news as often as you can. See if you can sorta
keep up with the people I have soldiered with or the people we know.
Write things to me so I'll not be too dumb about the people I used
to know.

Darling, you must love me now and forever for we really are matched
for this life on earth. The longer I live the surer I become of it, don't
you? We may have a lot of things to look forward to that we can't see
so live on the theory of today and don't worry about tomorrow—let
the engineers build your bridges as you need them. Just be happy and
think about all the things you and I have and will have as the years
go by. Stick to the theory of doing unto others as you want them to do
unto you and I am sure things will look up.

Live on my love and my regard for your purity and be as good to
Sandra Lee as possible. She is good enough to be spoiled so that you
can. Give her a hug and kiss from me and save a million for yourself.

Lovingly forever,   Charlie

Barbara's childhood home in Fairburn, Georgia.

Miss Mae and Mr. Bernie Wooddall, Barbara's parents, in Fairburn

Barbara on her way to work at Twentieth Century-Fox in Atlanta, August 1941. Virginia Kitchens, Charles, and Barbara at the Rainbow Roof in Atlanta, December 1941

Charlie

Charles's barracks, the first one on the right, at Fort Leonard Wood, Missouri, 1941. Charles and his buddies at Fort Leonard Wood, April 1942

Sunday P.M.

My dearest sweetheart,

It's 2:15 Sunday & I'm listening to Sammy Kay's "Swing & Sway" Program. They just played "Take Me" & it is more beautiful than ever.

I'm so lonesome for my dear husband today. It's a beautiful Georgia day — sun shining, nice breeze — reminds me of the times I made play-houses out in the back yard when I was a <u>child</u>. I'm definitely on the sentimental side today.

after church —

Hello again,

Well, some of the girls came by this afternoon so

A letter of August 24, 1942, from Barbara to Charles, written soon after returning from their honeymoon in Waynesville, Missouri

September 5
1942

My Dearest Darling, "Mrs. Taylor:"

I see by the Gainesville Sun, that you and I were married in St. Louis, August 1st. Now, what do you think about that? I think it is the best thing that ever happened to that Charlie Taylor, don't you? He was such a wild sort of a boy before August of 1941. Your picture was not in the paper. I wanted so very much for mother to wait and put your pix in but I guess we waited long enough after the wedding to announce it and so she that it best to go on and put the announcement in the paper when she could. I am so proud of you that I wanted all of the people to see who I married, guess we can show them after this ole war is over.

The boys are going to leave tomorrow and as yet I do not have a place to sleep or eat until I leave here Wednesday 2:45 PM. I am not worried for the army always sees that every man has quarters and board. By the way, do you know what a 2nd Lt. who is married makes per month? Runs around $250.00, not bad. A lot better than what I have been getting each month. I only hope I am capable of being a Lt. we shall see and we know it will not be long now.

A letter from Charles to Barbara, written when Charles was stationed at Fort Leonard Wood, Missouri

A Birthday Greeting

WITH LOVING THOUGHTS

My thoughts are with you
all the time,
Although we are apart,
And many are the loving words
That rise within my heart.
Today they form into the wish
That you'll be home next year,
So we can really celebrate
YOUR DAY together, Dear!

your loving wife,
Barbie

Barbara's birthday card to Charles, October 1942

The Dessells' house, on the left, where Barbara and Charles had a room
while he was at Fort Dix, New Jersey, 1943

Charles and Barbara in Gainesville, Florida, December 1942

"You mean it's not for Britain?"

Wartime cartoon on pregnancy that also refers to relief packages, "Bundles
for Britain." Barbara saved this when she learned of her pregnancy.

Barbara and Sandra Lee,
August 1943

Right: Charles and Sandra Lee,
September 1943. Charles in Lafayette, Louisiana, where he
was stationed for Primary Flight
Training, October 1943

Charles, Barbara, and Sandra Lee in Aunt Dot's yard, Fairburn, April 1944

Lieutenant Charles E. Taylor, 1943

Barbara Wooddall Taylor, 1945

Above: Barbara and Charles in New Brunswick, New Jersey, just prior to Charles's embarkation, June 1944. Barbara and Sandra Lee with Aunt Dot, 1944. *Left:* Sandra Lee and Judy in Miss Mae's front yard, November 1945

Opposite, clockwise: Charles in France, March 1945. Charles playing football in front of his quarters, near Reims, France, October 1945. An Atlanta *Journal* article announcing the return of troops from overseas, November 21, 1945. Among the ships listed is the *Wooster Victory*, the ship on which Charles returned to the states. Charles in Paris, France, 1945.

35,000 Vets Arriving in U. S.

NEW YORK, Nov. 20.—(AP)— Nearly 17,000 troops from several theaters of war were scheduled to debark Tuesday from 22 transports at three East Coast ports. At four West Coast ports, 17 vessels from the Pacific were due with more than 18,000 servicemen.

Ships and units arriving:

AT NEW YORK — Miscellaneous troops on following: (Tufts Victory from Le Havre), 2,056; (Zanesville Victory from Le Havre), 1,934; (Pomona Victory from Antwerp), 1,938; (Hawaiian Shipper from Calcutta), 1,888; (Colby Victory from Le Havre), 1,938; (Alexander Lillington from Marseilles), 616; (James B. Richardson from Naples), 617; (Santa Barbara from Caserta, Italy), 470; (Cape Poge from Cardiff, Wales), 38; (Amarillo Victory from Calcutta), 29; (William Cody from Antwerp), 646.

AT NEWPORT NEWS — Miscellaneous troops on following: (Miaulos, originally due Monday), 35; (Nathan Hale), 19; (Paul Hayne), 23; (Sea Snipe), 23; (Robert Bean), 23; (Anne Bradstreet), 114; (Hubert Bancroft), 16.

AT BOSTON—(Wooster Victory from Marseilles), 1,940 troops, including 290th Infantry (First Battalion) of Seventy-fifth Infantry Division; Second Battalion of Seventy-fifth Infantry Division and Seventy-fifth Counter-Intelligence Corps Detachment (George M. Bibb from Barry, Wales), 578 troops, including 444th Antiaircraft Automatic Weapons Battalion and miscellaneous personnel. (Montclair Victory from Le Havre), 1,955 troops, including Fifteenth Hospital Train; 999th Signal Service Company; 548th Quartermaster Depot Company; 301st Military Police Escort Guard Company; 768th Field Artillery Battalion with medical attendants; 957th Quartermaster Service Company; 3,189th Quartermaster Service Company; 4,000th Quartermaster Service Company, and miscellaneous personnel. (Henry Richardson from Barry, Wales, originally due Monday), 27 miscellaneous troops.

AT SAN FRANCISCO — Miscellaneous personnel on following: (Admiral H. T. Mayo), 5,088; (Bregen), 2,624; (Dauphin), 1,903; (Hendry), 1,743; (Albert A. Robinson), 287, (Esparita, Girasol, John P. Altgeld, Maunalei, Panaset, Saggitarius and William Moultrie) with a few each.

AT SEATTLE—Miscellaneous troops on following: (Dublin from Nagoya), 30; (Waukesha from Nagoya), 277; (General Butner from Nagoya), 4,892.

AT TACOMA—(Laurens from Yokohama), 1,322 miscellaneous troops.

AT PORTLAND, ORE.—(Alcoa Polaris from Tokyo-Okinawa), 1,132.

Print the complete address in plain letters in the panel below, and your return address in the space provided on the right. Use typewriter, dark ink, or dark pencil. Faint or small writing is not suitable for photographing.

From:

To:
MR & MRS. W.S. TAYLOR
P.O. BOX 2386
UNIVERSITY STATION
GAINESVILLE, FLORIDA

1st Lt. Charles E. Taylor O1301111
Co. H, 39th INF APO #9
% P.M. N.Y. N.Y.

(CENSOR'S STAMP)   See Instruction No. 2   (Sender's complete address above)

26 October 44
GERMANY

Dearest Folks:

Just a note to tell you that you are the owner of a son who has received a "Battlefield promotion" from second Lt. to first Lt. Now ain't you proud of him. Well actually I was surprised but happily so.

Today is a very pretty day, the sun is out and the sky is clear and I feel pretty good. Had a fine breakfast of pancakes and coffee and that starts the day off right. I am more or less just taking life easy. Had a very restful nite last nite also.

It has been cool and at times cold but we have enough clothes and blankets so it is ok. We actually are in good shape. I intend to go to church at the next service.

Have not had any mail for the past three days but then all of our mail has been all messed up for about that long. Really, though; it does not take so very long for my mail to get here after it is mailed there in the states.

Yep, I could sure enjoy a big box of good things to eat. a box last about two minutes after it is opened here. In fact— one man in the ETO ask another man what the fastest thing in the ETO is and he replied an opened box from home.

Well, I better stop and try to get ready for dinner.
Love to all
Charlie

HAVE YOU FILLED IN COMPLETE ADDRESS AT TOP?

REPLY BY
V---MAIL

HAVE YOU FILLED IN COMPLETE ADDRESS AT TOP?

16—28143-5 ☆ U. S. GOVERNMENT PRINTING OFFICE : 1943

Above: A letter from Charles to his parents, an example of a V-Mail that was not photographed, which was quite unusual. *Opposite, top:* A postcard from Charles to his parents, written during his service at the Western Front, where paper was often in short supply. *Bottom left:* Examples of stickers often placed on letters during the war. *Bottom right:* An example of the V-Mail form concerning mail delivery sent home when return of service personnel was imminent

21 Oct. 44

Dear Folks:
Out of paper so I'll just have to write you a card. I am fine and for a change the sun is out.
Please send a box and include some writing paper. I can get enough envelopes so don't bother about them.
I hope you all are well, please do write me real often for I enjoy all of your letters so much.
Give my love to all

Love
Charlie.

P.S. Hope you can find me the little gas stove I asked for.

UNITED STATES
★ ARMY ★

Find the complete address in plain letters in the panel below, and your return address in the space provided on the right. Use typewriter, dark ink, or dark pencil. Faint or small writing is not suitable for photographing.

To: Miss Charles E. TAYLOR

From: LT. CHARLES E. TAYLOR
109 Lar. Sprs. Com. 1971 L.S. Co.
APO 72, % PM, NY, NY.
8 October 1945
(Date)
Sender's complete address above

Dear Darbie :

I am scheduled to return to the United States sometime before the end of December, so please hold any Christmas parcels you have for me.

Until I advise you otherwise, continue to send my letters, but DO NOT SEND ANY MORE PACKAGES.

Charles E. Taylor
(Signature)

PD FORM 83
HAVE YOU FILLED IN COMPLETE ADDRESS AT TOP?

V - MAIL

HAVE YOU FILLED IN COMPLETE ADDRESS AT TOP?

Barbara and Charles in Miami Beach, January 1946

Barbara and Charles at the Clover Club in Miami, Florida,
January 1946

[Co. T., APO 51323, NY, NY]

England, 13 July 1944

My Dearest Barbie:

I was able to borrow this paper from Lt. Smeades, therefore I'll be able to write a better letter than on a V-Mail. Enclosed is a picture of a village.* At present, I am no more than a hundred yards from the nearest house in the picture. That is all I can tell you. No, I can't even tell you the name of the village. It would do you no good to know, would it? It's pretty but they can have it all. . . .

Barbie I sure do miss you, honest I do. Wish I could but see you for a few minutes this evening. It's about eight o'clock now and it looks like three in a day. The sun is up. I'd love to spend the winter with you in a land like this for they have about sixteen-hour nights (darkness)—bet we could have fun. You know, in a way, your letters cheer me up for while I am reading them I am body and mind back there seeing the things Miss "T" is doing and then the letter is over and then here I am in England, and oh, so all alone. Gee, I do want you so much. It is too bad that we have to give up this precious time. Time that we could have so much fun—guess it is just our part though. If God can but make this war get over and get all of the people who are apart back together once more. Every day or so a soldier comes in and tries to find out how he can stop his allotment to his wife or get a divorce. So many of the wives are doing their husbands wrong. Barbie, please be good and just stick by old Charlie 'til he gets back. I did not worry in the States, and now I don't worry, but it sure does make me think sometimes. I trust you completely so it really must be hard on the fellows who do not trust their wives. I can look back over my life so far, but there is but a small part of it that is worth knowing about except the part that has been known by you. . . .

Well, Barbie, I sure do know one thing—America is going to be pretty crowded after the war, for all the English people say they are going to the U.S., for it's such a wonderful place. They are right too. . . .

Lovingly,   Charlie

*Crewkerne, in Dorset, England.

[Co. H., 39th Inf. Regt.]

France, 29 July 1944

My Dearest Darling:

Today I am really tired but perhaps I'll get some rest. Darling, I am sorry that I had to let a few days slip by without getting a letter off to you, but at times there is no time or place to write and when there is time, there is nothing to write on. I'll try to do better for awhile, maybe I can carry a few V-Mail blanks with me. War or no war, there is really no excuse for me to let so many days get by without sending at least a note, is there?

We had a wonderful meal tonight for supper—fresh beef, corn, potatoes, bread, coffee and pears. I think it was the first meal I've eaten that was not out of a can since I left England. I just ate and ate and ate. Sure was a treat too, for my stomach was getting to be annoyed by the stuff it was having to use as food. Really, I think I am getting fat, but there are no scales near at hand so I don't know. . . .

Darling, our infantry regiment has a saying and letters—AAA-O— "anything, anywhere, anytime, bar nothing." It used to be a brand used on cattle on our Regimental Commander's ranch, but it sure holds good for our regiment. The whole regiment is proud of their saying and I am proud of the whole damn regiment 'cause I feel sure there is none better in the whole US Army. After the war you can feel sure that you are feeling right when you feel proud of the regiments that your Charlie fought with during this war. There are really a lot of brave men, you can bet on that.

The country here is really pretty and I guess every Frenchman that had a house had also a couple of cider barrels in his cider room. All of them raised a lot of rabbits too, for as I sit here there are four or five rabbits within a few yards of me. Most of the Frenchmen had cattle too, for there are cows all over the place. I just stopped and took a tent rope and roped one of those rabbits. They look like they would be good to eat. May try one some of these days. A few of the boys are cooking some fried chicken a few tents down from me, sure smells good too. I'd sure like some chicken that Mother used to cook. My, I'll bet it would taste good. . . .

Here are some clippings too, written about my outfit. Hope you enjoy it. It's mostly written by Ernie Pyle. He sure writes it straight. You can read about us in your Atlanta paper. . . .

Lovingly,   Your Charlie

[Co. H., 39th Inf. Regt.]

France, 10 August 1944

Darling:

I still have a few hours of daylight and I may not get a chance to write tomorrow so I will do some more today so you will not miss a letter, o.k.?

Bet it is almost as hot over here as it is there in Georgia. Sho' is hot —pretty cool at night. The country is real pretty and they have apple trees by the billions. You wouldn't like it half as much as you do good old Georgia, I don't. Most all of the people here wear wooden shoes and most of the shoes that are made of leather have wooden soles on them. The people here are definitely on the peasantry side, the same as they are in England. Would be good to be back to civilized people once more. Would be good to just sit down there at KITCHEN'S SODA fountain and drink about a dozen cokes, "the soda jerker who was Lt. Taylor at the time." My, oh, my, what beautiful memories I do have of days gone by—may God grant a million days more like them. They were all so beautiful, so pure, and so happy, that I'd hate to ever lose them. Really have had a lot to be thankful for and now I am quite sure we have a lot more to thank God for. He has looked out for us well.

You would sure like your husband with his hair all cut off and dirty as hell. I did shave last night and washed my face, so I am not so dirty after all. Now am I? I would have kept my hair as long as it was, but it really gets so dirty that you can't run a comb through it. It feels better short like it is now. I am getting tan hands and face, but the rest of me is still white as everything. . . .

Well, it's been about two months or more since I've seen you and I sho' do get lonesome every once in a while. Well, maybe it will not be too long before it is all over with and the Jerries are all dead or whipped and then we can all come home. When I say it may not be too long —it could be a year—I don't know, who does know? Let us hope it is weeks and not longer than months, for it is too bad for wars to spoil so many happy days. I sure do know that we are losing a lot of happy days, aren't we? We will sure make up for it, won't we? We will just have a honeymoon once more and this time we will take Sandra Lee along, won't we?

Darling, keep your chin up and your fingers crossed for it may take a lot of love to stretch over all of this war and all. We are sure a bunch of good people and we will always be that way.

I love you and Sandra Lee so much so give her a few big birthday kisses from her Dad.

Lovingly,   Your Charlie

[Co. H., 39th Inf. Regt.]

France, 22 August 1944

My Dearest Darling:

Sure is a pretty day today but did it rain yesterday all day long! I sure was glad to see the sun this a.m. for we sure did need drying out bad. . . .

My mail to you must have been forwarded to you on to Florida—the way you talked. . . . Most of the boys here get their mail in about ten to eleven days, so that will really be good. V-Mails are about four days slower than Air Mail and 6 cents will bring an Air Mail to or from an APO address, so there is no need to put 12 or more cents on one like you have done from time to time. O.K.? You can save money that way and be penny wise and dollar happy, ha.

You really should see some of these places these people over here have as homes. In places, part of the house is used as a barn, and the other part the people live in. Most of the houses are one story and the rooms have been added from time to time. Most of them are made of mud or cement, rock with shale roofs or straw thatched roofs. The people all work hard and look as though they never had a thing. Really they are land poor. Some of them have had no candy or chocolate for over about four years. We give them about all of the candy that comes in our rations. You should see how the kids chase after the candy we throw out to them. I really feel sorry for the kids. These GIs sure do have hearts of gold for they give everything they have away. I'll be glad when this damn war is over and everybody is back home once more. It will be a good feeling just to walk down your old main street in your own home town and for good. Pip just doesn't know how lucky he happened to be.* I am glad that our country does not have a war in it, aren't you? . . .

I lay there in the rain last night and thought about you and me and little Sandra Lee. You know, we were really lucky to have had the time we have had together. We honestly made the most of it too and I am glad even if we did stay broke most of the time. What is money anyway, just a false sense of security. Why, look what your dollar will buy now and then remember what you could buy with a dollar only two years ago. Sure could buy a lot more then than you can now, couldn't you? Even though it was a pretty hard job and mostly hard on you, I am glad we worked around and got Jr. He will be good for us to have when I do get back. Best of all he is all paid for in full. I hope you have gotten the title from what's his name. When it comes time to get a tag, buy a Georgia tag in my name, and that will take the place of a title in case we need to get rid of Jr. at anytime. How are your tires holding out and are you getting along on the gas you get? I hope he does o.k. Jr. sure is easy on gas and tires. A good type of transportation and cheap too. Wish he had a radio, maybe I'll be able to pick one up when I get back. Probably can talk Dad out of his radio if he starts to trade cars for I do not think he ever uses his any at all. . . .

Barbie, I sure hope that we can get ourselves a place out in the country where it is quiet and nothing to bother us. I'd like to own about a thousand acres and some cattle and a few horses and really live. I don't ever want to be cooped up in a city and really have to rush and push and fight to live. I want to be out where there is plenty of air and sun

*Charles's brother-in-law, John "Pip" Barrett, was classified 4-F and not eligible for military service.

and have a relaxed and unhurried life like I have seen a lot of people do. I'll not be afraid of a little work. I'd like to have about 80 acres of tillable soil. Oh, it would be hard for a year or two, but if we worked hard we could have it made. Maybe we could find a place like that somewhere where we could buy on time or just lease. Barbie, I don't think I'd ever be able to stand to be cooped up when I get back so let's try it, o.k.? I would like for us to get independent for once in our life, wouldn't you? We could make a go of it and if we did I am sure we would have a better life out in the country than we would if we were in a town working and paying out all we could make. That's the trouble with jobs and towns. You put money in one pocket and it goes out the other one. Guess too, I would sorta have no boss in the farming and cattle business, and that's much better too, don't you think? . . .

Barbie, keep your chin up and don't fail to take care of little Sandra Lee.

I love you both,   Charlie

[Co. H., 39th Inf. Regt.]

France, 30 August 1944

My Dearest Barbie:

I really am out of the habit of writing for there has not been any time to write in the past few days. We have not gotten any mail either, so I guess it all evens things up in the long run. Please forgive me but it is not my fault and I'll not let it become a habit, o.k.?

Sure has done a mean piece of raining in the last three days. Gee, I hate the rain, sure does make it bad at times. Pup tents are pretty good and we really do all right in them, 'course the ground is wet, but a nice shelter-half on it does o.k. Rain never stops a good soldier.

Guess I should not even try to write a letter tonight, for I just am not in the mood. I am sorta sour on the world tonight. The first place I am mad and the second, well, I just am in a real mean mood. You know what I mean, the sort of mood I used to get in and have to just get out and go to get over. I guess I am just tired of this damn war and all of everything else. Well, nothing will help me but some good chow and a night's sleep. Sooo, I guess I'll try that. Damn this damn war anyway. I wish it was over and I was home. My thoughts are that it will only last for a little while longer. I really think it will be only a short while. All I need is to see my darling and I know my mood would change a hundred percent. We know the impossibility of that for a while so I guess our letters will do. Barbie, you just don't know how much I miss you and Sandra Lee and everything. Only yesterday we were at a place and there was the cutest little girl a year old. She was walking good, but she could not talk yet. Gee, she was cute, had blond hair and blue eyes, and so sweet. She would just smile and laugh at me. Hung on to our pants leg the whole time we were there. Guess kids just sorta know who is a father etc., don't you think so, too. Well, anyway, I showed the people your picture and Sandra Lee on my pistol and they all said "belle madame" etc. whatever baby is—means pretty wife and baby and I say "oui, bien merci" which means, yes, many thanks. I sure do look at your pictures a lot, darling. If you only knew how much I really really love you, why you would never ever think of anything but your Charlie. I don't believe you ever think of anything but me anyway. . . .

I guess you can tell more about how things are coming than I can, for you see the papers. The papers are behind but you can tell a lot about it from them. Wish I got a paper every day, but I would not even get it 'til it was a month old. . . .

By the way I got a little scratch a few———ago, and it was nothing, so if you hear anything about me, it's a lie. I really haven't lost a day of duty. I'll always tell you the truth just so that you read my letters right and don't get too much out of them, o.k.? . . .

Lovingly,   Your Charlie

[Co. H., 39th Inf. Regt.]

Somewhere in Belgium, 7 September 1944

My Dearest Darling:

My, but it is wet today and it has been wet. Looks as though we just follow the rain around for we just stay wet—as if I have not always been wet, ha!

Well, a lot has happened since I last had a chance to write to you and today I am just taking life easy. I am really living like a big king. I slept in a beautiful house and you should see the furniture. I am sending a pix of the place so you can see. One piece of furniture cost sixty thousand francs—a lot of money. The dining room has an oil painting all the way 'round the room from top to bottom. The painting is about the scenery around the house. Really a beautiful piece of work. It was painted around the 17th century—guess the house was built about then too. My, I wish I could send some of these things home, but it is impossible but I'll bring home the stories and memories of all I have seen so I can tell you. O.K.? Really all of these things are wonderful to see.

I have but a little time right now, so I'll try to write more later.

Belgium, 8 September 1944

My Dear:

I am so sorry to have had to have such a delay on the mail situation for I know how anxious you get to hear from me. I get the same way. But as it was, I was up in the line companies and could not write for the time I was there. I started this letter back and now it is around ten o'clock and your Charlie boy is really tired and I do mean tired. I have just drunk two or three cups of coffee but I am just tired mentally and physically both. I had quite a lot of mail at the company when I got there, up through number nine.

Your letters: #4—The scrapbook (Army), you should go ahead and fix it up so it will be complete when I get home. O.K.? Sure do wish we were back together in the old town of Augusta, I get homesick, too. Those evening dresses should be good on a beautiful gal like you. Bet we do have a time with our kissing gal, don't you? By all means, I do know how much you love me and don't you ever forget to at least think of me every day, I am the boss.

Letter #5—Sandra Lee sure does love her Aunt Marcie* and I am

*Nickname for Martha Wooddall Gastley.

glad. Yes, you sure do have some full days and I am really glad for that will help to pass the days. Skeeter sure is pretty, he is a nice dog. Yes, darling, I am yours, all yours. . . .

Letter #6—Honey, you are a good soldier and I know you have been. You can bet our marriage is a sacred thing and I will never do a thing to mar it. It's funny, over here women and things of that sort never cross my mind. Yes, it is too bad we are wasting so much time, but we have a job to do and I am sure it will only take a little while longer. The Army Hour is a good thing,—so is Ernie Pyle's column in the paper so keep up on the news and you will know more about the war when Sandra Lee studies her history. Now, do not worry for I am very careful and I know the score. . . .

Always   Your Charlie

[Co. H., 39th Inf. Regt.]

Belgium, 12 September 1944

My Dearest Darling:

Well, after the rat race today I will try my best to get my mind on this letter. Today I got a lot of mail from you written in June and July —a letter from each, Dad, Mother and Ina. Sure am enjoying all the pictures and razor blades that you send in your letters. Don't stop, for you are doing a good job of keeping my morale up. . . .

I was sorry to read the clippings you sent about Fulton and Jackson both being dead.* Did you ever write to any of the other fellows like you said you were going to do?

Say, I sent you a letter yesterday with three pictures in it and some sort of a charm. The pix are of some man, wife and daughter I met here. Had supper with them. I am sending a box with an Iron Cross, Purple Heart, and some coins and paper money. Hope you are liking all of the souvenirs. I went into a town the other day and tried my best to buy some little shoes (wooden) about four inches long, but they were out. They said to come back in a week or two. You know, I am

*Persons with whom Charles had served prior to his being sent overseas.

getting to be pretty good with this French language plus all my hand and arm signals to boot. Sure do wish you could watch me at times. Of course there are a few Latin words in the French language and if you remember, I had three and a half years of Latin; wish it had been German or French.

Darling, I can really say that Belgium is far more advanced than France. We sure do get a much warmer welcome, too. The homes are so pretty. Really the thing that is so pretty to me is the countryside— the hills are all rolling and high, with a patch of woods here and there, and a lot of cattle all over. Sure is pretty country for cows. There are a lot of springs and things, with a few orchards here and there. All the main roads have tall pines or poplar or some kind of trees, that at some time or other were planted. Every fence has a hedge covering it so you can't see the wire. Most of the houses have electricity, but the disposal systems are very poor—like our country homes. You should see the inside of their houses, they are really spotless, and the floors are all (even in the poorest homes) square-cut inlaid linoleum or hard wood. Really pretty. Most of the stoves are coal or wood stoves, but they are really good to cook on. These people believe in good beds and, in the finer homes, they most all have two or three extra bedrooms, all with the best beds you've ever seen. Most of the homes are built in a court style. The home connected to the hay barn connected to the cow barn—to the milk room—and a manure rack in the center of the court. Sure does look funny or it did when I first saw it. Well, I guess I better stop, for chow is ready and good hot chow is rare. . . .

Lovingly,   Your Charlie

[Co. H., 39th Inf. Regt.]

Somewhere, 14 September 1944

My Dearest Darling:

Well, it is even raining here, has been raining since early this morning. Do hope it stops before in the a.m. I am not out in the rain now, but I have been all day, but it was not too bad. I had baked chicken for dinner and corned beef for supper and some good old coffee. Bet I'll be getting fat if I keep eating like that.

There is not any news for mail is hard to get and say, I did not tell you, but I got a lot of letters you wrote a month after I came over. They were old, but I assure you I was quite glad to get them. The pictures were quite good and the razor blades came in quite handy. I should shave now, for I have not had a shave for three days. . . .

You know, Barbie, as the days go by it seems like I want to be near you a little more. Honey, if there was a way in this world for me to tell you how much I honestly do love you. I think of you a million times a day, and, oh, how much I really do miss those little things you do, like tickling my back, and just generally looking after your Charlie. You are and have been the real light in my life and that you will always be. I really do love you with all there is in me. I hurt inside of me to even think about all of the sweet, sweet loving that I so well remember. My, oh, my, how I would like to be in that nice soft bed at Miss Mae's* with you to cuddle up to and not a thing to worry about but oversleeping and missing my eggs and bacon. Gee, that is sure a life. . . .

Say, I wish you would be sure and save this letter, for I want it kept, o.k.? . . .†

You know what I would like to do tonight? I know you do, in a way, but I'll just tell you everything.

First, I'd like to be—just for tonight—in New Brunswick or New York or Miami Beach, with a hotel and you the only other person in the whole city that I knew. We would start out and make a tour of all the night spots, until we had had about ten drinks, and a lot of hands across the table—and eying—and all of the soft sweet things I would like to tell you as we dance so nice around the dance floor. (Oh, Barbie, I love you so). Then we would find us a place to eat, and then all tired out and in love, we would get in Jr. and maybe visit a nice place and look at the moon. Then, guess what we would do?—yes, go to the hotel room,

*Barbara's mother, Mae Pearce Wooddall.
†Charles crossed into Germany for the first time on September 14, Barbara's birthday.

and, oh, Barbie, how I do miss you, really I do! We have so darn much to look forward to, don't we? We will really have one more wonderful time—you and me and Sandra Lee. I do not intend to ever worry over a thing once I get back, for I have had more worrying to do than I was to have, but I could have had more, couldn't I? Say, I sure am going to be just your slaphappy Charlie when I get back. I am quite sure that nothing will ever be able to change my outlook in life. The only one thing that would ever change my outlook on life and that would be to not have you as all mine, but I am not worrying about that, for I know that I don't have anything to worry about there. . . .

Lovingly,   Your Charlie

[Co. H., 39th Inf. Regt.]

Somewhere in Germany, 17 September 1944

My Dearest Darlings:

I am in Germany and the country is really pretty. That is all I can say. O.K.?

I am cool now for it is threatening to rain and the sun hasn't yet come out today. Wish I had a nice fire—someday when I get back when it gets cold all I am going to do is have a big nice fire in the fireplace and a good chair. Then, I'll just sit there and rest, o.k.? That's what I'll do, too.

Just had a good shave and washed up for the first time in weeks. When I say washed up, I mean my face and hands, that's all. I should wash my feet and change socks, but I guess I'll wait to do that.

Am up on your mail—but eleven and thirteen have not arrived yet —but through fourteen did. I was sure glad to get them too, for there are a lot of things that were in your letters that Charlie must talk to you about.

First, about this blood-giving business. I am trying to get you built up and in good shape and what do you do but start dragging yourself down by giving blood to the Red Cross. I think it is a splendid gesture, but I do not want you to give another drop, do you understand? There are too many persons who are more capable of giving blood than you.

You said that was the least you could do, well, I don't think so. You can buy all the war bonds you want too, but do not donate any more blood. I mean it. The bonds will be good after the war even if they do freeze them, but if you keep on giving blood you will just tear yourself down. Barbie, please do as I say, o.k.? Drink a lot of milk and now that you have given so much blood you should eat one green onion per day. Gee, I wish I was there to take care of you. . . .

Lovingly,   Your Charlie

[Co. H., 39th Inf. Regt.]

Germany, 18 September 1944

My Dearest Barbie:

Well, this is all the paper I have at the moment so I'll just try to use it. It's sorta damp and the ink does not look good on it, but it will have to do.

Just got three of the best letters you have ever seen. I did not expect to get them—so that's why they were so good—one was really a good letter. All about everyone being there in Fairburn and everything. Man, I would sure have liked to have been there with you people. I sure do miss old peaceful Fairburn and with you all. Bet that Labor Day dinner was good—most everything is or would be good to me now. . . .

I am really in good shape except I am a little homesick today. You know after a while, you more or less become numb from being homesick and then you get a real good letter and all the time you are reading the letter, your mind is back home and you see nothing around you. A letter is truly a "ten-minute furlough," as is said by the men. . . .

Your letter of the 4th of September was one of the best I have ever seen or ever gotten, I should say. Gee, when you sit down to it you sure can put out a nice sweet newsy letter. Wish I could write letters as well as you can. Probably if I had the time and the place as you have then I could really put out a much better letter. You understand, don't you?, when my letters are short or when there are no letters. Well, so much of the time I am busy and cannot write, and then there are times that the mail does not go out at all and it would do no good to write. . . .

Just you remember that I love you more than everything else and I know that Sandra Lee is a good gal, so give her a kiss for me.

Lovingly,   Your Charlie

[Co. H., 39th Inf. Regt.]

Germany, 22 September 1944

My Dearest Darling:

. . . Today has been a real pretty day, not any clouds, but a lot has happened. Was sorta my day off, but I slept 'til about eleven thirty, the first time I've done that in years. However, I was sorta ill—my stomach was sorta messed up and I felt as if I was getting a bad cold. I went to the medics this afternoon, but you know them, they only give you a few pills—(really that's all a man needs, but you know the soldiers have to have something to bitch about). . . .

Darling, sorry this one is so short but the stationery is not too easy to find just now. I use most of the letters that I get that aren't used on the back. Sometimes I have a lot of paper and then the rains come and then I have no paper. I am able to get stamped envelopes so don't worry about that. I told a lie 'cause I just borrowed a pile of paper—so that means I can write you a much longer letter, isn't that nice? Well, I sure am sweating this damn war out—well, all we can do is do our part and hope and pray, I know all will do o.k. in the long run. By the way, you know damn well that I am not an MP,* and I'll never be one. I was just lucky enough to get what I need your picture for. I am not allowed to tell you my job or what I do but I can say I hope I never have to take a platoon in a rifle company. I can say I am not in a rifle company. I sure wish that it would all be over soon and I know it will have to be over.

Sure do like the people I am with. My company commander has had a commission for two years this month, a captain—Captain Guice— sure is a swell guy. Say, I ran into my commanding officer's brother, the company commander of the company I was in in the 66th Inf. Regt. I think he said his brother was with Patton now. Sure would like to

*Military Police.

see him, but guess I'll never see him. The executive officer is a first—is Lt. Boyd. My platoon leader is a first—is Lt. Spunagle. We all get along fine and it is good too. Am glad I went to the Air Corps, 'cause if I hadn't my plight would have been like Fulton and Jackson. Was glad you wrote me about it all—wonder how Mr. Granger and Hickey* and all of the rest are? If you know, please write me. If I knew all that has gone on in the last year I know I'd be surprised. . . .

Well, goodnight, darling, for I love you,

Your Charlie

[Co. H., 39th Inf. Regt.]

Germany, 25 September 1944

My Dearest Darling:

Barbie, please go find and save the August 21st issue of the *Time* magazine. There is an article about "Paddy"† in it. A grand old man he was. I met him. In fact, I wish you would get all the *Time* magazines from August on and save them for me. It is a weekly magazine, you know.

Finally, we have the lights turned on in London. I am glad for I am really tired of them bellyaching about them being off. Wonder when the lights will go on again back there in the States. At least not 'til we all get back home, eh? Damn this war anyway, and I sure wish old man Hershey had to be here and get released under his plan.‡ Oh, some of these people make me sick and, in a way, remind me of Hitler. Do they to you? Well, I just won't cross that bridge of getting back home til I get to that bridge. I know however that the subject demands thinking about. First, though, we have to get these damn Germans whipped.

---

*Charles served with Chief Warrant Officer Granger and 1st Lt. Hickey while with the Fourth Division in Augusta, Georgia, and Fort Dix, New Jersey.

†Colonel Harry S. "Paddy" Flint, commanding officer of the 39th Infantry Regiment, who was killed in combat on July 24, 1944.

‡Charles was referring to General Louis B. Hershey, Director of Selective Service. He evidently thought that Hershey was also in charge of the point system for reassignment which was just then being discussed among the troops.

We have so much further to go too. It makes me sad when I read the papers and magazines from back there. Why, they have you people thinking that the war is over and really I don't think it is near over. This demobilization plan does not have a thing to do with the officers so there is really no use in our counting my honors or points 'cause they don't even count. I have an idea that they will need most all of the officers and especially the battle-tried officers for the Pacific theatre or over here for occupation, after this is all over. That is my idea and I know it is not very sunny, is it? I was sorta hoping that both theatres would be over about the same time. I guess we are just little people when you stop and think of the number of persons who will be wanting out. There isn't much that we can do about it either, except just hope and pray. It looks like a pretty dull time 'til all of these damn wars are over, doesn't it? Well, it is a good thing that you and I are young— for all we know it may be years from today before old Uncle Sam will let old Charlie come home. I hope not for I hardly see how I'll be able to stand it away from you and Sandra Lee and everything I love that long. . . . You know, I hope this is one war to end all wars forever, for I hope the next twenty years after this one that there is only peace and natural living for all. I'd hate to know I'd gone through all of this and then Sandra Lee would have to sit over there waiting for her husband, as you are having to do now. . . .

    Lovingly forever,   Your Charlie

[Co. H., 39th Inf. Regt.]

Germany, 26 September 1944
AAA-O

My Dearest Darling:

    Well, it is still wet and also still raining, but I am quite sure that it won't rain much for it looks pretty clear out tonight. We got our whiskey ration today, but it was only a pint of both scotch and gin, so you can see it will not go very far. Well, probably the war will be over soon and we can get a lot of stuff to drink. That's not really so important anyway, is it? . . .

Darling, there is so much noise it is really hard for a man to write a decent letter, but here I sit doing the best I can do. All I know to say is that it is not as rough as it has been, but you don't know where we have been so that gives you no information at all. What I do really know is that I love you and despise this whole mess and I do so wish it would all be over soon and too, I hope we would all be back home soon. I love you a million times I love you, and you and Sandra Lee are all in the world I am over here for. You know if it was not for you two I would not want a thing to do with all this. I've had a lot of unpleasant things to do and I have not shirked my duty. I'll always be the person you think I am. I have never tried to fool you and I will not lie to you about the things that happen over here. Don't you worry, you just pray hard and all will be all well. I love you and all I am waiting for is for the day I return. Give my little gal a kiss. She still is a good sgt. to me and so are you.

    Lovingly,   Charlie

[Co. H., 39th Inf. Regt.]

Germany, 6 October 1944

(Enclosed—piece of a tree from Germany)

My Dearest Darling:

Just got a letter from you and one from Mother, plus the box with the nice lighter in it. I sure do like the lighter too. In fact, everything is good. Guess I have enough blades to last me a year now, but I was glad to see those come in and especially liked the ciggs. I really did well in these last two days—three boxes I got in two mail calls.

Well, I asked for gloves, but don't send any, for I got some this a.m. from Uncle Sam. I don't need, nor can I use anything for Christmas, so just spend the money on yourself and Sandra Lee, o.k.?

I just can't wait for this war to get over and I get home to see you and Sandra Lee. I know she has grown a lot and looks more like a little girl than a baby. Gee, I'll bet when I do see her that I'll just eat her up.

Be sure to have a tree for her—we always want her to have a real good Christmas, for it means so much to kids after they get grown. Wish you would buy her a present from her Daddy, for I'll not be able to send her anything from here.

Jack Thomas's boys are really doing a job today, sure am proud of them, but I really wish I was one of them.* They sure do live, don't they? Oh, well, I know we envy them but they admire us. Ha! I must keep my morale up, you know. . . .

By the way, you should know our 1st Sgt., for he is a Taylor, from Virginia. A real soldier if I have ever seen one. He has the Purple Heart, three times, one DSC† and a Silver Star for two times, and has been in seven different things like France, Belgium, Africa, etc. He and I are exceptionally good friends. I think he is tops and I know he thinks a lot of me for he has said so at different times. All Taylors must stick together, mustn't they, so we do. . . .

Barbie, you say possible is suffering from lack of work, well, so is impossible. He really does need to go on extended maneuvers and I guarantee you that he shall do it as soon as he is near possible for as long as he wants. I do really need you, honey, I guess, more than I ever thought it humanly possible to need anyone. Barbie, we will sure make up for all of these things we have missed, but please let's both wait 'til I am back and it is you and I. It is funny but I do not think I could ever touch anyone but you. I am only in love with you and I am true to you alone and if I can't have you then I'll not have anyone. Oh, God, please let the day come soon when you and I are back in Georgia and starting out through life like we should have been able to do had this war not come up and deprived us of it. . . . Please let me know how you are and Sandra Lee too, for I do get anxious to know. By the way, I have not told you how much I love you (as if there was any way for me to express it on this paper). Well, I love you more than the sun or the moon or the bright little stars. I guess you are my shining love as you have been, my sweet, clean, beautiful, wonderful wife and eternal sweetheart. I love

*Jack Thomas, a boyhood friend, was a pilot in the Air Corps.
†Distinguished Service Cross.

you a whole lot more than life itself, so never do anything to dent our wonderful silver shining world. Oh, Barbie, I worship you, honestly.

Lovingly,   Your Charlie

WOW! What an incredibly wonderful letter from a man to his beloved wife and sweetheart?

[Co. H., 39th Inf. Regt.]

Germany, 11 October 1944

My Dearest Barbie:

I hardly know how to start this letter for my morale is low and I really am not in a good mood at all. Had a new boy I had to train Saturday and Sunday. Sent him back to the Company Sunday, and I came back Monday. Has not been such good fighting weather, rain and more rain. Everything is wet and mud up to your —— (you know what). It is just rough but it could be worse, I guess. . . .

Two days ago I had been in the Army three years, three months—been a 2nd Lt., two years less two months—and in three days I will be twenty-five. Yes, Charlie is beginning to get old and probably grey before he gets back to the good old USA. I guess I must be pretty healthy for I feel pretty good. I am a real good-looking fellow, though, even if my beard is five days long and dirt on me for at least a month. Could use a good haircut too. Other than having wet feet and low morale, I am in good shape. Well, old Jack Thomas's boys are there today which makes it a lot better for all concerned. . . .

Don't worry about me, honey, for I am o.k. . . . I'll try to write a long, long love letter to you tomorrow. I worship you and am praying for the day to get here soon when I can be there to love you and hold you near me forever on.

Lovingly,   Your Charlie

[Co. H., 39th Inf. Regt.]

Germany, 12 October 1944

My Dearest Darling:

My hand is not too steady this a.m., but I'll try my best to write so it can be read. Sho' did get a close call today, but it's all over now.

Never even touched me, thank goodness. Sho' did spoil my breakfast though. . . .

Young lady, you are getting on my black list for I got no mail yesterday and I should have. You know, I am going to just stop writing long letters and just write short notes if you don't stop sending short letters to me. That is fair. I know good and well if I can sit in a damn foxhole and dodge and still write long letters, so can you, now can't you? Anyway that is the bargain—compree? Honestly, I am pretty tired out and I am so damn tired of eating these cold C-rations but I am not alone, and it would be worse without C-rations. Forgive me for telling you my troubles, but I must have gotten out of the wrong side of my foxhole and besides that, I am damn well fed up with all of this anyway. What a life! Damn the Germans anyway. . . .

Barbie, I lay there in bed or in my foxhole last night for hours and all I thought about was us. . . . I love you too damn much to be over here away from you, I know.

Lovingly,   Charlie

[Co. H., 39th Inf. Regt.]

Germany, 12 October 1944

Hello Darling:

Well, old Charlie is in a lot better mood now as the day has dragged along. It is now a few minutes after four. . . . Wish I was there so you could scrub my back, for it is honestly dirty. Gee, you know how I hate to be dirty but how in the world can I wash? Can't heat the water and anyway it is a little too cold to bathe in a creek. Don't think I have even as much as washed my face or hands in a week. No, it does not worry me as much as it did at first—guess I am more or less used to it by now. I would really hate for you to see me in such a condition, I'll tell you how I look. My hair is dirty and needs combing and is all mashed down from this helmet—my face is real dirty and I have a heavy beard —with a good coat of dirt under it. My face is not too pretty now. I have on OD* pants and my OD shirt and shoes with boot tops sewed

*Olive Drab.

on them (combat shoes). They come made like that. I have on an old driver's jacket or mackinaw—that is dirty all over and real dirty at the collar. There are spots of mud on my pants and coat and the dirt on my hands looks as if it had been there for months—it's really in the pores of my skin. I still have my watch and it runs good and my ring looks as good as ever. What I need is a wedding band from you. My fingernails are unkept and they have dirt under the nails and the cuticles need fixing. Was just looking in a mirror that I borrowed and I really look rough, guess I am pretty rough at that, aren't I? Well, anyway, I am not looking as pretty as you used to think I looked. I still have the same old deep look in my eyes. One of my men said the other day, "Lt., you sure do look through a person when you look at 'em. When you look at me, I feel like you can see my whole past." Remember, you used to feel as if I could look right through your clothes, didn't you? Well, perhaps this old war won't last too long and then maybe they will let me come home to you.

You know we get an army paper called the *Stars and Stripes*, and I quote, "They say that the Ninth Division has been in contact with the enemy since July 9th." Now, that is a long time to be on the go night and day, isn't it? Sure is a nice paper, wish you people got them over there.

What a day, what a day, you should see me sitting in this foxhole. Sure is a nice one too, and old Jerry himself dug it for me. Back in France we hardly ever had to dig a foxhole, for he really did a good job of digging in those days. What a day!

Well, darling, I am growing older as the days go by, why in two more days I'll be twenty-five. Bet I'll be an old grey-headed man by the time all of this is over and the countries have decided to do away with the Army of Occupation. Every now and then I get to see an American paper and it seems to me that everybody is so worried about what is to happen after the War that they do not give very much thought to the fact that there is a long road ahead of us before the War is over. They should not do that. Like I always say—they should not cross the bridges until they get to them.

Tonight the mail has not come in, but my rations have—and included with my C-rations is a quarter of a loaf of white bread, baked by our own quartermaster—now isn't that nice??—well, it helps out, anyway, I guess. . . .

Lovingly,   Your Charlie

[Co. H., 39th Inf. Regt.]

Germany, 14 October 1944

My Dearest Darling:

. . . It is a pretty day, but it has tried to rain off and on all day. Hope it does not rain tonight, for it will be so messy. We had quite a hard wind blowing all last night and it broke the cut-up trees down all over the place. It's after noon now and I had oatmeal for breakfast and dinner, but it is all gone. Guess I'll have cocoa, cheese, K-ration biscuits for supper. Would have coffee, but it is all gone. See, we usually get coffee for one meal a day. Wish I had a little right now for it is cool, but I am honestly cold. A cup of coffee would do the trick of warming me up, I guess. Today being my birthday—so there has not been a thing to land near me all day and I am proud of that. (The day isn't over though, is it?) I have the sniffles and my nose will run and then I have to break the trend of thought and drag that dirty rag of a hank and blow hard. Oh, well, such is life, I guess. Sure would be a good surprise for me to get a big old box in the mail today. See, it's like this—the mail usually comes in at dark and we get it the next a.m., so as yet we have tomorrow's mail yet to get here, understand? It is quite confusing.

Now to straighten you out on a few other things here and there. When I say I am not busy I am not trying to convey any other meaning —I do not mean that the war has stopped or that I am going to USO dances, or that I am having fun. I mean that I am not working at that time, see? It is against regulations for me to say what type of work I do, but I can say that I work at my job for a couple of days and then am relieved for a few, understand? First you were worried about me and the Paris girls and I never did see any—then you, well, I don't know what you thought I came over here to do. Anyway, I think you can figure your way now. . . .

Darling, they just brought up coffee and it was so good, really in answer to a prayer. Wish this was over and we were both together and everything was normal once more. . . .

    Lovingly,   Charlie

[Co. H., 39th Inf. Regt.]

Germany, 19 October 1944

My Dearest Darlings:

    Yep, it rained all day yesterday, all last night, and is raining this morning. They say this is the worst weather they have had here in over eighty years and I believe them. I slept pretty dry last night, for I rebuilt my foxhole, and now the only rain that gets in is blown in the front door. No, I don't have a back door. While I am not too busy today I think I'll get in my jeep and run back a couple of miles to the kitchen and get my hair cut by one of the cooks. I sure need one. Might even help my morale some.

    Last night I got two letters—one unnumbered and no. 37. They were real good and I did so enjoy them both. . . . The mail came in after dark so I sat in the foxhole, put a raincoat over my head and used a flashlight to read the letters. They were sure good. I can see that you actually don't believe the war is over. I am glad you take a lot the papers say with a grain of salt. Honestly, they are overoptimistic about this whole thing. I hate to see them print a lot of the stuff they do print. . . .

    Just had some of, what they call, new rations. All they are is C-rations with more variety. For dinner I had some spaghetti with some K-ration cheese, white bread and cocoa. Not a bad lunch but sorta short. The spaghetti is o.k. except it is packed in the can too tight, which makes it look like glue. I put a little water in the can and sorta boiled it up a bit —all in all it was pretty good. . . .

    I love you truly,   Your Charlie

P.S. Kiss my little girl and give yourself a hug for me.

[Co. H., 39th Inf. Regt.]

Germany, 24 October 1944
(1st as of 19 October 1944)

My Dearest Darlings:

Today I was over at E. Company working and Bob Spunagle called and told me to go up to the Captain for the Colonel wanted to see me. Well, at first I thought that perhaps I could have messed up somewhere. Anyway, as soon as the Sgt. got there and my jeep, I jumped in the jeep and rushed up there. The Captain greeted me with a "Good-good morning." He called up Battalion, the Colonel said to send me right over. I went over, only about a hundred yards or so—and the Colonel was waiting for me. I went up and reported and he looked me over real good—(luckily I had gotten a hurried haircut this a.m., and also had shaved only day before yesterday)—then he began asking me about my work, etc. Then he told me that they had been watching my good work and he enlightened me about two incidents of my accomplishments. After that he took out an order and told me that I might be interested in it. I read it and a big broad smile broke out on my face and I looked up at him. He actually beamed and looked like he had just played Santa Claus—he didn't know it, for he actually had played Santa to me. The order was making me a 1st Lt., from 2nd—and the order read "battlefield promotion", which is better than an actual promotion. Now you can brag—eh? Sure was sweating it out though. He pinned the *Silver Bar* on my collar and handed me the old gold bar. The Battalion Commander was on his left and they both congratulated me, and I saluted them and left. Sho' was a proud little boy, as you can imagine. Well, that's that—yep, you can say, "My little hubby was promoted on the field of battle." Gloat—gloat—Ha!—listen to me brag, but after almost twenty-three months I think I deserved to gloat—seemed as if I was in a rut, didn't it? . . .

Today I received my Purple Heart for that scratch away back there, so I just packed it up and mailed it on to you to keep or show, etc. In the package is the medal and the ribbon and the civilian lapel insignia —all stand for the same thing, see? Also I put my 2nd Lt.—the last one I wore, the one the Colonel took off of me.

Darling, I am o.k. now but for the past week or so my sinus has bothered me and my kidneys and it seems like everything all at once. Had a couple of bad headaches, too. I am o.k. now. . . .

Give my love to all and do not forget that I love you truly.

Lovingly,   Your Charlie

Charles wrote the following three letters from a rear echelon hospital in Belgium where he was undergoing tests for his increasingly severe headaches. The doctors diagnosed them as migraines.

[Co. H., 39th Inf. Regt.]

Belgium, 4 November 1944

My Dearest Barbie:

. . . I am feeling fairly well today except I have a pretty bad headache and still my stomach is not quite up to par. I'll be o.k. in a few more days, and then I'll go back to that bad business once more. Am enjoying it here for it is quiet, get a lot to eat, and can rest a lot. Think I need more rest than anything else, anyway. The Doctor has not told me much, just feeding me pills all the time. I either have sinus trouble or migraine headaches and I think they are trying to find out which one. Don't think they can do much for either one but the rest will help some, will it not? . . .

There is no news here; they had a big inspection this a.m. Our ward passed o.k. and that is the only big thing that has happened that I know of. Oh, yea, we connected up the radio and it is banging away. I took a hot shower yesterday and sent all of the dirty clothes I was wearing to the wash. Will not know how to act with clean clothes on, will I?

They have a Red Cross room here and we get ciggs everyday and sometimes a bar of candy. We have all of the things we need to read or letter stuff. Sure is a different life altogether.

Guess all of my mail is still going to the company. That's o.k. for I'll be there in a few days and get it, I guess. However, I am missing it now.

Tell my little girl hello for I don't want her to forget her old Pop.

Lovingly,   Your Charlie

[Co. H., 39th Inf. Regt.]

Belgium, 7 November 1944

My Dearest Darling:

I had planned to write to you last night but I got one of my headaches at supper and the darndest stomach ache I have ever had. This morning my stomach muscles are all sore as everything and I only have a slight headache. I forget now if I told you what the doctor found as my trouble. He says I have migraine headaches and there is no medicine that will give you relief and there is no cure for them. Guess I'll be like Dad for the rest of my life. You know, I would not mind having these bad headaches, but it is sorta inconvenient up on the front to be sick like that. Well, such is life, I guess.

I was to be taken back to the 4th Convalescent Hospital this morning but due to the fact that I was sick last nite, they are not going to send me until maybe tomorrow. When I get there I'll probably stay there for a week and then go back to the company. It's funny after you get back and don't have to contend with dangers and then think about having to go back up you sorta get a case of cold feet. I know when I get back to the company I'll be more nervous than a bride on her wedding day. Guess you know what I mean? Enough of this chatter about myself. . . .

Barbie, we have been allowed to talk or write about places we have been to and seen as long as the places we mention are 25 miles away. I will try to write little stories that are not pertinent to military information, so you can keep them. Maybe after this is all over we can write a few short stories or maybe a book to cover my experiences over here.

Yesterday it rained off and on most of the afternoon, today it looks like rain. It must rain here all of the time for it has since I got here.

Back in France when we would go in and liberate a town, the French would all come out and hand out coffee, eggs, butter, or anything. Flags would spring out of every house and they would shower us with kisses. As soon as we would leave, all would be quiet. The same thing in Belgium, but in Germany after a town has been sentenced to die and become a battlefield there are no civilians. They leave their homes and go somewhere. When we go into a town and take it there are no others but us. Probably it will be different when larger towns are encountered.

The hills remind me a lot of Missouri, but the tremendous amount of planted timber—mile after mile—trees, trees, trees. 'Tis bad country to fight through. . . .

Lovingly forever,   Your Charlie

[Co. H., 39th Inf. Regt.]

Belgium, 7 November 1944

My Dearest Darling:

It's dark now, almost eight o'clock and they tell me I can't have any breakfast in the morning for I am to get an x-ray of my stomach taken. They didn't say what they are looking for, probably think I swallowed a part of their silver or something. I'll bet a pay day they don't find a thing 'cause I think all of my stomach disorders come from my headaches. When they were trying to find out what was Dad's trouble, they thought he had stomach ulcers, but he didn't. Well, at least we will know if they find anything or not, by tomorrow. . . .

Yes, we have been lucky, but I am getting a little fidgety for who knows when the chances are running out, and God knows I have used up my share of them in this hell. Possibly I am losing my nerve, but a man can't last forever—well, it all is in God's hands. I am quite certain there is no more than headaches wrong with me. I am not quite gold-bricking, but that would be a good idea. Maybe I love you too much and have too much to live for to be leading such an adventurous life.

You know, once upon a time there were some troops crossing a large river and they had to go across on a narrow footbridge. While crossing they ran into no type of resistance but a few machine guns firing on them at pretty long range. The reserve company was to go down the left side of the sector along the river 'til they had passed through a small town on the river bank. They started on toward their objective and out of a clear sky ran into an enormous amount of small arms, machine guns, and mortar fire. Due to the time of day, almost dark, the company was held up and the attack put off 'til the next a.m. During the night a well-found observation post directly over the town was found and the next day the observers flailed the town with mortar fire and artillery fire. Near dark of that day the town was taken and to one of the observers was given the credit of knocking out eleven enemy machine guns. What do you think of that? . . .

    Lovingly,   Charlie

[Co. H., 39th Inf. Regt.]

Paris, France, 14 November 1944

My Dearest Darling,

    Bet you can't guess where your old wandering boy is or doing or what he has been doing? Give up? Well, he is now in the gay city of Paris and it is some place! I got a three-hour pass from the hospital today around three and went to town. First I had to find a Finance Office so I could get a little money. It took me a little while to get to town on the subway. I got off of the subway at the opera and started looking for the Finance Office. I stopped a Lt. who had a French girl for a guide and what did he do but help me find the Finance. I waited around there and finally got two hundred dollars (app. 9950 francs) and then the three of us started looking through the shops. I was shocked and surprised both, for really Paris has so little to offer now. Of course it is so different when there is no war. There are a trillion little shops along every street. I had only about one hour to shop and get back to the hospital on time, and really I did see so little. I guess you are wondering what I was shopping for, well, I sorta want to send you and Miss T. a little something for Christmas. I got you two things but there was no more choice than there was back in Walnut Ridge, that is if you counted the shortness of time and the number of stores. You should have seen me in the stores trying to talk to these French people. It was really a sight to see me in a Paris perfume store smelling all the perfume 'til the proprietor blew his top. You probably will be a little bit disappointed at my choice of gifts, but please try to understand my lack of the language to tell them what I wanted. If it was not on display, I did not get to see it— see? Too, there is another factor—the prices of things are enormous. Pocketbooks like the one we gave your Mother for Christmas last year cost as much as twenty-nine hundred francs or around sixty dollars. I could hardly believe it, but it is true. An average dinner cost around fifteen dollars, I just can't believe it! I guess there is so much inflation, that's the cause.

The funniest part of my trip to the big city was the trip home on the subway. I had to transfer twice, and twice I went by my transfer station, and had to get another subway back to my transfer station, so actually I had to transfer four times. It is bad to be in a big city and get all lost— let alone not be able to ask questions—how to get where. I hope some day I can show you Paris, better study your French. Anyway, when I got off the subway it was dark and it took me about thirty minutes to find the hospital. Finally a priest came along and took me to the hospital. He could talk English—was glad to see him for I almost got picked up —you know these French women. Ha! No kidding, all my trip I saw no more pretty women than I would have seen had I been on Peachtree Street in Atlanta. Would have liked it a lot better had I been on any street in Atlanta.

Darling, I am pretty tired for I rode all night last night and most of the day yesterday, so I just must get to bed. Have about a thousand letters to censor before I go to bed—see, I have to do all the mail in this ward. . . .

Your Charlie

[Co. H., 39th Inf. Regt.]

Paris, France, 15 November 1944

My Dearest Darling:

. . . I have no idea what my boys are doing tonight, but they are fighting like hell and I am a damn yellow so-and-so to be here and not with them. After all, an officer is not supposed to be ill or ever feel bad. Guess I should have more intestinal fortitude so as to be able to have a sick headache and still do my duty as a machine gun platoon leader, don't you think? Why do I have to get sick and at a time that they need me, too. . . . I don't guess I have told you enough of why I am here, have I? Well, before I came overseas and a month after I came over, I had a bad headache nearly every month, then they began

to come twice, then, three or four per month, and now, from one to
two each week. The only thing that seems to relieve them is for me
to lose all I have eaten and sleep it off. Also in the past month I have
had frequent stomach aches and a tremendous amount of gas on my
stomach. We had a few dull days so I came back to get checked over.
The day I came back I had a bad headache and that nite I lost all I
had eaten. Soo, that started it, they have taken x-rays of my sinus, my
stomach, both negative and this a.m. they took one of my skull—you
should see my skull, it sure is pretty, no brains at all—ha! Anyway, this
is my fourth hospital, I hope they get on the ball and do one thing or
the other, fix me up or tell me to get the hell back to the front. I am not
sick, so don't get to doing any worrying—they are just trying to trace
down the headaches which was sinus and now is migraine. One doc
says one thing—another says another. . . .

If there was ever anything that you had done that you knew was not
right while I've been away, you would be decent enough to tell me,
wouldn't you, Barbie? Answer that. You would tell me those things even
though you knew I'd hate you, wouldn't you? had you failed me. We
are so far apart and I know how all the stories get to the soldiers about
how their wives back in the States are roving around, too, I know what
all the people back there think about the boys over here. Either one of
us has a bad thing in us called jealousy, and we are too often doing too
much wondering about each other's actions while we are apart.

Now, let's just stop and face this sexual situation for a minute: we are
both very passionate and you might say always ready to do something
when we are together, but I am quite certain we, neither one, could ever
think of sexual relations or any other type relations as long as we are
apart. No one could fill your sexual station with me. Sexual relations
are no good unless you feel that the person you do them with is clean,
above reproach, and to me you are the only clean woman in the whole
wide world. I am true to you because I want to be, not because you
want me to be. I love you because I want to love you, not because you
want me to. I hope you are the same way, I mean, I hope you are true
to me because you want to, not because you think I'd want you to be

true. You know I'd want you to be true, but you get what I mean, don't you? . . .

Your Charlie

P.S. Give Miss T. a big hug and a kiss from her Dad.

[Co. H., 39th Inf. Regt.]

"Our Day"

Paris, France, 19 November 1944

My Dearest Darling:

Today is our day even here in Paris, for the sun is out and it is a beautiful day. In the distance you can see a plane flying here and there in the clouds. What a pretty sight!

Yesterday I went on a sightseeing tour of the city—did not see too much, but I did enjoy what I saw. First we left the hospital right after we ate dinner. A Captain, a 2nd Lt., and myself got a ride to the subway on an ambulance—caught the subway to the Opera—changed—went to the Arch de Triumph. It was pretty yesterday, for there were so many flowers on the tombs of the unknown soldiers. You have seen pictures of the Arch de Triumph, well, under one side is the urn containing a blue flame. The flame is the flame of eternal life of the unknown soldier. The flame is at the head of the unknown soldier's grave. It was so very interesting, wish I could have had a camera. We walked a few blocks down to the officers' sales department for the Lt. with us wanted to buy a hat and shirt. . . . Got the buying done, and then went to another part of the town by subway to see the Cathedral.

Barbie, you should have seen it—it was so very beautiful and so large. We got an English-speaking guide and he took us all through it. Oh, it was so astounding—the beauty and the reality of all that work. There was such a lot of things in the art that didn't seem to me could possibly have been done away back there in the days that the Cathedral was built. It was almost dark when we got out of there and so we went onto the subway and got a ride to the Opera district for we had an idea we could get some supper at the Red Cross. We tried, but no luck, there is such a huge food problem that finally we had to go to a cafe and get a meatless supper. It cost us a hundred and twenty-five francs but we were hungry and the food was good and there was no other place to eat—so we ate. The place was a real ritzy place, "Cafe De Paris", right in the heart of the Opera district. Supposed to be for the aristocracy back in the earlier days of Paris. The waiters wore tails and "monkey suits" or tuxedos. We enjoyed the place for it was full of "Oui, Monsieur," and mirror-perfect waiters, etc. We had wine and soup, spaghetti, vegetables, bread (no butter) and water. We had finished supper and had decided to go and see one of the Cabaret Clubs. We found one around nine and went in. No admission charge and you readily see why when we ordered orangeade. Cognac was two hundred francs—for really only two thimbles full. Why my orangeade cost a dollar sixty cents—wow! Well, we stayed and listened to the orchestra and it was good. There were Negroes dancing with some of the French girls just like back in England. Finally we left—caught the subway to our station—got off—and were lucky enough to catch a G.I. truck to the hospital. That completes an afternoon in Paris.

I bought a present for Miss T., I hope she likes it. Really it is so cute. See, the stores close Sat. afternoon, Sunday, and Monday, but once in awhile you will see a store open. Hope I am still here Tuesday so I can get that perfume. Guess that was a good day, for I am already tired of Paris. I am tired of the hospital too, but it is a lot better than on the front. I hear the boys are going well. . . .

Give my love to all and don't forget to write to me.

Lovingly,   Your Charlie

P.S. I've still not seen a woman half as pretty as you, even in your Paris.

[Co. H., 39th Inf. Regt.]

Paris, France, 22 November 1944

My Dearest Barbara:

. . . Have had my final chat with the doc and I am to be marked up as non-combat and will be sent to a replacement pool for reassignment to a non-combat outfit. I feel sorta low about that, but I do not think it is my fault, so I'll just have to accept the change as one of those things. He says a man with migraine headaches should not be up front. Being under strain causes migraine headaches and nervous indigestion and even though the rest I have had has somewhat relieved the stomach trouble and caused the headaches to become less frequent and not as bad, if I went back to the strain of combat I would have this trouble occur, so that is the conclusion in a nutshell, see? I leave here tomorrow for a replacement pool and you will probably get the next letter from me there. It will probably be some time before I do get my mail from the company and my other stuff too. Most likely I'll never get a lot of my Jerry pistols and stuff from up there, but I guess that's my luck.

We sure had a good dinner today—baked chicken and was it good! Boy, oh, boy! Wish this damn business was all over so we could be home and get some good fried chicken with all of the trimmings, don't you?

Barbie, I have to run now and take a bath so don't fret at this short little letter, for I'll try to write tonight and tell you how I do love you.

Lovingly,   Your Charlie

[Co. H., 39th Inf. Regt.]

Paris, France, 2 December 1944

My Dearest Darling:

Today is another day but over here they all seem to look alike for I feel as if I am doing no more now than just sweating out the time. Days are not days as they used to be for up there one had accomplished quite a feat if he was sound and unharmed at the end of the day, but here a day is something that is standing between you and I. When one sits down and tries to think how much longer it will be or what tomorrow will bring, well, one just can't think about it, that's all. . . .

Barbie, I left my gun at the company—your picture and all of my stuff. I sure hated that too, and besides that I lost my leather bag, the one you and I looked for all over Atlanta. I put my bracelet, identification bracelet that you gave me in the watch pocket of a pair of dirty OD pants I had on before I took a tub bath in Lammersdorf and the

pants were in a jeep, but it's lost now. I put the bracelet in the pants to
keep from losing it 'cause the catch on it was always coming loose and
the bracelet would fall on the ground. I lost it at Mahn, but one of my
boys found it and I got it back. Sure hate to get all of my stuff lost and
scattered like I have. Can't say I did not do a good job of it though, can
you? Really all I have is the clothes I have on and what little equipment
that I have been issued around here. I still have my wallet, watch, ring,
pen and pencil, so I am doing o.k. Oh, yes, I still have those paratroop
boots, but there is a fellow here trying to trade me a pistol for them—
may trade. . . .

The dinner bell is ringing and I must stop and wash up. Give Miss T.
a big kiss for me and let her hug you for me.

Lovingly,   Charlie

P.S. You know I love you.

[GFRP 215 Co., 67th Bn.]

France, 6 December 1944

My Dearest Darling:

Have I worked pretty hard all day! Don't guess I have ever censored
more mail today than I ever have in a single day. The boys are all
sending Christmas cards and every one of them have to be checked
and signed too and that is quite a job. Really it was the first work I had
done in over a month. I actually get quite a kick out of the letters some
of the boys write. One wrote his wife that if she was tired of looking at
the four walls to look at them right on until he got home, for after he
got there she'd see nothing but the ceiling.

Don't think the GIs have the right idea of the war either for a lot of
them think the war will be over soon. Really I don't know how long it
will last, but it isn't over yet by a long shot. Damn, no one would like
more for it to be over than I would. It is true that a man back here in a
limited service outfit has a greater chance of going back to the States
in one piece but he will probably not get back home as quickly as a

combat soldier. That means your Charlie will probably have to stay over here a while after this is all over. . . .

We got a whiskey ration tonight but I don't seem to want any. I don't know but all I want is to go home to you and Miss T. Honey, I must stop and go to bed for it's ten o'clock and we have to stand reveille and I don't like it a————damn bit. These rear echelon 4-F bas————I hate their so-and-sos. We didn't have to stand reveille on the front so why here? I am one of these "I want to go home" soldiers. 'Cause all that matters is my Barbie and her little sgt.

    Lovingly,   Charlie

[GFRP 215th Co., 67th Bn.]

        "Our Day"

    France, 10 December 1944

My Dearest Darling:

Only a few more hours of guard and my tour of duty will be over and I'll be glad too. I am laughing to myself now cause every time I am on guard it seems like something is bound to happen. Remember back at Camp Gordon, the very first time I was ever Officer of the Guard, the Regimental Recreation Hall burned down—well, last night there were ten 5-gallon cans of gasoline stolen. I have tried to trace it, but with no success. Gas will sell pretty high here on the black market and I guess some GI did it.

They are really bucking around here, for some big shot is due here to inspect the place, even though it is Sunday—they are working like dogs. I'd sorta forgotten what the word buck or eager beaver meant until I got back here. Oh, well, that's the way it will be when it's over with everybody in the Army scared of the man above him. They act like a bunch of old women. I talked to the Company Commanding Officer and he is going to let me go to the Classification Officer, a major at Battalion, and see if he can help me get assigned to something other than MP or guard outfit. I'd like to work in Intelligence or something in the FBI, or along that line. . . .

Tell everyone hello for me and please write to me with the address on the return address and do it often.

    Lovingly,   Your Charlie

[Co. F., 118th Inf. Regt.]

France, 17 December 1944

My Dearest Darling:

At last my orders have gotten here and you may address my mail to Co. F, 118th Inf. Regt., APO 131, NY, NY, for I'll be there before Christmas, I am sorry to say. Was sorta hoping that my mail from the company would catch up with me a bit before I moved, but I guess not. Sure do need some mail about now for it has been pretty close to seven weeks since I got my last mail. Hope you have been getting mine regularly. Once more in the Army I get what I do not want, but I can't help it at all. Probably I am lucky to get this though. I will still be a non-combat soldier, so don't you worry a bit. Have had it pretty easy here, so I am just a wee bit lazy, but it won't take me but a short time to get over that. Only hope I can be placed in such a job that I can go up one more grade before the war is over and I come home. No matter what my job is I'll try very hard to do it in the best manner possible, I'll never let you down, honey, so don't you worry when I write a blue letter 'cause I am always a little blue when I change jobs. . . .

I must write to the folks for I don't think I have written them in days and days. Must let them know my address.

I sure hate it all too, for now I can be sure not to get my mail until maybe the middle of January, damn it, I need some mail too.

Darling, I love you and miss you so much so please write often and don't fail to think about me and the way I love you. Tell my little girl hello, for I love her too.

    Lovingly,   Charlie

[Co. F., 118th Inf. Regt.]

France, 30 December 1944

My Dearest Darling:

. . . Say, I still have my helmet with my regimental insignia on it. I am going to keep it as a souvenir now. I got me another helmet through supply. I just couldn't bear to take that ole AAA-O off of the sides. Anyway, I feel sorta sentimental over that damn helmet. I felt the same way about my pistol, but I'll never get it, I don't guess. Probably will not ever need a gun, but I'd like to have my pistol anyway. I wrote to Sgt. Taylor and told him to get it and send it to me but I don't know. Would like to see that boy after the war. . . .

Barbie, darling, I am only sweating out the day when all of this is over and you and I have "Our Days" and the talks we always have after we get in bed. I still have that last cigg every night—I smoke that cigg and think only of you. You must always love your Charlie for without your love he is not worth a damn.

Lovingly,   Your Charlie

[Co. F., 118th Inf. Regt.]

France, 30 December 1944

My Darling:

I am sorta lonely tonight and I thought that a short talk with you would do me a lot of good. No, nothing is wrong. I am just a little bit restless, I guess. The quietness and lack of excitement around a place sorta gives me an uneasy feeling. Perhaps I have had too much time to feel sorry for myself or to think about the last six months. So much has happened and all, that sometimes I stop and wonder if any of it really did happen. Maybe it is all a big dream or something; if only it were. I've relived every bit of action I have ever seen a million nights in a million dreams. At times I wonder will I ever get through dreaming or thinking of the things I'd like to not remember. Surely as the time goes by and new and better things come along I'll forget and be the same once more.

Barbie, don't you worry about me or anything I write, for you are the one I love and there really isn't anything at all wrong with me that time will not cure. Every soldier that comes out of combat has his dreams of the things that impressed him most. Things that he had not seen before. Eventually one forgets—it is just a period one has to go through with no matter. Of course some have a little stronger case of subconsciousness than others. A person who has strong premonitions has a worse case of it to get over. The army calls it battle fatigue, and that, I guess, is what it is, nothing more. . . . *Sept, 14th (see P. 258)*

I remember way back in the days or seven days before your birthday, we had a river to cross. I had been on the OP* with the left company of the leading company for around 15 days. I was tired, I was worn out. The company I had been attached to was put in reserve and I went with them. We were to be the last company to cross. We had tried the night before to cross at another place, but there was something there to change our plans. Anyway, we started across. There was a force of Germans on the other side of the river who were stubbornly defending a small town and also covering the small footbridges that we were to cross the river on. There was quite a lot of machine-gun fire and mortars being used on the footbridge by the Germans. Nevertheless, we started out. It was nearly an eight-hundred-yard run and away we went. We reorganized on the other side and this company I was with got orders to take the town. We attacked the town and were pinned down. I immediately established my OP and the Bn. CO† called me and asked me if I would observe for the artillery and the other attached weapons. Of course I did. It was pretty tricky business, but I got 'er done and in good shape. The next afternoon we took the town. I was given credit for eight machine-gun positions knocked out with my observing and three taken by me while we went into the town. That, Barbie, is what got me my Silver Bar. It wasn't hard, was it? I am not writing this to you to brag, but I thought you would like to know. Of course, I almost got mine twice that day. . . .

Please take extra good care of yourself and drink your milk and see

*Observation Post.
†Battalion Commanding Officer.

the doctor and the dentist and don't let anything ever change you, Barbie. You are my all and I know Sandra Lee will grow up to be as you have been, perfect.

I love you,   Charlie

[Co. F., 118th Inf. Regt.]

France, 3 January 1945

My Dearest Darling:

Sorry I did not write yesterday, but I guess early this a.m. will do as good. Of course there is no news and it is still cold and this damn heater still smokes. . . .

Honey, I am back. It's six o'clock now and I started this letter this a.m. The Captain came in and sent us to the Company to do the 1st Sgt.'s job—get the men to police up. What is this Army coming to, I wonder? After we got there, the Captain gets there and the clerks are looking through the men's service records to find who is most eligible to get a thirty-day furlough home. Don't you get excited for I don't have a chance now. Maybe later. Anyway, everything this Captain and I talk about we have an entirely different idea on it. He was telling me that if a man had been in the lines for a few months and had not gotten an up in rank, he just wasn't a good soldier. I called his hand on that, for I know of a number of cases where that is not true. Some of the replacements are already rated when you get them up there and so when you have an overage of rank in the enlisted men, you just can't make anymore. He said, well, if he was a commanding officer and got rated men in that he would bust them to private and make his men who had been with him. I told him he would not last long up there. He said no one would shoot an officer and anyway I'd been up for so long, why wasn't I shot—or in other words, I'd been up and hadn't been shot. I told him that I did not run it as he said he would have. Really, every day he tries to burn me up about one thing or another because I've been up and he hasn't, I guess. I'll really make him sorry that he ever saw me before I get through. Other than the above—things are going all right. This a.m. I got tired of this smoke and so I tore this stove down, rebuilt it a little, and now it is the best stove you have ever seen. No smoke in the room now. . . .

Barbie, I used to get letters from you saying how tiresome it was to have nothing to do all day but the same old thing, day in day out. I got letters like that when I was fighting. At the time I thought, oh, how good it would be to be there at home or back with the same thing to do every day, that would be a snap with no artillery to sweat or counterattacks or small arms or mortars, but now I wonder. The days up front were really short compared to the days here. Honestly, I have never seen days that dragged on so. I really get nothing done, but the days are long as hell. I know now how long they have been for you all along. Really you have been wonderful. Your letters came to me regularly while I was up front and they alone gave me the courage a man needs to endure the exposure of man-made things—the weather—and his own conscious or mind. . . .

Do not fail to tell me all about yourself and all about Miss T. and please send me pictures, pictures, pictures of you both. I sure would like to have a "date" with you tonight.

Good Night,   Your Charlie

[Co. F., 118th Inf. Regt.]

France, 6 January 1945

My Dearest Darling:

What do you know? I got mail today! Three letters from Major L. E. Work, who I met in a hospital, 15th General; the Fairburn Methodist Church, and last, but not least, a wonderful letter from you. Yours was written on the twenty-ninth of November and mailed the first of December. Yep, it was doing a lot of raining on me on the twenty-ninth of November. I was in a town called Lardy. . . .

Barbie, your letter was real sweet and I've read it quite a few times. Honestly your letters are always the best for there is a lot in them. I only wish my letters could be half as good as yours are, but they aren't. I hope to be able to dream of you tonight and I know I'll read your letter a dozen times more before next mail call.

Love,   Charlie

[Co. F., 118th Inf. Regt.]

France, 23 January 1945

My Dearest Darling:

I have been a bad boy for I have not written you in two days. Day before yesterday I had started your letter and Lt. Gardner came running in our room and said get your stuff and get the hell out of the house, it's burning down. I guess that was around eight-thirty at night. He wasn't kidding, three stories went to the ground 'cause the Fire Department wasn't on the ball. I fought fire until about eleven but we could have just stood by and let the damn thing burn down. The next morning I had to go on the range at eight o'clock for all day. Boy, it was cold! Ran across a covey of quail and killed one with my carbine at a little over two hundred yards. When we came in at noon yesterday, lo and behold I had mail. Boy, oh, Boy! From you I got October 25th, 6th, 13th, November 6th, 7th, 17th. One letter from Dad, Nov. 5th, one from Mother written back in June 23rd, one from Clay, October 19th. I sure did enjoy them, especially yours. Now I got a letter from you about two weeks ago written Nov. 13th. Today I got some more. . . . From you, darling, Oct. 28th, 27th, 19th, Jan. 5th. I know there are a lot of them yet to come and I will really be glad to receive them. . . .

Darling, I was really glad to get all of your daily reports on yourself and Miss T. Sorry to hear that the tires are going to give out on you so soon. . . . Yes, I do think it is a good idea to spoil our little sweetheart —am glad you are doing it too. . . .

Looks like the Russians are headed the right way, don't you think? Hope they get where they are going in a couple of weeks. Bet they are pretty rough people to deal with. . . .

Glenn Miller's band is on the air now—sure sounds good. Too bad about him. . . .

So you cut your hair. Boy, you are getting hard to handle, are you not? I'll have to bust your little bottom after this war is over and straighten you out. . . .

Lovingly,   Your Charlie Forever

[Co. F., 118th Inf. Regt.]

France, 24 January 1945

My Dearest Darling:

Lots and lots of mail came in today—twelve letters from you. . . .

Honey, I'll not answer all of the letters individually but as a whole and I'll try to remember most of the questions. . . .

One of your letters you had your feelings hurt by something I'd said in my letters about you not being very interested in writing your letters to me and also about wives running around back there at home. Honey, I can explain both of those insinuations. Probably I was writing from Germeter and maybe you had only written a page or two in quite a few letters. I do remember getting such letters with absolutely nothing in them and I guess I sorta blew my top and it landed in a letter to you from me. Sorry I ever wrote any such letters for I am sure I never really knew what you were having to put up with back there. From where I was sitting at the time, any place in the U.S. looked like a bed of roses. . . .

When you would say, "Well, you are in the news again"—How would you know? About the foxhole business. Not like in training. We have to put a top of some sort over a foxhole to keep tree bursts out of the hole. Therefore, one has to have a door to get in by. Most of the time we dug them that way to sleep in, so they had to be as long as they were tall and wide enough for two persons to sleep on their sides, see? . . .

'Bout possible, I am quite sure she will be like a bride—better be for she will have a lot of back work to catch up on (I have a big smile all over my face). . . .

Yes, I was a mortar observer and then I got a machine gun platoon. The cellar, I don't remember what it's all about. . . .

Keep your chin up, learn to cook, and always just think about and love only me.

Lovingly,   Charlie

[Co. F., 118th Inf. Regt.]

France, 30 January 1945

My Dearest Darling:

I have sure worked hard today. Was building targets for my range and I wanted to get through today for I have to fire tomorrow. We got through o.k. even to making target numbers out of gallon cans and putting them on stakes. Sure am going to have a nice range when I do get it fixed. Will be a lot easier to run a bunch of men through in a hurry with numbers on the firing line and numbers of each target. Have thirty-five targets now. At least I've done one thing, I've gotten my whole platoon interested in our range and their individual work on it. They are really arguing to see who is going out on the range detail, which is really unusual for most of the time men don't like range work. (Maybe they just like their new boss (me) Ha!) Anyway, they are enjoying the days as they pass now. . . .

Got rations today and now we are getting seven pkgs. of ciggs. Hope you are able to get plenty for your use. Seven pkgs. are all I need over here for a week 'cause it seems every day is a weekday. I never have smoked more than a pack per weekday. . . .

I really love you and I miss you so much. Every night I pray that the day is soon coming when we will be side by side once more.

    Lovingly,   Charlie

[Co. F., 118th Inf. Regt.]

France, 4 February 1945

My Dearest Darling:

It's funny, I feel like I've done my share and some more too, but I'd sorta like it back up there now. Guess the boys are having a good show. Hell, I'll never go back up, though, it's all over for me, and I feel it's God's will. Sometimes I feel guilty being back, but it isn't any fault of mine, is it? You know, it's all like a big game, but it is bad to kill, I guess. At first I did a lot of worrying but I guess I got used to it. Guess a fellow can learn to like most anything good or bad. Anyway, what's done is done, isn't it, Barbie? I hope God will not hold anything against me. . . .

It is pretty hard for a man to forget a lot of the things he has seen, but well most of us can. 'Course a fellow does a lot of dreaming and those dreams are not good, but if a fellow has a wife like I have he will be o.k. if he can ever get back to her. There are a lot of things I did up there that I never have talked to anyone about, and when I get home I'll be afraid to tell you for fear it will make you see me in a different light. It's hard to talk about such things. Now I know why the veterans of the last war wouldn't talk about it. I know that I'll have to talk about it to you and it might be the best for me too—maybe I could forget a lot then. Oh, don't you dare to think of me as mentally unbalanced for talking as I have. See, it is just that killing is something that is taught as a sin and it is bad to do. We are taught that every day in every way back home, then, bang! you are in a war doing the things you were taught you must not do. It amazes me to see how good one can become at the art. Sooo, now that I am LA* I don't do that anymore and now I have to forget these things I did to help keep our country a peace-loving nation. Big men are peaceful men, for no one will fight them, see? Do you understand me? I hope you do and don't think I am off of my nut or drunk or anything for I am just your Charlie, see?

Barbie, one of these days this war will be over and then old Charlie will come home and we will really make up for all this lost time. We will have that ranch, won't we? I know we will be in deep debt for a long time, but it will be worth it in the long run, will it not? I think so, but it will be a lot of hard work, not much luxury, can you take it?

Kiss my little gal for me and tell her that I truly love her and her Mother.

Lovingly,   Your Charlie

P.S. What does Miss T. call you?

---

*Limited Assignment.

[Co. H., 118th Inf. Regt.]

France, 20 February 1945

My Dearest Darling:

Was real foggy when I got up this a.m. and I did not get up until eight-thirty. Walked over to the orderly room and censored my boys' mail. . . .

Been down to see Captain Green (Regimental S-3) and we were talking about the medals and campaigns of this war. There are only three campaigns for the European Theatre and they are Normandy, Northern France and Germany. A person who was in these certain areas, Normandy, D-Day to July 25 got a star, Northern France between July 25 and September 14 got a star, Germany between September 16 til date not announced got a star. I get them all on an ETO* ribbon. I was awarded the Combat Infantry Badge. The Combat Infantry Badge is only given to officers and soldiers who have been awarded them in combat. It is strictly a badge given to combat soldiers. I was wounded on August 8 and it read like this on my 66-1.† (WIA‡ Severe in R. hand, foot, L. arm. DID NOT LEAVE DUTY.) Boy, I'll look like a medal man when I get my garb on.

Well, anyway, there is one thing I wanted you to know. Every man you see with an ETO ribbon has not been to combat. You receive this ribbon even for being only in England. Too, every time you see a star on an ETO ribbon does not mean he has seen combat. Some of the personnel of this outfit (old members) have the right to as many as two campaign stars on their ETO ribbon and they have never seen a fight at all. Damn it, the small bit of glory a fellow could get from being allowed to wear his campaign stars is torn down due to the conniving 4-F non-combat outfits and personnel. No one should be allowed to wear campaign stars but combat personnel or ex-combat men. . . .

People that have never seen combat have never known what a war was like or even that a war was on. I have been knocked out three

*European Theatre of Operations.

†Officer's official record.

‡Wounded In Action.

different times by enemy shells—only receiving a few small cuts at the time. I refused to have my name put in for the Purple Heart. I only wish I had known how the people back in the rear were getting all their glory, I'd have taken every Purple Heart I could have gotten, even for a scratch. Sorry, but I sorta burn at the indiscretion of some people. . . .

Boy, I rave on and on like an old maid, don't I? You sure have to listen to so much of my anger—and I really know you don't want to listen to all of this stuff. Well, I haven't got much else to do but blow my top and I only have you who will listen to my top blowing. . . . From now on out I am going to wear every ribbon etc. that I am qualified to wear. . . .

Lovingly,   Your Charlie

[Co. H., 118th Inf. Regt.]

France, 7 March 1945

My Dearest Darling:

. . . All of this adjustment business that you were mentioning and that one reads in the papers is a lot of bull. I'll tell you why I think so —at least for my part anyway. I am a leader, maybe not born as one, but I did learn to become one. The one quality that a leader should have is to be able to adjust himself *and* his men to cope coolly with the situation. After the war is over, the change from Army life will be no more drastic than from combat to non-combat, or from civilian life to Army life, or from being single to married. See what I mean? I agree with you that there has been a lot of time lapse and I am quite sure that you and I have both changed to a certain extent, but I'll be willing to bet my bottom dollar that you would never be able to tell if I am changed. Honey, it will be a very easy job for me to be boss and make you like it. Even if you have been making your own decisions and plans and being Father and Mother both to Sandra Lee. . . . Darling, people like you and I only change for the better or we do not change at all. We will always be to everyone just what we already are—Barbie and Charlie. We will not change, honey, for we are more or less one person, we work everything out to where that one thing suits both of us most. No, little Barbie, we haven't changed nor shall we even if we are apart for years. There is but one thing that I know that could change either of us, and that is death, but we do not control that, so be it. . . .

I love you truly,   Your Charlie

[Co. H., 118th Inf. Regt.]

France, 15 March 1945

My Dearest Darling:

Yesterday and today have been so pretty that it looks just like Florida over here. The sun is shining and there are birds out, the trees are budding, and really it makes a guy like me sorta homesick.

Don't have to work today and I am glad, for I am as nervous as a cat. See, it's like this—every time I am on a problem where my guns fire and where there are mortars and artillery firing, I get the jumps, and that night I have a pretty bad headache—then the next day I am jumpy all day. Guess it is natural for an ex-combat man to be that way. It will be funny after I get home after the war and you and I are up town walking down the street and a car backfires and I hit the ground and slide under the nearest parked car. Maybe by the time all of this is over I will have these jumps whipped—let's hope so. It is not that a fellow is afraid—it is that his subconscious mind has a heavy hold on his actions. It is like this: when a man goes to combat, he, at first, does things due to his conscious mind, but after he stays up there so damn long, he begins to let his subconscious mind take over a few of the jobs of his conscious mind—soon his subconscious mind has a strong hold on him and he does things without thinking. The doctors call this Psychoneurosis which can only be cured by time. The common name of P.N. is Battle Fatigue. Everyone gets it after so long up front. Here is an example of how it acts. Scene—battlefield: A man is standing up— a shell is coming in—his subconscious mind makes him hit the ground —but his conscious mind does not realize he has done it until he is on the ground. . . .

Please love me alone and write me long, love letters for I am so hungry for a lot of loving from you. Kiss my gal baby.

Lovingly,   Charlie

[Co. H., 118th Inf. Regt.]

France, 26 March 1945

My Dearest Darling:

It's nine o'clock and really it seems like years ago that I ate supper. We get our rations on Monday and generally we buy the *Collier's, Liberty,* and *Look* and a few other of the magazines, even though they are a month or two old. I was able to get a *Cosmopolitan* today and of all the damn stories in it you have never read. Every one, no matter what type, has something to do or say about some soldier making his readjustment to civilian life or coming home or well, why do they have to always rave on and on, on stuff like that. Things like that should only be thought about and not talked or written about and it would be a hell of a lot better for everyone. Most people or most American people are a little too melodramatic and they cater to the idea of being actors or actresses in their own little world. When they are wives or soldiers etc. the things they read seem at times to direct their actions or words in the future when they run up against things they have read about. The less a fellow reads about how hard it is to adjust himself after he gets back to the old ball game the better it will be for everyone concerned. Oh, maybe I am nuts, I don't know, but it is that way with me even now. Every fellow tries to forget what he has been in or through or seen or done. If most soldiers could have it so—they would rather have the years they were away from home in a war a complete blank—that's what I'd like even though I know it can't be so. We try to forget but always people ask questions or we read things—that's just the way it is. I think I know now why the men in the last war never liked to talk about it. I can see, now that I have been away from the fight, how absurd a true story would sound to the people back home, like my bedtime stories, they must really sound egotistical and highly improbable over there, even though the live memory will be with me for a long time to come. It is all so much like a dream that a fellow tries to make it seem as such—do you understand me, or do I sound insane? . . .

I have told you before, but the fact is still fresh in my mind: the letters you wrote and the trust and devotion you had in them was a big factor in this war. Every time I got a letter it cost the Germans the next day. . . .

The people back home have been cautioned on this or that or the other thing, and so when the soldier gets home he is watched constantly like a child or treated with the same aspect as an uncaged animal when in reality I would say the people in the States have been the people making the change in the soldier and the change is really all in the homefolks' own mind. All of these stories one reads in magazines or sees in a show is purely poppycock. The way I want to be treated is just like I was treated before I left. I am the same old Charlie and I'd venture to say I've had as many shells knock me flat as the next guy or I've been in as rough a spot as most of them that are still up and around. A fellow is either sane or insane, and the insane ones are still in the hospital, see?

Boy, can I rave on. I am just full of it now, aren't I? Really did not mean to make a lecture out of it or make you be my audience, but it is written now, so there, too. Anyway, I guess you will be able to understand my views. . . . Oh, I'd give so much to be able to be there and make love to you tonight. Barbie, tell possible to stay good 'til I can get my turn to come home.

Lovingly,   Your Charlie

[Co. H., 118th Inf. Regt.]

France, 1 April 1945

My Dearest Darling:

. . . Lt. Lowery was on a trip for a few days and he got my effects (stuff I left with H. Company of the 39th) when I was hospitalized, from effects Quartermaster. Boy, had it been ransacked. The only souvenir left was a Jerry knife and two coins. All I had was dirty clothes, two old letters from you, October 11 and 12. I was a little disappointed for I had quite a bit of money in my Valapac, and neither the Valapac nor the

money came. No pistols—no nuthin'. Oh, well, what's the difference?
. . . Did I tell you about the woman sniper I captured right after I got to
Germany? Or did I tell you how pretty a German town looks with white
sheets or flags out of two or three windows in every house? That's really
a sight and it makes you proud to see those people too. I pity them but I
hate to see them live—they are no good, even if they are smart. I wrote
you September 14th, your birthday, and said "Somewhere"—that was see p. 19, bottom — see p. 18
the morning I first put foot in Germany. You know the first thing I did
in there was to spit on the ground—so did all the other soldiers. It gave
one a good feeling to spit on the ground that held the people who were
always causing so much trouble. They will see how they have been be-
damned for this war. Really, I hate them all, and I fought them that
way. Maybe that is not right, but after you learn them, and see how
they fight, how hard they die, you learn to hate them, learn to like to
help kill them. It becomes a sport to outwit them even if the stakes are
high. They are soldiers because they don't know how to be civilians—
how well they fight—how poor they die. They have discipline, but no
teamwork—we have both. We fight just the same way we play football.

Barbie, it is very wrong to kill people, but a damn Nazi is not human,
he is more like a dog—he stinks and jabbers and is sheepish and hard-
headed and arrogant. It sounds bad to say to one's self—I am a trained
high paid killer and I have done my part when I was there. The damn
Germans sorta dreaded to see that white head shine on the front line,
for every time they did they had a big loss to support. I used to fire
more ammunition than both of the Battalions together, and that's the
truth. Bragging?? No. Just trying to show you that you had a hell of
a lot to do with winning the war too. You inspired me to do a lot of
things. Every morning I'd wake up and say, "Good morning, darling
Barbie—today will be a good day, pray for us." You would always pray
for I was kept safe a lot of time when as the incident happened I should
have gotten hurt. I really believe that. You took me to OPs that none
of the other observers dared to go to. Maybe I was crazy—maybe not. I
know I did my job and only because I was always afraid I was not doing
enough for you. Maybe I can't explain the above on paper so well, but

one of these years I'll get home and then I'll really explain it to you to a "T." . . .

Are you drinking that quart of milk and getting to bed by ten-thirty every nite? Have you sent me a picture yet? Please do.

Lovingly,   Your Charlie

[Co. H., 118th Inf. Regt.]

France, 13 April 1945

My Dearest Darling:

Today is Friday the 13th, and it has been really full of the so-called jinx, too. The first thing we hear this a.m. was that the president was dead. I could hardly believe it, for it did not seem possible. Someone heard the seven o'clock news and told us at breakfast. What a shock to hear. Were a lot of bleak faces at the breakfast table. Surely someone will be able to take his place, but no one can be the diplomat that he has been. Guess he will go down in history as the greatest president that ever lived. Truman will take over and I am sure he will do a good job for his political background is quite a long one. He used to be connected with the Pendergast machine, remember? . . .

Barbara, really though, I hardly see how I can possibly be able to make it home before maybe December and that would really be a record time even if the war in Europe was over this month and I had a high priority rating on the rotation business. I say all of this not to get you down, but so you will not get your hopes sky high, just to get let down with a bang. Let us only hope and pray that I am able to get home by Christmas, for that would really be wonderful, wouldn't it? . . . Oh, it's a big, big war, and I am such a small person in it. Wish it was all finished so we could start on home. . . .

Keep your chin up and keep on being the perfect Mother that you have been being for Sandra Lee. I love you, truly I do.

Lovingly,   Your Charlie

[Co. H., 118th Inf. Regt.]

France, 15 April 1945

My Dearest Darling:

My morale is up for I got two good letters from you, April 3rd and 4th, plus the package containing the three sets of bars and the hankie. The letters were wonderful, even if I did really catch the devil in one of them about that Paris trip. Think you will find that I did write you a long, maybe ten-page, letter while I was in that fair city. Told you all about everything in that place. Maybe I did deserve the lecture, I don't know, but I did enjoy it, really I did. . . .

That Paris trip, I think you have the wrong idea on that. Anyway, I did write you all about everything. Really, I don't think you were really thinking anything, were you? I didn't think so. That ten months is really really a long time to even do without the sight of you, let alone of all the physical attraction you have for me. Yes, it could be all in your mind, but tell me, what isn't just in your mind? Without a mind we do not know beauty, darkness, cold, or anything, do we? Sooo, I guess I am right as usual, huh? . . .

The last five pages are in answer to your three-and-a-half pages of April 3rd. See what I write when you write me a good snappy letter! It does me good. . . .

Lovingly,   Charlie

[Co. H., 118th Inf. Regt.]

France, 20 April 1945

My Dearest Darling:

Every day the war news gets better and better but along with the good news we read about the many German atrocities. Guess it is just to be expected though, for all this present generation—the Germans have been taught how to kill—and once a man kills he wants to do it again. I hope the ones responsible for any one atrocity have to pay for it with their life. People who kill for no reason do not deserve to live in this world. When both this war with Germany and the one with Japan is over I hope God will help us keep a peaceful world from then on. Wars actually do not get a country anywhere except kill off part of their population. Now, the way our armies keep going and with this all out for Berlin the Russians are putting on, it shall not be so long until the northern part of all Germany will be under our control. Then, with the Russians and Americans and Allied Forces all putting their strength together the rest of Germany will take only a short time—then what? We have a good Army and a good people behind it as we always have and always will have. I thank God for being an American for there are no better people.

Before dinner I was browsing through some of the little books we have stacked on the table in our room. Came across *Brave Men*, by Ernie Pyle. The book itself does not interest me. Guess I am a little bit cold to the most part of it due to the fact that only the last part of it could I figure myself in and know that I had seen or felt the same things Ernie had seen and felt. I had never looked at the book before today, but really he sure did a good job of putting on paper the things he saw. He had a style of his own, precise, clear, and brief, but thorough as he could be. I enjoyed the way he expressed his conception of the bombing at St. Lô, and the country further on—he really was a great man. I think he was a great man for he told mothers, fathers, children, wives and everybody else in the States the things "Joe" saw, did and felt, and he was not one-sided in his viewpoint of either Air Corps, tankers, artillery, or infantry, even though he did like the infantry best. He was like a letter from the fighting men to the people at home. We will miss him even as we will miss President Roosevelt for they both were the soldier's friend.* If you have not read *Brave Men* it might interest you. . . .

Lovingly,   Your Charlie

---

*On April 18, 1945, Ernie Pyle was killed by a Japanese sniper's machine-gun bullet on Ie Shima, a small island west of Okinawa.

[V-Mail to Sandra Lee]

France, 2 May 1945

Hi, Sweet Thing:

I'll bet you are the sweetest little girl in the state of Georgia. Your mother tells me that you went to a picture show the other day. Did you have fun? Why don't you make her take you more often—then maybe you would get to where you would like to sit and see the whole show.

Miss T., is your Mother drinking her milk these days and does she get to bed on time? Now you will have to watch out for her for she has been known to neglect herself and not always eat the things that are good for her to eat. You write and tell me how she is doing.

Bet after I get home you would like for me to take you to see Donald Duck, huh? Well, you can just count on your Dad to do that for you. How about the zoo at Grant's Park, bet you would like to go out there again, too. Your Mother said you had already been there, but I'll show you everything there, even the monkeys.

Take care of your pore old ma.

Lovingly,   Dad

[Combat Co. A, GFRC, 6980th School Bn. (Prov.)]

Fontainebleau, France, 8 May 1945
"V-E Day"

My Dearest Darling:

Today is that grand and glorious day that we all fought, worked, and looked for so long. It took us almost a year of hard long fighting to gain this mark which is really not half of the fight. May God grant that the Japs see the writing on the wall and soon throw in the towel, also. I am very happy tonight to be able to be here safe and sound in a good quiet room thinking about the past and feeling sorta sure that in Sandra Lee's generation there will be no such great war, bloodshed, or tears to get everyone so mixed up. Today is really a big day and we all should thank God many times. History has been the greatest thing changed by this war, for people will regenerate and continue to thrive war or no war. We can see this by this country of France.

As I was going to the field for my problem, and as I drove through town every window in the entire city had a flag, either French, British, American or Russian. Actually it was a pretty sight to see. The streets were very crowded with people waiting for what seems to be a parade. All of the sidewalk cafes were in full blast and looked quite packed. Every girl, woman, or man that our truck passed, waved, threw a kiss, or put up two fingers in the V-for-Victory sign. It made me feel good to know that I had helped to give these people of France the freedom that they are now enjoying and to see that they knew it. Yes, for them the war is over. All the stores are closed and have been all day. Truly, today is a day of celebration here in France. Even as I sit in my room with the clock just striking ten-thirty there are sky rockets, daygo bombs, firecrackers, and noises of the celebration of a long looked-for day. . . . I don't really think this is the time for the Americans to celebrate for their war is not over yet. . . .

Give my love to all and please send me a box—melba toast and cokes.

Lovingly,   Your Charlie

[Combat Co. A., GFRC, 698oth School Bn. (Prov.), APO 545, NY, NY]
Fontainebleau, France, 13 May 1945

I swear this is the correct address on the envelope, so please use this one in preference to all the rest. CET

My Dearest Darling:

. . . You know, the war being over and everything, and now to have to stay over here, it really is getting on my nerves. I feel more and more that every day is just another day wasted, don't you? Actually a few months of it and I am sure that it will get your old Charlie down. All I can do is just sit around and think about going home and wonder when I'll really get to go. Too, we don't know yet how or if they will let any of us officers out. I can tell you this though, when they come to me with that title card and ask if I desire to stay in the Army until all hostilities are over, or do I want to get out, I'll put that I want to get out. I have had all of the combat I want and I am fed up with the Army as a steady

job. I am one of these "I-wanta-go-home" boys, but bad. As far as the
South Pacific is concerned, I feel that that war is someone else's not
mine. Oh, it's mine too, but really and truly I do not want any part of it
at all. . . .

Talking about catching up, I am sure that we had better be a jump
ahead of Mother Nature and see about getting some good birth control
ideas. As I have said before, why don't you go to some doctor and get
him to measure and fit you with a diaphragm. They cost pretty much,
but are really worth what you will have to pay (fifteen dollars, I think).
Probably you know more about them than I do, so don't laugh at me
for telling you all about them. . . . What do you know about diaphragms
and do you think it would be a good idea for you to get one for my
homecoming if and when I do get to come? Ans. please. Really though,
honey, I think that sexual intercourses are natural with persons who
are together and married. But, when there are intercourses, there are
bound to be children and as I see our future of the next few years,
we actually can't afford any more children and be fair to ourselves
and Sandra Lee, too. Sooo, I think we had better be using a device to
control Mother Nature in the way of baby birthrates for a little while
anyway, don't you? I do hope though, that not too many years will
pass until we can afford another little baby for we do want to raise
two children, don't we? It seems like every married couple should have
two children, anyway, huh? Well, I am getting away ahead of myself
I know, but I think it is good for us to do some prior planning, for I
know, and you know, too, how it will be for the first few weeks of our
second honeymoon, and you would feel funny getting pregnant on your
honeymoon, wouldn't you? I know I would. Ha! . . .

   Lovingly,   Your Charlie

[Combat Co. A., GFRC, 698oth School. Bn. (Prov.)]
                    Fontainebleau, France, 27 May 1945
My Dearest Darling:
   Just before I went to dinner the mail came in and I received a letter
from you with my new address on it, dated the 17th. Nine days—and I

was sure glad to get it, too. Seems like the weeks do go by so slow when I don't get mail. It is easy to see though that I have got to give you a nice long talking to, so you may take it all for what it is worth. . . .

Now, about this Paris business—you seem to be so damn annoyed by. You must have a contorted idea as to my relation with Paris, the women and the wine, etc., over here. Honey, I want you to know that I do not have a thing to do with any women nor do I go to the town bars and get myself all drunked up. You asked, "What do cocktails have to do with a stage show?" Well, in the first floor of the show house where they had the show, there was a bar, and it seems to be the custom in France to drink a glass of wine after or before a show, as we usually do drink a coke back home. I do not remember at the time what I wrote about the damn thing. . . .

Lovingly,   Your Charlie

[Combat Co. A., GFRC, 698oth School Bn. (Prov.)]

Fontainebleau, France, 15 June 1945

My Dearest Darling:

Finally and at last I am moved. Got it all done this morning. Moved to a hotel called "Pavilion Blues" and the place is true to its name, for it is blue all over and not at all pretty. I had to move in with a tactical (bird dog) officer and he has just gotten over here in March. Seems to have quite a chip on his shoulder 'cause he's been sent overseas and he is one of these wise guys who drinks hard and thinks he knows the answer to everything. He definitely does not have any use for combat or ex-combat officers. . . . Don't think he was ever in a division, so he knows nothing about being a soldier. He doesn't want to cross me though or I'll get him straight pretty fast. I'd like to get him mad enough to move for he is not what I'd call the higher type of officer, but who am I to judge? I guess there are some people that I do not like when I first meet them and he is one. . . .

There is no news or new news. I'd like to come home but I don't think I have half a chance of getting there anytime soon. I should know something in a couple of months—maybe by the last of August or sometime in September. Really it does not look as if I'll get home until '46, unless I get a real break some way or other. It's only six months till '46 now, but to be away from you that long sure is a hell of a big job. Oh, we can't say I will not be home 'til this or that time, but we can't say when we will be home 'cause we know nothing at all. But the way things like transportation, classification, and a few other things are at present and especially the lack of information on officers, well, a guy just can't see getting home in less than six months and that would be fast at that, huh? Well, if a fellow was unlucky enough to be put in this Army of Occupation, then the Lord only knows when he would get home. That would just be old Charlie's luck though. I tell you all of the possibilities 'cause I don't want you to be disappointed about what does happen to me because I did not tell you that it could happen. See what I mean? . . .

Lovingly,   Your Charlie

[189 Labor Supervision Center AAC, 1951 Labor Supervision Co.]
Reims, France, 21 July 1945

My Dearest Darling:

Well, here I am at last assigned and at a home once more. I really do think I'll like it here. The commanding officer in this company is really nice and a 1st. Lt.—ex-combat guy from the 28th Division—he has 99 points. I don't know how much he ranks me though. Can't rank me very much though. He is a southerner from Texas—a real good-looking man, too. We are billeted in what looks like part of an old one-story rambling French home. There are two officers in the Company—the CO and I, but we have a 2nd Lt. who has a platoon of guards to guard the PWs.* He is a real nice fellow too. Kentucky boy. He and his boys are out of the 75th Division. I will act in the capacity of an Executive Officer. We really do not have a hell of a lot to do, just be up and around every day. We actually do not have to really supervise the work of the PWs but they work for camps, like Camp Cleveland, Camp Brookland,

*Prisoners of War.

and a few of the others. I really think this will be a pretty nice setup. Only something like fifty miles from Paris. I am really glad I was not sent to be stationed in Germany. . . .

There is really no way to tell how long this job will last or how long I'll have to stay over here, but I'll try to keep you up-to-date on all of the information that I get. . . .

Honey, keep your fingers crossed and don't ever let a single thing change you in the least, 'cause you and Miss T. are the only life I really want to have. You are all mine and I am honestly all yours, forever.

    Lovingly,   Charlie

[189 Labor Supervision Center AAC, 1951 Labor Supervision Co.]
Reims, France, 1 August 1945

My Dearest Darling:

Three years ago today was sure one happy day for us, wasn't it? Really though, it seems like it has been ten years instead of only three and that's because you and I have been so long apart, eh? Yes, it's been a long time ago and still there are a great many things that I remember about it. I remember meeting you at the train—getting a cab —stopping for flowers—and going to the hotel—getting locked out of the bathroom by no other person but the new Mrs. Charles E. Taylor. In those days our title was PFC and Mrs., remember? Well, I guess I have not gone as high in this Army as I should have gone, but I can blame no one but myself, right?

Do you remember what we had for supper that night in the hotel? Yep, fried chicken and all the trimmings. (and I am not so forgetful that I really do not remember that it was the second time that you officially changed your name to Mrs., but I am just playing like it was the first). You got ill at supper and went to the room and I ate by my lonesome. Of course you had had a hard trip and everything but I did not enjoy my supper. Too, I had ordered champagne, but I had to cancel my order, for I was worried about you really being ill. I don't guess it mattered but anyway I love you for every moment you and I have known each other. You gave me the prime motive to live and now I never want to

die, nor do I want to have to live away from you. All I want is to be there
with you forever. Barbie, if only you knew how I feel—I have tears in
my eyes this minute for I really hurt inside for you forever. You are my
girl and I love you. Please always be true as I want you to and do not
ever let me down, for I love you too much. I am counting on you too
much to be all I want you to be and I only hope and pray that I have not
made up in my mind too much that you are a super-being, but I know
all that I have tried to just see you as you are. . . .

    I love you truly,

    Your Loving Husband,   Charlie

Incredibly fine letter.

    P.S. Kiss my little girl for me. CET.

[189 Labor Supervision Center AAC, 1951 Labor Supervision Co.]
Reims, France, 6 August 1945

My Dearest Darling:

    . . . Just heard about the new bomb. What a thing it really must be.
Sure hope it does the trick, don't you? If so, it will not take but a few
of them and Japan will say, "stop—we give up." What a grand day that
will be for everyone, huh? . . .

    I love you truly and am as good as gold.

    Lovingly,   Your Charlie

[189 Labor Supervision Center AAC, 1951 Labor Supervision Co.]
Reims, France, 9 August 1945

My Dearest Darling:

    It's pretty late now, almost eleven. Did not have a chance earlier
for we had a detail of about a hundred men working over on the new
stockade 'til almost ten and I had to check them every once in a while.
Can't say that I really did much all day, but I was busy. Messed around
from the new stockade (which I call the job) to the office. . . .

    What do you think of this new bomb? Wow, it is really a new and bad
thing for the Japs, isn't it? I do hope that it is kept in the right hands for

even a little nation could surely harness the world with a destructive weapon as that. I feel sure that if it is as powerful as the papers state it is then the War with Japan will be short from here on. They will surely give up soon with a weapon like that against them—plus Russia declaring war on them, all within 48 hours. They will be extremely foolish if they don't give up, eh? If they do, let us just stop and see what will happen or shall I say let us stop and *try to imagine* what will happen: Naturally when the Japs give up be it soon or distant from now we will be forced to police the country and control the situations that arise from a beaten nation. So, that will take care of a lot of the so-called low-point men now in the Pacific. Too, the troops that now are leaving from here to the Pacific direct will be stopped and due to the unneeded fighting men they will naturally start sending the highest-point personnel home for discharges perhaps. Then they will announce a new number—like four million—as the minimum number to be kept in the Army as Peacetime Army.

Of course, replacements with low scores will be sent to the South Pacific to replace the high-point men as they are now doing. Still, all in all, the transportation facilities will be getting better all of the time. Really, though, if the War with Japan was over, I do not really think it would get me home any faster, not much anyway. It would save a lot of American lives though, and after all, that is a wonderful thing with itself, isn't it? . . .

Say, I'll just bet that you are getting to be a good cook. From the things you talk about you must have really learned a lot about the kitchen business, haven't you. And truly I do love vegetables alone, honest!

    Lovingly,   Your Charlie

[189 Labor Supervision Center AAC, 1951 Labor Supervision Co.]
Reims, France, 15 August 1945

My Dearest Darling:

   . . . They say the war is over but it is truly hard to believe for it has been so very long, hasn't it? Almost four years and that is a long time.

I only hope it does not take them too long to get around to sending us high-point men on to our home. Guess I want to come home pretty bad now that it's all over and I really feel that they do not need me—a private could do my work, really! . . .

Barbie, just keep up your chin and remember that I am only living so I can come back to you and Sandra Lee. Maybe I can come home by Christmas if we pray hard for that or maybe it will be sooner, let's hope so. I love you truly—you could for the time being plan on getting me that diaphragm for Christmas, eh? Ha!—Well, I may get to come by then, now that the War is over.

I love you,   Your Charlie

Chapter Five

HOMECOMING

September 1945–January 1946

Overleaf: Barbara and Charles in Miami Beach, Florida, January 1946

With that first glimpse of you
    Shouldering through the throng
Straight and tall and khaki-clad—
    Love, the time was long.

With that first tiptoe hug
    All tears and heartache cease
And for one breathless moment
    The whole world is at peace.

    May Richstone,
    Ladies' Home Journal, June 1943

The end of the "duration" finally came in August 1945.[1] With the war over, the focus of Barbara and Charles's letters shifted to discussions of the future. There was no longer as much need for reminiscence, for their attention was now directed toward difficult questions about their postwar world. Should Charles apply for a commission in the Regular Army, or should he become a civilian, return to college, or perhaps find a job? Where should they live? When should they have more children? Would they have enough money? How would Charles, Barbara, and Sandra Lee react to each other? How had Barbara and Charles changed and what would this mean to their relationship?

Charles worried about the myriad problems associated with adjustment to civilian life. He talked of getting a job, but wrote that he had "come to the conclusion that I just don't know what in the world I am

going to do. . . . I am sorta lost as to how I am going to make a living."
His anxiety about the civilian world led him to contemplate application
for a Regular Army commission, remarking that "maybe I am afraid of
civilian life when I think it possibly is as close as it really is to the Taylor
family now. . . . One does feel secure in the Army. . . . so much so that
I know it will be hard for me when I leave it."[2] Further complicating
these problems was his deep concern about their financial situation. He
discussed automobiles, trips, clothes, Christmas presents, insurance,
his mustering-out pay, war bonds, saving accounts, and other details of
their prospective finances over and over. He moaned, "Money, money,
that's all I seem to be talking about." All of this was so overwhelm-
ing that he eventually concluded: "Oh, well, I'll worry about all of that
when I get home."[3]

One particularly vexing issue which troubled all of the troops in
Europe was the uncertainty shrouding their return to the United States.
As Charles complained to Barbara late in August, "If I knew I had to
be over here a certain length of time I am sure it would be a lot better
than not knowing for it just about gives me the jitters not to know and
seem to wait and wait like we are now having to do."[4]

Planning for demobilization had begun in 1942 by the National Resources Planning Board (NRPB). The work of the NRPB was expanded
by the civilian agency, the Office of War Mobilization, later the Office
of War Mobilization and Reconversion. The Army also recalled Brig.
Gen. (Ret.) John A. Palmer to head a study group of demobilization
matters. Gradually, a plan was developed which recommended discharges on the basis of service longevity, overseas duty, combat, and
parenthood. During 1943 and 1944, the Army surveyed servicemen
stationed throughout the world in order to determine their opinions
about what weight should be given to these categories. On the basis
of the findings, the War Department constructed a point system of
demobilization. On V-E Day, the point system was as follows:

Combat—5 points per campaign star or combat decoration.
Parenthood—12 points for each child under 18 with 36 as a maximum.
Overseas service—1 point per month.
Army service—1 point per month.[5]

Eventually, seventeen redeployment camps were established in an area fifty by one hundred miles near Reims, and later five more "temporary" staging areas were created in Le Havre. The large numbers of troops passing through these installations made for housekeeping difficulties, and storage space was at a premium. Morale was also something of a problem as such issues as enlistments for "the duration and six months" did not specify what duration.[6]

The Army commissioned a film, *Two Down and One to Go*, directed by Frank Capra, and a companion booklet explaining the system. Well over 80 percent of all Army troops saw the film, and many read the pamphlet, which appeared as a supplement to the *Stars and Stripes*. Charles Taylor saw the film as he waited for further news of the plans to send him and his fellow soldiers back to the United States.

As military personnel throughout the world impatiently waited to be shipped home, the amount of griping about and general dissatisfaction with the point system increased. The greatest opposition came from combat men who felt that the method used to determine combat qualification did not give them sufficient advantage over non-combatant men in the same area. Single and childless married men also felt that they had not been treated fairly. Politicians at home, sensing an issue that might benefit their standing in the polls, began to call for quick release of the troops. Even so, eleven "mutinies," the biggest at Manila in January 1946, occurred as troops showed their disappointment at not getting home.[7]

Charles groused at length about the point system and redeployment. He felt that his ninety-seven points qualified him as a "high point man" and could not understand why so many men with fewer points and less combat experience had already returned to the United States. He and his fellow officers continually discussed their situation, and his letters described new rumors about points and his return nearly every day. Among the complaints he lodged was one of September 4, 1945, in which he carefully detailed his dissatisfactions with the system:

> They say we will get all of the high point men home by Christmas, and then what do they do? Go and give everybody enough points for all the men to be high-pointers. Now, who is going home first, a guy that had 78

points the day before yesterday, and then the government gave him eight more yesterday because he has still been overseas since V-E Day, or some other joker that had eighty-five points since before May 12th, and does not get these new eight points, 'cause he already had eighty-five? No, I do not know, and you do not know either, and who in the hell does know —I'll bite?? Wait a minute, Charlie horse, don't blow the old top yet, old boy, for you are still young. It does make me sorta sore to sit and watch all [these] stupid things.

Because of the strains felt by servicemen like Charles Taylor, the entire well-planned process for redeployment and discharge underwent some modification. Points continued to be assessed and reassessed and always provided the basic guide for determining the return of military personnel to the United States. However, other matters, such as special skills needed by the military, availability of transport, and location of the unit, came into play. Given the immense job, the large numbers of troops involved, and the great pressures created on those in charge, it appears that demobilization worked very well. A Gallup poll taken in June 1945 reported that 73 percent of the public believed the point system to be fair. In actuality, the frustrations expressed by troops in general and Charles in particular came from their unhappiness at not getting out of the Army faster, rather than the fairness of the point system.[8]

Questions about civilian life, postwar jobs, finances, and the point system for redeployment home could be terribly frustrating. Even more perplexing were a number of other less tangible, but equally important, issues concerning Charles's personal relationship with Barbara and Sandra Lee. He was unsure about his role as a husband and a father, telling Barbara that "I guess I am in for a lot of learning how to become a good father, and a good husband, both at the same time." He was anxious about what their first reunion would be like. "Oh, I get so mixed up about coming home and what I'll do," he wrote on September 24, "how will things be and all!"[9]

Barbara shared many of Charles's concerns about the future, but she was reluctant to devote too much attention to questions about the postwar world. While stating that she was "anxious to . . . start getting things ready for your homecoming," she also wrote that it "sorta scares me when I think of it—and yet I know that as soon as I look into your eyes, and read all the lovely things that you have there for me, and me alone—then I know that everything will be all right." In an effort to prepare Charles for his reunion with Sandra Lee, she included detailed information about their daughter's activities in her letters. Barbara also offered her opinion on the role fathers should play in raising children: "I think a Daddy should have the respect of a child that a Mother never seems to have." [10]

During the eighteen months Charles and Barbara were apart, they frankly discussed their needs for sexual release while reassuring each other that they would remain faithful and true. Once the war was over, this topic permeated Charles's letters. While he told Barbara that he did not want "to sound vulgar or anything like that," he also candidly acknowledged that he was "sex-starved, love-starved, and Barbie-starved." Comments such as "my whole body cries to be near you" and "when I get home I'll be making love to you every time I look at you" appeared in nearly all of his letters. He repeatedly pleaded with Barbara to be fitted for a diaphragm before he returned, reminding her that "we both know that we will be unable financially to have another addition to our little family until we get out of the Army and well on our feet." He even suggested that the purchase of a diaphragm would make an excellent Christmas present for him. [11]

While Barbara was reticent about discussing her sexual needs in such detail, she occasionally made reference to the topic. Relating an incident about a friend who good-naturedly teased her about getting "plump," she stated, "Oh, well, when you come back—I imagine you can work some of this fat off of me—huh? You know, the lack of exercise? and all!" [12]

All of the readjustment and reunion problems which Barbara and Charles discussed during the late summer and fall of 1945 were topics of intense interest across America. Books, advice manuals, government pamphlets, articles in the popular and scholarly press, magazine covers, novels and short stories, and even advertisements addressed the subject. The voluminous literature covered every conceivable topic including wounded veterans, postwar housing, jobs for veterans, "Rosie the Riveter," family readjustment, the role of women, divorce dangers, sexual adjustment, and the GI Bill of Rights.[13]

War correspondents traveling on planes and ships with stateside-bound troops reported on the trips home. Other articles described how American towns and cities were preparing for the homecoming and how individual veterans had weathered the storm. Feature stories about reunited families were popular.[14]

Articles about the special problems of physically and emotionally disabled veterans advised family members and friends not to be condescending and reminded them that the seriously wounded were still "the same inside." Writers dealt with artificial limbs, plastic surgery, and blind soldiers. Information on "repairing war-cracked minds" also appeared. Although most veterans would deny that they had suffered from any psychological impairment, at least one author concluded that "the first few months of a serviceman at home will try the nerves of the whole family."[15]

The question of jobs for returning veterans was exhaustively examined. This complex issue involved the displacement of war workers, especially women, who found that veterans could exercise a claim on jobs they had held prior to the outbreak of the war. An informal poll conducted by *Good Housekeeping* revealed that American women were equally divided over whether women war workers should remain in the labor force after hostilities ended, but a report in *Ladies' Home Journal* suggested that most women still preferred "keeping a home to keeping a job." Margaret Culkin Banning was hopeful that the postwar "economy of plenty [would] provide work for men and women too." Yet other observers were convinced that "GI Jane will Retool with Ruffles."[16]

Postwar housing for veterans and their families was another frequently discussed topic. Popular magazines featured articles on the housing shortage, prefabricated houses, building techniques, financing, and interior furnishings. After surveying veterans about the type of postwar houses they preferred, *House Beautiful* reported that functional, maintenance-free, privately situated homes rated high.[17]

In order to ease the transition from military to civilian life, Congress passed the GI Bill of Rights in June 1944. This landmark legislation provided veterans with funds for education and training, low-interest loans, unemployment insurance, and job guarantees. By 1955, approximately 7,800,000 veterans, about 50.6 percent of those World War II veterans in civilian life, had begun education and training under the GI Bill. The readjustment allowance helped 5,322,000 veterans, and 3,782,000 ex-servicemen had taken out guaranteed loans. About three-quarters of the 16 million non-disabled veterans found readjustment benefits at least adequate.[18]

With the passage of the GI Bill, a plethora of articles on the training and education of veterans was published. While some educators initially expressed caution or even fear about the student veteran, they later praised veterans who took advantage of the educational benefits of the bill as "the best college students ever." Few Americans recognized the significance of the GI Bill at the time of its passage. Yet it was largely responsible for the 75-percent increase in college enrollment between 1940 and 1948. In 1947, the peak year of veteran enrollment, veterans made up 49 percent of the total enrollment in higher education.[19]

Most people still insisted that for families, "Home Coming Isn't Easy." Discerning observers urged reunited couples to enjoy the "first excitement of the homecoming," but they also warned that "after the first few whirlwind hours, the actual problems of readjustment begin. It is a little like the letdown that follows the honeymoon, when jobs and finances compete with hugs and kisses."[20]

Magazine writers reminded women that "your hero won't be the same person you kissed good-bye," and encouraged service wives to become well-informed about the potential problems of readjustment. Glossaries of military slang appeared "for girls who won't know what he's talking about when he comes back."[21] Similarly, writers advised returning veterans that homes, wives, sweethearts, and parents will have changed. As Christopher LaFarge stated: "The home front doesn't know what war is." An article published in *Ladies' Home Journal* aptly cautioned:

Home-coming isn't as simple as a homesick man getting off a train, hanging his hat in the hall, and eating all the shortcake and devil's food his wife can wring out of her sugar allowance. Human relations are never static. Living with other men, crossing oceans, experiencing fear and destruction have engendered many deep and ineradicable changes in him. Working at a drill press, living with in-laws, making her own decisions have certainly remolded her. After the first glad flush of reunion, these differences work their way to the surface, disturbingly, delightfully, hatefully, unpredictably.[22]

Dozens of short stories and novelettes in the "romance" genre explored the changes which war had brought to servicemen and their wives. Frequently they suggested that married life would never be the same once the war was over and that "love should not labor to make time stand still."[23]

The visual representations found on magazine covers provided further evidence of the significance of wartime changes. The January 1945 issue of *House Beautiful* portrayed a soldier returning to a lovely home surrounded by a white picket fence and the heading, "Will You Be Ready When Johnny Comes Marching Home?" *Collier's* of November 10, 1945 featured on its cover an exhausted, but obviously happy soldier and his bride, asleep on a crowded train. *Ladies' Home Journal* depicted a young girl on its December 1944 cover with the message: "My mommie told me to wish you a specially Merry Christmas because our Christmas is going to be specially merry because Daddy, we think, will be home pretty soon."[24]

Advertisers also recognized the importance of these changes. An ad for Maytag washers and ironers showed a letter from a housewife to her soldier husband saying: "I know what I'd like to buy first . . . when we can. Guess! You're right . . . a Maytag!" An advertisement for Floor-Plan Rugs included the caption, "Darling, remember our bare-floor Living Room? . . . wait 'til you see how a Floor-Plan Rug will change it!" General Electric's message took the form of a letter from a service wife to her husband, gently informing him that their postwar house would be built "for comfortable, *convenient*, living for a long, *long*, time!" and would include a "General Electric dishwasher that does the dishes without my getting a drop of water on my hands or *you* touching a dish towel."[25]

Barbara and Charles both recognized that homecoming would not be easy, but they cautioned each other not to worry too much about the discussions that filled the pages of the popular press. After overhearing a conversation between two women she did not know on how "to handle" returning loved ones, Barbara wrote: "Heck, they'll drive everybody insane if they start that—and it's just people like that, that make everything so complicated."[26]

Throughout their long separation, Charles and Barbara had kept each other informed about the changes that were occurring in their lives. Their honest and lengthy correspondence about both private and public matters meant that they had less to fear about homecoming than many others. Professionals who wrote about readjustment problems between husbands and wives acknowledged the important role which letter writing could play in paving the way for a smooth reunion. The well-known sociologist, Reuben Hill, noted that the "crises of separation and reunion may be cushioned and even used to strengthen the relationship if the processes of communication are adequate and the avenues kept open."[27]

Receiving letters from each other remained as important to Charles and Barbara during their last months apart as when they were first separated, but writing them became much more difficult. Barbara described her letters as "dull" and fretted because there "really isn't much to write." Charles, by the fall of 1945, found the monotony of waiting to be shipped home was beginning to wear on his nerves. The boredom was almost too much to bear. Late in October he wrote: "Now I am in my tent and all there is to do is to write or talk to you. This place is truly getting on old boy Charlie's nerves, but bad. I want to move from *see p 304* here and be on my way real soon." He described his letters as "silly and stupid," but said that he had to write them that way to "keep from just breaking down and crying." In almost every letter, Charles talked of his intense desire to return home. He candidly began one letter with "Yep, it's your old 'I-wanta-come-home-Charlie' back to chat with his one and only once more before he goes to bed." But on other occasions, his tone could be quite desperate as when he admitted that he was "possessed with the idea of wanting to come home and truly it is nearly running me nuts." [28]

During his last anxious months in Europe, Charles busied himself by writing long, occasionally three-hour, letters to Barbara. He also sent her packages and souvenirs, including some German soil which he shook off of the boots he had worn while with the Thirty-ninth Regiment. He even took a "wonderful," seven-day, Army-sponsored trip to Switzerland. All of this, however, was simply a way of "killing time" until he could go home.[29]

The last months of separation were also difficult ones for Barbara. The question of writing to Charles became more perplexing as his departure date drew near, but, despite the confusion about when he would be home, she continued to write; she mailed her last letter on October 30. This letter was returned to her, for by the time it arrived in France, Charles had finally departed for the United States.

The return trip across the Atlantic was more difficult than Charles had anticipated. Shipboard conditions were so crowded that the troops were forced to sleep in three eight-hour shifts. The convoy with which they were traveling was painfully slow. Midway through the voyage, the upper deck of the *Wooster Victory* (his ship) began to split apart, and the ship's crew spent the remainder of the trip trying to weld it together.

The convoy finally pulled into Boston Harbor on the evening of November 20, seventeen days after having left France. As Charles had promised, he immediately wired Barbara and informed her of his arrival. The next day he was assigned as a commander of a troop train headed for Camp Gordon, where he and the other troops were to be processed and discharged from the service. Now only a two-day train ride stood between him and his reunion with Barbara.

Before Barbara had even received Charles's wire, she had learned the date his ship was to dock from the listings published in the Atlanta *Journal*. At the time, she was taking care of her niece, Judy, and Sandra Lee on the front porch of her parents' home. When she read of the scheduled arrival of the *Wooster Victory* ship, she began screaming, crying, and jumping up and down with joy all at once. Her mother immediately ran out to see what had happened. Upon discovering Barbara's state of excitement and the source of it, she decided to relieve her temporarily of her parental duties. It was clear that Barbara was in no condition to take responsibility for the children.

Charles's troop train pulled into Camp Gordon at 11:00 a.m. on November 23. Barbara, who had driven their car, "Junior," to Augusta, was at the post to greet him. The couple spent one night in Augusta, and then headed to Fairburn to visit with family and friends for a few days. Sandra Lee was especially thrilled to see "Daddy," which convinced Charles that she actually remembered him. After shopping in Atlanta for some civilian clothes for Charles, the reunited family headed for Gainesville, Florida, to be with his parents.

When Charles and Barbara arrived in Gainesville, they were unsure what direction their future would take. Charles's father began to discuss the possibility of college. Charles, however, did not like the idea of returning to school, for he continued to feel it would be "too slow" for someone who had experienced the ravages of war. Rather than press the issue, his father invited Charles and Barbara to join him on a vacation in Miami. By the time they returned to Gainesville, Charles had reconsidered and had decided that college was the only sensible avenue available, since he, like so many other returning servicemen, had no particular training for a civilian job. In addition, the small house behind his parents' would be a nice place to live. Taking advantage of the educational benefits of the GI Bill, Charles, in the spring of 1946, enrolled in the University of Florida.[30] Although many questions about Charles and Barbara's future remained unanswered, they could at least find contentment in the knowledge that during the next three years they would be together in Gainesville while Charles earned his college degree.

They had survived the stresses of the war years and were stronger and surer individuals because of it. As one contemporary astutely observed:

> This is it—here—now. The future we've been promising ourselves has already begun. Will it really be our golden hope? It was the collective individual wills of this world that won the military victory over evil. . . . And if we are to win the future and all its potential good, we must continue

to know what we want and to demand it. We can't afford to muff this chance.[31]

Charles and Barbara would not "muff this chance." They were ready to take on the challenge of "the future and all its potential good."

Letters, September 1945–January 1946

Fairburn, Georgia, August 16, 1945

My dearest sweetheart,

THE WAR IS OVER—oh, Charlie baby, this is what we waited for so long. Even yet, I can't believe it. I'm so grateful to God. Let's be humble and live such a life that we can show Him how thankful we are. Mother and I were listening to the radio when the news first came on—and we were laughing and crying together. I kept saying, "I want to go to Paris"—meaning, I wanted to go on the air by radio—and sure enough—we did go to Paris—and I felt as if we were there together. I've been wondering if you did go into Paris.

We could hardly settle down to eat—and Mother wanted me to go to the Community Meeting at the church. So, I quickly took a bath and dressed, listening to the radio all the time. . . .

Well, I sat in the choir at church and felt good all over singing "My Country 'Tis of Thee" etc. Mr. Cheeves said all the things that were in our hearts—and I was glad I went. Jenny, Martha B., Emily, Jean and I had planned to go to Jenny's after church. So, over we went and soon someone called us to come to the Square Dance. And sure enough— right in the middle of town—was a real ole fashioned square dance. We stayed around awhile—and then went back over to Jenny's. I took some cokes—and Jean bro't enough whiskey (some kind I'd never heard of) for us to have a short drink. We then cooked bacon, eggs, and coffee— and oh, I tho't about how many times you and I had done the same— and we got home about two a.m. Maxine, Emma, and Eleanor went to Atlanta, and I would have liked to only I tho't about what you said— with Mother's help—that wherever I was on V.J. day to go home and quick.

Everyone has a holiday today of course—so we're going swimming this afternoon. And, gasoline is NOT rationed—man, that's wonderful. Honestly, things are happening so fast, well, I just can't grasp it all.

Always,   Your Barbie

Fairburn, Georgia, August 17, 1945

My dearest sweetheart,

Your birthday letter to Sandra Lee was beautiful. She understood almost every part of it. . . . Daddy always hands her the mail—and she in turn hands it to me. She's learned to 'feel' for chewing gum—and gets so excited when she actually finds some. I hit the jackpot today too —two August 7th letters and one August 10th. I'm not even thinking about your coming home—really, this time I'm just gonna wait 'til I hear that you are on the way. . . .

You should hear your daughter sing "When Charlie Comes Marching Home Again." She says and does everything. Says 11- and 12-word sentences now—and it makes sense, too. Her memory is a mile long— so she'll do o.k., always. Really you do have something to be proud of —and you won't really know how much until you are with her. I just can't wait for the three of us to be together. Oh, what a happy day that will be!

Remember that I love you, I love you, I love you!

Always,   Just Your Barbie

[189 Labor Supervision Center AAC, 1951 Labor Supervision Co.]
Reims, France, 17 August 1945

My Dearest Darling:

Well, Barbie, I go to see the Swiss—I leave by jeep to Chalons at nine—catch the train at midnight—and go to Mulhouse—then on to Switzerland. I can't believe it is me that's getting to really go any place, you know, sorta on a vacation in a way, it is a vacation for it (7 days) counts against my leave time. Well, I know it will do me good to go to a country that has seen no war at all. I'll probably get a chance to get a big glass of milk, eh? Captain Flannigan is sending his jeep by for me at nine and it's seven-thirty now. I have yet to clean up and shave. I have all of my junk packed and everything. You, I hope, will enjoy my letters from there. I bought a little notebook to take notes down in as I go on my tour, so I shan't forget any of the names of the places etc. Will do my best to get some souvenirs for you and Sandra Lee too. Of course I'd rather be coming home, but maybe I'll be home in two months, who knows?

The *Stars and Stripes* stated that 200,000 high-point men would be sent home by the last of September, but gosh sakes, over 85,000 of that number have already been taken up with those five divisions who have been alerted, not even taking into consideration the 30th, 35th, and 45th Divisions. If their numbers have not been counted then that's most of the quota right there. You can count something like 19,000 to a division. By that I really do not feel that we people who are assigned but who are not in a division will not be getting a quota or rather not a quota *large* enough to affect us 'til maybe in the first of November or December. Of course I may be very wrong like I have been for the past few predictions. I did not miss V-E Day far, did I?

Talking about leave time, I have almost seventy days' unused leave time that the government either pays you for or gives you that much leave before discharging you. That's almost three months, right? At least we shall not starve for a while after I get out for I too will get $300.00 mustering-out pay. Say, they are going to open Regular Army Commissions up to some AUS* officers (I am an AUS officer) and if we thought it best when I got back home, we could think about me signing up with the Army. . . . Oh, I am not very serious but it is a good thought if we see I am unable to do so well outside—maybe I am afraid of civilian life when I think it possibly is as close as it really is to the Taylor family now, right? When they say you can have a Regular Army Commission it is quite a temptation, for 300 bucks a month steady looks fair when I think of what people worked for in the Depression days, remember? Oh, I guess I shouldn't even think about it, should I? After I get home and get out of the Army and get a taste of *good?* old

*Army of the United States.

civilian life once more I'd not even think of this damn Army anymore. One does feel secure in the Army, though, so much so that I know it will be hard for me when I leave it. Maybe I have taken the Army too serious, huh? Don't mind me, honey, I only think I'd like to stay in the Army for a minute a day and for 1439 minutes a day I cry to get out, so there!

Barbie, are your eyes really as pretty and expressive as they look in this picture you sent me. This picture looks just as I remember you, and it renews my spirit, for I feel that all of the memories and thoughts of the past that I have are not dreams but are really the truth. God, I love you, honey, so please be mine forever, can you? . . . Please tell Sandra Lee all about her Pop. Oh, he is a hell of a Dad for a little girl, but after we are home again, I am certain he can learn all of the tricks of being a Dad and a good husband that he does not know.

Lovingly,   Your Charlie

Fairburn, Georgia, August 27, 1945

My dearest sweetheart,

It's been sixteen months today since you saw Prissy—and gee, I wish you could see her now. She is really a cute li'l gal—not really pretty, but just cute as pie—and the daintiest little thing you've ever seen. She's a real little girl—except when she climbs, and I don't encourage her tomboyish ways one bit! I know you will tho'—eh? . . .

Charlie, I'm sure looking old these days anyway—I'll just bet you'll want to ditch me for some young gal when you return. But—I'll always love you anyhow. Maybe I just feel old—I don't know. But, oh, I want you so—just to be able to relax again—how will it be when we know that we're together, never to part again. I can't even imagine. . . .

Jenny, Martha, Emily, Jean, and Bess came down tonight. Sandra Lee was so sweet about going to bed. I told her to run kiss Grandmother goodnight—and she did, and said, "I love ya." Mother and Daddy really worship her. Then I put on her gown and held her about five minutes on the porch and to bed she went. Oh, she's a dear!

Jenny thinks Freck will be here with a discharge in a month—so she's hitting the ceiling! He has forty-nine Navy points. If you could only come home, I wouldn't worry about a discharge, right? You won't ever know how long these months have been with you away. I love you so very much and it's getting me down. How about you? I'm all yours, Charlie, so believe me!

Just,   Your Barbie

[189 Labor Supervision Center AAC, 1951 Labor Supervision Co.]
Reims, France, 28 August 1945

My dearest darling:

. . . Did not have as much mail waiting for me here when I got back as I had thought I'd have, but I did have four letters from you—July 26, 17, August 10 and 13. I guess you must have been busy, as usual. I did not write you while I was in Switzerland 'cause it cost about 75 cents to mail a letter there and of course I could not buy stuff and mail letters too, understand? Anyway, I kept a notebook and took notes all the way through the whole trip for you. I will send it to you with all of the pictures and things I did buy. . . .

Thanks for that lock of pretty silk blond hair of Miss T. 'cause I really had no idea as to how light it really is. She is sure a wonderful baby, isn't she? I'd like to see her face when she gets what I am sending her. You will like what I am sending you too. I am sure.

I'll write another letter tonight so—

Lovingly,   Charlie

Fairburn, Georgia, August 29, 1945

My dearest sweetheart,

I'm ready for some mail now—but I've been so fortunate these fourteen months 'til I won't fuss at all. Yesterday Joe Mc's* wife, Barbara, and their four-months-old baby (Jo Ann) came for the day—and Barbara had just received a letter from Joe—written July 28th—and that

*Joe Mc Wooddall was Barbara's cousin.

was the first she had heard in four weeks. Therefore I don't dare gripe about missing a few days. I keep thinking you'll get home pretty soon now—and I hope I'm right. Gee, I need you so, Charlie. You are so wonderful—I'm thankful that you love me—ever so thankful. . . .

[Sandra Lee] . . . did something this a.m.—I couldn't quite figure out. She was building a train with her blocks and started saying "Hey, Daddy"—over and over. All of a sudden she jumped up, ran to the door and yelled, "Hey, Daddy, hey!"—then she came back and said, "That's the way I do." Perhaps she was pretending you were coming up the walk. Anyway, it's darling the way she talks about you. Sometimes I feel as if she actually remembers you.

Skeeter is the same ole dog. . . . He's almost human, Charlie, and just as humble as he can be. I'll be happy when we have a place so he can run around as he should. . . .

If I hear of anyone else getting home or getting a discharge I'm just gonna blow up. Really I'm awfully jealous! But, I'm glad you have such a nice setup, as long as you have to be over there.

Soup's on—so I'll stop for now. Will write more this p.m.

I love you truly,

Always,   Your Barbie

[189 Labor Supervision Center AAC, 1951 Labor Supervision Co.]
Reims, France, 4 September 1945

My Dearest Darling,

Well, today was another day, but no mail. Yea, that is all that I do is gripe about my mail, but I really do not have anything else to do all day but think about the things that I will gripe about at night to you. (Believe me?) Well, that is not just the way it is, but there is a lot of truth in the statement, for the days I do not have so much to do I find that I really do a lot more griping, but I don't mean half of it. . . .

I did not mind not having things in the War, or having to be here away from you and Miss T., and fighting, eating C-rations, smelling blood, not getting to bathe, or just doing without in general, but the end of the emergency is now here and I think that it is a shame the government can't muster enough ships to get all of the home-hungry boys and just kids home faster than they are. If they can't get the ships, then why don't they stop all of these promises and state facts as they are. These people over here are quite grown-up, even if some of them do not look like it. . . .

Darling, I'll have to stop for there are a lot of other people that are ready to hit the sack and they are yelling at me to stop the noise and go to bed. Joe says for me to tell "her you still love her and that you will be home in a few years, and get the hell to bed," but he doesn't bother me in the least, so there! I do love you, Barbie, and you know that I can hardly wait to get there to you and tell you all of the things that look so cold and expressionless on a piece of paper. I know that you are tired of all of this chatter for it has taken me about three hours to compose all of this and I am getting sorta tired myself. Please see me in your dreams and think of me all day—and the time will just fly by 'til I am there to hold you in my arms every night and look at you all day every day and every night. Use your little head until your Charlie gets there to take over all that you are. . . .

Your loving husband,   Charlie

Gainesville, Florida, September 5, 1945

My dearest sweetheart,

Your li'l wife really should be in bed right now, for it's late and I'm, oh, so tired—but I just had to drop you a line to let you know that Prissy and I are in Gainesville. . . .

Honey, I was really glad to get your letter Monday a.m. before we left home. It was written the 28th and I had been under the floor I was so low because of no mail. Also received your notebook and then I knew why I hadn't received any mail. I know you had a wonderful trip and I'm so glad you could take it. It was not only good to see Switzerland, but just getting away did you a world of good, I know. Have read your notes over and over and have really enjoyed them. Just can't wait to get the box and especially the watch—boyoboy!!—that's wonderful—thanks a million!! Hope you already have the box on the way. . . .

Won't it be just grand when everyone is out and on their feet. Lord only knows what we'll do—but we'll manage someway, won't we? I want you home so very much that I'd settle for bread and water. Tomorrow will be fifteen months without my one and only—and that's too long. . . .

I love you, I love you, I love you, Charlie baby—so don't ever forget it.
Always,   Your Barbie

Sandra Lee says "Thank you" for the gum and she loves you!!

Gainesville, Florida, September 6, 1945
15 months without you!

My dearest sweetheart,

Have just had a good bath and feel all nice, clean and comfortable. . . . Heard over the radio today that *all* men in Europe with 70 points and over would be in the States by December 25th so, 'course I'm 'cited about that! Fifteen months is long enough—now—I'm ready for you to get home now.

September 7th, Friday a.m.—Didn't get to finish this last evening—for it was late and we had some coffee before going to bed. It's almost 12:00 now and I've gotten out some washing and praying it won't rain. Pop has gone to Jacksonville—and Priss is running around and playing up a storm.

There really isn't much to write, but we think of you and talk about you all the time—so I just want you to know it. And Sandra Lee was the cutest thing this a.m. She went up to your pix and said, "Hey, Daddy, I love you"—and she came running in the bedroom and said, "I petted my Daddy, I love him berry much." . . .

Mama Taylor and Pop are continually talking about "us" living in the house back of them—I bet that's what we do. Really it's up to you and if that's the best thing to do—and we'll be happy, then I suppose it'll be fine. Just don't ever quote my viewpoints, for really I'll be content to do what you say.

Honey, I love you more than ever. . . . I miss you so much and pray that it won't be long before you get home.

Always,   Your Barbara

P.S. When we were riding in the car Monday, I wrote down what Priss was saying for several minutes. 'Course I missed a lot—but it will give you some idea of how she chatters all the time. Just be so glad when you are here to hear her—I know you're just going to eat her up: "Give Cora two cards." (Cora is her doll.) "Where are your cards? Are you going to give me your pencil? Oh, I hurt my foot, I hurt my foot so bad! Did it hurt, Nursey?" (Nursey is a doll.) "Give her one of these cards. I put 'em in her lap. They like cards, don't they? Can't you see, Mama? You can't see, can you, Mama?" (Dancing and singing.) "I almost fall down." "It's raining on me. I play, I play, I play. Oh, Mama, I can't see, Mama, I can't see. Can you see for me, Mama? I hit my head. That ole phone won't answer, Mama. I hurt the li'l baby, Mama. Oh, Oh, Oh, Mama, it's raining on me—it's raining on me." (Jumps up and down.) "You didn't buy me any crackers, Mama" (over and over). "Let me write—let me write to my Daddy, Mama" (over and over). "Let me write to my Daddy." (She yells that, so I gave her the pencil.) . . .

[189 Labor Supervision Center AAC, 1951 Labor Supervision Co.]
Reims, France, 7 September 1945
My Dearest Darling:

Lots of news today—I have been transferred to the 75th Division. . . . I got orders for my transfer today, but I do not think I will physically be with them for a few days, possibly a week, but I really do not know. I do know that they are replacing all of the 75th low-score personnel with high-pointers and that we will be sent to the States as the 75th Division people by not later than 30 November. That definitely means that your Charlie is finally going to get to come home to his Barbie and Sandra Lee. Honey, all of the above information is all that I know. It was a surprise to me to be transferred so soon to the 75th, for I thought, as I said the other night, that it would be at least the 1st of October, but wham! in it came this afternoon. I am sure that I'll be home to you before Christmas now. Please hope and pray real hard, will you? Do not stop the letters, but do stop the packages. Do not send me any more packages for I'd never get them. I'll get the letters possibly right up 'til just before I leave this area here—I don't know, but I think that will be around the 1st or later, Lord, I just do not know. Anyway, don't stop the letters for it will not hurt much if they get lost, for some day some of them will come to me at home and we can enjoy them there. . . .

Well, I will try to write you as soon as I find anything out for sure. Will try to wire you before I leave the continent.

Love,   Charlie

[189 Labor Supervision Center AAC, 1951 Labor Supervision Co.]
Reims, France, 13 September 1945
My Dearest Darling:

. . . I wrote you a long five-page letter last night, but after I finished it, I tore it all up. It was one of those mean letters that I can write when I am the least bit mad or in a bad mood or what have you. You really did not miss a thing by my not mailing it, in fact, you are a lot better off. . . .

I know all of my letters sound dry and real dull, but, hell, I am tired of writing letters and trying to tell you something, and sitting and sitting, and no mail hardly, and hell, I am just tired, I guess. Maybe I am crossing too many bridges before I get to them for no reason at all. When I do that it makes me give up too easily. Oh, I know it's going to be rough when I get back and try to work for a living instead of accepting donations like I am for the Army now, but I really make it seem like it is going to be a lot worse than it is, and I think about it entirely too much. . . .

Young lady, do you realize that this will be your fourth birthday as a married woman? Well, it is and I only wish I had gotten your birthday package off sooner so it could have gotten there to you on time. Gee, I love you! I really do hope that your watch gets there in good shape though, for I do think it is a nice one. I'll bet you don't look a day older now than you did the day I married you, do you? You have sorta neglected me the past few months with no pictures of you and Sandra Lee, why? Well, I guess there is always no film at the drug store. Maybe now you will be able to get just lots and lots. Barbie, I hope tomorrow you have a wonderful birthday, for I am sure you deserve the best, for I know you are the best.

Love, Charlie

Gainesville, Florida, September 14, 1945

My dearest sweetheart,

Well, this is my "Happy Birthday." Wouldn't it be just too wonderful if we were someplace together today. But I'm happy in thinking that you'll soon be here—and then we'll never have to be apart again. Oh, Charlie, I do love you so very much. You are my Charlie—nobody else's —*all mine*, and I am just as much Your Barbie. Had two letters from you yesterday—31st and 1st. Pop and Mama Taylor had one today written the 6th—so we were glad to get new news. Am glad your mail got to you at last—for the days really drag by without mail, don't they? . . .

Wednesday afternoon I went to Camp Blanding with the Red Cross to help in the canteen—make sandwiches, serve the boys, etc. I really enjoyed it, although I got awfully tired. Kept thinking how wonderful it would be should you walk in—but I wouldn't have lived to tell the tale! No siree—I like surprises, but not like that. So, give me plenty of warning when you get your orders.

Sandra Lee is as darling as ever. She's growing so—and acts like a big girl. Talks all the time—and I just can't wait for you two to see each other.

We're feeling fine—and everything's o.k.—just wanted you to know that I love you very much—even on my birthday. I could eat you up —and I nearly wore those two letters out yesterday—reading and re-reading them. You naughty man! But I love it! You are a sight, Chas. E. Taylor!

I love you truly,

Always, Your Barbie

[189 Labor Supervision Center AAC, 1951 Labor Supervision Co.]

Reims, France, 24 September 1945

My Dearest Darling:

Boy! what a good afternoon this was for mail!! I got three letters from you and one from Mother, now, wasn't that good? The best day for mail I've had in over two months. One of your letters was written on the 6th and finished on the 7th, but not mailed til the 9th; the next one was written on the 9th and mailed on the 10th; the latest one was written on the 15th and mailed on the same day. Just think, a letter from you in only nine days, not too bad, eh? . . .

Barbara, please if you haven't, go on and get yourself fitted with one of those diaphragms 'cause I really have thought about it and it is the best thing. We both know that we will be unable financially to have another addition to our little family until we get out of the Army and well on our feet. Think we had better try to control the birthrate for at least a year or more and then maybe we can see our way clear. Besides let's sorta plan for the next one and everything, o.k.? Barbie, I really do love you and I hope you will always love me just the way I want you to. I am sure you love me for I sorta feel it, deep down inside of me. Maybe I am too vulgar in my talks to you, I don't know. I guess I just feel that there is no part of your body that is not pure and wholly mine for a lifetime. Am I taking too much for granted? I hope I am not for I have always tried to guard against ever taking you for granted. . . .

Just like you said in one of your letters talking about the day I'd get home as being a great day, but that you were a little afraid of it, but even so, when you looked into my eyes and saw all of the beautiful things there that you knew I'd have in them for you and you alone forever. Darling, I am afraid of that day too, but when I am able to look into those big brown eyes and touch you and know you are real, I am afraid I'll have to borrow a shoulder and have myself a cry. Don't know when I've cried since I came over here. Oh, I've had tears in my eyes, but I have not cried, doubt if I could cry. Maybe I have gotten a wee bit hardened or maybe I grew up. Whichever it is I know I'll almost cry if I don't, so there too!

I love you so much and, Barbie, I hope I am a good father to Sandra

Lee and the rest of them that will come along some of these days. Got a long way to go, but I'll get there as long as I have you. I'll make you a good husband and a good provider too, I hope. Oh, I get so mixed up about coming home and what I'll do—how will things be and all! Oh, I know that if everything is all right between us, as I expect them to be, then we can always make a living at one thing or another. Can't see going back to school though, for I have wasted too much time now in the Army. Every time I think about coming home I get afraid of something. I guess maybe I have been trying to find too much to worry about—not enough to do around here to keep me busy and keep my mind busy. Anyway if I get a terminal leave of thirty days and see that I will not be able to make a go of it outside, then maybe I could take on some more of the Army. At least it would be a sound and honest way to make a living. Maybe I'd be able to keep at least a 2nd Lt. bar, huh!

Well, you and I will have our vacation, or should I say a honeymoon, and then after that we can look at the working and planning part of life. O.K.? I am pretty moody tonight and I know this letter sure shows it. When I get moody I just write as things strike me. Don't plan what or how I'll say it at all. Don't take my fussings too serious, honey, 'cause all I know is that I love you with all my heart, body, and soul and I am just so afraid some guy will try to steal you away from me while I am still over here. Promise me that no one will steal you from your mean old husband, will you? . . .

Your loving husband,   Charlie

[189 Labor Supervision Center AAC, 1951 Labor Supervision Co.]
"Our Day"
Reims, France, 30 September 1945

My Dearest:

Today is a real Sunday, nice brisk day and lots of sunshine. Sorta reminds me of those days we spent in Louisiana for they were the same kind of days. . . .

Say, I asked you if the tires were still rationed and I see by the paper that they are, darn it! Looks like they would turn them loose too, doesn't it? Do you think there is a chance of us getting a new set by any chance? Just what do you have to have to get tires. Boy, we will really be hurting for tires when we start on our trip. Oh, well, we have gone further on worse tires, haven't we? Maybe we can pick up some old used tires someplace if new ones can't be had. Say, you might try to find out though just how we can get them when I do get home so we can start in to work on getting some. I'll tell you right now, there are a few things that we are going to do when we get out of the Army (before our money runs out). Get the car in shape for at least a year's running, tires and all. Next see about clothes for us both, put an emergency fund in the bank and then (me) get a job of some kind to keep us on top of the water for the time being. Guess I can do all of those things including the work, with your help of course. There is one thing we do not want to do and that is have to go to our folks for money, for I am sure that both our mothers and fathers need what money they have. We want to be on our own so we can do and say what we please. I think I share the same feeling as you do about *our* being independent to the rest of the world but I am not sure. . . .

Honestly, though you know it may be a lot different than I am looking at it, still we will just have to wait and sorta let nature take its course and figure all of these problems out as we come to them. To tell you the truth, I am up a stump as to what I am going to do or how I will do it, but I feel that things will work out. I know I'll be lost and more or less spinning when I get discharged, but all we can do is to use our best judgment and I feel sure that I'll have to forget about my desire to be a gentleman farmer until I become a millionaire or something and instead become a hard-working husband and father, for now we have a lot more to do than just fulfill our quaint desires for we have Sandra Lee's future and background to look out for. I think I'll get Dad to look around and place me in a job of some sort, not in Gainesville, maybe in South Florida. A job that has some future in it and then we can be alone and start life out on completely new plans, huh? Do you think that's a good idea? . . .

Honey, I will stop now, but just you remember that I love you and only you. Darling, you please take real good care of yourself and Sandra

Lee and old Charlie will be home before you know it. Darling, did you get your Charlie that Christmas present that he asked you to get? Well, you better just run on up and get yourself fitted out with one! Will you, please? Honest, honey, I am very serious about that, so don't put it off another day, for if you aren't fitted when I get there I'll really be mad. It's for the best, so believe me.

Lovingly,   Your Charlie

Gainesville, Florida, October 1, 1945

My dearest sweetheart,

Honey, I should have written you last evening—but I just couldn't. Don't know what was the matter with me yesterday—guess it was just "Blue Sunday"—for I certainly wasn't a very good sport about anything! And late in the afternoon I cried like a baby, over nothing—and kept it up off and on until bedtime. Sure was sorry to make such a fool of myself, but it couldn't be helped. Think I'm just excited inside about your coming home. Oh, Charlie baby, I just can't wait—really!! I'm, oh, so lonesome for you and I love you so very, very much! . . .

'Course there's no way to plan just how we'll spend your first leave —but I wish it could happen this way. Say you get thirty days—well, I wish we could spend the first ten days at home—for that would give you and Priss both a few *quiet* days to get accustomed to each other— then, come down here for ten days. Then go back to Georgia—leave Prissy, and me and you go somewhere for a week right by ourselves. Sounds good, doesn't it!

Oh, just to be with you will be heaven! No matter where we are or who is with us. I love you truly, so don't let me down.

Always,   Your Barbie

[189 Labor Supervision Center AAC, 1951 Labor Supervision Co.]
Reims, France, 5 October 1945

My Dearest Darling:

My, but your Charlie was in a bad mood last evening. I actually wrote thirteen pages to you, but I tore the first seven pages up 'cause they did not sound like Charlie. They were cold, blue, lonely, hateful pages. Yes, honey, it looks like you were right. I have been using you for a punching bag for the past month, when I'd get blue and feel sorry for myself. Will you forgive me? I have my chin up high and I can hang on for a few more weeks like you asked me to do. Gee, you sure are a swell person for a fellow to have to come home to and I am proud, so proud, for I really do know how lucky I've been to have you and Sandra Lee as a wife and daughter. . . .

Nothing new in news, but I hope to be on a boat by the 25th at least. Boy, I'll be so happy when I get that boat for home. Maybe I am a sissy, so don't tell anybody, but I am sorta scared of that boat ride. You know to tell you the truth, I never did like big boats and transocean trips, 'cause I am a landlubber, I guess! Anything though, I'll ride a bathtub home if I could, I've just got to get there. Oh, I'll be there before either of us know it! . . .

Barbie, won't it be too good to be true when we have some place to live, a job, and at night we can sit by the fire and talk, listen to the radio, and have a real cozy time all of the time. I'll bet there will never be a dull moment around our house. Then about every nite if we want we can go to the kitchen and cook, say, coffee, eggs, toast, and I'll kiss you between each pop in the frying pan or each perk of the percolator. What happy days those will be. I can hardly wait. . . .

I love you truly,

Your loving husband,   Charlie

[189 Labor Supervision Center AAC, 1951 Labor Supervision Co.]
"Our Day"
Reims, France, 7 October 1945

My Dearest Barbie:

. . . Barbie, do you know the song, "I don't care if I never dream again"? Don't you think that's a pretty song? Don't guess I ever heard the words until this afternoon. Is it an old or a new song? I am just now able to catch up on all of the songs that I missed. This radio we have goes all day long and lots of time into the night. Sure do like to hear good music on the radio. You know what I am really wanting to do?

Well, I want us to go out to some real up-to-date night club and hear a good orchestra, where the lights are low, and we are all alone. How would you like to do that? Would you like it, really?

Another thing, let's you and I take some nice long walks in the woods and maybe wade in a creek and go out somewhere and roast wieners and sit by the fire under the blue-black sky with that pretty Florida moon up there like a ball of fire. There are so many little things I want to do—smell the lake at night, feel the air, drink in just lots of sun, be on the beach and feel the sand between my toes, get all burned and feel the sting of the sheet on my back, or sit in church and hear the preacher with my ears, and think about where I'll be hunting the next day. What I want most is to feel a saddle under me and smell horse flesh. To be out riding and hear the rush of the quail as they take off; to look around and see nothing human but maybe a house a mile away or so. Want to be able to watch a dog work after a covey of bird and see him point and get backed by the other dog. Just to watch the dog awhile and see him hold the covey and see his muscles twitch and see the real spark in his eyes. What an exciting moment! Oh, it's more exciting to kill a man than it is to kill a bird but not as much pleasure, for most of the time the damn man shoots back and up 'til you get him you don't know if you are the bird or the hunter. . . .

Well, I repacked yesterday and if I repack again and throw any more stuff away, I'll not carry a footlocker. Don't want to carry one unless I do not have to handle it myself. I feel the less I carry myself, the better off I'll be in the long run. My clothes may be all dirty by the time I reach the States, but still that's o.k. for I guess one can easily get clothes cleaned there now, right? . . .

I love you truly and everything is on top of the world. Give my love to Sandra Lee.

Lovingly,   Your Charlie

Fairburn, Georgia, October 8, 1945

My dearest sweetheart,

Sure hope you don't get this letter. What I mean is—I hope (unless you get your mail in seven days) that you'll be leaving dear ole France before you have time to get this. I really think you will sail on the 15th and I'll be a lost li'l gal if you don't! Every one of us are 'cited over your coming home. Even Priss tells everyone (of her own accord) that "my Daddy's coming home."

Yes, we're home again—and is it cool in Georgia! A fire feels good at night and early morning. In a way I'm sorta glad you're coming in cool weather, for it's so good to snuggle up close then, eh? Remember how doggone hot it was in August 1942! We didn't mind, tho'. Oh, honey, what's it gonna be like when we really are together again! Gosh, it's really more than I can imagine—oh, I do love you so good! . . .

Had a good time in Florida but am glad to get home. Mother is already sewing on my p.j.s.—isn't she a sight anyway.

Charlie baby, you don't know how my heart skips a beat whenever I think of you. Judy Canova (on the radio) is singing, "I'm gonna love that guy like he's never been loved before"—and *"them's my senti-ments."* I just can't wait, Charlie, oh, I'm so happy.

Be real good, and real careful, and remember that I love you very, very much.

     Always,   Your Barbie

"Our Day"
Fairburn, Georgia, October 14, 1945

My dearest sweetheart,

Oh, my darling, have I wonderful news—and I only hope it is correct! —that the 75th leaves the 20th for the good ole USA. It was announced over the radio yesterday along with many other divisions and dates— and I don't know how many people called to tell me about it. Oh, I get goose pimples when I think of it. Just think, Charlie baby, you'll soon be home—with me and Sandra Lee—and oh, what more could we ask for. I'll keep on writing 'til I hear something definite from you —because I know with this ole Army anything can happen—and I'd hate for you to sit over there without mail! My latest news from you is the 27th (you had it dated the 26th, but I think you were wrong)—and I keep thinking every day that I'll get a recent letter from you. Honey,

I love you so very much—and now, I'm counting the minutes until you return.

Have bought Priss four sweaters, and two pair of coveralls, and a skirt. It's sure a job to find clothes for her—and oh, they cost like everything. Not leaving much petty cash on hand for me—but I have quite a few clothes left from last year—and I don't think you'll mind too much if they aren't brand new. Priss has outgrown all her last year's clothes except one pair of coveralls. . . .

Martha, Eleanor, Jenny and I played cards here last night. Sandra Lee had supper with Fafa,* and it was 11:00 before she went to bed! . . .

Charlie, I hope I don't worry you when you come home loving you so much. But the way I feel now I could love you for twenty-four hours and then start all over again! You are really wonderful, honey—and all mine, aren't you?

Always,   Your Barbie

[Co. G., 290th Inf., 75th Div.]
                              Camp Pittsburgh, France, 14 October 1945
My Dearest Darling:

Yep, today I am 26 years old and I feel much older. Can imagine that I look a lot older than that too, but that is beside the point.

Even though today was Sunday we still had things to do. Had to get shots, get processed, and well, lots of things. I was fortunate enough to get a letter five pages long from you, written on the 3rd and 4th of October. Yes, one letter. You had just received four letters from me, but still you did not mention if you had received the boxes or not, and I am anxious to know if the watch got there yet or the other things too. Probably if it had you would have mentioned it in the letter, though.

Don't know a thing more as to when we leave here other than what we have been hearing, the 20th Port Call. I sure do hope it is the 20th for I am like a child waiting for a time like Christmas. In fact, I am

---

*Nickname for Barbara's sister, Martha Wooddall Gastley.

ready and waiting to go home and I get more impatient as the days go by. Do not think I could stand another delay either. . . .

I am glad you are now *thinking* about going to the doctor and also thinking about getting a diaphragm. At least you have thought about doing two of the four things that have been special requests of mine, thanks. Forgive Charlie but he is blue and lonely and everything. The shot has hit me pretty hard, I guess, but I am just as tired as hell of all this damn ETO, Army, and all. I just want to go home. The uncertainty of all this redeployment has beat the hell out of my mental state too. I can take it, but I have gotten to the state that I just don't want to take it any longer. Maybe you can do a brace job on me when I get home. Even the future scares me, honest it does. Maybe I need a lot of just plain old loving, huh? Think you could take care of that job, too? Barbie, there are a lot of things I am counting on you for and I hope you can do them all. . . .

I know all of the waiting is worth the waiting for what joy and happiness we shall get out of it in the end. Please wait for me and be as good as your Charlie.

Lovingly,   Your Charlie

Fairburn, Georgia, October 20, 1945

My dearest sweetheart,

This is the day that the radio said you would sail! Boyoboy!! Don't we hope you did. Oh, honey, I've got all my fingers crossed, and I'm praying hard. Just don't feel as if I can wait—I'll just have to swim out and meet the boat. Oh, I love you so very good, and honestly, Charlie baby, all I think about is your coming home to me and Sandra Lee. Just to be near you every day and every night—and to know that we'll never have to be apart again. I'm surely looking forward to putting my head on your shoulder and having your arm about me. I believe I could sleep forever and never wake up, that way. Just to really relax—oh, Charlie—how I love you—you'll never really understand. I hope you won't think I've grown into an old maid—not too much anyway—for I've just done the same ole 1–2–3 everyday for so long, until I'm afraid you'll think me awfully dull. Really I feel years older—but I guess when we're together again we'll be o.k., don't you? . . .

Just nothing new to write about—and I hope soon we'll be telling and showing each other everything, don't you. . . .

Darling, my own Charlie, I do love you so—I'll bet I just wear you out loving you when you do get here. Oh, honey, you are *all* mine, aren't you? And I am yours for as long as you want me.

Always,   Your Barbie

[Co. G., 290th Inf., 75th Div.]

Camp Pittsburgh, France, 21 October 1945

My Dearest Darling:

"Our Day" has been all a usual Sunday, except it was sunny and warm, not a cloud in the sky. I didn't get up until nine, had breakfast, and then wrote to the folks. Just messed around until dinner—then went to dinner and a show that was not very good, *The Lady in Green.* Well, then I came back here and had a hot shower and a shave and put my ODs back on, and then walked over to the company. Sent the jeep driver over to see if there was any mail at the Labor Supervision Center but no, there wasn't, so I came back to the Officer's Mess for supper. We had fried chicken and it was pretty good.

Now I am in my tent and all there is to do is to write or talk to you. This place is truly getting on old boy Charlie's nerves, but bad. I want to move from here and be on my way real soon. Gee, I hope something breaks soon, honest I do. Oh, something will break and we will up and move out. I hope so anyway. I have a feeling that we will for sure leave this week, but I do not know. . . .

I have often wished that I could sit down and so completely describe myself to you that you could get a clear picture of me to compare with all the varied pictures you carry in your memory. I'll try, huh? To be truthful, I am your guy and if you looked closely you couldn't help but see stamped all over me, even in my eyes, the words, "I belong to Barbie." That has been a secret motto of yours truly ever since the morning I left you. I have not changed, my sweet. My hair is just as unruly as ever with that faithful cowlick standing up in back, waving at everything I pass. My eyes are the same even though some different look seems to have crept into them somewhere in the past—it's not a look of hate or despair, maybe it's only the look of a tired being. One who is tired of waiting, of fighting, of doing without the spirit of life, you. I guess I am the same weight, for all my clothes sizes are as usual and my shoe size hasn't changed a bit. I may look a little older now. I cannot tell, but two years ago people used to think I was about twenty, now they call my age on the head. I am still the old hard-headed guy you used to know, but maybe I talk less now than I remember I used to. Actually I am your same old Charlie, old sleepy-headed Charlie. Hope you always love me for I am afraid you are stuck for life with me. You could probably have found a better bargain than me, but I'll bet never a more willing one. Want to bet? I know we have a long road in front of us, Barbie, and it will not be an easy one in the least, but you will have the hardest job of being a mother to Miss T. and a morale builder for me. . . .

Barbie, I pray that I get home real soon and please take care of yourself and Miss Sandra Lee for I'd not want my life without you both.

Lovingly,   Your Charlie

P.S. Did you do anything about going to the doctor and getting that diaphragm yet? If not go on up today, o.k.!!

[Co. G., 290th Inf., 75th Div.]

Camp Pittsburgh, France, 24 October 1945

My Dearest Darling:

Today is Wednesday and guess what? We are going to leave here Saturday for the Port. . . . Now what do you think of that, old gal? Boy, I am about to believe I'll get to come home, aren't you? They say it's darkest just before dawn and they are right for I had all but given up a few days ago. Maybe my letters showed it, if so please excuse me, o.k.? . . .

Honey, we sure better not have to sit up all the first night talking to your folks or my folks, 'cause I'd really be mad if we had to. Why do I love you like I do? I don't know unless you are so sweet—that must be it, huh?

Darling, I will stop for I am tired and want to go to bed pretty early tonight. Give my love to all and Sandra Lee. I love you better than all the rest of the world, so there too.

Lovingly,   Your Charlie

Fairburn, Georgia, October 24, 1945

Hello darling Charlie,

I really don't know how well this will suit you—but I've taken the liberty of just not writing you anymore—until I hear something definite from you. Then, if something should happen and you don't come home right away—well, I'll just pack up these words and send them on. That way, you'll get them just as quick[ly] and will be more certain of getting them. If you do come on home—then you'll have these to read when you please—o.k.? . . .

Monday: Almost a week has passed—but I've tho't of you a zillion times I know. I'm sorta sickish all the time—and I guess it's just nerves. Isn't this suspense just terrible!! . . .

This afternoon I got two letters from you—Oct. 22 and 23! Boy, was I low! But, gosh, I shouldn't have built myself up so—and just waited like a sane person. So, I'm going to mail this on in the a.m. and henceforth keep writing nightly. Sorry my letters aren't up to standard—sorta let you down, haven't I? Oh, Charlie baby, I love you so—and I want you to always love me. I want to do everything right—but looks as if I've really done everything backwards since you've been away. But, that just proves that you should have stayed here and kept things in line, doesn't it? At any rate, maybe it won't be too hard for you to get me straight when you return. . . .

Do you think you'll get discharged upon your return to the states— or will you get a leave first? I've just been wondering. Sorta hard to make plans without knowing what—but, heck, we'll be having such a good time just being together we won't know what we had previously planned anyway, will we?

If you're just one-half like the Charlie baby you were when you went over, I'll be happy forever. Oh, honey, I just love every li'l ole bit of you. You are good-looking, not too rough—but rough so I like it—and you have such character—and everyone loves you at sight—and honey, the best part is that you are all mine. That means so much to a dumb li'l ole country girl like me—really it does. . . .

I want to mail this on to you in the a.m.—and hope you get it. Gee, I want you, Charlie baby—but we've waited this long, so what's a few more weeks. We can take it, can't we?

I love you,   Your Barbie

[Co. H., 290th Inf., 75th Div.]

Calais Staging Area, France,
3 November 1945

My Dearest Darling:

Well, it will not be too long now—possibly a dozen more days and I'll be there in Fairburn, Georgia, if all goes well. A matter of hours before we are on a ship. Boy, I'll really be glad to put foot on the boat. I took the Bns. hold baggage down to the boat last night. The boat wasn't in, but it's supposed to be in now, and if that's the case, then we should load sometime tomorrow. Yep, always moving on a Sunday. We will ride the *Wooster Victory* ship and I guess we will have about as good a ship as they have on victory ships. If we get loaded, then we may pull out by Monday, and, boy, I'll really be glad! Have not written here lately for I have really had a big job that has kept me busy. I have all my stuff up-to-date, so I am ready to get on the boat. Been waiting a long time on this ride, haven't I, or should I say we both have been waiting a long time, haven't we?

Oh, Barbie, it's going to be so good to get back home again and have you and Sandra Lee there with me all of the time. Oh, if you could hear my heart go bumpidy-bump every time I think about getting to be home there with you all. That day I get there will truly be a great day to me. We have such a bright future to look forward to, don't we? We are really going to be able to enjoy life for a little while. There are so many things that we have missed and have to catch up on now and we will too, just you wait and see.

Yea, we left Pittsburgh on the 29th and rode two days on a sorry French train. I had it pretty good—had a compartment on the 40-and-8 we used for the baggage car, and I unrolled my bed roll and slept most of the way down. Those long train rides really are no good, though, for anyone. Have really worked long and hard to get ready here though!

Still I have to go to Camp Gordon, Georgia. Couldn't get it changed so it will be as good, I guess. I'll get there and phone or wire you from there what and how we will get together. May have to meet me in Atlanta, but that will be o.k. We will decide all of that after I get there and see how long I have to stay in the center.

Darling, I love you and I have really missed you. Please be good and kiss my little girl.

Love,   Charlie

WESTERN UNION

Mrs. Chas. E. Taylor   fm. Boston, Mass
Phone 2771—Fairburn, Ga.   20th.

Arrived safely expect to see you soon. Don't attempt to contact or write me here.

Love, Charlie

Epilogue

Dearest Family:

Here are copies of the "FAMOUS LETTERS" that we have talked about for so many years. These letters started forty-three years ago—and it is a 'miracle' that they were kept through thirty-two years of 'Army-moving-about'!! They were stuffed in an old trunk (in no order whatsoever) along with souvenirs, coins from Europe, newspaper clippings, and pictures. Most of the time this trunk was stored in a warehouse by the Army—and of all the barrels, boxes, bikes, furniture, etc., that were lost . . .

THIS TRUNK ALWAYS CAME BACK TO US.

We hope that by your reading these letters, you will not only have a better insight as to why your Mom and Dad think as they do—why they sometimes act a little strange—why they sometimes *are* very strange, but also, perhaps you will get the 'feeling' of the USA population in time of WAR. Bear in mind that we (the USA) had been through many years of depression—we survived that—and try to go back in time and feel the patriotism of all the boys in the services and the patriotism of the ones back home who were waiting for them. Also, remember that most of these service men had never been more than a hundred or so miles away from home before they were drafted and sent to all corners of the world by Uncle Sam. Times were so different—radios, songs, movies, family, and friends were such important parts of our lives.

With all our love,   MOM and DAD

P.S. We would say the rating is "P.G. 18"; however, parents use your own judgment.

Barbara and Charles sent this letter to their children as an introduction to the first installment of the letters which are the basis
for this book. The strength of the letters remains. The relationship of their correspondence to life in the United States during
World War II, "the duration," so confidently stated in the Christmas
letter of 1984, has become a part of the material which now accompa-
nies our selection of the letters.

Reading and rereading these letters reminds one of watching a 1940s
movie, except that this is a real life story. Barbara and Charles really did
live "happily ever after." Early in 1946, the reunited family moved to
Gainesville, Florida, where they lived in a small house located behind
Charles's parents. Charles spent the next three years at the University
of Florida, graduating in 1949 with a double major in agricultural
engineering and animal husbandry. Barbara typed his papers, helped
organize his class notes, looked after Sandra Lee, tended to household
chores, and, in January 1947, gave birth to their second child, a son
whom they named Charles.

In 1949, after Charles graduated from the University of Florida, he
and Barbara decided to follow the army way of life again. He applied for
and received a commission in the Regular Army. Over the next dozen
years, he instructed ROTC units at the University of Hawaii, graduated
from the Infantry Officer's Advance Course at Fort Benning, and served
for fifteen months in Korea. In 1961, he graduated from the Command
General Staff College and was then assigned as the Assistant Chief
of Staff, G-4, Third Infantry Division in Germany. While stationed in
Germany, Charles lost his right lung as a result of cancer. Despite his
physical limitations, he continued in a command position, serving as
Chief of Training at Fort Benning for three years. In 1968, he requested
and was assigned a tour of duty in Vietnam. Charles served thirty-two
years in total, retiring in 1972 as a highly decorated lieutenant colonel.

The Taylors were a true military family, moving every three or four
years from one post to the next. While Charles pursued his military
career, Barbara took on the responsibilities of the officer's wife. She
managed post thrift shops, took a leadership role in the Officers' Wives
Club, served the Girl Scouts and Cub Scouts for over two decades, and

remained very active in church work, serving as President of Protestant Women of the Chapel while they were stationed in Germany. Their family continued to grow, and eventually Barbara and Charles had six children, three boys and three girls.

During Charles's assignment in Korea, Barbara and the children returned to Fairburn to live. As they had during World War II, Barbara and Charles wrote each other virtually every day they were separated. This time, however, their letters were supplemented with audio tapes, a new technology.

After Charles retired from the service in 1972, the family settled in Gainesville, where he began a second career with the Florida Department of Agriculture. He retired from this position in 1987. Now that the children were growing older, Barbara used her "free" time to complete a series of courses at a local community college and at the University of Florida.

Barbara and Charles, like most parents, experienced the joys and frustrations of watching and helping their children grow and mature. One of the most difficult times in their lives came in January 1972 when their oldest son was killed in an automobile accident. All of the children have graduated from college, and today they all live in Florida, where they have begun raising their own families. Hardly a day goes by that at least one child or grandchild does not make a visit. One daughter, Mary Helen, has followed in her father's footsteps with a career in the Army.

As Barbara and Charles worked on this book, they took the opportunity to re-live the days of World War II. Barbara found that as she transcribed the letters, music and films—the sounds of the period—helped recall the time and create an illusion of returning to the early days of her marriage. She has since written:

> After organizing and reorganizing the letters in some kind of order, I began to transcribe them on my faithful IBM. (What a blessing a word processor would have been at that time!!)
>
> I would sit for hours on end, reading, typing, and re-typing. As I typed

the letters, I would listen to Big Band tapes of the '40s and would literally go 'back in time' in my thoughts and feelings—actually experiencing the joys and sorrows of the World War II days.

After many hours in my office, I would come out to the world of the '80s —my whole being would do an "about face" when I realized that it was so many years later—the world of today.

Charles and I have had a good life—we have no regrets. Sandra Lee was joined by longed-for brothers and sisters, and we are very happy with our seven grandchildren.

For Charles, as he reread the pages that brought back his youth, and as he recalled his "old buddies," the various camps at which he had served, and the seventeen months of combat, retraining, and garrison duty in Europe, the experience was also very personal. But it was not so much the sounds of the big bands which flooded into his mind as his relationship to his family, the "home country" from which he had been taken. Early in this project, he wrote down his feelings:

> I was just sitting here in my office reading letters that Barbara wrote to me January/July 1942—and delighting in the tone and all of the excitement and love that they conveyed. God! I remember those days so well and can still feel the flush of passion I got then, and, as a matter of fact, still get now, over forty years later. I am not egotistical enough to think that I have ever been successful professionally, but I do know I would never have gotten anywhere or had anything without that gal. Life on this earth is both heaven and hell, but it's Barbara that has made my heaven part for me.
>
> I hope our life together has meant and still means as much to her as it does to me. I must admit that even today I am jealous of the time she spends with other people—I want her all to myself. She is exciting to talk to—to look at—and even more so to love. She really does make the problems I have in living worth all of the pain I go through, or I would probably have given up the ghost long, long ago! She is the "Best of my life."

These are the ways the two letter-writers look at their lives, these letters, and the meaning they all convey. The other duet, who have known their excitement, observed and shared their love, and been privileged to read, use, and discuss this remarkable series of letters are equally moved by the experience. How could we ever forget the February day in Gainesville when we first met as a group to work on this book? There on the dining-room table stood a vase with a dozen long-stemmed red roses. The message on the card simply stated, "To Barbara—Just because I love you—Charlie."

Life has been good to all of us, and among the grand memories are the hours and days when we have been part of *Miss You*.

Notes

Abbreviations

American Journal of Sociology	*AJS*
American Sociological Review	*ASR*
Annals of the American Academy of Political and Social Science	*AAAPSS*
Better Homes and Gardens	*BHG*
Good Housekeeping	*GH*
House Beautiful	*HB*
Journal of Marriage and the Family	*JMF*
Journal of American History	*JAH*
Ladies' Home Journal	*LHJ*
Saturday Evening Post	*SEP*
Woman's Home Companion	*WHC*

Excellent reference works

Chapter One. Courtship by Mail: August 1941–August 1942

1. Charles and Barbara's first date was arranged by Charles's cousin, Virginia Edwards Kitchens, who lived in Fairburn. Charles's grandparents, Edna and Charles Lancaster, were also Fairburn residents.

2. For an examination of the origins and early history of the 1940 Selective Training and Service Act, see J. Garry Clifford and Samuel R. Spencer, Jr., *The First Peacetime Draft* (Lawrence: University Press of Kansas, 1986).

3. Charles E. Taylor, memoir, "July 1941—Basic."

4. Ellen K. Rothman, *Hands and Hearts: A History of Courtship in America* (New York: Basic Books, 1984), 12. For a general introduction to wartime romance, see John Costello, *Virtue Under Fire: How World War II Changed Our Social and Sexual Attitudes* (Boston: Little, Brown and Company, 1985), esp. chapter 1.

5. Charles E. Taylor to Barbara Wooddall (later Taylor), February 24, March 2, 1942. Hereinafter referred to as CET and BWT.

6. Good advice on protocol when out with a serviceman is in Henrietta Ripperger, "Are You Going with a Serviceman?" *GH*, June 1941, 121. See also Jo Anne Healey, "Nice Girls Go On Military Weekends," *GH*, June 1942, 4, and Henrietta Ripperger, "Gone with the Draft," *GH*, November 1941, 70, 225.

7. A good general introduction to the history of dating in the twentieth century is John Modell, "Dating Becomes the Way of American Youth," in *Essays on the Family and Historical Change*, ed. Leslie Page Moch and Gary D. Stark (College Station: Texas A&M University Press, 1983), 91–125. On dating practices in the 1920s, see Paula S. Fass, *The Damned and the Beautiful: American Youth in the 1920s* (New York: Oxford University Press, 1977), esp. pp. 262–63; Emily Post, *Etiquette* (New York: Funk and Wagnalls Company, 1922, 1929, 1939, 1945, 1960). Also useful is Beth L. Bailey, *From Front Porch to Back Seat: Courtship in Twentieth-Century America* (Baltimore: Johns Hopkins University Press, 1988), and Joseph F. Kett, *Rites of Passage: Adolescence in America: 1790 to the Present* (New York: Basic Books, 1977).

8. Frederick Lewis Allen, *Only Yesterday* (New York: Harper and Brothers, 1931); Robert S. Lynd and Helen Merrell Lynd, *Middletown in Transition: A Study in Cultural Conflicts* (New York: Harcourt, Brace and Company, 1937); and Willard Waller, "The Rating and Dating Complex," *ASR* 2 (1937): 727–34. For rejoinders to Waller, see Samuel Harman Lowrie, "Dating Theories and Student Responses," *ASR* 16 (June 1951): 334–40, and Michael Gordon, "Was Waller Ever Right? The Rating and Dating Complex Reconsidered," *JMF* 43 (February 1981): 67–75. Another source on dating and courtship in this era is Francis E. Merrill, *Courtship and Marriage: A Study in Social Relationships* (New York: William Sloane Associates, 1949).

9. A debate on dating between Philip Wylie and Sarah-Elizabeth Rodger appeared as "The Girls They Left Behind Them: Should They Have Dates?" *Cosmopolitan*, November 1942, 32–33. Also of interest is Florence Howitt, "How to Behave in Public Without an Escort," *GH*, September 1943, 40, 160–61.

10. BWT to CET, April 13, 1942.

11. BWT to CET, December 11, 1941. On the cancellation of Christmas furloughs after Pearl Harbor, see "Soldiers Say Farewell to Girls as Christmas Leaves Are Cancelled," *Life*, December 15, 1941, 40. Information on the unheralded military movement at this time is discussed in "Troops on the Move," *Life*, December 29, 1941, 22–23.

12. CET to BWT, December 25, 1941.

13. "Love in Wartime," *Collier's*, July 25, 1942, 70; Gretta Palmer, "Marriage Under the Microscope," *Collier's*, May 15, 1943, 12, 74, 76; Walter John Marx, "What About Marriage," *Commonwealth*, July 10, 1942, 270–72; Eleanor Harris, "Don't Stop, Don't Look, Just Marry," *Cosmopolitan*, April 1941, 28–29, 95; Gretta Palmer, "ABCs of Love in War," *Cosmopolitan*, April 1942, 34–35; Dean Jennings, "Cinderellas of War," *Cosmopolitan*, September 1943, 62–63, including information on special counseling at the San Francisco YWCA; William C. Headerick, "To Wed or to Wait?" *Current History*, October 1943, 115–20; J. F. Nelson, "War Brides," *Independent Woman*, January 1942, 7–8; "Marriage and War," *LHJ*, March 1942, 110–11; Leslie B. Holman, "Married Strangers," *LHJ*, October 1944, 156–57; K. W. Taylor, "Are They Too Young to Marry?" *Parent's Magazine*, January 1944, 16–17; "Will War Marriages Work?" *Reader's Digest*, November 1942, 14–18. "I Married My Soldier Anyway," *GH*, June 1942, 33; A. Maxwell, "Should Marriages Wait?" *WHC*, November 1942, 58–60; Elizabeth Gordon, "The Triumph of Little Things," *HB*, March 1943, 35–37; Randolph Ray, "For Better or For Worse," *Atlantic*, March 1944, 62–65; P. Popenoe and D. Eddy, "Can War Marriages Be Saved?" *American Magazine*, November 1944, 40–41; Elizabeth Shepley Sergeant, "What Is War Doing to Modern Marriage?" *Cosmopolitan*, December 1944, 64–65, 173; Samuel Tenenbaum, "The Fate of Wartime Marriage," *American Mercury*, November 1945, 530–36; "Soldiers' Wedding: Seven Couples Marry All at Once," *Life*, May 4, 1942, 82–87; "Life Visits New York's Marriage License Bureau," *Life*, June 21, 1943, 98–101; and Harry Henderson and Sam Shaw, "Marriage in a Hurry," *Collier's*, July 17, 1943, 22–24.

14. "War Brides," *SEP*, June 12, 1943, 28–29, 84; Dorothy Marsh, "Here Comes the War Bride," *GH*, June 1943, 82–85; Martha Strout, ed., "Fashions: Destinations Matrimony," *GH*, March 1944, 45–51; Nancy Shea, "A Call to Arms," *WHC*, June 1942, 96–97; Alexander S. Potts, "How to Get Married," *Collier's*, May 19, 1945, 66, 68; Dr. Joseph R. Sizoo, "Faith in Wartime," *WHC*, October 1942, 15, 74; Louise Andrews Kent, "Mrs. Appleyard . . . Masterminds a Service Wedding," *HB*, March 1944, 92–93, 126; Louise Andrews Kent, "Mrs. Appleyard Plans a . . . Wartime Wedding Breakfast," *HB*, April 1944, 50–51, 123, 125, 127; June Rainard Hunting, "Comfort for All In-An-Uproar Brides," *HB*, April 1944, 78–79, 83, 93; and "Furlough Brides: The Newest Fad in Bridal Bouquets is the Victory Stamps Corsage," *Life*, June 22, 1942, 37–40.

From a volcano of romantic fiction, good examples include Vina Delmar, "The Home Front," *Cosmopolitan*, August 1942, 26–29, 75–77, 79; Eleanor

Mercein, "School for Wives," *Cosmopolitan,* October 1943, 67–70, 73–76, 78, 80, 82, 86, 88–89, 91–92, 94, 96, 98, 101–2; Leona Mattingly, "G.I. Wedding," *SEP,* August 21, 1943, 14, 52, 54, 56, 59; Sarah-Elizabeth Rodger, "War Bride," *WHC,* February 1943, 28, 110, 112–24. Will F. Jenkins, "Crazy Marriage," *Collier's,* October 2, 1943, 17; and Hope Hale, "Straight Answer," *Collier's,* May 27, 1944, 14, 65. The February 1944 issues of *Collier's* contained a novel-length piece, "War Wedding," by Margaret Culkin Banning.

15. James H. S. Bossard, "War and the Family," *ASR* 6 (June 1941): 330–44; Ernest W. Burgess, "The Effect of War on the American Family," *AJS* 48 (November 1942): 343–52; and H. J. Locke, "Family Behavior in Wartime," *Sociology and Social Research* 27 (March–April 1943): 277–84. On the increase in the marriage rate during the early war years, see Karen Anderson, *Wartime Women: Sex Roles and Family Relations During World War II* (Westport, Conn.: Greenwood Press, 1981), 76–79.

16. E. M. Mudd and M. M. Everton, "Marriage Problems in Relation to Selective Service," *Family* 22 (June 1941): 129–30; Ruth Zurfluh, "Impact of the War on Family: Wartime Marriages and Love Affairs," *Family* 23 (December 1942): 304–12; Evelyn Millis Duvall, "Marriage in Wartime," *Marriage and Family Living* 4 (November 1942): 73–76; Katherine Whiteside Taylor, "Shall They Marry in Wartime?" *Journal of Home Economics* 34 (April 1942): 213–19; and Robert G. Foster, "Marriage During Crisis," *Journal of Home Economics* 35 (June 1943): 329–32. The importance of this topic was further highlighted when the prestigious *Annals of the American Academy of Political and Social Science* devoted an entire issue to it. Ray H. Abrams, ed., "The American Family in World War II," *AAAPSS* 229 (September 1943), entire issue. See especially John F. Cuber, "Changing Courtship and Marriage Customs," 30–38; Gladys Gaylord, "Marriage Counseling in Wartime," 39–47; and Ernest R. Mower, "War and Family Solidarity and Stability," 100–106. The topic of war marriages was even the subject of university team debates. E. M. Phelps, ed., "War Marriage," *University Debater Annual,* 1942–1943, 159–91.

17. BWT to CET, March 19, 1942.

18. CET to BWT, April 5, 1945, provides an account of the events of the night they were married.

19. CET to BWT, June 18, 19, 1942.

20. The quotation comes from John D. Millett, *The Army Service Forces: The Organizational Role of the Army Service Forces* (Washington, D.C.: Department of the Army, 1954), 107. Additional information on the family allowance system can be found in Denzel C. Cline, "Allowances to Dependents of Servicemen

in the United States," *AAAPSS* 27 (May 1943): 51–58, and Phyllis Aronson, "The Adequacy of the Family Allowance System as it Affects the Wives and Children of Men Drafted into the Armed Forces" (Master's thesis, Wayne State University, 1944). Discussion of this subject in the popular press includes Harry Henderson and Sam Shaw, "Pay for Soldiers' Families," *Collier's*, May 22, 1943, 18, 76; Gretta Palmer, "Army's Problem Wives," *Reader's Digest*, July 1944, 66–68; J. C. Furnas, "They Get 'Em Paid," *SEP*, June 5, 1943, 22, 105, 106; Brig. Gen. Harold N. Gilbert, "Green Checks for the Folks Back Home," *American Magazine*, January 1944, 94–97; and Nell Giles, "That Army-Navy Paycheck: Answers to Many Problems," *LHJ*, March 1944, 4–5.

21. BWT to CET, June 18, 1942; CET to BWT, July 10, 1942.

22. BWT to CET, July 29, 1942.

23. The Atlanta *Journal*, September 2, 1942, carried the announcement of their "official" marriage.

24. Frances Hall, "Lovers—1941," *SEP*, September 6, 1941, 35.

much research by the authors! I'd love to read some of the articles.

Chapter Two. Marriage on the Move: August 1942–June 1944

1. CET to BWT, February 23, 1942, "These Yankees—you insult them as much as you please and they will not do a thing." CET to BWT, March 2, 1942, on "Yankee" girls. CET's memoirs and his conversations with the other authors describe his experiences; see especially "The Draft and Related Memories," "Camp Wheeler—1941," "July 1941—Basic," "The Fort Leonard Wood Bridge," and "December 7, 1941."

2. The extent of this material is remarkable. The most easily accessible books are Elbridge Colby, *Army Talk: A Familiar Dictionary of Soldier Speech* (Princeton, N.J.: Princeton University Press, 1942); Marion Hargrove, *See Here, Private Hargrove* (New York: Henry Holt, 1942); Pvt. E. J. Kahn, Jr., *The Army Life* (New York: Simon and Schuster, 1942); Park Kendall, *Gone with the Draft* (New York: Grossett and Dunlap, 1941); Maj. John D. Kenderdine, *Your Year in the Army: What Every New Soldier Should Know* (New York: Simon and Schuster, 1940); and "Old Sarge," *How to Get Along in the Army* (New York: D. Appleton Century, 1942). On the distribution of paperbacks throughout the armed services, see David G. Wittels, "What the G.I. Reads," *SEP*, June 23, 1945, 11, 91–92. William J. McChesney, "How to Get Along in the Army," *American Magazine*, January 1941, 24–25, 106–7. "Where Our Servicemen are Training," *American Magazine*, January 1942, 104–5, includes a double-spread

map of the new military bases. *Collier's* ran a weekly feature, at first called "Our New Army," later called "Our Fighting Men," as well as another, "Wing Talk." *Ladies' Home Journal* had a monthly column, "Your Men in Uniform." Other magazine articles include Dorothy Dunbar Bramley, "They're in the Army Now," *New Republic*, January 6, 1941, 13–15; Dale Kramer, "What's It Like in the Army," *Harper's*, June 1943, 12–19; "What Soldiers Are Thinking About," *Harper's*, December 1943, 68–75; Vernon Pope, "Do You Know Army Slang?" *GH*, December 1942, 11; "Keep Up with Your Soldier," *WHC*, November 1943, 12–13; "This Is What the Soldiers Complain About," *Life*, August 18, 1941, 17–21; Joseph Kastner, "Top Sergeant Bruce Bieber Makes Soldiers out of Citizens," *Life*, July 7, 1941, 64–71; "A Good Soldier: Bill Brady Is an Infantryman in the Famous First Division," *Life*, October 27, 1941, 69–70; "U.S. Army Private Charles E. Teed of Effingham, Illinois Typifies Draftee Trained to Fight," *Life*, March 16, 1942, 96–98, 101–2, 104, 106, 109–13; Frederick Elkin, "The Soldier's Language," *AJS* 51 (March 1946): 414–22; August B. Hollingshead, "Adjustment to Military Life," *AJS* 51 (March 1946): 439–47. On the emergence of the GI hero, see John Morton Blum, *V Was for Victory: Politics and American Culture During World War II* (New York: Harcourt, Brace, Jovanovich, 1976), esp. chapter 2, "Homely Heroes." Blum's article, "The G.I. in the Culture of the Second World War," *Ventures* 7 (Spring 1968): 51–56, is also useful. A recent, very good addition to the literature is Lee Kennett, *G.I.: The American Soldier in World War II* (New York: Charles Scribner's Sons, 1987).

   3. CET to BWT, November 4, 1941, and August 29, 1942.

   4. Robert R. Palmer, Bell I. Wiley, and William R. Keast, *The Army Ground Forces: The Procurement and Training of Ground Combat Troops* (Washington, D.C.: Department of the Army, 1948), 91–110, 325–64.

   5. "Officer Candidate School: Leadership in Art of War Is Taught Well at Fort Benning," *Life*, January 7, 1943, 73–80; "Private Murphy Teaches Candidates at Fort Benning's Officer School," *Life*, December 21, 1942, 86–88; Major Gen. James A. Alio, "How to Get a Commission," *American Magazine*, July 1942, 32–33, 107; Captain Robert H. Collins, "Backbone of the Army," Atlanta *Journal Magazine*, August 1, 1943; and Henry F. Pringle, "Bottom of the Barrel," *SEP*, October 9, 1943, 24–25, 44–47.

   6. CET to BWT, August 21, 25, 1942.

   7. CET to BWT, December 21, 1942. BWT to CET, September 16 and 18, November 2, 1942. When thinking back on their first Christmas together as a married couple, Barbara recalled that they "had dinner at Camp Gordon with

the Regiment," and that she was thrilled "to eat in an Army Mess Hall." BWT memoir, "Christmas 1942."

8. Vance Packard, "Millions on the Move," *American Magazine*, October 1944, 34–36, 97, has a good map of the migratory routes. Bertram B. Fowler, "You're Moving July 1st," *SEP*, June 12, 1943, 20–21, 105–6; "Soldiers' Wives Give Up Home and Job for Camp Life with Husbands," *Life*, October 12, 1942, 56–62; "Fort Sill Welcomes an Officer and Bride," *Life*, March 3, 1941, 34–36; Constance Bennett, "Blue Star Wife," *Cosmopolitan*, July 1943, 54–55, 65.

9. Dorothy Thompson, "Women and Army Morale," *LHJ*, September 1941, 6; Ethel McCall Head, "Old-Fashioned Neighborliness," *American Home*, September 1944, 4, 6, 8; Ruth W. Lee, "Attic Home for Two Navy Wives," *American Home*, October 1944, 52, 54, 57; Dorothy Draper, "Share Your Home— Cut Your Rent," *GH*, January 1943, 133–35; "Tripling Up: Wives of Servicemen Pool Resources," *Life*, December 13, 1943, 69–70, 72, 74. The January 1943 issue of *House Beautiful* included three articles on "war guests": "Invite a War Guest for the Duration," 15–19; "There Are Four Ways to Get Ready for War Guests," 20–21; and "Could You House a War Guest in Your Attic?" 8. See also *House Beautiful*, February 1943, for additional articles on this topic: Elizabeth Gordon, "Nice People Everywhere Are Inviting War Guests," 30–31; "Boom-Town Decorating," 22–25; "War Guests in Washington, D.C.," 32; and "How to Make More War Accommodations," 54.

10. "A Question of Wives," *Magazine War Guide* (Office of War Information), October 1944, 27–29. Leslie B. Hohman, "Don't Follow Your Husband to Camp," *LHJ*, September 1943, 108–9, and Helen B. Sweedy, "I'm Following You," *New York Times Magazine*, October 3, 1943, 32.

11. Barbara Klaw, *Camp Follower: The Story of a Soldier's Wife* (New York: Random House, 1943; reprint, 1944). The articles appeared under the same title in the *Atlantic*, October, November, and December 1943, but were severely condensed from the book. As Klaw explained in her preface, her title bore a double meaning, as prostitutes and "Victory Girls" also followed men to camp. Elizabeth R. Valentine, "Odyssey of the Army Wife," *New York Times Magazine*, March 5, 1944, 14, is another excellent piece on this subject. Other discussions occur in Agnes Meyer, *Journey Through Chaos* (New York: Harcourt, Brace and Company, 1944); "Whither Thou Goest," *Time*, August 30, 1943, 66, 68; and Terry Morris, "Armytown, U.S.A.," *New Republic*, March 20, 1944, 375, 378. Two short stories on this topic are Sarah-Elizabeth Rodger, "Temporary Widow," *Cosmopolitan*, February 1942, 79–92, and Margaret Weymouth

Jackson, "Never Forget Spring," *Cosmopolitan*, November 1944, 69–106. A recently published memoir which discusses the dilemmas wives encountered as they followed their husbands to military bases is Virginia Mayberry, "Draftee's Wife: A Memoir of World War II," *Indiana Magazine of History* 79 (December 1984): 305–29.

12. CET to BWT, June 28, September 22, 23, 30, 1942.

13. A very useful advice book was Ethel Gorham, *So Your Husband's Gone to War!* (Garden City, N.Y.: Doubleday Doran and Company, 1942). See esp. chapter 7, "Week-end Marriage." See also "How to Live in a Trunk," *GH*, January 1942, 106–9, and Elizabeth Gordon, "The Triumph of Little Things," *HB*, May 1943, 35, 37, 100–101, 104–5. Both of these articles have lists of things to take. The quotation is from the latter. Other advice appears in Christine Holbrook, "You Can Take It with You," *BHG*, July 1944, 18–19; "Navy Bride Gilds the Shoestring," *HB*, April 1943, 42–43, 72–75; "An Expandable Home for the Bride Who Lives Alone," *HB*, August 1943, 56; "Decorations for Army Wives," *HB*, July–August 1942, 52–57; Helen Markel Herrmann, "What an Army Wife Did to a Furnished Room," *HB*, March 1944, 66–67, 102; "Wartime Renters *Can* Live Gracefully," *HB*, November 1944, 72–73; "The Army Life for Me," *GH*, March 1944, 50–51; Nancy Titus, "Permanent Couple Only," *Collier's*, November 27, 1943, 28, 72–74, 76; Florence Kas and Betty Thompson, "A War Bride Equips Her Kitchen," *LHJ*, February 1944, 116; and Elizabeth Beveridge, "Cooking in Cramped Quarters," *WHC*, June 1944, 98–99. On the growth and history of disposable paper products, see David C. Smith, *A History of the Paper Industry in the United States* (New York: Lockwood Trade Journal Company, 1971), esp. chapter 14.

14. For statistical information on the number of service wives in the labor force during World War II, see Mary Elizabeth Pidgeon, *Changes in Women's Employment During the War*, Women's Bureau Special Bulletin no. 20 (Washington, D.C.: Government Printing Office, 1944), 18–29. The subject of working women during World War II has been treated by several authors including Eleanor F. Straub, "United States Government Policy Toward Women During World War II," *Prologue* 5 (1973): 240–54; Sheila Tobias and Lisa Anderson, "What Really Happened to Rosie the Riveter? Demobilization and the Female Labor Force, 1944–1947," MSS Modular Publications, Module 9 (1974): 1–36; Leila Rupp, *Mobilizing Women for War: German and American Propaganda, 1939–45* (Princeton, N.J.: Princeton University Press, 1978); Anderson, *Wartime Women;* Susan M. Hartmann, *The Home Front and Beyond* (Boston: Twayne Publishers, 1982); Maureen Honey, *Creating Rosie the Riveter: Class,*

Gender, and Propaganda During World War II (Amherst: University of Massachusetts Press, 1984); and Ruth Milkman, *Gender at Work: The Dynamics of Job Segregation by Sex During World War II* (Urbana: University of Illinois Press, 1987).

15. J. C. Furnas, "Lady at the Lamp," *SEP*, September 27, 1941, 12–13, 78, 80–83, is a good article, with photos, on Traveler's Aid. Robert M. Yoder, "Chicago Throws a Party," *SEP*, July 18, 1942, 22–23, 62–63, describes and shows photos of a Chicago servicemen's center which catered to 25,000 people a week. The role of these agencies in morale-building is covered in "Soldiers Get Service!," *SEP*, March 20, 1943, 24–25. Also see Gerald Frank, "Off-Duty Where Boys Meet Girls," *Cosmopolitan*, October 1941, 28–29, 116–17. This article discusses the impact of sophisticated life on small-town women. Madeline Carroll, "Why I Joined the United Seaman's Service," *Cosmopolitan*, April 1943, 46–47; Bette Davis, "Canteen Christmas," *Cosmopolitan*, January 1944, 64–65, 138; and "USO: In Peace and War It Has Proven Its Worth," *Life*, June 29, 1942, 70–79. The cover of the June 29, 1942 issue of *Life* featured a picture of a USO "Victory Belle." Julia H. Carson, *Home Away From Home: The Story of the USO* (New York: Harper & Brothers, 1946); *Rainbow Corner, USA* (London: n.p., [1946]); Gorham, *So Your Husband's Gone To War!* chapter 4, "She's Only a Volunteer." The December 23, 1944 issue of the *Saturday Evening Post* has a wonderful Norman Rockwell cover of the Chicago railway station crowded with Christmas travelers. William F. McDermott, "Wartime Joy Riders," *Collier's*, August 7, 1945, 22–24, and William Ashley Anderson, "Day Coach to Washington," *SEP*, June 23, 1945, 22–23, 95–96. CET's memoir, "Train Ride from St. Louis to Atlanta," discusses his experiences as a wartime traveler. Government publications also paid considerable attention to this matter. See, for example, *Defense*, later *Victory* (the weekly bulletin of the Office of War Information), November 1, 1940; April 25, May 20, July 22, December 23, 1941; March 10, 1942. Service clubs were also important to the women who remained at home. For instance, Charles's mother and sister were very involved in the Gainesville Service Center.

16. Dorothy Thompson, "Soldier's Wife," *LHJ*, February 1945, 6, 78.

17. Patricia Davidson, "Back Home to Mother," *HB*, August 1943, 16–17, 55; "These Two Army Wives Went Home to Mother," *HB*, October 1943, 48; and Billie Maye Eschenber, "While His Address is APO," *BHG*, February 1945, 12, 65, an especially good article on the benefits and drawbacks of living with mother while he is overseas. Judith Walzer Leavitt has demonstrated that from the eighteenth to the early twentieth century pregnant women often

returned to their childhood homes for their confinements. See Judith Walzer Leavitt, *Brought to Bed: Childbearing in America, 1750 to 1950* (New York: Oxford University Press, 1986), 91–93.

18. BWT to CET, July 12, 1943. Barbara's letters of July 22 and July 29 also contain favorable descriptions of the prenatal care she received at Fort McPherson. The federal government recognized the importance of providing quality care for the pregnant wives of servicemen. In 1943, Congress adopted a program aimed at reducing the risks of childbearing to military wives. This Emergency Maternity and Infant Care (EMIC) Program provided free medical care to the wives of enlisted men and their children under the age of one. The average cost to the taxpayers was $82.00 per confinement. By 1946, approximately one million babies, or one out of every seven births in the country, had been born under the protection of EMIC. See, for example, Martha Eliot, "The Kids of G.I. Joe," *American Magazine*, November 1944, 135; Amy Porter, "Babies For Free," *Collier's*, August 4, 1945, 18–19; Martha M. Eliot and Lillian R. Freedman, "Four Years of the EMIC Program," *Yale Journal of Biology and Medicine* 19 (March 1947): 621–35; M. M. Eliot, "Maternity Care for Servicemen's Wives," *Survey*, April 1943, 113–14; and Nathan Sinai and Odin W. Anderson, *Emergency Maternity and Infant Care: A Study of Administrative Experience*, Bureau of Public Health, Health Economic Research Series No. 3 (Ann Arbor: University of Michigan, 1948).

19. CET to BWT, July 22, 24, August 20, 1943.

20. CET to BWT, September 8, 1943. Wesley Frank Craven and James Lee Cate, eds., *The Army Air Force in World War II: Men and Planes*, 7 vols. (Washington, D.C.: Office of Air Force History, 1983), 6:559–61, describes preflight training. A first-person account which describes the rigors of air cadet training is Corey Ford and Alastair MacBain, *From the Ground Up* (New York: Charles Scribner's Sons, 1943).

21. BWT to CET, August 22, 24, September 1, 2, 3, 15, 1943. Virtually every letter was filled with details about the baby.

22. CET to BWT, September 9, 12, 1943. A good short story about a soldier who made a long train ride in order to spend a short weekend with his wife and young child is George Harmon Coxe, "Week-End Pass," *Collier's*, February 19, 1944, 82.

23. *If Your Baby Must Travel in Wartime*, Children in Wartime No. 6, United States Department of Labor, Children's Bureau Publication No. 307 (Washington, D.C.: Government Printing Office, [n.d.]). See also Josephine H. Kenyon, "Traveling with Baby," *GH*, January 1945, 59, 142–43; Arthur L. Bantam,

"Children of War Marriages," *Survey*, July 1944, 198–99; Vance Packard, "Give the War Babies a Break," *American Magazine*, June 1945, 24–25, 112–15; Helena Huntington Smith, "G.I. Babies," *Collier's*, December 12, 1943, 11–12, 54; Alfred Toombs, "War Babies," *WHC*, April 1944, 32, 76; "Boom in Babies," *Life*, December 1, 1941, 73–74; "Children in Wartime," *Life*, March 30, 1942, 58, 61–62; Gladys Denny Shultz, "If Baby Must Travel," *BHG*, July 1943, 30, 59–60; and Gladys Denny Shultz, "Hints for Tiny Travelers," *BHG*, June 1945, 40, 98–99.

24. CET to BWT, September 19, 1943; BWT to CET, October 7, 11, 1943.

25. Craven and Cates, eds., *The Army Air Force in World War II*, 6:561–78. The quotation occurs on p. 578. CET to BWT, January 17, 19, 20, 21, 1944. On January 21, Charles described his instructor as a "yelling expert too," and then went on to state: "Oh, I can fly it OK for myself, but everyone flys differently, and to get by you have to suit your instructor and I hope I can suit him." Unfortunately for Charles, he did not pass. Articles in the popular press dealt with the Air Corps in tremendous detail, discussing such matters as esprit de corps, the rigorous training, and the instructor problem. In *Collier's* weekly "Wing Talk," see, for example, Jim Marshall, "For Freedom's Skies," July 12, 1941, 17–21; Duddley Haddock, "Keep 'em Flying," November 8, 1941, 21, on naval aviation; Devon Francis, "We Win Our Wings," June 13, 1942, 20–21, 58–60, which included details on training and the demanding and exacting instructors; Robert McCormick, "Save That Pilot!" July 18, 1942, on how Col. Sam Harris was attempting to keep pilots from being too foolhardy; W. B. Courtney, "Born to Fly," August 8, 1942, 13, 38–39; Kyle Crichton, "The Flying Hawks," January 16, 1943, 36, about the movie *Air Force;* Alistair MacBain, "One Foot on the Ground," February 27, 1943, 52, on mechanics; Robert McCormick, "The Army Spreads Its Wings," March 20, 1943, 33–34, on the phenomenal growth of the Army Air Force. Other examples include Gen. Henry H. Arnold, "Is Your Son an Army Flier?" *WHC*, September 1943, 26; "Air Training," *Life*, May 24, 1943, 50–51; and George Sessions Perry, "Flying Cadet," *Life*, May 11, 1942, 50, 52–54, 57–58.

26. BWT to CET, February 14, 1944.

27. A large number of Army Student Training Program (ASTP) personnel had been assigned to the Sixty-sixth Infantry Division when the ASTP experiment was discontinued in early 1944. It was evident to Charles that an enormous amount of training was in store for this division before its level of esprit de corps and discipline would be suitable for an overseas move or a combat mission.

28. BWT to CET, April 30, 1944; CET to BWT, April 28, 30, May 7, 12, 1944. During Charles and Barbara's stay at Fort Dix, they had gone to Camp Kilmer to see a cousin who was about to leave for overseas. Barbara realized that Charles must have been directing her to come to Camp Kilmer, a well-known port of embarkation, rather than Fort Dix. CET to Martha Wooddall Gastley, May 17, 1944. Codes by which "sensitive" information was provided appear to have been a feature of much homebound military correspondence.

29. Howard Whitman, "How to Say Good-bye," *GH*, February 1943, 34, 153–54; Sylvia F. Porter, "What Every Woman Should Know About Her Husband," *GH*, August 1944, 39, 163–64; Ray Giles, "What if Uncle Sam Calls You?" *BHG*, February 1943, 16–18, 62–65; Elizabeth Janeway, "Meet a War Widow," *LHJ*, January 1945, 97–100, 120; Gorham, *So Your Husband's Gone to War*, chapter 8; and Palmer, Wiley, and Keast, *Ground Troops*, esp. Bell I. Wiley, "The Preparation of Units for Overseas Movements: The Period of Accelerated Movement, 1944–45," 561–618. CET to BWT, June 12, 1944, is filled with the details of insurance, cars, health, and other personal instructions.

30. Gorham, *So Your Husband's Gone to War*, 124–25.

Chapter Three. The Home Front: June 1944–August 1945

1. Most of the war correspondents who survived wrote some sort of memoir. Perhaps, of all these, the ones which might most warrant remembering are those of Jack Belden, Margaret Bourke-White, Eric Severeid, Edward R. Murrow, Howard K. Smith, Otto Tolischus, Hallett Abend, and William Shirer. A good book which discusses the correspondents' training is Eric Hawkins, *Hawkins of the Paris Herald* (New York: Simon and Schuster, 1963). Books about war reporting on radio include David Holbrook Calbert, *News for Everyman: Radio and Foreign Affairs in Thirties America* (Westport, Conn.: Greenwood Press, 1976); Philip T. Rosen, *The Modern Stentors: Radio Broadcasters and the Federal Government, 1920–1934* (Westport, Conn.: Greenwood Press, 1980); and David M. Hosley, *As Good as Any: Foreign Correspondents on American Radio* (Westport, Conn.: Greenwood Press, 1984). Also useful is Sherman H. Dryer, *Radio in Wartime* (New York: Greenburg Publishing, 1942).

2. The standard source on V-Mail is George Rayner Thompson, Dixie R. Harris, Pauline M. Oakes, and Dulany Terrett, *The Signal Corps: The Test* (Washington, D.C.: Department of the Army, 1957), 407–408. See also Mary E. Boswell, *A Study of Signal Corps Contribution to V-Mail Through December, 1943*, Signal Corps Historical Monographs, F-4 [1944], and *Supplement*,

December, 1943 to August, 1945, F-5 [1945]. Another useful source is a post-office study of mail movement, Roland K. Abercrombie, *Mail Matter: A Survey of United States Overseas Mail, September 1943* (Washington, D.C.: United States Postal Service, 1944). Information on the RAF plane crash may be found in *Victory*, February 24, 1943. On the role of the letter carrier and the National Association of Letter Carriers in World War II, see *The Postal Record*, 1940–1946.

3. CET to BWT, July 10, August 1, 1944. Contemporary comment appears in "V-Mail," *Life*, December 14, 1942, 151–53; "V-Mail—Letters to Our Boys Via Film," *Collier's*, October 17, 1942, 33; "V-Mail," *Fortune*, November 1942, 72, 84; Jackie Morton, "Will He Get My Letter?" *WHC*, May 1943, 7–8; and Lt. James Dougland Johnson, USNR, "We Censors Are Frustrated Humans," *SEP*, September 22, 1945, 34, 99; *Annual Report of the Postmaster General, for Fiscal Year Ended June 30, 1944* (Washington, D.C.: Government Printing Office, 1945), 4. The Office of War Information produced a 3-by-11-inch placard in November 1944 which stated: "A War Message: Use V-Mail Today! FAST, SAFE, SAVES CARGO SPACE." The OWI distributed dozens of other V-Mail posters.

4. *Annual Report of the Postmaster General, for Fiscal Year Ended June 30, 1942* (Washington, D.C.: Government Printing Office, 1942), 5–6.

5. *Annual Report of the Postmaster General, for Fiscal Year Ended June 30, 1944* (Washington, D.C.: Government Printing Office, 1945), 2–4, and *Annual Report of the Postmaster General, for Fiscal Year Ended June 30, 1946* (Washington, D.C.: Government Printing Office, 1947), 5. The *Annual Reports of the Postmaster General*, 1940–46, provide detailed statistical information on the enormous increase in the volume of mail during World War II. See also Carl H. Scheele, *A Short History of the Mail Service* (Washington, D.C.: Smithsonian Institution Press, 1970), 172–75. A good history of the postal service prior to World War I is Wayne E. Fuller, *The American Mail: Enlarger of the Common Life* (Chicago: University of Chicago Press, 1972).

6. William Kenney, *The Crucial Years: 1940–1945* (New York: Macfadden Books, 1962), 30–32, is the source for the mail plane incident. Bill Mauldin, *Up Front* (New York: Henry Holt and Company, 1945), 23–24; George Baker, *The Sad Sack* (New York: Simon and Schuster, 1944), esp. "The Package," "Mail," and "V-Mail." The quotation appears in John Monks, Jr., *A Ribbon and a Star: The Third Marines at Bougainville* (Washington, D.C.: Zenger Publishing Company, 1945; reprint, 1979), 129; Eleanor "Bumpy" Stevenson and Pete Martin, *I Knew Your Soldier* (New York: Penguin Books, 1945), 142. Ernie Pyle, *Here Is Your War* (New York: Henry Holt and Company, 1943), 35.

7. *Saturday Evening Post*, June 17, 1944, cover. The January 1945 cover of
American Magazine depicted a sailor receiving V-Mail. The October 4, 1941
cover of *SEP*, the September 1944 cover of *LHJ*, and the May 26, 1945 cover of
Collier's featured young women sending letters overseas. Anne W. Buffum, "Up
Goes Morale," *WHC*, April 1943, 108, and Dr. Irwin Edman, "You *Can't* Be
Too Busy to Write," *HB*, November 1943, 60–61, 111–12. Among the dozens of
pieces that describe the importance of the mail, we should also cite Henrietta
Ripperger, "The Hum Front," *GH*, April 1942, 13; Paul Popenoe, "If You're
a War Bride," *LHJ*, September 1942, 24; Jo Anne Healey, "Nice Girls Go on
Military Weekends," *GH*, June 1942, 4; Alan Dunn, "Letters from Home,"
SEP, January 22, 1944, 12–13; Mary K. Browne, "He Lives for Your Letters,"
American Magazine, October 1944, 102–7; Vance Packard, "Mail Call," *American Magazine*, October 1945, 46–47, 122–23; Lt. Gen. Mark Clark, "Letters
from a General," *Collier's*, December 4, 1945, 14; "Dear Mom," *HB*, December 1943, 58–59, 107; "Excuse My Handwriting: More Letters from Overseas,"
WHC, March 1943, 93, 116; and "These Are the Pictures They Like to Get,"
WHC, March 1943, 100. The importance of letter writing was also a theme
often stressed in short stories in popular magazines. See, for example, Virginia
Spiker, "New World," *WHC*, September 1943, 21, 43–45; John Wells, "Final
Letter," *Collier's*, October 30, 1943, 48; and J. D. Salinger, "A Boy in France,"
SEP, March 31, 1945, 21, 92. This last piece is a very good story about a soldier
in a foxhole in France reading a letter from home. Two novels, written in the
form of letters to servicemen, are Margaret Halsey, *Some of My Best Friends
Are Soldiers: A Kind of Novel* (New York: Simon and Schuster, 1944), and Margaret Buell Wilder, *Since You Went Away . . . Letters to a Soldier from His Wife*
(New York and London: Whittlesey House, 1943). See also Therese Benedek,
Insight and Personality Adjustment: A Study of the Psychological Effects of War
(New York: Ronald Press Company, 1948), 153–55; Jeane Patterson Binder,
One Crowded Hour: The Saga of an American Boy (New York: William Frederick Press, 1946), 162 and elsewhere; Mina Curtiss, ed., *Letters Home* (Boston:
Little, Brown and Company, 1944), viii; Ethel Gorham, *So Your Husband's
Gone to War!* chapter 13, "The Lost Art of Letter Writing"; John J. Hogan, *I Am
Not Alone: From the Letters of Combat Infantryman John J. Hogan* (Washington,
D.C.: Mackinac Press, 1947), 47, 90; Armais Hovsepian, *Your Son and Mine*
(New York: Duell, Sloan and Pearce, 1950), 33, 61, 84, 132, 201–2; Isaac E.
Rontch, ed., *Jewish Youth at War: Letters from American Soldiers* (New York:
Marsten Press, 1945), 71, 243; Howard Kitching, *Sex Problems of the Return-*

ing Veteran (New York: Emerson Books, 1946), 78–80; Charles B. MacDonald, *Company Commander* (New York: Ballantine Books, 1947), 48 and elsewhere. Mail call photographs and their captions in the official history of the Army during World War II are further evidence of the significance of the mail. [Capt. K. E. Hunter], *The Pictorial Record: The War Against Germany, Europe, and Adjacent Areas* (Washington, D.C.: Department of the Army, 1950), 41, 152.

8. George Clark, "The Neighbors," Atlanta *Constitution* and elsewhere, early 1945. Louise Paine Benjamin, "Safe Conduct: The Dos and Don'ts of Keeping Him Loving You Always," *LHJ*, January 1943, 71, 90. The art of good letter writing is described in Mary K. Browne, "He Lives for Your Letters," *American Magazine*, October 1944, 102–7; Frances Fenwick Hills, "Letters from Home," *GH*, June 1942, 69, including the "do's and don'ts" of writing a good letter; Frances Russell, "What You Can Do for Him," *Cosmopolitan*, August 1942, 140; Margaret Cousins, "The Art of Writing a Good Letter," *HB*, November 1942, 55, 96–97; Pvt. John G. McCullah, "When You Write to Us," *Cosmopolitan*, December 1942, 6; Dorothy Speare, "Don't Mention Other Men," *Collier's*, December 19, 1942, 15, 22–24, 26–27; Reuben Hill, "The Returning Veteran and His Family," *Marriage and the Family* 7 (May 1945): 33, including six important ingredients for successful letter writing; Reuben Hill, *Families Under Stress: Adjustment to the Crisis of War, Separation, and Reunion* (New York: Harper and Brothers, 1949), 141; Kitching, *Sex Problems of the Returning Veteran*, 78–80; Institute for Psychoanalysis, *Women in Wartime* (Chicago: n.p., 1943); and Albert Parry, ed., *What Women Can Do to Win the War* (Chicago: Consolidated Book Publishers, [1943]), 27–28.

9. For information on how not to run afoul of the censors, see Dick Gerry, "Stopped by the Censor," *American Magazine*, May 14, 1943, 100, 102–3, and Jonathan Wake, "The Censor Reads Your Letters," *GH*, November 1942, 117. On how to pack, wrap, and address packages, see Frank C. Walker, "Christmas Mail for Members of Our Armed Services Abroad," *Cosmopolitan*, November 1942, 138; Dorothy Marsh, "Christmas Boxes for the Folks Away from Home," *GH*, December 1942, 140–42; James Gardner, "Wrap It Up for Joe," *American Magazine*, November 1944, 120–22; Eve Hatch, "Hurry! It's G.I. Christmas Time," *WHC*, September 1944, 116–17; Louisa Comstock, "Make Christmas Boxes Good Travelers," *BHG*, September 1945, 38–39, 76; and "Will Your Gift Get There?" *Collier's*, September 8, 1945, 8.

10. The covers of *Saturday Evening Post*, May 8, 1943; *Good Housekeeping*, August 1943; *Woman's Home Companion*, September 1943; *House Beautiful*,

November 1943; *Ladies' Home Journal*, January 1944; and *American Magazine*, February 1944, featured mothers, children, and war brides receiving mail from their loved ones overseas. "Share Your Mail," *WHC*, May 1942, 37; "Share Your Mail," *WHC*, January 1943, 32; and "Mail Call," *WHC*, June 1943, 8–9, provide information on the contest rules and include the publication of winning letters. Ernest O. Hauser, "Are There Any Blondes at the Front?" *SEP*, June 17, 1944, 6.

11. See, for example, "Speaking of Pictures . . . These Lips Send Kisses to U.S. Fighting Men," *Life*, July 20, 1942, 8–9, 11; "Christmas Gifts for Army and Navy," *Life*, October 5, 1942, 45–46, 48; John Field, "Letters from Home," *Life*, September 27, 1943, 102–4, 106–10; "General Vandegrift Writes His Wife," *Life*, November 16, 1942, 83–84, 86, 88, 90; "Colorful Romance," *Life*, October 18, 1943, 76–77; "Dear Martha," *Life*, December 6, 1943, 93–99; and "War Wife," *Life*, September 25, 1944, 75–76. "Picture of the Week: Christmas Presents for Servicemen Overseas Go to Pieces in the New York Post Office," *Life*, October 4, 1943, 34–35, and "Christmas Packages Which Never Reached Dead or Missing U.S. Servicemen," *Life*, January 1, 1945, 20–21.

12. The Sheaffer's Pens advertisements can be found on the inside front cover of *Life*, November 23, 1942, and August 23, 1943; and the inside front cover of *Collier's*, October 24, 1942; August 28, 1943; and November 27, 1943. Parker "51" appeared in *Life*, September 4, 1944, inside front cover and *Life*, December 13, 1943, 6. Crane's Fine Papers frequently advertised in *House Beautiful*, for example, May 1942, 42 and March 1943, 1. Montag's Coronet, *HB*, March 1945, 10.

13. One place where the Chesterfield ad appeared was *Collier's*, November 20, 1943, back cover. The Camel advertisement can be found in *Good Housekeeping*, November 1942, back cover, as well as in many other popular magazines. For the Coca-Cola advertisement, see *Life*, August 2, 1943, back cover. The Brewing Industry Foundation ads appeared in *Collier's*, October 30, 1943, 75, June 10, 1944, 74, and August 5, 1944, 52; *WHC*, October 1944, 111; and *Life*, September 25, 1944, 107. Martin Aircraft, *Collier's*, June 9, 1945, 45; Dole Hawaiian Pineapple, *LHJ*, December 1944, 7; Hamilton Watches, *Life*, November 5, 1945, 7; Borden's milk products, *Life*, September 3, 1945, 19; Kotex Sanitary Napkins, *WHC*, June 1944, 8; Scotch Tape, *WHC*, October 1944, 109; Pacific Sheets, *Life*, August 2, 1943, 5; Kodak Film, *Collier's*, July 11, 1942, 39; Nescafe, *Life*, February 14, 1944, 51; General Electric dishwashers, *Life*, March 16, 1944, 21; AC spark plugs, *Life*, November 27, 1944,

7; Sergeant's Dog Medicines, *Life*, May 29, 1944, 111; Maytag washers, *Life*, August 7, 1944, 8; International Sterling, *Life*, January 15, 1945, 6; and Listerine Antiseptic, *Life*, May 24, 1943, 1. This is merely a sampling; similar advertisements appear throughout the popular press.

14. The standard work on the government's role in propaganda during World War II is Allan Winkler, *The Politics of Propaganda: The Office of War Information* (New Haven: Yale University Press, 1978). Four good specialized studies of propaganda are Frank Fox, *Madison Avenue Goes to War: The Strange Military Career of American Advertising, 1941–1945* (Provo, Utah: Brigham Young University Press, 1975); Clayton R. Koppes and Gregory D. Black, *Hollywood Goes to War* (New York: Free Press, 1987); Leila Rupp, *Mobilizing Women for War*; and Maureen Honey, *Creating Rosie the Riveter*. The issues of *Victory* which dealt with mail were September 15, November 10, 24, December 10, 1942; January 6, 13, February 17, March 3, 31, May 12, 1943. A list of propaganda campaigns appeared in *A Service for War: Advertising in Newspapers* (Washington, D.C.: Office of War Information, 1943). The *Magazine War Guide* and its *Supplement*, publications of the Office of War Information, occasionally published short articles on the importance of using V-Mail. See, for example, "The V-Mail Campaign," June 1944, 3; "V-Mail Always Carries Through," July 1944, 12; and "V-Mail," July 1945, 8. James Webb Young, *The Diary of an Ad Man: The War Years, June 1, 1942–December 31, 1943* (Chicago: Advertising Publications, 1944). The material for this book first appeared in *Advertising Age*, a Chicago-based trade magazine. It consists of observations on advertising and the war effort by a senior advertising official. Young makes no comment on any deliberate use of the mail theme in advertising.

15. Not all mail was necessarily uplifting. The "Dear John" or even the "Dear Jane" letter did occur and could pose emotional problems for the recipient. For a discussion of "Dear John" letters, see Lee Kennett, *G.I.: The American Soldier in World War II*, 75–76.

16. For a general introduction to the lives of service wives, based largely on secondary sources, see D'Ann Campbell, *Women at War with America: Private Lives in a Patriotic Era* (Cambridge, Mass.: Harvard University Press, 1984), chapter 7, "War and Victory Inside the Home: The Service Families." Statistical information on the number of women married to servicemen is on pp. 90–91. A discussion of the historical and literary uses of the private writings of women can be found in Leonore Hoffmann and Deborah Rosenfelt, eds., *Teaching Women's Literature from a Regional Perspective* (New York: Modern

Language Association of America, 1982), and Leonore Hoffmann and Margo
Calley, eds., *Women's Personal Accounts: Essays in Criticism and Pedagogy*
(New York: Modern Language Association of America, 1985).

17. Edward and Louise McDonough, "War Anxieties of Soldiers and Their
Wives," *Social Forces* 24 (October 1945–May 1946): 195–200; Milton Rosen-
baum, "Emotional Aspects of Wartime Separation," *Family* 24 (January 1944):
337–41; Florence Hollis, "The Impact of the War on Marriage Relationships,"
Proceedings of the National Conference of Social Work (New York: Columbia
University Press, 1943), 104–25; Carol Bauman Lefevre, "The Satisfactions
and Dissatisfactions of One Hundred Servicemen's Wives (World War II)"
(Master's thesis, University of Chicago, 1948). This work is based on interviews
conducted in the summer of 1945 and was directed by Evelyn Millis Duvall.
Duvall herself wrote "Loneliness and the Serviceman's Wife," *Marriage and
Family Living* 7 (Autumn 1945): 77–81. The popular press also dealt with this
issue. See, for example, Maxine Davis, "Women Without Men," *GH*, March
1942, 30, 180–81; Howard Whitman, "How to Say Good-bye," *GH*, Febru-
ary 1943, 34, 153–54; Florence Howitt, "How to Behave in Public Without an
Escort," *GH*, September 1943, 40, 160–61; Charlene Wynns, "Now That I'm
Alone," *GH*, September 1943, 92–93; Dorothy Thompson, "Soldier's Wife,"
LHJ, February 1945, 6, 78; George C. Marshall, "A Message to the Women
of America," *LHJ*, August 1941, 6; Alexander Woollcott, "To Loving Young
People Apart," *Reader's Digest*, December 1942, 1–2; E. O. Krausz, "For the
Duration Widow," *Parent's Magazine*, March 1944, 31–32; Leah J. Rienow,
"You Can Face It, Says War Wife," *American Home*, January 1944, 4, 6, 8;
"Heartsickness," *Time*, January 1945, 65; Gretta Palmer, "Your Nerves and the
War," *Cosmopolitan*, July 1942, 20–21, 93–95; "Credo of an American Wife,"
Esquire, April 1942, 42; Florence Paine, "Don't Stop Entertaining Just Be-
cause He's Away," *HB*, May 1944, 72–73; James Gordon Gilkey, "If He Isn't
Coming Back," *WHC*, April 1943, 23, 44; Elizabeth Ambrose, "It's Fun to be
a Wall-flower," *WHC*, September 1943, 22–23; Dr. Clifford R. Adams, "The
Companion Marriage Clinic," *WHC*, May 1945, 35; Hannah Lees, "Mothers
Without Fathers," *Collier's*, April 14, 1945, 19, 35; Gladys Denny Shultz, "Cited
for Courage," *BHG*, May 1944, 44, 78, 80. In addition, see Dr. Frank Howard
Richardson, "Wartime Worries Department," *BHG*, March 1945, 8, 84; April
1945, 10; May 1945, 80; June 1945, 12; July 1945, 8; and Gladys Denny Shultz,
"We Regret to Inform You," *BHG*, August 1944, 12, 59–60. At least one prac-
tical guidebook for the wartime wife was published: Ethel Gorham, *So Your
Husband's Gone to War!* A feature article on this book was published in *Life:*

see "Lonely Wife," *Life*, December 21, 1942, 71–73, 75, 77–78. More recently, the theme of wartime separation has been examined by John Costello, *Virtue Under Fire*, esp. chapter 12, "The Girls They Left Behind."

18. BWT to CET, November 12, 1944, April 30, 1944.

19. BWT to CET, August 24, September 17, 1944; February 7, March 25, May 8, August 8, 29, and September 6, 1945.

20. BWT to CET, January 31, April 29, 1945; see also Sandra Lee's letters to Daddy, February 7, October 6, 1944, and March 12, 1945. On raising young children alone, see Dorothy W. Baruch, "Home Without Father," *WHC*, August 1944, 69; Gladys Denny Shultz, "Life Without Father," *BHG*, June 1944, 12, 76–79; Gladys Denny Shultz, "If Your Daddy's Gone to War," *BHG*, October 1943, 14; "Be a Wartime Foster Daddy," *BHG*, October 1943, 7; and "How America Lives: Meet the Andrew Micklos, Draftee-Father Family of New York," *LHJ*, March 1944, 141, 143, 174.

21. BWT to CET, December 13, 1944; April 1, July 23, September 17, 1945. Barbara mentioned Pyle's writings when Charles first went into combat. See *see p. 153* BWT to CET, August 14, 1944.

22. BWT to CET, July 10, 1943; May 14, December 13, 15, 1944; January 1, 17, August 1, September 5, 1945.

23. BWT to CET, July 15, 18, 20, 1943; January 16, 31, 1944.

24. BWT to CET, November 2, 1942; December 10, 20, 1944; and March 8, 1945. Romantic fiction covered virtually every aspect of wartime life, but three short stories which mirrored Barbara's situation are Ernest Haycox, "Always Remember," *Collier's*, July 4, 1942, 11–12, 67–68; Nancy Moore, "He Told Her to Have Fun," *Cosmopolitan*, March 1943, 46–47; and Loraine Fielding, "Alone They Wait," *Cosmopolitan*, June 1943, 36–39, 121–31. *I'd like to read all three stories.*

25. BWT to CET, January 17, June 19, July 8, October 1, December 10, 19, 1944; January 7, 10, May 4, 20, July 15, 29, August 19, 29, September 9, 1945. The need of wives for a vacation from the stress of wartime life received attention from Eleanor Roosevelt in an article entitled, "How About Your Vacation?" *Cosmopolitan*, April 1942, 28–29. The Office of Defense Transportation, because of shortages of tires and gasoline, urged people to take "vacations-at-home." *Victory*, June 16, 1942.

26. Elizabeth R. Valentine, "Odyssey of the Army Wife," *New York Times Magazine*, March 5, 1944, 14. See also "Island of Navy Wives," *SEP*, September 5, 1942, 26–27, 68–69; Mary Ellen Green and Mark Murphy, "No Mamma's Girls," *SEP*, April 3, 1943, 20–21, 83–84; Vernon Pope, "War Brides," *SEP*, June 12, 1943, 28–29, 84–85; "Navy Wives at Key West," *Life*, June 2, 1943,

58–60; Louise Paine Benjamin, "Safe Conduct: The Dos and Don'ts of Keeping Him Loving You Always," *LHJ*, January 1943, 71, 90; and Ann Maulsby, "War Wives: The Four Types," *New York Times Magazine*, May 6, 1945, 20. A formal organization, War Brides of America, was founded in 1943 at Fort Meade, Maryland. "Interesting People: Brides They Left Behind Them," *American Magazine*, February 1943, 108. Another club formed at Lookout Mountain, Tennessee. "They Think of the Moment," *Time*, February 26, 1945, 18–19.

27. BWT to CET, October 5, 1943; November 22, December 12, 1944; January 10, February 19, June 3, 5, July 15, August 9, 1945.

28. BWT to CET, October 25, 1944.

29. Paul Popenoe, "If You're a War Bride," *LHJ*, September 1942, 24, 70, encouraged war brides to develop their homemaking skills while their husbands were away.

30. BWT to CET, February 14, March 12, 1944; March 15, September 18, 1945.

31. BWT to CET, June 10, 1945.

32. Tom Siler, "Paris: The G.I.'s Silver Foxhole," *SEP*, January 27, 1945, 26–27, 66. See also "Speaking of Pictures . . . Some Iowa Girls Didn't Like That Kissing in Paris," *Life*, September 25, 1944, 16–18, and Arthur Gordon, "Folies Bérgère," *Collier's*, July 21, 1945, 22–23, 42.

33. BWT to CET, April 3, 1945.

34. Louise Paine Benjamin, "Safe Conduct: The Dos and Don'ts of Keeping Him Loving You Always," *LHJ*, January 1943, 71; "This is the Voice of Our Daughters in Wartime," *PM*, September 25, 1942. This anonymous article was reprinted in Victor Robinson, *Morals in Wartime* (New York: Publishers Foundation, 1943), 153–54. Another war bride, Gertrude Blassingame, put it this way: "I felt terrible, I felt alone. But I would say it was one of the best things that ever happened to me, because I learned to depend on myself." Roy Hoopes, ed., *Americans Remember the Home Front: An Oral Narrative* (New York: Hawthorne Books, 1977), 256.

35. Sherna B. Gluck, *Rosie the Riveter Revisited: Women, the War, and Social Change* (Boston: Twayne Publishers, 1987), 269.

36. D'Ann Campbell, *Women at War with America*, 212, 228. For a general history, see Eugenia Kaledin, *Mothers and More: American Women in the 1950s* (Boston: Twayne Publishers, 1984). On the women's rights movement and the politics of women's issues, see Leila J. Rupp and Verta Taylor, *Survival in the Doldrums: The American Women's Rights Movement, 1945 to the 1960s* (New York: Oxford University Press, 1987), and Cynthia Harrison, *On Account of Sex:*

The Politics of Women's Issues, 1945–1968 (Berkeley: University of California Press, 1988). A sociological assessment of the lives of working-class wives in the 1950s is Lee Rainwater, *Workingman's Wife* (New York: Oceana Publications, 1959). *I'd like to read this book.*

Chapter Four. Western Front: June 1944–August 1945

1. An example is CET's letter of August 21, 1944, written on the back of BWT's July 25 letter to him. He also used the letters of others as a source of stationery to write what he called "second hand letters." CET to Sandra Lee, July 31, 1944.

2. CET to BWT, June 29, July 1, 2 (two letters), 3, 4, 5, 7 (this enclosed postal cards of Crewkerne, with the name censored), 8 (two letters), 9, 10 (three letters), 11, 12 (two letters), 13, 14, 15, 18, 1944. CET memoir, "England—June 1944." Clarence Woodbury, "The American Revolution in England," *American Magazine*, October 1944, 40–41, 118–20, describes the impact of the invasion army in the south of England. This is also treated in a novel by a man who was a boy in the area at the time. Leslie Thomas, *The Magic Army* (London: Penguin Books, 1981). See also "Red Cross Fun," *Life*, February 8, 1943, 85–93; Robert Arbib, *Here We Are Together* (London: Longmans, 1946); William Bostick, *England Under G.I. Reign* (Detroit: Congress House, 1946); and Norman Longmate, *The G.I.'s: The Americans in Britain, 1942–1945* (New York: Scribner's, 1975). David Glaser, in "The Sentiments of American Soldiers Abroad Toward Europeans," *AJS* 51 (March 1946): 433–38, remarks on the Americans' reverence for the old European culture, the absence of the color line, the soldiers' surprise that women smoked in public and that men were provided with pissoirs; he observes that most American troops relied heavily on nostalgia when facing this unknown and quite different area. Charles reacted in much the same way as Glaser's subjects to the people of England, France, and Germany.

like to read

3. Samuel A. Stouffer, et al., *The American Soldier*, vol. 1, *Adjustment During Army Life* (Princeton, N.J.: Princeton University Press, 1949), 165, and vol. 2, *Combat and Its Aftermath*, 61–62.

4. Russell F. Weigley, *Eisenhower's Lieutenants: The Campaigns of France and Germany, 1944–1945* (Bloomington: Indiana University Press, 1981), 101.

5. George Hicks, "This Is How It Is," *Cosmopolitan*, April 1945, 34–35, 189–90. See also Sgt. Milton Lehman, "Nothing Ahead But Krauts," *SEP*, March

10, 1945, 34, 101–2, and Ernest Hemingway, "The G.I. and the General," *Collier's*, November 4, 1944, 11, 46–47. Hemingway, speaking of this division, said that "there was no rest for the tired men in the line, nor for their leaders."

6. This story is best told in Martin Blumensen, *Breakout and Pursuit* (Washington, D.C.: Department of the Army, 1961), especially 141–42. On the heavy casualty rate of the Thirty-ninth, see Stouffer, *The American Soldier*, 2:26–27.

7. The issue of the shortage of combat-trained troops appears in bits and pieces in more general discussions. The best of these is Max Hastings, *Overlord: D-Day and the Battle for Normandy* (London: Pan Books, 1985), 197–99, which criticizes the training of riflemen and their replacements. Hastings also discusses the air cadet retraining. He claims that in Normandy only about 37 percent of the replacement troops actually had rifle and infantry training sufficient for the job they were given to do. He remarks that dependence on those who survived and became leaders was very high; their casualties were also high, as command was reluctant to transfer them to the rear. This book is very important also on morale and combat fears. Charles Taylor had had very good training, prior to the Air Corps episode, including participation in prewar maneuvers. See also Kennett, *The G.I.: The American Soldier in World War II*. Hanson W. Baldwin, "The Queen Is Dead," *SEP*, February 28, 1942, 9–11, 78, 80, is an early discussion of new weapons, relationships to armored troops, and modern transport; another is Henry F. Pringle, "Bottom of the Barrel," *SEP*, October 9, 1943, 24–25, 44–47.

8. Blumensen, *Breakout and Pursuit*, 141–42, 231. Charles's account of Flint's ordering Patton about can be found in CET's memoir, "The Unforgettables." On Flint and his death, see Hastings, *Overlord*, 187–88, 296–97. Also CET to BWT, July 25, 1945, and his memoir, "St. Lo—Périers Road, July 25."

9. Stouffer, *The American Soldier*, 2:242–89, contains some very useful information on replacement troops, especially since much of this material was based on interviews with men of the Thirty-ninth. See also Kirson S. Weinberg, "Problems of Adjustment in an Army Unit," *AJS*, 50 (January 1945): 271–78. The Army's account appears in Leonard P. Lerwill, *The Personnel Replacement System in the United States Army*, Department of the Army Publication 20–211 (August 1954), and Bell I. Wiley, *Redeployment Training* (Washington, D.C.: Department of the Army, 1948). The popular press also carried articles on replacement troops. See, for example, Richard C. Hottelet, "Orphans of Battle," *SEP*, March 17, 1945, 18–19, 91–92, and "U.S. Army Replacements," *Life*, April 2, 1945, 81–84.

10. Roland G. Reppenthal, *Logistical Supply of the Armies*, vol. 1, May 1941

to September 1944, and vol. 2, September 1944 to May 1945 (Washington, D.C.: Department of the Army, 1953, 1959), especially 1:451–63, 475–583, and 2, chapters 10, 11, and 20. The popular press made a special point of describing the Army's efforts to provide food for combat soldiers. See, for example, "If the Army Can, So Can We," *WHC*, May 1943, 95, and "Army's Iron Ration," *Life*, April 6, 1945, 82–85.

11. Blumensen, *Breakout and Pursuit*, 231–448, 468–71, 474–75, 487. The Ninth Division suffered 850 casualties in the first push and 1000 in all at this time. Many of these came from the Thirty-ninth, which received most of the enemy's blows. The Falaise Gap decision is discussed in Kent Roberts Greenfield, *Command Decisions* (Washington, D.C.: Department of the Army, 1960); see especially Martin Blumensen, "General Bradley's Decision at Argentan," 401–17. Blumensen concluded that, on the basis of available knowledge, the decision was proper.

12. CET memoirs, "First Combat Light," "The Rock War—July 1944," "What Is a Hero?" and "Back Fence Post Problems." Most of these events were described in Charles's "bedtime stories" to Barbara. For contemporary comments on this life, see "How a Soldier Faces Fear," *Life*, January 25, 1943, 11–12, and Private Dale Kramer, "What Soldiers Are Thinking About?" *Harper's*, December 1943, 68–75. John Keegan has written two very good accounts of combat from the point of view of the "ordinary" frontline soldier, *The Face of Battle* (New York: Viking Press, 1976), and *Six Armies in Normandy* (London: Cape, 1982). Another useful article is the anonymously written "The Making of the Infantryman," *AJS* 51 (March 1946): 376–79. Other works that focus on the experiences of "ordinary" soldiers in combat in this area include Charles Cawthorn, "Pursuit, Normandy, 1944: An Infantryman Remembers How It Was," *American Heritage* 29 (February–March 1978): 80–91; Charles B. MacDonald, *Company Commander;* Ralph G. Martin, *The G.I. War, 1941–1945* (Boston: Little Brown, 1967); Harold P. Leinbaugh and John D. Campbell, *The Men of Company K* (New York: Morrow, 1985); Kennett, *The G.I.: the American Soldier in World War II*. For the official Army view, see Kent Roberts Greenfield, Robert R. Palmer, and Bell I. Wiley, *The Organization of Ground Combat Troops* (Washington, D.C.: Department of the Army, 1947).

By this time the military had revived a Revolutionary War decoration, instituted by George Washington as an award to those who were wounded in action, and Charles received the Purple Heart for "his little scratch." The medal replaced the wound stripe which had been sewn on the sleeves of the tunic. See Donald P. Keyhow, "The Purple Heart," *Cosmopolitan*, November 1943, 19.

13. CET to BWT, July 18, 21, 22, 25, 29, 30, 31, August 13, 18, 19, 20, 1944.

14. Extensive coverage of the fighting in France appeared in *Life*. For example, see "War Comes to the People of Normandy," July 3, 1944, 11–19; "The Fall of Cherbourg," July 10, 1944, 30–34; "Cherbourg Trial," July 24, 1944, 32–34; "Battle of the Hedgerows," August 7, 1944, 17–21; "Break-Through in France," August 14, 1944, 19–25; "The Battle of France," August 21, 1944, 34–37; and "The French Get Back Their Freedom," September 4, 1944, 19–25. *Collier's* also carried a number of articles on these battles. See, for example, Ernest Hemingway, "How War Came to Paris," October 7, 1944, 14, 65, 67; Gertrude Stein, "Liberation, Glory Be!" December 16, 23, 1944, 14–15, 61–63, 71, 74, 76; and Archbishop Francis J. Spellman, "Liberated France," April 28, 1945, 24, 33. Ernie Pyle's dispatches covering the Normandy fighting are datelined June 22, 23 (from the Ninth Division), 24, 26, 28, 29, July 13 (on the Ninth readying itself for the battles to come), 14, 15, August 4, 5, 8, 9, 10, 11, 12, and September 5, 1944. These dispatches were later published in Ernie Pyle, *Brave Men* (New York: Grosset and Dunlap, 1944). The relevant chapters are 25–35.

15. Greenfield, Palmer, and Wiley, *The Organization of Ground Combat Troops*, 19, 190, 193–95. Even though the war was fought with savage new weapons, advances in medical science, most importantly the development of blood plasma transfusions and penicillin, as well as the new sulfa drugs, made it possible for more of the wounded to survive than ever before. For popular discussion of medical advances see Ruth Carson, "Blood for the Wounded," *Collier's*, February 6, 1943, 14–15; "Penicillin," *Life*, July 17, 1944, 57–61; Ross T. McIntire, "New Medical Miracles Save Thousands in Battle," *American Magazine*, November 1943, 26–27, 108–9, 112; and Gordon Gaskill, "Life Line for the Wounded," *American Magazine*, October 1944, 44–46, 82–85.

16. CET to BWT, June 10, 1944.

17. CET to BWT, July 19, 1944.

18. CET to BWT, August 3, 13, 22, 1944. For contemporary comments on the relationship between American soldiers and French civilians, see Jefferson Caffrey, "What the War Really Did to France," *American Magazine*, April 1945, 20–21, 110–11; Frank Gervan, "At Last You Have Come," *Collier's*, September 6, 1944, 15, 74; and Robert Metzger, "Normandy Interlude," *Collier's*, September 23, 1944, 24, 27.

19. CET to BWT, August 30, 1944. Although Charles would have laughed at the idea, he was beginning to exhibit the classic psychology of combat neuroses.

First came anxiety, followed by headaches, stomach aches, and later, memory losses. S. Kirson Weinberg, "The Combat Neuroses," *AJS* 51 (March 1946): 465–78.

20. CET to BWT, October 3, 1944 (two letters). The second was written on the back of Barbara's letter that he had complained was too short.

21. This information is based on Blumensen, *Breakout and Pursuit,* 444, 448, 693–95, and CET, "Charleroix," "About September 10 or 11, 1944," and " 'Tis a Shame—September 13, 1944." This last memoir tells of meeting a civilian who showed Charles photographs of his soldier son, killed in the war, who looked like Charles.

22. These events are covered in Charles B. MacDonald, *The Seigfried Line Campaign* (Washington, D.C.: Department of the Army, 1963), especially pages 23, 66–68, 84–85, 90, 92–94. MacDonald, a company commander during the fighting, wrote that in late October, the Thirty-ninth and parts of the Sixtieth were not fit to continue until they received some food and reinforcement. He also stated that this was only the first time the U.S. forces were savaged in the Huertgen Forest, a reference to the later massacre at Malmedy and the battles of the Bulge. Other important references in this volume are on pp. 323, 326–29, 331–34, 336–40. MacDonald attributed the Schmidt failure, in part, to improper reinforcements, as well as to the command problems. During this vicious fighting, the Allies gained about 3000 yards at a cost of 4500 men, while capturing 1300 Germans and inflicting close to 2000 casualties on the enemy. MacDonald remarked: "The victor thus far was the Huertgen Forest" (p. 340). Another useful account is Charles B. MacDonald and Sidney T. Mathews, *Three Battles: Arnaville, Altuzzo, and Schmidt* (Washington, D.C.: Department of the Army, 1952). This book is a study of command failure at several levels; none of these failures concerned the Thirty-ninth directly. Press reports include Ernest Hemingway, "War in the Seigfried Line," *Collier's*, November 18, 1944, 18, 70–71, 73; Richard C. Hottelet, "The Victory at Aachen," *Collier's*, December 30, 1944, 17, 47; "The Coming Battle For Germany," *Life*, October 2, 1944, 25–26; Hanson W. Baldwin, "Our Army in Western Europe," *Life*, December 4, 1944, 86–92, 95; Jack Belden, "Where Is the Front?" *Life*, December 4, 1944, 28–29; and William Walton, "The Battle of the Huertgen Forest," *Life*, January 1, 1945, 33–36.

23. CET's memoirs of these battles include, "Germany—14th September 1944," "Lammersdorf (September 1944)," and "Huertgen Forest." In addition to receiving the Purple Heart, Charles was twice nominated for the Silver

Star. He was recommended for the Bronze Star as well, for his actions of October 15, 1944, but it was not awarded until long after his combat tour. The Bronze Star was a decoration given for combat excellence. The Silver Star, the third highest decoration given for combat by the United States, denotes extraordinary gallantry under fire.

24. CET to BWT, October 7, 12, 13, 14, 15, 18, 1944.

25. CET to BWT, October 16–18 (a long serial letter written in his foxhole), 22, 24, 27, 1944.

26. CET to BWT, November 2, 10, 1944.

27. CET to BWT, August 22, October 13, November 10, December 4, 27, 1944; January 7, February 6, 14, March 25, 1945, contain the most important descriptions of the ranch.

28. CET to BWT, November 14, 15, 18, 19, 23, 25, 26, 27, December 9, 10, 12, 17, 24, 1944.

29. For information on the *Stars and Stripes*, see *Life*, February 15, 1943, 36, 38–39. Information on Mauldin and his "Willie and Joe" characters can be found in *Life*, March 27, 1944, 9–10, 14; February 5, 1945, 49–53; and July 9, 1945, 30–31. The best of Mauldin's World War II cartoons were reprinted in Bill Mauldin, *Up Front* (New York: Henry Holt and Company, 1945). Another important Army publication was *Yank*, a magazine intended for enlisted personnel but widely read. It featured the famous George Baker, another gifted cartoonist that Charles appreciated, and his character, "The Sad Sack," as well as a gripe column called "B-Bag," useful for indicating enlisted men's morale. An article on *Yank* was published in *Life*, November 15, 1943, 118–21. A good collection of the articles appearing in *Yank* is *Yank: The Story of World War II, as Written by the Soldiers* (New York: Greenwich, 1984, originally published in a smaller edition in 1946). Also relevant is Sgt. George Baker, *The Sad Sack* (New York: Simon and Schuster, 1944).

30. CET to BWT, October 19, 1944, and January 24, 1945 (second letter). When he retired from the Army, Charles wrote about his combat experiences in the memoirs cited generally throughout this work.

31. "Little Benning" is described in Ruppenthal, *Logistical Supply of the Armies*, vol. 2, chapters 10 and 11. This school was established on January 21, 1945, as an overseas OCS and training base. CET memoir, "Little Benning—Fontainebleau—1945."

32. CET to BWT, January 1, 3, 6, 17, 23, 24 (two letters), 26, 30, 1945.

33. CET to BWT, January 29, 30, February 2, 12, 15, 20, 26, March 2, 5, 7, 15, 19, 25, 27, April 10, 11, 20, 21, May 15, 27, June 16, 25, 29, 1945. The

encounter with De Gaulle is also discussed in CET's memoir, "The Salute
—1945."

34. CET to BWT, October 6, 13, 1944, April 10, 12, 1945. For professional
discussion of these matters, see Edward and Louise McDonagh, "War Anxieties of Soldiers and Their Wives," *Social Forces* 24 (October 1945–May 1946):
195–200, written by a sociologist soldier and his war bride. See also Henry
Elicin, "Aggressive and Erotic Tendencies in Army Life," *AJS* 51 (March
1946): 408–13.

35. CET to BWT, May 1, 1945, August 13, 1945.

36. CET to BWT, April 23, 1945.

37. CET to BWT, May 7, 1945.

38. CET to BWT, April 23, 24, 30, May 1, 2, 9, 10, 11, 13, 17, 20, 24, 1945.

39. CET to BWT, August 9, 10, 1945.

Chapter Five. Homecoming: September 1945–January 1946

1. Eric F. Goldman, *The Crucial Decade—and After: America, 1945–1960*
(New York: Vintage Books, 1960), chapter 1, "Mood Maybe," describes the
national mood during and immediately after V-J Day. *Like to read this book*

2. CET to BWT, August 13, 17, September 11, 1945.

3. CET to BWT, September 13, 20, October 4, 24, 1945.

4. CET to BWT, August 29, 1945.

5. John C. Sparrow, *History of Personnel Demobilization in the United States
Army*, Department of the Army Pamphlet 20–210 (Washington, D.C.: Department of the Army, July 1952), 23–103. Stouffer, et al., *The American Soldier*, vol. 2, chapter 11, "The Point System for Redeployment and Discharge."
David R. B. Ross, *Preparing for Ulysses: Politics and Veterans During World
War II* (New York: Columbia University Press, 1969), esp. 166–70. Also useful
is Joseph C. Goulden, *The Best Years, 1945–1950* (New York: Atheneum, 1976),
1–36. On V-E Day, persons with 85 points were eligible for discharge. After V-J
Day, this score was progressively lowered. Officers also accumulated points,
but their discharge was first determined by the needs of the military.

6. Sparrow, *Personnel Demobilization*, 178–228.

7. CET to BWT, October 20, 21, 1945. Sparrow, *Personnel Demobilization*,
103–228, esp. 112–17, 162–69. Photos of some of the mutineers appear on pp.
165, 166, and a painting done by a combat artist is described on p. 344. *Stars
and Stripes*, September 7, 1944; New York *Times*, September 8, 24, Decem-

ber 10, 1944. R. Alton Lee, "The Army 'Mutiny' of 1946," *JAH*, 53 (December 1966): 555–71. Stouffer, *The American Soldier*, 2:531. Ross, *Preparing for Ulysses*, 171.

8. Sparrow, *Personnel Demobilization*, 297. Goulden, *The Best Years*, 23. Stouffer, *The American Soldier*, 2:547, states that "there can be little doubt that opinions as to the fairness of the point system were confused by frustrations in not getting out of the Army faster." The point system was phased out and a length-of-service method substituted for it in January 1946.

9. CET to BWT, September 24, October 4, 27, 1945.

10. BWT to CET, September 11, 15, 1945. Reuben Hill, "The Returning Father and His Family," *Marriage and Family Living* 7 (March 1945): 31–34, deals with the impact of separation on the family and talks about psychological problems returning fathers might have. Edward C. McDonagh, "The Discharged Serviceman and His Family," *AJS* 51 (March 1946): 451–54, wrote that "in many cases responsibility for the family is hardest on the soldier who married while in the Army, for most of the obligations of a husband and father are unknown to him" (p. 452). Coleman R. Griffith, "The Psychological Adjustments of the Returned Servicemen and Their Families," *Journal of Home Economics* 36 (September 1944): 385–89. Magazine articles include Anna W. M. Wolf, "Daddy's Here," *WHC*, December 1945, 106–7, and Patricia Guinan, "Getting Acquainted with the Children," *HB*, January 1945, 30–31. Magazine covers which used the theme of returning servicemen and their children include *LHJ*, December 1944 (Daddy coming home for Christmas), July 1945 (a serviceman being greeted by his wife and child), and *Collier's*, May 19, 1945, which shows a pigtailed child wearing her father's military hat.

11. CET to BWT, September 6, 9, 16, 24, 1945. Howard Kitching, *Sex Problems of the Returned Veteran* (New York: Emerson Books, 1946), v, wrote that "one of the greatest of all the ills that accompany warfare is the abnormal sex situation it creates."

12. BWT to CET, September 26, 1945.

13. On the literature of veterans' social adjustment, see Susan M. Hartmann, "Prescriptions for Penelope: Literature on Women's Obligations to Returning World War II Veterans," *Women's Studies* 5 (1978): 223–39. Among the many books and advice manuals published for returning veterans, three of the most widely circulated were Charles G. Bolte, *The New Veteran* (New York: Reynal and Hitchcock, 1945); Willard Waller, *The Veteran Comes Back* (New York: Dryden Press, 1944); and Jack Goodman, ed., *While You Were Gone: A Report on Wartime Life in the United States* (New York: Simon and Schuster, 1946).

The standard Army view is reported in William G. Weaver, *Demobilizing the Ground Army*, Special Study Series, Historical Section, Army Ground Forces (Washington, D.C., 1948); Robert Coakley, Ernest F. Fisher, Karl E. Cocke, and Daniel P. Griffin, *Resume of Army Roll-Up Following World War Two*, Office of the Chief of Military History (Washington, D.C., 1968); and Wiley, *Redeployment Training*. Modern monographs are Ross, *Preparing for Ulysses*; Golden, *The Best Years;* and Keith Olson, *The G.I. Bill, the Veterans and the Colleges* (Lexington: University Press of Kentucky, 1974).

14. Correspondents' reports include Martha Gellhorn, "You're on Your Way Home," *Collier's*, September 22, 1945, 22, 39, and Quentin Reynolds, "The Trip Home," *Collier's*, December 22, 1945, 23, 66, 68 (a lovely story of coming home on the *Queen Mary*). Robert Moses, "Postwar Blueprint," *SEP*, March 13, 1943, 27, 64, 66, 69, described how New York City was preparing. See also "Birmingham [Alabama] Gets Jobs for Its Veterans," *SEP*, June 3, 1944, 34; Patricia Lochridge, "A Town to Come Home To," *WHC*, November 1944, 29, 106. *Cosmopolitan*, June 1944, featured a major section on homecoming; the lead article was Meyer Berger, "G.I. Joe Comes Back," 43–46. Franklin Peck, "Bart Wall—Soldier to Civilian," *BHG*, August 1945, 32, 56–58, 60–63. John Hersey, "Joe Is Home Now," *Life*, July 3, 1944, 68–72, 76, 78, 80, reported on 43 discharged soldiers. Family stories include "Life Comes Home with Jimmy Stewart," *Life*, September 24, 1945, 126–28, 131; "Pappy Boyington Comes Home," *Life*, October 1, 1945, 29–31; "Christmas at Home," *Life*, December 24, 1945, 15–19; and Kyle Crichton, "Captain Bong Comes Home," *Collier's*, February 26, 1944, 22–23, 54. *I'd like to read all the articles. Photos would be fun to see!*

15. Stanley Frank, "Helping Hands and Feet," *Collier's*, May 6, 1944, 19, 46, 49; "A Wounded Veteran Gets a New Face," *Life*, November 6, 1944, 79–80, 82, 84; Enid Griffis, "How Can I Help the War-Blinded Soldier?" *LHJ*, March 1945, 62, 64–65; Franklin M. Beck, "What Does He Want of You?" *BHG*, October 1944, 15, 88–93; Dr. Clifford R. Adams, "The Companion Marriage Clinic," *WHC*, July 1945, 28; Helena Huntington Smith, "They're Still the Same Inside," *WHC*, October 1945, 32–33; Kyle Crichton, "Repairing War-Cracked Minds," *Collier's*, September 23, 1944, 22–23, 54; Coleman R. Griffith, "The Psychological Adjustments of the Returned Servicemen and Their Families," *Journal of Home Economics* 36 (September 1944): 385–89. The quotation appears on p. 388; William Best, Jr., "They Won't All Be Psychoneurotics," *SEP*, April 14, 1945, 112; and "Give Us a Break!" *WHC*, October 1944, 27, 80–81.

16. "Soldiers and Civilians," *Life*, September 25, 1944, 36; "What *You* Can

Do to Help Provide Jobs for Johnny," *HB*, January 1945, 79; "How to Make Jobs for Johnny When He Comes Marching Home," *HB*, January 1945, 40, 68–70, 77; "The Big Money—It Isn't There," *Collier's*, April 28, 1945, 22, 40, 42; Stanley Young, "What Will Happen in Detroit the Day the WAR Is Over?" *Cosmopolitan*, January 1944, 28–29, 139–40; Helena Huntington Smith, "When It's Over, Over Here," *WHC*, November 1943, 4; and Miles Hollister, "Careers for G.I. Joe," *American Magazine*, March 1945, 40–41, 109–10, are a sampling of the many articles on postwar jobs for veterans. In March 1945 the *Annals of the American Academy of Political and Social Science* (vol. 238) devoted an entire issue to the theme.

Writings on the postwar situation of women workers include Cecil Brown, "What's Going to Happen to Our Women Workers?" *GH*, December 1943, 42, 78, 80, 82–83; Nell Giles, "What About the Women," *LHJ*, June 1944, 22–23, 157; Margaret Culkin Banning, "Prizes of War," *GH*, May 1943, 23, 210; "G.I. Jane Will Retool with Ruffles," *HB*, January 1945, 32. Also of interest is "Give Back the Jobs," *WHC*, October 1943, 6–7; "American Women," *Life*, January 29, 1945, 28; Constance Roe, "Can the Girls Hold Their Jobs in Peacetime?" *SEP*, March 4, 1944, 28–29, 37, 39; Amram Scheinfeld, "How 'Equal' Are Women?" *Collier's*, September 18, 1943, 15, 73–74; and Mary Elizabeth Pidgeon, *A Preview as to Women Workers in Transition from War to Peace*, Women's Bureau Special Bulletin no. 18 (Washington, D.C.: Government Printing Office, March 1944). There is a growing body of secondary literature on the subject of working women during and immediately after World War II including Eleanor F. Straub, "United States Government Policy Toward Women During World War II," *Prologue* 5 (1973): 240–54; Shelia Tobias and Lisa Anderson, "What Really Happened to Rosie the Riveter? Demobilization and the Female Labor Force, 1944–47," MSS Modular Publication, Module 9 (1974): 1–36; Karen Anderson, "Last Hired, First Fired," *JAH* 69 (June 1982): 82–97; Leila Rupp, *Mobilizing Women for War*; Maureen Honey, *Creating Rosie the Riveter*; and Ruth Milkman, *Gender at Work*.

17. *House Beautiful* carried a number of articles on the general topic of postwar housing for veterans. The first appeared as early as 1943. See, for example, "A Forerunner of the Way You'll Buy Furniture After the War," August 1943, 72–73, 75; "Here Is a Picture of Tomorrow's Home," November 1943, 78; "What the G.I. Wants in His Postwar House," August 1944, 31; "The Veterans of World War II Say They Will Want," August 1944, 32–33. "A Proper Dream House for Any Veteran," January 1945, 34–35; "The Complete Facts About Home Ownership for Veterans," May 1945, 68; Marion Gough, "If You Have

Enough War Bonds Anything Will Be Possible," July 1945, 31; "First of the Postwar Prefabricated," November 1945, 127–35. Other articles on this topic include "The Great Housing Shortage," *Life*, December 17, 1945, 27–35; Dan Eddy, "How to Build Your Postwar House," *American Magazine*, March 1945, 47, 99–100; Dorothy Draper, "A Postwar House with a One-Room Wing," *GH*, May 1943, 175–82; Richard Pratt, "A Home for the Veteran," *LHJ*, May 1945, 146–47; and "We Plan Homes for G.I. Joe," *WHC*, April 1945, 38–39.

18. Ross, *Preparing for Ulysses*, chapter 4, "The G.I. Bill of Rights," 89–124. The 1955 statistics can be found on p. 124. Also useful is Olson, *The G.I. Bill*.

19. On the "dangerous" implications of the education clause of the G.I. Bill, see Robert M. Hutchins, "The Threat to American Education," *Collier's*, December 30, 1944, 20–21. Hutchins argued that unqualified veterans would go to college in order to draw the $50 to $75 monthly allowance, and this would lead to the creation of educational hobos. For a rebuttal to Hutchins, see Alfred E. Kuenzli, "The Challenge to Education," *Collier's*, March 3, 1945, 37. Also relevant are Willard Waller, "Which Veterans Should Go to College?" *LHJ*, May 1945, 137–40; "G.I. Gripes and G.I. Bill," *American Magazine*, August 1945, 28–29, 106–8; Kyle Crichton, "G.I. Bill of Complaints," *Collier's*, June 2, 1945, 14–15, 72; and "When You Come Back," *Life*, September 25, 1944, 53–58, 63, 64. The statement that veterans were the "best college students ever" appears in Olson, *The G.I. Bill*, 43. On the increase in college enrollment, see Olson, *The G.I. Bill*, 43, 72.

20. Arch Soutar, "Home Coming Isn't Easy," *SEP*, December 24, 1944, 35–36, 38; Maxine Davis, "Now That He's Home," *GH*, January 1945, 36, 69–70; Lt. Frederick Robin, "When Your Soldier Comes Home," *LHJ*, October 1945, 183, 204; and Emory Ward, "The Road Back," *Stars and Stripes Magazine*, September 19, 1945.

21. S. M. Hahn, "Will You Be So Nice to Come Home To?" *Independent Woman*, March 1944, 69, 88; Capt. Alfred Friendly, "'Almost Good Enough' Won't Be Good Enough For Him," *HB*, January 1945, 38–39, 81, 90, 92. This article included a glossary of military slang. Willard Waller, "What You Can Do to Help the Returning Veteran," *LHJ*, February 1945, 26–27, 92, 94–100; "When He Comes Home: A Father's Advice to His Married Daughter," *WHC*, December 1944, 38; "Will You Be Ready When Johnny Comes Marching Home?" *HB*, January 1945, 27; Marion Gough, "Home Should Be Even More Wonderful than He Remembers It," *HB*, January 1945, 28–29. Franklin M. Reck, "Will He Be Changed?" *BHG*, December 1944, 15, 53–56; Irene Stokes Culman, "You Married Him, Now Stick with Him," *GH*, May 1945, 17; Leo

Cheine, "The Army Changes Men," *Collier's*, May 27, 1944, 23, 69–70; and Master Tech. Sgt. Samuel Shaffer, "How to Torture a Returning Serviceman," *LHJ*, August 1944, 70.

22. Christopher La Farge, "Soldier into Civilian," *Harper's*, March 1945, 339–46; Mona Gardner, "Has Your Husband Come Home to the Right Woman?" *LHJ*, December 1945, 41, 72, 74, 76. Other articles of interest include Gertrude Schweirzer, "Since You've Been Away," *Cosmopolitan*, February 1944, 30–33, 151–52, 154–60; Henry Meade Williams, "The Question," *Collier's*, May 6, 1944, 15, 54–55, 57–58; "The Kind of Girl I'd Like to Come Home To," *WHC*, January 1945, 86; Mary Parker, "A Girl to Come Home To," *WHC*, August 1945, 88–89; and Corporal Marion Hargrove, "The Girls We Are Going to Marry When the War Is Done," *GH*, November 1942, 39, 128. The changes experienced by some couples during the war years often led to divorce; for information on the postwar increase in divorce among veterans, see Harold M. Wayne, "G.I. Divorce Dangers," *Collier's*, October 21, 1944, 13, 180–81, and Samuel Tennenbaum, "The Fate of Wartime Marriages," *American Mercury*, November 1945, 530–36. Also relevant is Margaret Mead, "What's the Matter with the Family?" *Harper's*, April 1945, 383–90. Two secondary sources which examine this complex issue are D'Ann Campbell, *Women at War with America*, 88–90, and Susan M. Hartmann, *The Home Front and Beyond*, 164–65.

23. Two excellent examples appeared in *Collier's:* Lucian Cary, "Home Again," November 20, 1943, 30, 73–74, and Ware Terry Budlong, "When You Come Home," February 12, 1944, 15–16, 57–58. Others are Frederick Laing, "A Husband Comes Home," *WHC*, November 1943, 24–25, 37–38, 43; Mona Williams, "What's Happened to Mary?" *LHJ*, April 1945, 22, 104–6; Gladys Tabor, "Not Quite Like the Books," *LHJ*, September 1945, 22, 111; Vina Delmar, "Coming Home," *Cosmopolitan*, 20–21, 60, 62, 64, 65, 67, 68, 70–71; "When I Come Back Darling!" *HB*, May 1943, 53, 112–14; Katherine Albert, "The Promise," *Cosmopolitan*, March 1945, 58–59, 124–26; Richard English, "Melody in G.I.," *Collier's*, August 12, 1944, 20, 62–64; Ernest Buckler, "David Comes Home," *Collier's*, November 4, 1944, 24; Robert Fontaine, "The Home-Coming Heart," *Collier's*, November 24, 1944, 18; Ware Terry Budlong, "Look Back at Love," *Collier's*, December 9, 1944, 19, 28, 30–34; Marian Sims, "Homecoming," *Collier's*, January 13, 1945, 42–44, 46; Norma Bicknell Mansfild, "Something to Build On," *Collier's*, January 13, 1945, 26, 51–54; S. L. Gomberg, "When Leo Came Marching Home," *Collier's*, May 12, 1945, 20–21, 77, 79, 81, 83. For an analysis of the significance of popular

fiction, see Janice A. Radway, *Reading the Romance: Women, Patriarchy, and Popular Literature* (Chapel Hill: University of North Carolina Press, 1984). *I'd*

after this book

24. Other relevant covers include *HB*, May 1945, *Life*, May 1, 1944, and *SEP*, May 26, 1945.

25. Maytag, *Life*, August 7, 1944, 8; Floor-Plan Rugs, *HB*, June 1945, 11; General Electric, *Life*, March 6, 1944, 21. Other relevant advertisements include Hamilton Watches, *Life*, November 5, 1945, 7; Listerine, *SEP*, September 29, 1945, 1; Grand Rapids Furniture Makers, *HB*, November 1943, 2; Chesterfield, *Collier's*, November 18, 1944, back cover; Kelvinator, *GH*, June 1945, 10; Community Silverware, *GH*, May 1944, 135; Metropolitan Insurance, *GH*, October 1945, 69, and hundreds more.

26. BWT to CET, July 5, 1945.

27. Reuben Hill, *Families Under Stress*, 141. For a similar discussion of the importance of letter writing in easing the strains of separation and reunion, see Kitching, *Sex Problems*, 60–80; Robert James Havighurst, et al., *The American Veteran Back Home: A Study of Veteran Readjustment* (New York: Longmans Green and Company, 1951), 49–50; and Therese Benedek, *Insight and Personality Adjustment*, 153–55.

28. BWT to CET, September 6, October 3, 1945; CET to BWT, August 30, September 3, 13, 17, October 20, 21, 1945.

29. Examples of the long letters which Charles wrote are September 4, 9, 1945. His letter of August 13, 1945, included the German soil and the comment: "The sand is German soil. Want to spit on it—yes—start a business—10 cents to spit on German soil. Ha!" Charles's letter of August 28, 1945, described his trip to Switzerland. He did not write to Barbara while in Switzerland because it cost 75 cents to mail a letter. He did, however, keep a diary/notebook of his experiences which he sent to Barbara upon his return to France.

30. CET memoir, "March 1945 to 1947—War End and School" and interviews with the letter writers.

31. Marion Gough, "Will It *Really* Be a Brave New World?" *HB*, November 1945, 97. *I'd like to read this article.*

For Further Reading

A wealth of information about the lives of "ordinary" individuals appears in published World War II letter collections. In addition, there are hundreds of collections which have yet to appear in print. Most of the published collections were written by men in combat. A good recent anthology is Annette Tapert, ed., *Lines of Battle: Letters from American Servicemen, 1941–1945* (New York: Times Books, 1987). There is no comparable anthology of letters written by women on the home front in the United States. A few volumes based on letters written by women in the military exist. One such anthology, long out of print, is Alma Lutz, ed., *With Love, Jane: Letters from American Women in the War Fronts* (New York: John Day Company, 1945).

From the plethora of works on the military history of World War II, both "official" and "personal," those which speak most directly to Charles Taylor's experience in the United States and Europe include Martin Blumensen, *Breakout and Pursuit* (Washington, D.C.: Government Printing Office, 1961); A. Russell Buchanan, *The United States in World War II* (New York: Harper and Row, 1964); Max Hastings, *Overlord: D-Day and the Battle for Normandy, 1944* (London: Cape, 1982); Lee Kennett, *G.I.: The American Soldier in World War II* (New York: Charles Scribner's Sons, 1987); Charles B. MacDonald, *Company Commander* (New York: Ballantine Books, 1947); Charles B. MacDonald, *The Seigfried Line* (Washington, D.C.: Government Printing Office, 1963); David Nichols, ed., *Ernie's War: The Best of Ernie Pyle's World War II Dispatches* (New York: Random House, 1986); Eleanor Stevenson and Pete Martin, *I Knew Your Soldier* (New York: Penguin, 1945); Samuel A. Stouffer, et al., *The American Soldier*, vol. 1, *Adjustment During Army Life*, and vol. 2, *Combat and Its Aftermath* (Princeton, N.J.: Princeton University Press, 1949); and Russell F. Weigley, *Eisenhower's Lieutenants: The Campaigns of France and Germany, 1944–1945* (Bloomington: Indiana University Press, 1981).

Although the vast majority of works on World War II have focused on military and political detail, historians have recently begun to address the question of the impact of the war on the home front. Useful accounts are David

Brinkley, *Washington Goes to War* (New York: Alfred A. Knopf, 1988); John Morton Blum, *V Was for Victory: Politics and American Culture During World War II* (New York: Harcourt Brace Jovanovich, 1976); John Costello, *Virtue Under Fire: How World War II Changed Our Social and Sexual Attitudes* (Boston: Little Brown and Company, 1984); Roy Hoopes, *Americans Remember the Home Front—An Oral Narrative* (New York: Hawthorn Books, 1973); Richard Lingeman, *Don't You Know There's a War On?: The American Home Front, 1941–1945* (New York: G. P. Putnam's Sons, 1970); Geoffrey Perrett, *Days of Sadness, Years of Triumph: The American People, 1939–1945* (New York: Coward, McCann Geoghegan, 1973); Richard Polenberg, *War and Society: The United States, 1941–1945* (Philadelphia: J. P. Lippincott Company, 1972); and Studs Terkel, *"The Good War": An Oral History of World War II* (New York: Pantheon, 1984).

In the area of public information, entertainment, and propaganda, one should consult Frank Fox, *Madison Avenue Goes to War: The Strange Military Career of American Advertising* (Provo, Utah: Brigham Young University Press, 1975); Maureen Honey, *Creating Rosie the Riveter: Class, Gender, and Propaganda During World War II* (Amherst: University of Massachusetts Press, 1984); Clayton R. Koppes and Gregory D. Black, *Hollywood Goes to War* (New York: Free Press, 1987); Leila Rupp, *Mobilizing Women for War: German and American Propaganda, 1939–1945* (Princeton: Princeton University Press, 1978); and Allan Winkler, *The Politics of Propaganda: The Office of War Information* (New Haven: Yale University Press, 1978). Much more on this topic may be accomplished by analysis of *Defense*, later *Victory*, the weekly magazine of the Office of War Information, as well as the monthly *Magazine War Guide* and its *Supplement*, also published by the Office of War Information.

Historians have only recently begun to examine the effect of World War II on family life. Many come to the study of the family and World War II through their interest in women's history. The following works have significant sections on family life during World War II: Karen Anderson, *Wartime Women: Sex Roles, Family Relations and the Status of Women During World War II* (Westport, Conn.: Greenwood Press, 1981); D'Ann Campbell, *Women at War with America: Private Lives in a Patriotic Era* (Cambridge: Harvard University Press, 1984); Susan M. Hartmann, *The Home Front and Beyond: American Women in the 1940s* (Boston: Twayne Publishers, 1982); and Margaret Randolph Higonnet and Jane Jensen, eds., *Behind the Lines: Gender and the Two World Wars* (New Haven: Yale University Press, 1987).

Most historians who have investigated the subject of women and World War II have concentrated their attention on "Rosie the Riveter" and the public role of wartime women. Recent works include William Chafe, *The American Woman: Her Changing Social, Economic, and Political Roles, 1920–1976* (New York: Oxford, 1972); Sherna B. Gluck, *Rosie the Riveter Revisited: Women, the War and Social Change* (Boston: Twayne Publishers, 1987); Ruth Milkman, *Gender at Work: The Dynamics of Job Segregation by Sex During World War II* (Urbana: University of Illinois Press, 1987); and Mary Martha Thomas, *Riveting and Rationing in Dixie: Alabama Women in the Second World War* (Tuscaloosa: University of Alabama Press, 1987).

There is much less material on the private lives of women during the war period. Four useful primary sources are Ethel Gorham, *So Your Husband's Gone to War* (New York: Doubleday, Doran, and Company, 1942); Barbara Klaw, *Camp Follower: The Story of a Soldier's Wife* (New York: Random House, 1943); Katherine L. Marshall, *Together, Annals of an Army Wife* (Atlanta: Tupper and Love, 1946); and Agnes Meyer, *Journey Through Chaos* (New York: Harcourt, Brace and Company, 1944).

Historical works which discuss the issue of reunion and readjustment include Eric F. Goldman, *The Crucial Decade—and After: America, 1945–1960* (New York: Vintage Books, 1960); Joseph C. Goulden, *The Best Years, 1945–1950* (New York: Atheneum, 1976); Keith Olson, *The G.I. Bill: The Veterans and the Colleges* (Lexington: University Press of Kentucky, 1974); and David R. B. Ross, *Preparing for Ulysses: Politics and Veterans During World War II* (New York: Columbia University Press, 1969). We would also recommend Susan Hartmann's pathbreaking article, "Prescriptions for Penelope: Literature on Women's Obligations to Returning World War II Veterans," *Women's Studies* 5 (1978): 223–37.

Index

Public Journal: Marginal Notes on Wartime America (Lerner), 137
Purple Heart, 195, 203, 254
Pyle, Ernie, 139–40, 144, 153, 189, 196, 211, 217, 261

Red Ball Express, 193
Red Cross. *See* American Red Cross
Replacement troops, 190–91, 193, 203
Repple-depples, 190
"Reunion at Grand Central" (Richstone), 273
Richstone, May, 273
Roosevelt, Franklin D., 173–74, 205, 259, 261
ROTC, 28, 310

"St. Louis Serenade," 83
Saturday Evening Post, 55, 65, 140
Scharnhorst Line, 200
Second Armored Division, 195
See Here, Private Hargrove (Hargrove), 66
Seigfried Line, 200
Selective Service, 192, 223
Selective Training and Service Act (1940), 4
Servicemen's Dependents Allowance Act (1942), 14
Sicily, 191
Silver Star for Valor, 202
Sixth Infantry Division, 66
Sixtieth Division, 201
Sixty-sixth Infantry Division, 76
Sixty-third Infantry Regiment, 66
Smeades, Lt., 209
Smith, PFC, 42, 43

Soviet Union, 183, 205, 269
Spunagle, Lt. Robert, 223, 232
Stars and Stripes, 204, 229, 275, 286
Strickland, Lt., 93–94
Supply shortages, 193–94

Taylor, Barbara Wooddall, x–xi; meets Charles, 4, 5; and letters, 6, 36, 281, 282; social life, 7, 8–10, 23, 35–36, 39; secret marriage, 8–9, 13–15, 16, 31, 37, 40–41, 49–50, 51–52; works at Twentieth Century-Fox, 9, 13, 23, 46, 85, 92, 93; on marriage, 10–11, 12, 22, 44, 46–47, 168; on the war, 10–11, 18–19, 46, 158–59, 183, 184–85; public marriage, 15–16, 54–55, 62, 66, 267; courtship of Charles, 18–20; as war bride, 68, 143, 144–46; pregnancy, 71–72, 98, 99–100, 145; follows Charles to Louisiana, 74, 113–15; returns to Fairburn, 76–77, 117, 119; joins Charles in Augusta, 94; and birth of Sandra Lee, 95, 96, 97, 103–4, 105, 112–13; and Charles's washout from Air Corps, 124–25; worries about Charles, 144, 162; considers getting a diaphragm, 147, 177–78; chides Charles about letters, 147–48; on daily routine, 170, 178–79, 180–81; and Charles's return, 276–77, 282–83, 291, 298; and sex, 277; on end of war, 284–85; postwar life, 310–11
Taylor, Charles E., xi; courtship of Barbara, 3–4, 5, 7, 17–18; and letters from Barbara, 6, 33, 138, 189–